Business Law

Garry P. McMurry
Robert W. Packwood
Educational Research Associates

 Canfield Press   San Francisco
A Department of Harper & Row, Publishers, Inc.
New York Evanston London

BUSINESS LAW

International Standard Book Number: 0-06-453003-5

75   76   10 9 8 7 6 5 4 3 2

Contents

Business Law

1 Introduction to the Law

LEARNING OBJECTIVES

To introduce you to basic law.
To acquaint you with its origins and modes of enforcement.
To indicate the basic uses of the law.

CHAPTER CONTENTS

Definition of the Law   Basic Law   The Various Forms
of the Law According to Their Sources   Criminal Law   Civil
Law   Property Rights   The Court System   Enforcement of
Property Rights   Summary   Glossary   Self Test

Business law directly or indirectly enters the everyday
lives of just about everyone in a modern industrial society.
Before we begin our study of business law, however, we can
benefit from some familiarity with the idea of law in general and some acquaintance with various legal concepts and
distinctions that will later be part of our understanding
of business law.

DEFINITION OF THE LAW

The law can be defined as legal rules of conduct enforceable
in courts of law. Such a definition distinguishes the law
from such other sets of rules as religious rules, the rules
of physics or laws of nature, and rules of social conduct
such as courtesy, politeness, and the rule that we all follow, the rule of fair play. Although the law takes many such
concepts into account in the rules that it follows, it is
not based exclusively on them.
        Thus, only in passing will we discuss the rules of mor-
ality, the rules of honesty and integrity, even though
the law is founded upon these rules over centuries of practice and refinement. While the law is based in large part
upon moral rules, legal rules are nevertheless somewhat different from moral rules. For example: If Mary borrows a
coat from Sarah, the law says that Mary must return the coat
to Sarah in the same condition as when she received it. But
say next week Sarah wants to borrow Mary's coat. Sarah says,
"Mary, I lent you my coat last week, now, you must lend me
your coat this week." The law makes no such requirement on
Mary, whereas fair play or courtesy might very well do so.
So there is a distinction: Once the coat has been lent,
certain legal rules come into play. But social rules are
different from legal rules and Mary has no responsibility,
legally, to lend her coat to Sarah even though Sarah has
been courteous and generous in lending her coat to Mary the
week before.

BASIC LAW

In its most basic sense, the law includes in its general definition reciprocal rights and obligations, or reciprocal
duties. We have certain rights and certain obligations.
Basically, our obligations are to protect our rights in others. You may not do something to me that I may not do to

you. It is the legal definition of the Golden Rule. One
of the great Supreme Court Justices of this country once
said, "Your right ends where my nose begins."

Our rights and obligations may be broken down into two
great bodies of law: criminal law and civil law. When
someone transgresses my right by conduct that the state or
the Constitution prohibits, this is a crime. When someone
transgresses my private rights, this is a civil wrong, or a
tort.

THE VARIOUS FORMS OF THE LAW

The law in this country may be found in five places: (1)
Constitutional Law. The supreme law of the land is set down
in the United States Constitution which guarantees us our
individual rights as well as the rights of the states and
the separation of powers. Each state has a constitution
which sets forth the people's rights within the state as
well as the power of the state to act. (2) *Statutory Law.*
There are also statutes which are passed by our legislative
representatives. Statutory law applies not only to criminal
law but to all forms of law that a state enacts to govern
its and its citizens' affairs. Both Houses of Congress--the
Senate and the House of Representatives in conjunction--enact
statutes to govern the United States of America and its business and the business of the people. Every legislature in
each state also passes statutory law. (3) *Common Law*. The
common law is not statutory but instead is made up of decisions over many many years by courts and judges in every
state in the union, and by the federal courts. The common
law, then, is the law that has been passed down from court
to court over the years and which governs our conduct and
the rights and obligations of the people. The common law
may interpret the Constitution, as the Supreme Court does,
or may interpret statutes, as all state and Federal Courts
do, or may describe the rights of people who live together.
Lawyers and judges spend their lives seeking to understand,
analyze and interpret the common law for our day-to-day
activities. (4) *Administrative Law.* In every state the
state legislature grants to various administrative agencies
such as the Highway Commission or the Commission of Higher
Education, and so on, rights to make rules and regulations
for the government of their specific agencies. The federal
government also gives to federal agencies the right to pass
rules and regulations on subjects that they are responsible
for. For example: the Federal Communication Commission

passes rules and regulations governing the rights of radio
and TV stations to have licenses before they may broadcast
and rules and regulations as to what they may and may not
broadcast in the interest of the public.   (5) *International
Law*.   International law governs the behavior of nations with
one another.   This law is found in treaties, customs, and
international common law.

So, briefly then, let's look at the kinds of law that
we have: (1) the Constitutional law of this country and the
states, (2) the statutes passed by the U.S. Congress and by
the state legislatures, (3) the common law as defined and
described and as changed by courts throughout the land over
the years, (4) administrative law that is passed by administrative agencies within both state and federal governments
and (5) international law, which governs the conduct of nations with one another.

CRIMINAL LAW

Let's look for a moment at the criminal law.   Crimes are
divided into two basic types: (1) felonies and (2) misdemeanors.   The simple definition of a felony is a major crime
which is punishable by death or by imprisonment in a state
or federal penitentiary.   Felonies are such crimes as murder,
kidnapping, embezzlement, robbery.

Misdemeanors are crimes of a less serious nature than
felonies, and are usually punishable by fine or imprisonment
in a county or city jail.   A misdemeanor may be punished by
fine or imprisonment or both.   Examples of a misdemeanor
are improper operation of a motor vehicle (although that can
also be a felony), or violation of such city ordinances
as those against loitering or those imposing curfew.

Whether a felony or only a misdemeanor, a crime may
sometimes also violate a person's private right.   When the
commission of a crime also violates personal rights, the
criminal may be guilty of a tort.   To recover for the damage
to the personal right requires the institution of litigation
by a private citizen, the person whose rights were violated.
For example, an intoxicated person driving down a public
highway may be guilty of a felony or misdemeanor.   But if
that drunken driver so operates his car as to collide with
yours or to injure you, he is liable, or responsible, to
compensate you for the loss you have suffered.

You may recover this loss by bringing suit against him
for his negligent conduct.   This is a recovery in the <u>civil</u>
court for a violation of your private right.   At the same

time that person may be tried for violation of state or local criminal statute.

We see something interesting: The criminal law is always enforced by the state, or government, the federal government, the state government, or county or city, depending upon which statute has been violated, because the criminal law is always written in statutory form.

CIVIL LAW

The civil law, our subject for the rest of this book, has two main parts: (1) the law of torts and (2) the law of contracts.

Torts

The word "tort" means wrong. A tort consists of a person doing an act or failing to carry out a legal duty and thereby interfering with the private rights of another. Whenever a person·fails to do what the law commands and causes injury to an innocent person, the law requires him to pay damages for the injury sustained, as we discussed earlier. Such injury may have come from an act performed negligently, that is, without due regard or due care, or it may have come from the failure to perform an act which is required by the standard of care imposed upon a reasonable, prudent man. Or the tort may be the malicious or willful doing of an act or failing to do an act required by legal rules. For example: A person may be guilty of a tort if he says, without justification, that "Joe is a no-good thief." This would be a willful act. Torts will be discussed briefly elsewhere in this book.

Contracts

The law of contracts is the legal area of most concern in the study of business law. Quite simply our social system is based primarily on the concept of property and the protection of property, and contracts are the primary means by which individual rights in property are determined. There are, of course, other means of determining rights in property, such as wills and inheritance laws and taxation. But most property rights are acquired and disposed of by contract. Private property rights are so fundamental to our system of government that they are guaranteed by the Constitution of the United States. In addition, the Constitution forbids

any state to pass a law interfering with the contract rights
entered into by individuals.

PROPERTY RIGHTS

Property rights are those legally enforceable rights one has
in anything subject to ownership. Such rights include possession, use and enjoyment, as well as disposal during life
or at death. Therefore, if you purchase an automobile under
a legally binding contract, no law or person can take that
automobile from you except by contract terms or upon paying
you adequate compensation for this right to the use and enjoyment of the car.

There are two kinds of property: real property and
personal property. Real property is land and anything which
is permanently attached to it, such as a house, or trees.

Sometimes personal property may become real property
when it is so attached and fixed to the land as to become
permanent. For example, Sam bought a lot that he was going
to grow crops on. He also bought some fence posts and barbed
wire. Now the lot is real property; but Sam dug post
holes, put the fence posts in and covered their bases and
strung the barbed wire around the field. Once he had put
the fence posts into the ground and attached the barbed
wire to them, that fence, or the posts and wire, became a
fixture, and thus part of the real property.

Personal property is simply all property that is not
real property. Personal property includes tangible personal
property (also known as chattel), that is, things we can see
and touch such as radios, clothes, cars, etc. Intangible
personal property includes our rights, such as the right
to have contracts we've entered into performed by the other
party. This is both a right and a part of your personal
property.

THE COURT SYSTEM

When a person has been badly injured or his business has been
badly damaged by the unforgivable conduct of another person,
we need some tribunal to establish the nature of the damage
or injury, and the extent of compensation required to adequately compensate the person injured or whose interests
were damaged. We enforce and administer laws through our
courts.

Let's look briefly at our court system in this country. The court system is in three basic parts: federal, state, and local.

Federal courts

At the top of the federal court system is the United States Supreme Court, our highest legal authority. It is the court of last resort; that is, the Supreme Court rules upon the constitutionality of laws passed by both Congress and the states. The Supreme Court hears appeals from both state and federal courts, and--with rare, special exceptions--hears only appeals.

Beneath the Supreme Court in the federal system are the federal courts called United States Circuit Courts of Appeal. These courts hear appeals from the United States District Courts, the courts immediately below the Appeals Courts.

In the United States, federal cases are tried in the U. S. District Courts. These courts have original jurisdiction to hear questions relating to federal statutes and the admiralty law. They also have the power to hear questions between citizens of different states if the amount in controversy is in excess of $10,000. For example: A resident of the state of Ohio sells an airplane to a resident of the state of Texas for $25,000. If dispute arises out of this contract of sale, the parties can litigate the question in a United States District Court.

State courts

In every state there is a State Supreme Court. Although it may not be called that in every state, nevertheless every state has a highest tribunal which hears only appeals from lower courts within the state on private or civil, as well as criminal, cases.

Beneath the State Supreme Court in some, but not all, states there is an Intermediate Court of Appeals, or Appellate Court, which hears appeals from the trial court of the state.

The state trial courts are generally found in the various counties of the state. These courts try the great percentage of all litigation, both criminal and civil, in the United States of America.

In many states there are also specialized courts: Probate courts concern themselves exclusively with wills and the estates of deceased people. Many states have juvenile courts, concerned exclusively with matters relating to minors

and infants of specified ages in each of these states. Most
states also have tax courts, which consider only matters of
taxation.

Local courts

Finally, there are local courts: County Courts; City or
Municipal Courts within cities; and Justices of the Peace
Courts. Local courts are courts of limited jurisdiction.
They concern themselves with violations of ordinances and
statutes passed by the government within their jurisdiction.

ENFORCEMENT OF PROPERTY RIGHTS

We mentioned the courts as the instruments of law enforcement, for both criminal and civil cases. But what <u>particu-</u>
<u>lar</u> forms does such enforcement take in civil cases?
    Enforcement is through either litigation or settlement.
Now obviously settlement (that is, out of court) of a dispute
is always better than litigation. But if a dispute cannot
be settled amicably by the parties, then they must go to
court to have their rights adjudicated: That is, the applicable rights and responsibilities must be defined by a court.
A dispute is adjudicated by a court and a decision is rendered based upon that adjudication. For example, assume
that Sam has a legal dispute with a neighbor, either in
business or in his own neighborhood. They cannot agree to
an amicable settlement of the dispute. Sam must therefore
file a complaint in a court. (If he is wise he will do so
through the services of an attorney, who will draw the complaint so that it sets forth only the important facts and
law relating to this dispute.) After the complaint, having
been sworn to by Sam, under oath, before a Notary Public, is
filed the defendant must answer the complaint and admit or
deny certain allegations made by the plaintiff and must
make allegations in his own defense. (He may in addition--
but <u>not</u> <u>instead</u>--file motions or charges of his own against
the plaintiff.)
    If the case cannot be settled by complaint and answers
to the complaint, then the case is set down for trial, either
before a judge only or before a judge and jury. (But here
is an important point: The right to a jury trial is guaranteed only in criminal matters.) If Sam and the defendant
waive a jury trial, the matter will be decided before a judge.
But if the court sits with a jury, the court's (the judges)
function is to decide matters of law and the jury's function

is to decide matters of fact in the dispute, and the amount
of damages, if any, that Sam has suffered and for which
he seeks recovery.

Some disputes are tried exclusively before a judge.
For example: Sam has made valuable improvements on property
that he purchased from his neighbor. The neighbor then decides that he doesn't want to go ahead with the contract.
Sam brings the man into court in the manner described above
and asks the judge for an order that the seller of the property proceed with the contract or specifically perform it.
The case will then be tried before a judge without a jury.

SUMMARY

The law was defined as legal rules of conduct enforceable in
courts of law. The law imposes reciprocal rights and obligations, which are to protect our right in others. Criminal
law covers government statutes and common law, and civil law
covers personal rights. The law takes one of five forms:
constitutional, statutory, common law, administrative, and
international law. Civil law has two main parts: torts
and contracts, both pertaining to personal rights. Contracts
are inseparable from the rights of private property. The
courts administer and enforce the law, and thus the ultimate
recourse for protection of property rights and settlements of
disputes related to such rights is the courts.

GLOSSARY TERMS

Common law Law that has developed from court decisions and practice rather than from statute.

Complaint An attempt to have a court redress a claimed wrong.

Contract A binding agreement between two or more parties; the basic form of protection of property rights.

Court A tribunal authorized to administer and enforce the law.

Defendant The person against whom a complaint is made before a court.

Felony A serious crime incurring punishment by death or imprisonment.

Law Legal rules of conduct enforceable in courts of law.

Misdemeanor A crime less serious than a felony, incurring punishment by fine or imprisonment or both.

Personal property Any property that is not real property.

Plaintiff The person making a complaint to a court.

Property rights The legally enforceable rights to hold and use property.

Real property Fixed property, specifically land and anything attached to it such as a building.

Reciprocal rights and obligations The legal obligation to protect our rights in others.

Statute Law enacted by a government legislature.

Tort Transgression of a private right; a civil wrong.

SELF TEST

CHAPTER 1

NAME_____

DATE_____

1.1 The concept of law used for these lectures could be defined as legal rules of conduct enforceable in
_____.

1.2 The law, in its general definition, includes reciprocal_____and reciprocal_____.

1.3 The two main bodies of law are_____law and
_____law.

1.4 Under criminal law, a major crime which is punishable by death or imprisonment in a state penitentiary would be considered a/an_____, whereas a crime of less serious nature, usually punishable by fine or imprisonment in a county jail, would be considered a/an
_____.

1.5 Criminal conduct may violate not only a criminal statute, but also a person's private rights. True_____
_____False_____.

1.6 The criminal law is always enforced by the_____.

1.7 What is the source or type of law for each of the following conditions:
(a) The law of the land which sets forth and guarantees the individual rights of citizens, the rights of states, and the separation of power_____;
(b) The law established by state legislature or the Congress of the United States_____;
(c) The law that is based on prior court decisions over a long period of time_____;
(d) The law set forth by rules or regulations of various state commissions or federal agencies_____;
(e) The law between nations_____.

1.8 Criminal law is usually written in_____form.

1.9 The highest legal authority in the United States is the_____court.

1.10 The court that hears appeals from the U. S. District courts is called the_____.

1.11 U. S. District Courts have the original jurisdiction to hear questions relating to_____Statutes and the
_____Law.

1.12   U. S. District Courts have the power to hear cases be-
       tween citizens of different states if the amount of
       the controversy is over_____.

1.13   The State_____Courts, generally found in the
       various counties of the state, try both criminal and
       _____litigation, and also try the greatest
       percentage of all litigation in the United States.

1.14   The two main parts of Civil Law are the Law of_____
       _____and the Law of_____.

1.15   A/An_____consists of a person doing an act, or
       failing to carry out a legal duty, thereby interfer-
       ing with the private rights of another, and may be
       committed either negligently or_____.

1.16   _____are the primary means by which individual
       rights in property are determined.

1.17   _____are those legally enforceable rights one
       has in anything subject to ownership.

1.18   The two kinds of property are_____property and
       _____property.

1.19   Personal property may also be known as_____.

1.20   The system of enforcement of a person's legal rights
       is through_____or_____.

1.21   _____is a word used for the definition of rights
       and responsibilities by a court.

1.22   The right to a jury trial is only guaranteed in_____
       _____matters.

2 Contracts

Introduction

LEARNING OBJECTIVES

To define the contract.
To define mutual assent.
To examine the five basic elements of a valid contract.
To discuss competency and disaffirmance.

CHAPTER CONTENTS

The Importance of Contracts   Definition of the Contract
Mutual Assent   The Five Basic Elements of Enforceable Contracts   Competency   Disaffirmance

THE IMPORTANCE OF CONTRACTS

In the Introduction we spoke briefly about contracts and the
law of contracts and about the large part that contracts
play in the law generally. Contracts are immensely important because just about everyone enters into at least one
contract everyday. Without some means of enforcing contracts
and knowing which contracts are enforceable, which are not,
business would be conducted only with great difficulty, and
it would be virtually impossible to conduct the affairs of
our everyday lives.
     Contracts and the law underlying them prevent problems
from arising because contracts create <u>certainty</u>. Unless
promises made by you to others, and promises made by others
to you, can be enforceable, our society just couldn't function.

DEFINITION OF THE CONTRACT

To most of us the word "contract" conjures up a lengthy paper document with seals and ribbons and stamps, which is
loaded with legal terms like "now therefore" and "to wit"
and "whereases" which most of us don't really understand.
However, very few contracts are even on paper, and those
that are on paper are usually quite simple and informal.
     Exactly what, then, is a contract? Basically, <u>a con-
tract is a promise made by one person to another to do or
not to do something in the future, and which is enforceable
in a court of law</u>.
     If we examine our definition of a contract carefully
we can see that a contract can be resolved into five basic
and essential elements. If a so-called contract lacks any
one of these elements it is not a true contract. The five
separate elements of a true contract are:
1. A contract is a <u>promise.</u>
2. A promise made by <u>one person to another.</u>
3. A promise <u>to do or not to do something.</u>
4. A promise to do or not to do something <u>in the future.</u>
5. A promise that is <u>enforceable in court.</u>

Contracts and promises

Can it properly be concluded from our definition that every
promise is a contract? No, because not every promise is enforceable in a court of law. For example, <u>social promises</u>

are not contracts, as we can illustrate: The plaintiff (the person, remember, who makes a complaint in court about someone else's conduct) is a girl.

Your Honor, the defendant asked me for a date last Friday night and because I accepted I went ahead and turned down a babysitting job which was offered to me. Defendant did not come to pick me up for the date, and now I feel he should be held responsible for the money I could've made on that job.

But Your Honor, I admit that I had a moral duty to appear for our date, but I do not feel that I was legally obligated to appear because neither of us had any actual intent to legally bind the other. In other words, I did not expect the plaintiff to be legally bound to be at home when I arrived, and she didn't intend that I be legally bound to come and pick her up.

If courts should be expected to hear controversies of this type, court calendars would be so crowded that legitimate and meaningful disputes would not have a chance to be decided by the court. Also, Defendant's argument is generally correct. People do not generally intend to legally bind themselves when they enter social agreements. In this case, therefore, I find for the defendant. We see from this example that not all promises are contracts.

Contracts and persons

The second element on our list of essentials of a contract--that it be a promise by one person to another--means that a man or woman may not contract with himself or herself. A contract requires <u>two or more</u> people to agree to be bound by their promises given one to another. (Note that a contract may have more than two people. You or I could contract with literally thousands of people, as we will see later in this book.) But suppose a person tried to make a contract with himself. Let's say he promises himself that he is going to give up smoking cigarettes--an excellent promise, by the way, and one that should be enforceable but is not, because he has not legally bound himself to any other person. He has merely made a promise to himself to do something. It's something that should be done, but it is not a legally binding contract because it does not have another person who is relying, or has paid, for his prmise to perform as he has undertaken to do.

Contracts and actions

The third item on our list of essentials for a contract is
that the promise is <u>to do or not to do something</u>. Obviously,
a contractual promise must be to do something, for if no action, or restraint from action, is involved, then there can
have been nothing to promise. For example, two students are
walking across a campus:
<u>Joe</u>:   Hi, Dick, are you walking to chemistry?
<u>Dick</u>:   Sure am, Joe.
<u>Joe</u>:   Can I walk with you?
<u>Dick</u>:   Be my guest.
These two people are having a conversation, but neither <u>pro-
mised</u> to do something for the other. Joe wanted to walk with
Dick, but Joe didn't agree that he would walk to class with
him and Dick didn't agree to do anything either.

Contracts and time

As item (4) on our list of contractual essentials stipulates,
contract is an agreement to do or not to do something in the
future. You and I cannot contract or promise to do something
in the past; the past is beyond our control. So the law of
contracts says that the promise for performance must be in
the present or in the future but it cannot affect the past.

MUTUAL ASSENT

From these examples you should see that contracts are promises
made by one person to another, with the intent to legally bind
one another to perform. This mutual intent to legally bind
each other is known as mutual assent. Mutual assent can be
expressed by words or by acts. When mutual assent is expressed
by written or spoken words, it is known as express mutual assent. The contract which results from that express mutual assent is known as an express contract. For example,
<u>1st person</u>:   I'll give you my radio if you'll give me your
<u>water skis</u>.
<u>2nd person</u>:   All right. Let's trade.
Here the parties gave mutual assent through express promises--
an express, oral contract. Of course, they could have agreed
expressly in writing to the trade.
    When mutual assent is expressed by the acts of the parties,
it is known as an implied in fact contract. For example,
<u>1st person</u>:   Taxi Driver, take me to the York Hotel.
<u>2nd person</u>:   Here you are, Ma'am. That will be $2.35.

When a person gets into a taxicab and asks for a service--
here, to be taken to the York Hotel--the person implicitly
agrees to pay for the service that was rendered.

There are also situations in which the courts will imply
mutual assent even though the parties gave no real assent
either express or implied in fact. This form of contract
is used by the courts to prevent the unjust enrichment of
one party at the expense of the other, even though no real
contract was intended to be entered into. These contracts
are called contracts implied in law. For example,
<u>1st person</u>: Your Honor, I am a doctor, and as I was driving
home one night last month I came upon the scene of an automobile accident. I found the defendant lying on the street
near death and I performed some immediate surgery which en-
abled me to save her life. I then drove her to the hospital
and performed further surgery, and then I cared for her until she was out of danger. Because medicine is my liveli-
hood, I feel the defendant should pay me a reasonable value
for the services I performed in saving her life.
<u>2nd person</u>: I do not feel that I owe the plaintiff any money,
because I did not ask him to treat me, nor did I assent when
he began treating me. Therefore, I had no intent to enter
into a contract with the plaintiff and I feel that I should
not pay him any money,
<u>Judge</u>: Defendant, you have been enriched at the expense of
the plaintiff. It is only fair that the plaintiff, since
medicine is his occupation, recover from you the reasonable
value of the services rendered to you. In this case, therefore, I will render judgment for the plaintiff.

You can see that the doctor would have been unfairly
treated if he was not paid for his expert services, and the
woman would have been unjustly enriched for having received
the free services. So the court implied a contract in law,
which really didn't exist, to avoid unjust enrichment.

Now that we know basically what a contract is and why
we have it, let's discuss which contracts are valid and enforceable and which are not.

A valid contract is one which the courts will enforce
against either party.

A voidable contract is one which the courts will enforce
against one of the parties but not against the other.

A void contract is an agreement which the courts will
not enforce against either party.

We shall now attempt to determine which contracts are
valid, which voidable, and which void.

THE FIVE BASIC ELEMENTS OF ENFORCEABLE CONTRACTS

There are five basic elements that every contract must have in order to be valid and enforceable:

1. <u>Two or more parties</u>, each party legally capable or competent to contract.
2. <u>Mutual assent</u>, which means, again, that each party must freely and voluntarily intend to enter and be bound by the contract.
3. <u>A lawful object</u>, which means the contract must not require the performance of an illegal or unlawful act.
4. <u>Consideration by each party</u>, which means, briefly, that each party must obtain some benefit or incur some detriment in the contract.
5. For some contracts <u>a required form</u>. For example, any contract involving land must be in writing.

   Now we will look more closely at these five basic elements of a contract.

COMPETENCY

Let us look first at the competency of the parties. Basically, anyone is competent to enter a contract unless the law denies such a right to that person. If a person does not have the competency to contract, it simply means that contracts which he enters cannot be enforced against him. Therefore, an incompetent person may enter contracts and can actually perform them, but if he fails to perform, the other party cannot force him to perform the contract at law. Most states have laws which require an individual to be of a certain age in order to be competent. In most states this age limit is 21 years. But some states set a lower age limit, and others distinguish between men and women. Most states also provide that mentally ill persons are not competent, and some states include persons who are drunk when they enter the contract as being incompetent. Contracts made by persons while in prison are unenforceable against the person in prison, or may be in some states. An incompetent person who has entered into a contract may enforce the contract against the other party, but the other party cannot enforce it against him. This does not mean, however, that the incompetent party can require the other party to perform without performing himself. And if he wishes to avoid the transaction or get out of it, he must return to the other party any benefit he has received under the contract.

Let us use an example of a person who has contracted
but who is not of legal age to enter into the contract in
question. The law calls such a person, a person not of legal
age to contract, an infant. (This is a legal term; it does
not mean the infant in a mother's arms.)
1st person: Your Honor, I am a used car dealer and last week
I sold a car to the defendant and she now refuses to pay for
it.
2nd person: Your Honor, I bought the car thinking that I
had a job lined up for after school. But the job fell through
and now I have no way of paying for the car.
Judge: How old are you, Defendant?
2nd person: Nineteen years old, Your Honor.
Judge: Since the age of legal competency in this state is
21 years, and the defendant is only 19, I find in this case
for the defendant, provided, however, that defendant return
the automobile to the plaintiff.

Now, some states require not only that the benefit received be returned but that it be returned in the same condition in which it was received. If that is impossible, the
incompetent party may have to pay the difference between the
value when received and the value when returned. So if our
fortunate 19-year-old girl had been unfortunate enough to
have an accident with her car, the court may well have required her to return the car, plus the difference in value
for what she paid for it and the value after it was returned
destroyed or damaged.

A minor's parents are not usually liable for the contracts entered into by the minor, or infant, unless the
parent co-signs the contract. This is why if you purchase
anything of considerable value while you are incompetent
by reason of age, the seller requires one of your parents
to co-sign the contract.

DISAFFIRMANCE

The fact that a contract is voidable in favor of one who is
not competent under the law means that that person may disaffirm the contract. Disaffirmance is a statement or an act,
such as return of the goods, showing an intent not to perform the contract. For example, a minor may disaffirm contracts involving personal property up until the time of his
majority--that is, the time he reaches the legal age at which
he could contract--or within a reasonable time thereafter.
If a contract made while the person was a minor is not dis-

affirmed upon that person's reaching his or her majority or
shortly thereafter, the contract may then be enforced against
him or her.

In contracts involving real property (that is, land and
things permanently fixed to the land), a minor cannot disaffirm the contract until he or she reaches majority. When
majority is reached, the law will consider the contract disaffirmed unless the minor who has just become an adult then
agrees in writing to be bound by the terms of the contract.
This agreement by an adult to be bound by the contracts entered into while a minor is called <u>ratification</u>.

In most states, contracts involving personal property,
are automatically ratified upon reaching majority unless the
contract is at that time disaffirmed. For example, suppose
that while a minor Jim Johnson purchased a television set
and a lot upon which he was going to build a house someday.
He purchased the lot and the television set on the time payment plan. If upon reaching majority Jim fails to say anything to the seller of the TV set, the seller will be able
to enforce the contract against him. However, if Jim says
nothing to the seller of the lot, he will be deemed to have
disaffirmed the contract and it cannot be enforced against
him.

There are exceptions to the general facts given above
about contracts. Some states have laws which allow certain
contracts to be enforced against certain minors; for example,
a minor engaged in a legitimate business activity may not
be able to avoid contracts entered into in pursuance of that
business. Most states also include insurance contracts in
bank deposits and withdrawals also. And many states will not
allow a minor who misrepresents his age as an adult to later
avoid his contracts.

Another common exception to the rule occurs if a minor
contracts for a <u>necessity</u>. A necessity is anything a person
buys which is required to maintain a station in life, such
as food, clothing, lodging, medical care, and education.
There are other examples: An automobile may be a necessity
if without it the minor could not earn his living. This is
really not an exception to the rule in that the contract
itself can be enforced against the minor. But the seller
may recover the reasonable value of the services rendered
to the minor for necessaries under the implied in law contract theory; for example:
<u>1st person</u>: Your Honor, the defendant contracted with my
business school for a course in shorthand. The course took
six weeks and the defendant promised to pay $200 for it. She
completed the course but now refuses to pay the $200.

2nd person: Your Honor, I'm only 18 years old and therefore
may not be bound to perform my contracts.
Judge: Defendant, what is your occupation?
2nd person: I'm a student now, but I hope to be a secretary.
Judge: In this case the course in shorthand is considered a
necessity because it is part of defendant's plan for readying
herself for a good job. She entered into the agreement with
this plan in mind, and it would be unjust to allow her the
benefit of the course which she completed without paying the
reasonable value, therefore.

Again, we see that a legally incompetent person may avoid
his obligations under the contracts he enters into. However,
that legally incompetent person may be liable for the reasonable value of the benefit he or she received and cannot return
to the other party.

GLOSSARY TERMS

Competency   The ability to enter into contracts.

Contract   A promise made by one person to another to do or not do something in the future, and which is enforceable in a court of law.

Disaffirmance   Intent expressed by statement or act not to fulfill a contract.

Express contract   A contract resulting from written or spoken words of mutual assent.

Implied in fact contract   A contract in which the mutual assent of the parties has been expressed by their acts.

Implied in law contract   A contract that is implied by the law to be entered into by certain parties in certain situations.

Incompetency   The condition of not having contracts entered into enforced against oneself, because the law has denied one the right to enter into contracts.

Infant   In legal terminology any person not of the legal age to enter a contract.

Majority   Legal age at which contracts can be entered into.

Minority   Any age below that which is legal for entering contracts.

Mutual assent   The expressed mutual intent of two or more persons to legally bind one another to perform.

Ratification   Agreement by an adult to be bound by contracts entered into while a minor.

Valid contract   A contract enforceable against either party.

Void contract   A contract not enforceable against either party.

Voidable contract   A contract enforceable against one party but not the other.

SELF TEST

CHAPTER 2

NAME_____

DATE_____

2.1   Contracts, and the law underlying them, prevent problems from arising, because contracts create_____.

2.2   A promise made by one person to another to do or not to do something in the future which is enforceable in a court of law is a/an_____.

2.3   _____promises are examples of promises which are not contracts, because they are not enforceable in a court of law.

2.4   In the definition of a contract, reference was made concerning "one person to another" which implies that a person may not_____with himself.

2.5   The promise in a contract must be for present or future performance, but it cannot affect_____ performance.

2.6   The mutual intent for two parties to legally bind each other is known as _____.

2.7   When mutual assent is expressed by written or spoken words, the contract resulting from this expressed mutual assent is known as a/an_____contract.

2.8   The contract resulting from mutual assent implied by the acts of the parties is known as a/an_____ contract.

2.9   When the courts imply mutual assent where no mutual assent is present, but do so to prevent the unjust enrichment of one party at the expense of another, the contract is a contract implied in_____.

2.10   A/An_____contract is one which the courts will enforce against either party.

2.11   A/An_____contract is one which the courts will enforce against one of the parties, but not the other.

2.12   A/An_____contract is an agreement which the courts will not enforce against either party.

2.13   List, in spaces_____,_____,_____, _____, and_____,the five basic elements that every contract must have in order to be valid and enforceable.

2.14   The element that requires that each party must be
        legally capable to contract is referred to as_____
        ____.

2.15   Basically, anyone is considered competent to enter a
        contract, unless the_____denies such a right
        to that person.

2.16   Contracts entered into by an incompetent person would
        be an example of a/an_____contract, because the
        incompetent party cannot be made to perform the con-
        tract but he can make the other party perform.

2.17   A/An_____is considered incompetent to enter con-
        tracts because he has not reached the age required by
        law to be considered competent to enter contracts.

2.18   Before an infant can disaffirm a contract it has en-
        tered, it must return the_____received under
        the contract.

2.19   Generally speaking, an infant's parents are not liable
        for contracts the infant enters, unless they_____
        the contract.

2.20   _____is a statement or act showing an intent
        not to perform a voidable contract.

2.21   The agreement by an adult to be bound by the contracts
        entered into while a minor is called_____.

2.22   In contracts involving _____property the majori-
        ty of the states consider ratification to occur auto-
        matically when the minor reaches his majority, unless
        the contract is disaffirmed within a reasonable time.

2.23   A minor cannot disaffirm a contract involving_____
        property until he or she reaches their majority, at
        which time the law considers the contract disaffirmed
        unless the minor, who has just become an adult, then
        agrees in_____to be bound by the contract.

2.24   If a minor contracts for a/an_____; most states
        will not allow the minor to later disaffirm the con-
        tract.

2.25   A/An_____is anything a person buys to maintain a
        station in life, such as food, clothing, medical care,
        etc.

3

Contracts
Mutual Assent

LEARNING OBJECTIVES

To discover the essentials of the offer and acceptance necessary for mutual assent.

CHAPTER CONTENTS

Some Offers Not Binding   Communication of Offer
Duration of Offer   Revocations and Options   Acceptance
Unilateral Contracts   Bilateral Contracts   Acceptance of
Unilateral and Bilateral Contracts   Summary   Glossary
Self Test

The second basic element of a contract is mutual assent:
the offer made by the *offerer* and the acceptance made by
the *offeree*.

SOME OFFERS NOT BINDING

An *offer* is an expression of intent to be legally bound by
certain terms if the other party will assent to the same
terms; it expresses or appears to express the attempt to
enter a binding agreement, and thus it must create in the
other party the power to accept, and to do this the offerer
must lead the other party to believe that he is the recipient
of a power to accept. To reasonably create this belief in
the other party, the offer must be sufficiently definite
rather than vague or uncertain, and must not be made in
obvious jest, excitement, or the heat of anger. A few examples will help:
1. "Your Honor, defendant offered to sell me his Stingray
yesterday for $10, and now he refuses to go through with the
transaction."
   "Your Honor, the plaintiff and I were in a hurry to get
to school yesterday and when my Stingray wouldn't start I
became angry at it and I said to the plaintiff, 'If
you have ten bucks, you can have the darn thing.'"
   Such an offer is obviously made in anger, and no reasonable person would think that anyone intended to be
bound by it.
2. "Your Honor, defendant advertised Beatles records for
sale in the paper for 50 cents. But when I went to his
store to buy a Beatles record, he refused to sell one to
me for 50 cents."
   "Before plaintiff came into my store, I had sold 50
Beatles records at 50 cents each and I was losing so much
money that I decided not to sell any more for that amount."
   Most newspaper advertisements are not offers, but are
merely an <u>invitation</u> to the public to make an offer to the
seller: A newspaper ad is usually merely a request for an
offer, unless it is so specific, clear, definite and complete that there could be no mistake that the advertiser
intended to make a binding offer. Since the storekeeper
specified neither which Beatles records were for sale for
50 cents nor how many were for sale, this was clearly a
mere invitation to the public to come into the store and
offer 50 cents for Beatles records.

3. "Your Honor, while attending defendant's auction yesterday, I submitted the highest bid on a piano that was being auctioned off, but defendant refused to sell me the piano."

"The owner told me not to sell the piano for less than $60, and since plaintiff's bid was only $45, I refused her bid."

In auction, unless it is expressly stated that the auction is for sale without reserve, it is the bidder who makes the offer and the auctioneer who accepts. Therefore, the plaintiff's bid was an offer, not an acceptance, and the auctioneer had the right to refuse the offer.

An exception to the rule that offers made in newspapers are not really offers but only invitations is the offer of reward for lost or missing goods, animals, etc.: Rewards published in newspapers are offers, that is, binding. So the finder who returns the goods to the owner is entitled to the reward.

COMMUNICATION OF OFFER

Offers must be communicated, either by words or actions, by the offerer to the offeree. Sometimes communication may be deficient:

"Your Honor, last week I took my shoes into the defendant's shoe repair shop. I received a piece of paper which looked like a receipt for them, with the price for the repair written right on its front. But when I went back in this week to pick my shoes up, the defendant couldn't find them. Now I think he should either give me my shoes back or pay for them."

"Your Honor, I admit that the plaintiff left his shoes in my shop, and that I can't find them. But on the back of the receipt which I gave him it stated: NOT RESPONSIBLE FOR LOST OR STOLEN ARTICLES. By leaving his shoes and taking the receipt the plaintiff thereby agreed to all the terms of my offer."

Now, the test as to whether or not terms printed in small letters on a written contract are communicated to the offeree and thereby become a part of the contract is whether or not a reasonably prudent man or woman would see, understand, and assent to those terms. Such a person who has taken his shoes into a shoe shop to be repaired would not notice these terms, and if he did could not be expected to assent thereto. Thus the judgment would be for the plaintiff.

DURATION OF OFFER

How long does an offer stay open before the power to accept
is cut off? Often the duration of the offer is expressly
provided for in the offer itself; however, if no time is
specified, or if the offer says "anytime," the courts will
construe a reasonable time, taking into account the facts
of the particular situation. Under this rule, a reasonable
time for offers made over the telephone or in a face-to-
face conversation is at once, or during the conversation
itself. If the offer is made by wire or special messenger
the time is lengthened to one or two days, and if by letter
even longer.

The death of either party revokes the offer. And of
course a rejection communicated by the offeree to the
offerer terminates the offer. An acceptance which states
different terms from those contained in the offer terminates
the original offer and the power to accept thereafter
(unless it is expressly stated otherwise)— for example:

"Your Honor, defendant offered to sell me his car for
$200 as is, and I declared that I'd buy it for that price if
he would guarantee it for 30 days. He then said that he
couldn't do that and told me he would no longer offer it
for sale at $200."

"I merely changed my mind and decided to get more for
my car."

The plaintiff's statement that he would buy the car for
two hundred dollars if the offerer would guarantee it for
30 days constituted a counteroffer, not an acceptance,
since it varied the terms of the original offer. As such
the plaintiff's counteroffer terminated the original offer
and the plaintiff's power to accept the original offer;
that is, the counteroffer prevented enforcement of the
original offer. Mere inquiries in separate offers are not
counteroffers, thus the question "Is this your lowest
price?" is a mere inquiry and does not terminate the offer.
Such a statement as "You may send me the goods offered but
I assume you'll sell me more at another price" is both an
acceptance of the original offer and an offer back to buy
more at the price stated.

REVOCATIONS AND OPTIONS

Most offers may be terminated by the offerer before the
offeree has accepted. This is known as *revocation*, a rule

that generally applies even though the offerer stated in
his offer that it would remain open for a certain period of
time—unless the offeree gave the offerer something of value
to hold the offer open. This separate agreement to hold the
offer open for a given period of time is a separate contract,
and is called an *option*.

ACCEPTANCE

Generally speaking, only the person designated in the offer
as the offeree has the power to accept it. If Sam offered
to sell his horse to Joe for $30 and Pete overheard the offer,
Pete could not accept the offer for himself. If Pete had
said, "I'll buy the horse for 30 dollars," that would have
been an offer, not an acceptance; Sam could reject or accept
Pete's offer as he pleased.

But there are two exceptions to this rule: 1) if the
offer states on its face that it is open to anyone; 2) if
the offer is a reward, because a reward is by its terms open
to anyone.

Generally, a person must have knowledge of the offer
before he may accept. Although unusual, it is possible to
unwittingly accept an offer—for example:

A couple of weeks ago a person found my dog. I had already put an ad in the newspaper, but the fellow came over
as a good citizen and neighbor and said, "Here's your dog
back." The next day he called me and said he'd read my ad
the following day in the paper. Now he wanted the $25 re-
ward. I told him, "You had no knowledge of that offer prior
to the time that you acted, so you are not entitled to a
reward because you couldn't have accepted it."

Well, that was a pretty strong statement because you
know perfectly well that there is an exception to that
rule—and that is when REWARD is offered by a public body.
If the FBI is offering a reward for the capture of a dangerous criminal, the person who turns in the criminal may
collect the reward whether or not he knew it was offered
at the time he captured and turned over the criminal.

Acceptance of an offer must take certain forms to be
proper. First, the acceptance must be exactly in accordance with the terms of the offer. Otherwise it will be
construed as a counteroffer, as we saw in our earlier
example of the car offered for sale as is, the offeree
wanting a 30-day guarantee, and the withdrawal of the offer.

Second, acceptance must usually be indicated by some word or act, for only in rare cases will silence be construed as an acceptance. Generally, there is no duty to reply to an offer, and most courts would hold this true even if the offer is framed so as to make silence an acceptance. For example: I write a letter to a stranger offering to send him 30 widgets for 10 cents apiece and that unless I hear from him in ten days, I'll send them and he's to pay for them. If I don't hear anything by mail from the stranger I may send the widgets to him, but he won't have any obligation to pay for them. For he and I are strangers and had not had any dealings in the past with one another, so the offer was not accepted by his silence. But if in the past he and I had established the usage of trade whereby I sent him offers which could be accepted by his silence, and when I sent the goods he then accepted and paid for them, then this contract for widgets could be enforced.

Another instance in which silence is not acceptance is in the receipt of unsolicited goods by mail accompanied by instructions to send a certain sum or return the goods by mail. The law is that the recipient has no obligation to pay for unsolicited goods nor to return them— as long as he doesn't use them. To use them would be acceptance.

UNILATERAL CONTRACTS

Further modes of acceptance are authorized in the law, but before these are discussed two types of contracts must be distinguished: The first type of contract is an exchange of a promise or an act. In other words, the offerer is not seeking a promise to perform from the offeree, but is seeking actual performance. This type of contract, known as a *unilateral contract*, is accepted when the offeree performs what the offerer asked for in his offer.

In an example in a previous chapter a woman got into a taxi cab and said, "To the York Hotel." The taxi driver didn't say, "Yes, I'll take you to the York Hotel for $2.35," he took her to the York Hotel and then made a charge. The woman did not want the driver's promise to drive her to the York Hotel, she wanted to be driven there, and when she was the contract was entered and she was bound to pay the fare. She implicitly made a promise to pay upon his performance.

Or, for another example of a unilateral contract, suppose Sam wrote to George: "Ship me 500 lbs of birdseed at $3 per lb at once." If George ships the birdseed immediately, then the offer has been accepted and a unilateral contract has been entered and at that point Sam's promise to pay can be enforced in a court of law. Thus, no "contract" arises in a unilateral contract until the act which is bargained for is performed.

BILATERAL CONTRACTS

In the second type of contract, known as a *bilateral contract*, a promise is exchanged for another promise. The bilateral contract is enforceable as soon as the offeree promises to do what was asked of him in the offer. For example, if Bill writes to Hal, "I will buy 300 lbs of widgets if you will sell them to me at $3 a lb," Hal needs only agree to the terms of Bill's offer to create a binding contract. In other words, Bill is bargaining for Hal's <u>promise</u> to sell him 300 lbs of widgets at $3 a pound, rather than for the widgets themselves.

To reiterate the difference between a unilateral contract and a bilateral contract, in a unilateral contract the offerer seeks <u>performance</u> from the offeree, once performance is made then the contract is deemed accepted by the offeree and the offerer's promise to pay can be enforced; but a bilateral contract seeks a <u>promise</u> from the offeree: It is an exchange of one promise for another ("I promise to pay you if you will do, and first <u>say</u> you will do, something for me").

ACCEPTANCE OF UNILATERAL AND BILATERAL CONTRACTS

As we saw, unilateral contracts are accepted by the offeree's performing what was asked by the offerer. But bilateral contracts can be accepted in different ways— for example, the mode of acceptance may be specified in the offer. This specification of mode is sometimes binding on the offeree and sometimes not, as two examples will show: If I send a letter offering to sell you my stamp collection for $75 and state that you may accept my offer by letting me know by telephone within the next 2 days, but before you could telephone you saw my brother on the street and told him that you will accept my offer, which

my brother then tells me, you may claim that a valid contract has been entered; but you are incorrect because I
specified that you must telephone me within 2 days of your
acceptance.   Since you did not do this, no contract has been
entered.

However, the Uniform Commercial Code specifies that
any mode of acceptance will be sufficient so long as the
offerer has actual notice of the offeree's acceptance—even
if another means of acceptance was specified in the offer.
Thus, if the Uniform Commercial Code is in effect in your
state, any mode of acceptance can be used for the sale of
goods so long as the offerer receives actual notice of the
acceptance, and the contract is binding.

If no mode of acceptance is stipulated in the offer
the general rule is that actual notice to the offerer by
the offeree of his acceptance will create a binding contract.   However, in some cases, acceptance can be binding
before the offerer has actual notice—for example, if an
offer *not* specifying any mode of acceptance was made by
mail, the acceptance may be made by mail also; and it is
effective when it is deposited at the Post Office.

If a friend writes me a letter telling me that he'll
sell me his skis for $50, and I write him back saying I'll
buy the skis for $50, and deposit that letter in the mail
with postage on it, we have a binding contract the minute
I drop it in the mail chute.   Acceptance may be sent in
the same way that the offer was received, so long as no
other method was specified in the offer.   And if the offer
is sent by mail, or even telegraph, and the same manner
of acceptance is used, acceptance is valid when it is
mailed or deposited at the telegraph office.

SUMMARY

Thus, mutual assent consists of two essential elements:
offer and acceptance.   The offer must be definite and
certain, must be made with the intent by the offerer to
be bound by it, and must be directed and communicated to
the offeree.

An offer may be accepted only by the party to whom
it was made; the acceptance must be unconditional and
identical with the offer; it must be indicated by some
word or act; it may be made by performance of an act when
the offer calls for such (the unilateral contract); when
the offer requires a promise, the acceptance must be communicated to the offeree (the bilateral contract).

GLOSSARY TERMS

Bilateral contract A contract accepted by the offeree's promise to perform as requested in the offer.

Offer An expression of intent to be legally bound by certain terms if the other party will assent to those terms.

Offeree The party who receives an offer.

Offerer The party who makes the initial offer.

Option A separate agreement to hold an offer open.

Revocation Withdrawal of an offer by the offerer before acceptance by the offeree.

Unilateral contract A contract that can be accepted only by the offeree's performing what is asked for in the offer.

SELF TEST
CHAPTER 3

NAME_____

DATE_____

3.1 An expression of intent to be legally bound by certain terms if the other party will assent to the same terms is an _____.

3.2 In order to create the _____ to accept in the other party, the offer must be sufficiently _____ so as not to be vague, and must not be made in _____.

3.3 Newspaper advertisements are usually not offers, but merely _____ to the public to make an offer to the seller.

3.4 In auctions, unless it is expressly stated that the auction is for sale without reserve, it is the _____ who makes the offer, and the _____ who accepts.

3.5 _____, which are published in newspapers, are offers, which is an exception to the rule that offers in newspapers are invitations for offers.

3.6 Offers must be communicated, either by words or actions, by the _____ to the _____.

3.7 The test as to whether or not terms printed in small letters on a written contract are communicated by the offerer to the offeree depends upon whether or not a _____ man or woman would see, understand, and assent to the terms.

3.8 If the duration of an offer is _____ provided for in the offer itself, then that will control how long an offer remains open; however, if no time limit is specified in the offer, the courts will construe that the offer is open for a _____.

3.9 _____ of either party, or _____ communicated by the offeree to the offerer, terminates an offer.

3.10 A _____, which is an acceptance of different terms than those contained in the offer, terminates the original offer unless it is expressly stated otherwise.

3.11   Most offers can be terminated if the _____
        is received by the offeree before he has accepted.

3.12   A separate agreement in which the offeree gives the
        offerer something of value to hold an offer open
        for a given period of time is known as a/an

        _____.

3.13   Generally speaking, an acceptance may be made by the
        person to whom the offer was _____, and who
        has _____ of the offer, except in a/an
        _____ situation that is made by a public
        agency.

3.14   If the acceptance of an offer is not made exactly
        in accordance with the terms of the offer, it will
        be construed as a/an_____.

3.15   Acceptance of an offer must usually be made by
        some word or _____, and only in rare cases
        will _____ be construed as acceptance, because
        generally, there is no _____ to reply to an
        offer.

3.16   If two parties because of their past dealings with
        each other, had established the usage of
        _____, then silence could possibly be
        construed as acceptance.

3.17   If goods are sold unsolicited to someone, that
        person has no duty to pay for them or return them,
        unless that person _____ them.

3.18   A contract whereby the offerer is seeking actual
        performance, rather than a promise to perform, is
        known as a/an _____ contract, and performance of
        what was asked by the offerer by the offeree would
        constitute _____.

3.19   No contract arises in a unilateral contract until
        the act which is bargained for is _____.

3.20   A contract that is enforceable as soon as the
        offeree promises to do what was asked of him in the
        offer is known as a/an _____ contract.

3.21   The Uniform Commercial Code specifies that any mode
        of acceptance is sufficient as long as the offerer
        has actual _____ of the offeree's acceptance.

3.22   To communicate acceptance of an offer when no mode
        of acceptance is specified, the general rule is
        that acceptance may be sent in the same manner it is

        _____.

3.23   An offer must be made with the _____ of the
        offerer to be bound by it for a valid offer to exist.

3.24   When an offer is made and accepted, the parties have
        indicated their _____ to be bound.

4 Contracts

Defective Agreements

LEARNING OBJECTIVES

To define in detail the elements that make some contracts unenforceable.

CHAPTER CONTENTS

Involuntary Contracts Defined   The Elements of Fraud
Remedies for Defrauded Parties   Methods of Inducing Invol-
untary Contracts   Erroneous Contracts   Glossary   Self
Test

We have seen that mutual assent is comprised of the offer
and acceptance, and we have seen what constitutes a valid
offer and acceptance.
   Mutual assent must be freely given: The offer and
acceptance which comprise it must be made with the intent
to enter a binding contract. Some agreements appear to be
perfectly valid on their face but may not be enforceable,
either because one of the parties did not freely and
voluntarily intend to enter the agreement or because the
contract actually entered was not the one intended to be
entered by one of the parties, even though both parties
did intend to enter some kind of contract.
   Two concepts are involved in such unenforceable contracts: One of the parties may have entered a contract
even though he had no intent to enter a contract at all;
or one of the parties may have entered a different contract
from the one he actually intended to enter.

INVOLUNTARY CONTRACTS DEFINED

There are several ways one may be induced to enter a contract with no intent to enter. The first one is by the
fraud of the other party. Legally fraud is a false representation or concealment of a present or past material
fact made by a person who has knowledge of its falseness
or who makes it in reckless disregard of the truth with
the intent to have the other person rely upon it and which
actually induces such reliance. Let's see if we can break
fraud down into its component parts.

THE ELEMENTS OF FRAUD

A *false representation* is an affirmative false statement,
such as "There's nothing wrong with the transmission in this
car," when it is known that the transmission is faulty. An
example of *concealment* would be putting heavy oil in the
transmission to muffle the sound of grinding gears. Concealment is a rather slippery term because, say, the seller
of a car may not have a duty to disclose the fact that the
transmission is bad even if he knows it. But he may not
actively conceal the fact that a bad transmission is bad.
Thus, the key word is concealment rather than mere nondis-
closure. The false representation or concealment which we
have just discussed must be of a present or past material

fact; that is, the fact must already be in existence.
The law presumes that no one can predict the future as a
matter of fact. Thus, a prediction cannot be considered
fraudulent. For example, if someone is trying to sell
you a convertible and tells you that it's not going to
rain for the next six months, and you are foolish enough
to rely on his prediction and buy the convertible because
he told you it wasn't going to rain for six months, this
would not be fraud and you would not be able to avoid the
transaction.

The term material, as used in the law, means a fact
that influenced the decision to enter the contract.

To be fraud, a statement must falsely represent or
actively conceal a *fact*—this excludes mere opinions,
judgments, and beliefs about things. For example, a car
salesman's telling you that this is the best 1950 Chevy in
town is not fraud because it may be his opinion, his judgment, his belief, or perhaps mere puffing—his effort to
make his wares more valuable in the eyes of the potential
buyer.

The law presumes that an ordinary reasonable and prudent man can distinguish between statements of fact and
statements which are calculated to only psychologically
affect a person but are not meant to be taken seriously.

To commit *fraud* the person making the statement must
know that the statement is false or must make the statement
in reckless disregard of the truth—that is, the person
who makes the statement should have known that it was
false, even though he may not. actually have known. Thus,
if a used car dealer tells you that the brakes on the car
you are thinking of buying were just relined and they were
in fact not, the statement would be fraud because he
should have known whether or not they were relined before
he made the statement.

Again, to commit *fraud* the person making the statement
must intend that the other person rely upon it. Thus,
if Jerry overhears Bill tell Jim that the brakes were just
relined and Jerry buys the car, no fraud was committed
because at the time only Jim, not Jerry, was meant to rely
on the statement.

For *fraud* to have been committed the false statement
or concealment must actually have induced reliance by the
other party; the other party must have been *deceived* by the
statement and have truly relied upon it in entering the
contract. Thus, in our example, if the salesman tells you

that the brakes have just been relined but you know that in fact the brakes have *not* been relined, then there is no fraud because you are not actually deceived by the seller's statement.

To summarize, the five elements of fraud are as follows: (1) a false representation or concealment of a (2) present or past material fact, (3) made with knowledge that the statement is false or made in reckless disregard of the truth, with (4) the intent to have the other party rely thereon, and (5) which actually induces the other person to rely upon it by deceiving him.

REMEDIES FOR DEFRAUDED PARTIES

Contracts induced by fraud can be *voided*, which you will remember means that the contract may not be enforced against the party upon whom the fraud was practiced. The party upon whom the fraud is practiced may also *disaffirm* the contract by returning what he has received. By returning what he has received, he could, of course, get back what he has paid the other party.

However, a party induced to enter a contract by fraud may elect to ratify the contract; that is, he may demand that the other party go through with the contract. He then must also perform himself, but he may be able to obtain damages from the other party for the actual damage the fraud created. For example, the used car salesman fraudulently tells John that the brakes have just been relined and John relies upon this representation in his decision to buy the car. He pays cash for the car and intends to drive it home; on the way he tries to stop at a stop sign but finds that the brakes don't work. He then discovers that the brake linings are worn to the drum. John can do one of two things: He can return the car to the seller and demand his money back; or if he likes the car otherwise and wants to keep it he may force the seller to put the car in the condition that the seller represented it as being in—that is, force the seller to put new brakes on the car or at least pay the cost of a new brake job.

Thus, fraud generally applies to the situation in which the party intends to enter a contract, but not the contract which he actually entered: John intended to enter a contract when he bought the car, but he intended to buy a car with new brakes, not defective ones.

METHODS OF INDUCING INVOLUNTARY CONTRACTS

But fraud may be used to induce a person to enter a contract when he really didn't intend to enter a contract at all. John tells a car salesman that he is just shopping around for a car, but then says, "I would like to see if I can buy that Ford convertible on your lot for about $500." The salesman tells John that if he will sign a piece of paper the salesman will see if the sales manager would be willing to sell the car for $500. The salesman tells John that the paper is not a contract or an offer, but merely a request for an offer from the sales manager, when in fact the salesman knows full well that the paper is an offer. If the sales manager accepts, John was induced to enter a contract by fraud when he really did not intend to enter a contract at all.

The threat of force or an act of violence, known as *duress*, may be used against a person to induce him to either enter a contract when he did not intend a contract at all or enter a different contract from one he intended to enter. Duress may occur if the other party threatens to harm a person or his property, or to take away his liberty, or threatens the person, liberty, or property of a near relative. The classic example of duress is kidnapping: Suppose Mr. Brown's son is kidnapped, and the kidnapper threatens to harm the child unless Mr. Brown contracts with the kidnapper to pay the kidnapper $500 a month for 2 years.

Duress can occur only if the threat is to do an illegal act. For example, Jake runs into Larry with his car; Larry's threat to sue Jake unless Jake will contract to pay Larry a certain amount of money is not duress, because Larry has a legal right to sue Jake for his injuries.

A third type of contract is voidable because of lack of intent if a person in a confidential relationship to another uses that relationship to influence the other to enter a contract. This is known as *undue influence*.

Confidential relationships are those in which one person is peculiarly subjected to the influence of another as in a family relationship where one person has a mental weakness or in a business relationship involving trust and confidence. A few example relationships are parent and child, attorney and client, physician and patient. Undue influence occurs when the person who has the trust and confidence of another uses it for his benefit at the expense of the other person.

ERRONEOUS CONTRACTS

Being human, people make mistakes, even when they enter contracts. The general rule is that a person is bound by what
he signs, even if he was unaware by his own mistake that he
was entering a contract or was entering one different from
what he intended to enter.

The law presumes that in the absence of fraud, duress,
or undue influence, people generally know what they are doing and they do not enter transactions which they do not
intend to enter. Thus, if only one of the parties is mistaken as to the agreement, or some of its terms, this unilateral mistake will not affect the agreement and it may be
enforced against him.

The only real exception to this rule is when one party
is mistaken as to the identity of the other party. For instance, if Keith is talking on the telephone with a man
named Jack Jones but is unaware that it is the wrong Jack
Jones, and enters into a contract over the telephone with
the wrong Jack Jones, his mistake in identity may result
in no contract at all being entered. However, if Keith
were talking face-to-face with the wrong Jack Jones thinking that he was the right one, even if he did not know
what the right Jack Jones looked like, the law would not
afford relief, because the law would assume that Keith
intended to contract with the person to whom he was talking
face-to-face.

In two situations a *mutual* mistake—that is, both
parties are mistaken as to the same fact—of the parties
may allow the contract to be avoided: First, if both
parties are mistaken as to the *identity* of the subject
matter; second, if both parties are mistaken as to the
existence of the matter. An example of the first is if
John negotiates with a used car salesman for a 1963 Ford
sedan, but there are two 1963 Ford sedans on the lot and
John is thinking about one of them but the salesman is
thinking about the other, there would be a mutual mistake
as to the identity of the subject matter and no contract
would be entered. As an example of the second mutual error,
the object of the contract had been destroyed, but neither
party knew it: John says to the used car salesman, "I
want to purchase that 1959 Chevrolet," and points to a
specific car. The salesman says, "Fine, I'll sell it to
you." But if in fact another salesman has already sold
the car to another party, John would not be able to buy it:
The object of the contract would not exist insofar as the
salesman did not have the power to sell it.

Thus, we see that even though there has been an offer and acceptance and an apparently valid contract has been entered, it may be voidable if there was fraud, duress, or undue influence, or void if there was a mistake in the identity of the parties, a mutual mistake as to the identity of the subject matter or a mutual mistake as to the existence of the subject matter.

GLOSSARY TERMS

Concealment   The active concealing or disguising a fact.

Duress   Threat of force or an act of violence to induce a party to enter a contract.

Fake Representation   A statement made that is known by its maker to be false.

Fraud   Legally, a false representation or concealment knowingly made with reckless disregard for the truth and designed to produce reliance.

Material   The property of a fact that influences the decision to enter a contract.

Undue Influence   The use of a confidential relationship to induce a person to enter a contract.

SELF TEST
CHAPTER 4

NAME_____

DATE_____

4.1   To have a binding contract, mutual assent must be
_____ given, and the offer and acceptance
which comprise it must be made with the
_____ to enter a binding contract.

4.2   _____ of the other party is one way to induce another person to enter a contract that he did
not _____ to enter.

4.3   The legal definition of fraud is a false
_____ or _____, of a present or past
_____ fact made by a person who has knowledge of its falseness, and induces another person
to rely on this falsity.

4.4   A/An _____ is an affirmative false
statement.

4.5   A present or past fact means that the fact must already be in _____.

4.6   The law presumes that no one can predict the future
in fact, so a/an _____ cannot be fraudulent.

4.7   A fact is _____ if it influenced your decision to enter a contract.

4.8   To be fraud, a statement must falsely represent or
actively conceal a fact, which would exclude a
person's judgment, _____, or a salesman's
_____.

4.9   The third element of fraud is that the person making
the statement must know that the statement is
_____, or make the statement in reckless
_____ of the truth.

4.10   A statement is made in _____ of the truth
when the person who makes it should have known that
it was false, even though he may not actually have
known that it was false.

4.11   The fourth element of fraud is that the person
making the statement must _____ that the
other person _____ upon it.

4.12   The fifth element of fraud is that the false statement or concealment must actually induce
_____ by the other party.

4.13   Fraud is a false _____ or _____
        of a past or present _____ fact, made
        with _____ that the statement is
        _____ or made in reckless disregard
        of the truth, with the _____ to have
        the other party rely thereon, and which actually
        _____ the other person to rely upon it by
        deceiving him.

4.14   Contracts which are induced by fraud are
        _____, which means that the contract may not
        be _____ against the party, against whom the
        fraud was practiced.

4.15   The party upon which the fraud was practiced may
        _____ the contract by returning what he has
        received from the fraudulent party, and getting
        back what he _____ the other party; or, he
        may _____ the contract and demand that the
        fraudulent party perform the contract.

4.16   If the party against whom the fraud was practiced
        elects to ratify the contract and demands the per-
        formance by the fraudulent party, then he must also
        _____ himself, but may still be able to obtain
        _____ from the fraudulent party for _____
        damages created by the fraud.

4.17   As we can see, fraud generally applies to a
        situation where the party _____ to enter
        a contract, but not the contract which he
        _____ entered.

4.18   _____ would occur if a person is induced to
        enter a contract·under the threat of force or acts
        of violence.

4.19   The classic example of duress is _____.

4.20   Duress can only occur when there is a threat to do
        a/an _____ act.

4.21   The use of a confidential relationship by one person
        to induce the other party of the confidential rela-
        tionship to enter a contract is known as
        _____.

4.22   A confidential relationship would be one whereby
        one person is peculiarly _____ to the
        _____ of another.

4.23   Undue influence occurs when the person who has the
        _____ or confidence of another, uses it for
        his _____ at the expense of the other party.

4.24   The general rule is that a person is _____
        by what he signs.

CHAPTER 4

NAME_____

4.25   A unilateral mistake usually does not affect the
        validity of a contract, except when there has been
        a mistake by one party as to the _____
        of the other party.

4.26   The two situations where a mutual mistake of the
        parties may allow the contract to be avoided, is
        where there is a mutual mistake as to the identity
        of the _____, or the _____ of the
        specific subject matter.

4.27   Contracts may be _____ if there was fraud,
        duress, or undue influence present or _____
        if there was a mistake as to the identity of the
        parties, or a mutual mistake as to the identity
        or existence of the subject matter.

5 Contracts

Lawful Object

LEARNING OBJECTIVES

To understand that a contract has force only if it has a lawful object.

To define lawful object.

CHAPTER CONTENTS

Contracts Affecting Public Policy   Contracts Violating Statutes   Contracts Partly Enforceable   Summary   Glossary   Self Test

A contract may be illegal in two different ways: First,
if the object of the contract is made illegal by stature,
a law passed by a legislature; second, if the object of the
contract is against *public policy*. Here the contract
violates no written law but the court declares that the
object of the contract is so harmful to the public good
that it will not be enforced.

CONTRACTS AFFECTING PUBLIC POLICY

There are several ways in which contracts can violate
public policy. For one, they might affect the administration of justice, such as contracts not to prosecute someone
who has broken the law for money, or contracts with a witness
to influence him to testify in a certain manner, or contracts encouraging the commission of a crime or encouraging
litigation are all against public policy.

If you should run into and injure me with your car I
could not sell my right of action against you to a third
person because it encourages litigation. You may ask,
"What's wrong with encouraging litigation? What are courts
for if not to litigate disputes?" Courts are designed to
be used only as a *last resort* in the settlement of disputes. Our social structure favors parties solving their
own problems without the aid of outside influences. Therefore, where a contract tends to prevent the parties from
settling their own disputes the court will hold that such a
contract is against the public policy.

Thus, we see that any contract which tends to obstruct
or corrupt justice or encourage litigation will not be enforced by the courts. Another type of contract which is
against public policy is a contract affecting marriage,
such as a husband paying his wife money to give him a
divorce. Contracts which tend to disrupt existing contract
obligations are also unenforceable: If you should contract
with Carl to sell him your car for $400 and I then agree to
pay you $25 to breach your contract with Carl and sell me
the car for $400, you could not collect the $25 from me and
I could not force you to breach your contract with Carl in
a court of law.

Another type of contract which violates public policy
is one which tends to cause a neglect of duty or injures
public service, such as by bribery of a public servant or
of a private citizen who has public duties. Thus, any contract is void which tries to stop a person from performing

duties which he is legally obligated to perform. No
actual corruption need result to void such a contract; for
example, if I paid $50 to a policeman for his promise never
to give me a ticket if he catches me breaking the Motor
Vehicle Laws, this contract would be void, whether or not
I'm ever caught by him breaking a traffic law. If I am
caught breaking the law he can give me a ticket and I can't
get my $50 back, because even though my payment to him did
not in fact corrupt him, its object was corruption, and the
contract was therefore illegal.

A final object of contract against public policy is
that of facilitating an illegal purpose. If an illegal
purpose can be suspected, the contract may be unenforceable, such as when a person sells a gun to another person
knowing that the buyer intends to use the gun to shoot
someone.

CONTRACTS VIOLATING STATUTES

If a statute prohibits the act required to be performed by
the contract, the contract is unenforceable. Thus, a contract to commit a crime or a tort is unlawful and unenforceable. For example, if you paid me $10 to beat up Joe, our
contract would be unlawful because assault and battery is a
statutory crime as well as a tort. Therefore, you could
not get your $10 back if I refused to beat up Joe.

Most states have laws against gambling, wagering, or
engaging in lotteries. However, some states do not consider
a contest, which is a matter of skill rather than chance,
as gambling. If you enter and win a contest where a
prize is awarded merely by chance—for example, if everyone
who enters gets a number and all the numbers are dropped in
a hat and the drawing is then made—you could not force the
contest holders to give you the prize because the contest
was based merely upon chance. But in states which recognize
the skill exception, if the contest you entered was to
write a jingle or draw a picture then you could recover the
prize if you won because your winning was based upon skill.

Where the contract is for gambling and the state prohibits it, you usually can't even get back the amount you
paid to enter the contest, even if you win. Many states,
of course, have exceptions to their gambling laws such as
state-run horse racing, dog racing, and lotteries.

Another type of statute which may be violated by contract is a usury statute. Most state legislatures have

declared that an annual interest rate over a certain percent
is unlawful. A greater rate than allowed by statute is
usury. Most states, however, do not follow the "leave the
parties as you find them" rule when usury is involved. The
person who was injured by the usurious rate usually can recover the difference between the contract rate and the lawful rate in his state in a civil action.

Statutes are frequently violated that prohibit agreements which unreasonably restrain trade. Under our form of
social and economic system, competition is highly desirable,
and recognizing this, legislatures have attempted to protect competition; contracts which fix prices, limit production, allocate territories, or otherwise tend to create
monopolies are forbidden. Thus, a contract between two
competing manufacturers promising each other not to sell
their goods below a certain price is illegal and unenforceable because it unreasonably restrains trade.

Although ordinarily a contract between two competitors
not to sell their goods in certain areas is also illegal,
some contracts which appear to limit trade are held by the
courts to be not unreasonable and therefore not illegal.
For example, an agreement by one person to sell his
business to another and not to open a competing business
within a reasonable area for a reasonable period of time
may be valid and enforceable. Or an employee can promise
his employer not to work for a competitor for a reasonable
time after his termination of employment. Some states
also allow manufacturers of products to specify a price
below which his goods may not be sold in retail stores.
Also, patents and copyrights protect inventors from having
their inventions copied for a reasonable period of time.

Such restraints as a promise not to compete or not to
work for a competitor may be found unreasonable by the
court if the restraint produces undue hardship upon the
person subjected to it, or if it is greater than necessary
to protect the person benefiting from it. Also, such restraints must be connected with the sale of a business or
other property, or with a contract of employment. Under
these rules, then, a contract containing a restraint from
ever opening a competing business or from *ever* working
for a competitor would be unreasonable.

A restraint may also unreasonably limit the transfer
of property. A promise never to sell an item which you
purchased is unreasonable. However, a promise not to sell
it to certain persons or for a reasonable length of time
could be enforced.

Most states have many other laws prohibiting certain acts,
such as prohibiting certain activities on Sundays, prohibiting the sale of certain drugs except by prescription,
and prohibiting certain occupations except by license, such
as pharmacology, law, and medicine. Many states and
localities which prohibit certain activities on Sunday make
it illegal to enter into or perform a contract on Sunday,
but probably religious or charitable contracts or those involving necessities are excepted, as are many forms of
entertainment. Some jurisdictions also allow contracts
which are entered on Sundays but are to be performed on
a weekday to be valid if they are then ratified on a
weekday. Also, the law usually allows that although a
contract requires payment on a certain calendar date,
payment can be made the following regular business day
if the stipulated date falls on a Sunday or holiday. Thus,
if you have a contract whereby you are to pay $100 on the
4th of the month, and the 4th of July falls on Wednesday,
you would have until the close of business on Thursday to
make your payment without being in default.

CONTRACTS PARTLY ENFORCEABLE

Some contracts can be legal in some parts and illegal in
others. For example, if I contract to buy your grocery
store from you, and you promise not to open another grocery
store within three blocks of my store *and* never to work for
any other grocery store, what will be the status of the
contract? Since a reasonable limitation on opening a competing business within a certain geographical area may not
be against public policy or a statute it may be valid in
most courts. However, the promise never to work for any
other grocery store would be considered unreasonable and
therefore illegal.
    Most courts would separate the two promises and enforce
the legal one but *not* the illegal one; the court would
sever the illegal clause from the contract and enforce the
rest of it. (Thus, the court would probably enforce in the
contract of sale the promise not to open a competing store
within the three block area, but it would *not* enforce the
promise not to work for any other grocery store.) If
clauses which are valid and others which are not can be
separated without destroying the entire bargain, the contract
is a *severable contract*. If the contract is *not* severable,

that is, if the illegal part cannot be removed without destroying the whole contract, then the court will not enforce any part of the contract.

SUMMARY

To have a lawful object, the acts which a contract requires to be performed must be legally capable of being performed; the object of the contract must not be against a statute or public policy. If a contract is illegal it is void, and as a general rule the courts will leave the parties as they find them; the courts will not aid either party to the agreement.

Contracts that violate public policy—that affect the administration of justice by obstruction or corruption by encouraging litigation—are illegal. Contracts affecting marriage, such as between a husband and wife to get a divorce, are illegal. Contracts to breach an existing contract are illegal. Contracts, such as forms of bribery, which cause a public servant or a private individual acting in a public capacity to neglect his duty are illegal and void. Finally, contracts which facilitate an illegal purpose are illegal.

A contract with another to commit a crime or a tort violates a statute and is therefore illegal. Second, most states have laws which prohibit gambling, wagering, or lotteries; however, some states distinguish between gambling and contests, which require skill as opposed to mere chance, and will allow contest contracts to be enforced. Third, most states limit by law the amount of interest that can be charged on the loan of money; more than the lawful rate of interest is *usury*. In usury cases most states make an exception to the rule that courts will leave parties to illegal contracts as they found them, and will allow the contracts to be enforced up to the lawful rate of interest. Fourth, statutes make contracts which restrain trade illegal—unless the restraint is reasonable and is connected with the sale of a business or employment, or the transfer of property. Fifth, some states and localities have laws making it illegal to enter or perform contracts on Sundays or holidays. Most of these laws make exceptions for contracts involving necessities and sometimes entertainment. Some states also will allow contracts which are entered on Sunday to be enforced if they are ratified on a weekday, and others will allow contracts which are to be performed on calendar dates that fall on a Sunday or a holiday to be performed on the next regular business day. Most states require contracts that control the licensing of businesses and prohibit the sale of drugs except by prescription.

Finally, some contracts which are partly legal and partly illegal will be enforced as to their legal part *if* the illegal part can be removed from the contract and the rest of the contract enforced. Such a contract is known as a severable contract.

GLOSSARY TERMS

Public policy   Objects and conditions which though not
protected by statute the courts consider essential
to the public good.

Severable contract   A contract in which parts are considered unenforceable but the contract is not thereby
destroyed.

Usury   Unreasonably high interest rates on loaned money.

SELF TEST

CHAPTER 5

NAME_____

DATE_____

5.1   The two different ways in which a contract may be
       illegal are when the contract is made illegal by
       _____, or when it is against_____.
5.2   A contract that is against _____ does not
       violate any written law, but the court declares the
       object of the contract to be harmful to the public
       good, and that the contract will not be
       _____.
5.3   Contracts encouraging the commission of a crime, or
       encouraging litigation, would be examples of con-
       tracts that violate public policy, because they
       affect the administration of _____.
5.4   Any contract which tries to stop a person from per-
       forming _____ which he is _____ ob-
       ligated to perform is against public policy, and
       _____.
5.5   If a/an _____ purpose can be suspected, a
       contract may be unenforceable.
5.6   A contract to commit a crime or _____ is
       _____ and unenforceable.
5.7   Some states do not consider a contest which is a
       matter of _____, rather than chance, as
       gambling.
5.8   _____ results when a greater rate of interest
       is charged than is permitted by statute.
5.9   Contracts which fix prices or tend to create mono-
       polies would violate statutes which prohibit agree-
       ments which unreasonably _____ _____.
5.10   Restraints connected with the sale of a/an
       _____, or with a contract of _____,
       if reasonable, can be considered valid contracts
       and not in violation of the law.
5.11   Some jurisdictions allow contracts which are entered
       on Sunday but are to be performed on a weekday, to
       be valid if they are _____ on a weekday.

5.12   In a contract where one part of a contract is legal, and the other part is illegal, the courts will separate the two parts, and _____ the legal part, but not the _____ part.

5.13   If a contract is not _____, that is, the illegal part cannot be removed without destroying the whole contract, then the court will not _____ any part of the contract.

5.14   In order to have a lawful object, the acts which the contracts require to be performed must be _____ of being performed.

5.15   If a contract is illegal, it is _____, and as a general rule, the courts will _____ the parties as they find them.

5.16   An exception is taken by most courts regarding usury, and will allow the contract to be enforced up to the _____ rate of _____.

5.17   Contracts to breach _____ contracts are illegal, and therefore _____, and are examples of contracts which violate _____.

5.18   A/An _____ is a law established by a legislature.

5.19   A contract intended to corrupt a public servant or private individual acting in a public capacity is called _____.

5.20   If a contract is considered void, and the courts leave the parties as they find them, then the court will not _____ either party to the agreement.

6 Contracts

Consideration

LEARNING OBJECTIVES

To know fully and in detail what constitutes valid consideration.

CHAPTER CONTENT

Consideration   Elements of Consideration   Size of Consideration   Formal Contracts   Recognizing Consideration   Glossary   Self Test

As we have seen, to enter a valid contract the parties must be competent, must mutually assent to the terms of the contract by proper offer and acceptance, and must have a lawful object in entering the contract.

CONSIDERATION

The fourth essential of a valid contract is *consideration*. In its most basic sense consideration is the price one pays for the promise or the act which he receives. This price may be simply a promise to do something or the actual performance of something which you are not already bound to do.

To be valid, a contract requires mutuality of consideration: The promisor and promisee must both incur a *legal detriment*: They must promise to do something or actually do something which they are not already bound to do. And each must gain a *legal benefit*: Each party must obtain from the other party a promise or an act that the other party is not already bound to do. Thus, mutuality of consideration requires each party to incur a legal detriment and gain a legal benefit.

Therefore, a promise to give someone something is not enforceable as a contract if the other person did not promise to do something in return. Here again the distinction between bilateral and unilateral contracts is important. In a bilateral contract one party promises to do something in return for the promise of the other party to do something. In a unilateral contract, one party promises to do something in exchange for an act of the other party, whereas the other party performs an act in exchange for the promise of the other party: For example, John enters a contract with a new car dealer whereby the dealer agrees to order and obtain a certain model and sell it to John, and John agrees to pay cash upon delivery. This is a bilateral contract, because each party has promised to perform an act which he was not obligated to perform before the contract was entered. John is detrimented by his promise to pay money and is benefited by the dealer's promise to obtain and sell him the car. The dealer in turn is detrimented by his promise to obtain and sell the car to John and is benefited by John's promise to pay him the money.

Thus, there is consideration for the promise made by one to the other, and the binding contract is entered at the time the promises are exchanged. But suppose instead that

John promised to pay the dealer the price of the new car upon the dealer's delivering the car to John's home by Wednesday. Further, assume that the dealer did not promise John that he would obtain and deliver the car to his home by Wednesday. At this point, there is no valid contract, for the dealer has incurred no detriment; he has not acted or promised to act in any way: He has neither *promised* to do something nor *done* anything which he was not obligated to do. Now assume that the dealer obtains the car and delivers it to John's home on Tuesday night. At this point, a valid contract arises and John is obligated to perform his promise—that is, to pay for the car.

Thus, in a unilateral contract there is no mutuality of consideration until the *promisee performs the act for which the promisor bargained*. So far, we have defined consideration as the promise to do an act, or its actual performance, which one is not already bound to do.

But consideration may also be a promise to refrain or the actual refraining from doing something that one has a legal right to do. This is know as forbearance. For example, if I have a legal right of action against you for a breach of contract or a tort, my promise to not sue you may be good consideration for your promise to pay me a certain amount of money out of court. This agreement not to sue for a sum of money is known as a *compromise*. If it involves a contract or a settlement, it involves a tort.

ELEMENTS OF CONSIDERATION

In order to be good consideration a promise to act or to forbear must:
1. be definite and certain in its terms,
2. be legally and physically possible to perform,
3. require conduct not already required by law or pro- hibit conduct not already prohibited by law.
For example, suppose you and I got into a disagreement over which of us was going to date MaryAnn on Friday night. The argument got a little heated, and when I threatened to strike you, you offered to pay me $5.00 tomorrow if I would promise to refrain from striking you. The next day you re- fuse to pay me the $5.00. My promise to refrain from striking you was definite and certain and was also physically possible of performance. However, since it is illegal to strike someone it was not legally possible of performance; and since a promise to forbear striking someone is conduct

already required by law, my promise to forbear striking
you or my actually forbearing from striking you is not
valid consideration for the promise to pay me $5.00.
Therefore, no valid contract was entered, and you are under
no legal obligation to pay me the $5.00.

SIZE OF CONSIDERATION

As a general rule, as long as some price was paid, how ever
small, the law will consider the amount unimportant. If
all other requirements of a valid contract are met and the
amount is what was actually bargained for, no matter how
small, it will be adequate.

Where a great disparity exists, as where the value of
one party's promise is far greater than the value of the
other party's promise, this fact may be evidence of fraud,
bad faith, or lack of intent to enter the contract, such
as jest or even a gift. For example, the sale of a piece
of property having a market value of $5000 for $1.00 could
be a valid contract if the court is satisfied that $1.00
is really what the seller bargained for. Although, in
extreme cases, if there is any evidence that the promisor
did not really intend to enter a binding contract, the
court will usually set it aside, but the court's grounds
for doing so would not be that the consideration was inadequate, but rather it would be on some other grounds,
such as lack of intent.

FORMAL CONTRACTS

Some contracts, known as *formal contracts*, need no consideration to be binding; validity depends upon the form alone.
Checks, notes, and bonds are formal contracts.

Another type of formal contract is known as a "contract
under seal." The seal, originally an official mark, in the
early days was either an impression in wax affixed to the
back of the envelope containing the contract or a gold seal
on the face of the contract itself. In modern times, no
formal official seal is needed, but instead the letters
LS, or the words "Witness my hand and seal" at the end of
the document are alone sufficient as a seal. At common
law the seal took the place of consideration, and a sealed
contract did not need to be signed.

Under modern law about half the states have abolished the effect of seals, and in the other states the fact that a document is sealed merely raises the *presumption* of consideration. A presumption is a legal rule whereby courts assume something to be true unless the contrary is proved. Thus, today in half the states the only effect of the seal is to make it harder for the other party to prove that there was no consideration. But the seal does not take the place of consideration. It still must be proven. For example, in any one of the states which allow the seal to raise the presumption of consideration, if a person conveys land to another without stating the value he received in return in the deed, having the contract sealed would merely raise the presumption that some consideration was given in return for the conveyance.

RECOGNIZING CONSIDERATION

We have seen that promising to give up or actually giving up a legal right to do something may be consideration, called forbearance, such as giving up the right to sue. And promising to do something or actually doing something which one is not bound by law to do may be sufficient consideration. Now let us look at some specific situations to see whether or not they constitute consideration.

Carl and Frank entered a contract whereby Frank agreed to build a house for Carl for $15,000. As work progressed on the house, Frank discovered that he had underestimated his costs of construction. When the house was about half finished, Frank approached Carl and told him that unless Carl would pay him an extra $5000 he would not finish the house. Since Carl's lease expired on his existing residence at about the same time that the house was supposed to be completed he agreed at the time to pay the extra $5000 to get Frank to finish the house for him.

But when the house was completed, Carl refused to pay Frank more than the original $15,000 contract price. Could Frank force Carl to pay him the extra $5000? No: Frank could not force Carl to pay him more than the original $15,000. As you recall, we earlier stated that consideration was the doing of an act which one was not already legally bound to do. Since Frank had contracted with Carl to build a house for $15,000 he was legally obligated to build that house for $15,000. Therefore,

Carl's promise to pay an additional $5000 was not supported by consideration and there was no contract. The rule this example illustrates is that a contract cannot be modified without further consideration by both parties—and for good reason, as the example shows; that is, it prevents contract blackmail.

One exception to the rule, however, is found in the Uniform Commercial Code, which states that no consideration is necessary to change the terms of a sales contract so long as both the parties have acted in good faith. And the courts will often recognize another exception—an unforeseen hardship, which would make it inequitable to force one party to perform. For example, if in our previous example Frank had encountered an underground stream on the property which had to be dammed or diverted before the house could be built and neither party had known of the stream before the contract was entered, the court would probably allow Frank to force Carl to pay an extra amount to cover the additional cost.

In the previous examples one party did not promise to do any more than he had already promised to do. However, if for example Frank had agreed to build an extra room for Carl's agreement to pay an extra $5000, this then would be a valid modification of the contract, because both parties would now be promising to do something more than they were already obligated to do.

The general rule that a contract cannot be modified without further consideration by both parties applies to creditors also. So, an agreement by a creditor to accept less money than a debtor actually owes is generally not binding, and the creditor can still sue for the full amount. However, if the debtor agrees to pay the debt sooner in return for the creditor's agreement to reduce the debt by a certain amount, this would also be valid consideration. Here again, the amount of change or the extent of it is unimportant. An agreement to pay even one day sooner by the debtor may be sufficient consideration for the creditor's promise to accept as complete payment less than the total amount that was originally due, in addition, a creditor's promise to extend the time for payment is consideration, because it is a forbearance in return for the debtor's promise to pay, say, additional interest.

The distinction between unilateral and bilateral contracts is important in the area of consideration. If one party bargains for the other party's promise to forbear exercising a legal right, but instead of receiving a promise to forbear he receives actual forbearance, the actual forbearance would not be consideration for the first party's promise. In other words, if one bargains for a bilateral contract to forbear—that is, one bargains for a promise to forbear—and instead receives a unilateral contract—that is, does not receive a *promise* to forbear but instead the actual forbearance—then there is not any consideration, and the party who actually refrained from exercising his legal right could not force the other party to honor his promise to pay. For example, if I ran into you and injured you with my car you would have a legal right of action for damages against me in tort. Now, if I approach you and offer to pay you $1000 in exchange for your promise not to sue me and instead of promising not to sue me you merely don't sue me, then you will not be able to force me to pay you the $1000. This is because I bargained for your *promise* not to sue me and I did not receive it even though you did not sue me: There was no consideration.

Can an act which has already been performed be consideration for a present promise? For example, suppose I find your watch on the street and return it to you and you tell me that you're so grateful you will pay me $5 on the next payday. Can I hold you to your promise? No, to have a valid contract each party must promise to or actually perform either in the present or the future. Since I already returned your watch to you, you cannot bargain for either my promise to return your watch to you or for my actually returning it, since I've already returned it. Therefore, past acts or promises are not consideration for a present or future act or promise.

However—and this is an important distinction—past consideration may be sufficient consideration for a new promise to perform a previously unenforceable promise. For example, suppose you fraudulently induced me to enter a contract. We have already learned that this contract is voidable and you could not force me to perform, but *if* after learning of your fraud I tell you that I will perform anyway, now a valid contract is entered and can be enforced against me. In other words, you need not give me any new consideration for my new promise to perform the voidable contract.

This same theory applies to contracts made by incompetent parties. You will remember that a person who is incompetent because of age may affirm his contract upon reaching legal majority without further consideration from the other party. This new promise to perform a previously voidable contract is known as *revival*. Revival may occur either by an acknowledgment of the old contract, such as a statement that you will perform it even though it was not enforceable when made, or a part-payment of either the principal or interest. Thus, if you bought a car on a time payment plan while still a minor, and if you made a payment after reaching your age of majority, you will be deemed to have revived the contract, and it can be enforced in total against you.

One situation in which courts have found promises to be binding, even though there is no consideration for them in the traditional sense, is when a person promises to charity or an educational institution or the like that he will donate a certain amount of money. This exception is known as a Charitable Subscription. Even though there may be no personal benefit received, the courts find consideration for this promise to donate money to a charity in two ways: First, the recipient of the promise to donate implicitly promises to use the money for certain purposes; second, and more frequently, the promises of other persons to donate are the consideration for an individual's promise to donate.

GLOSSARY TERMS

Compromise   A contract, for consideration, not to sue for breach of contract or a tort.

Consideration   Basically, the price paid for the promise or act received.

Forbearance   The promise to refrain or the actual refraining from doing something one has a legal right to do.

Formal contracts   Contracts in which validity depends on form alone.

Legal benefit   The obtaining of a promise from a party to do something he is not already bound to do.

Legal detriment   The promise in a contract to do something one is not already bound to do.

Presumption   A legal rule by which the courts assume something true unless it is proved otherwise.

Revival   An expression or action by a party validating a contract not previously enforceable against that party.

SELF TEST

CHAPTER 6

NAME_____

DATE_____

6.1 The fourth element necessary to have a valid contract is _____.

6.2 The price one pays for the promise or the cost which he receives is known as _____.

6.3 Most easily defined, this price may be simply a/an _____ to do something, or actually doing something, you are not already _____ to do.

6.4 To be valid, a contract requires _____ of consideration.

6.5 _____ of consideration requires each party to incur a legal _____, and gain a legal _____.

6.6 In a bilateral contract, one party promises to do something in return for the _____ of the other party to do something.

6.7 In a unilateral contract, one party promises to do something in exchange for a/an _____ of the other party, whereas the other party performs a/an _____ in exchange for the _____ of the other party.

6.8 There is no mutuality of _____ in a unilateral contract until the promisee _____ the act for which the promisor bargained.

6.9 Consideration may also be a promise to refrain or actually refraining from doing something one has a/an _____ right to do. This is known as _____.

6.10 A contract to not sue is known as a/an _____ if it involves a contract, or a/an _____ if it involves a tort.

6.11 In order to be good consideration, a promise to act or to forbear must be _____ and certain in its terms; it must be legally and physically _____ to perform the promise; and, it must require _____ which is not already required by _____ or it must _____ conduct not already prohibited by law.

6.12 If the amount of consideration is something of _____, even though it may be very small, if all other requirements of a valid contract are met and the amount is what was actually _____ for, it will be _____.

6.13 Where a great disparity in the value of consideration exists, and it is evident that the promisor did not

really intend to enter a binding contract, the court
will usually set the contract aside, not on the grounds
of inadequate _____, but on some other grounds.

6.14   _____ contracts need no consideration to be
binding.

6.15   Examples of formal contracts are _____,
_____, _____, and contracts under
_____.

6.16   Under modern law, about one-half of the states have
_____ the effect of seals.

6.17   A legal rule, whereby courts assume something to be true
unless the contrary is proved is known as _____.

6.18   An existing contract cannot be modified and still remain
valid without _____ consideration by both
parties, except in states where the Uniform Commercial
Code has been adopted; it states that _____
consideration is necessary to change the terms of a/an
_____ contract, so long as both the parties have
acted in good _____. Courts will also recognize
and make an exception when _____hardship arises,
which would make it inequitable for one party to perform.

6.19   An agreement by a creditor to accept less money than
a debtor actually owes is generally not _____,
and the creditor can still sue for the _____.

6.20   A creditor's promise to extend the time for payment
is consideration, because it is _____ for the
debtor's promise to pay, say, additional interest.

6.21   _____ acts or promises are not consideration for
a present or future act or promise; however, past
consideration may be sufficient consideration for a new
promise to perform a previously _____ promise.

6.22   The new promise to perform a previously voidable contract is known as _____, which may occur either
by _____ of the old contract, or a/an _____
of either the principal or interest.

6.23   Consideration is not necessary for a binding contract
when a person promises an educational institution or
a/an _____, that he will _____ a certain
amount of money. This exception to the general rules
of consideration is known as a/an _____.

7

Contracts
Required Form—Statute of Frauds

LEARNING OBJECTIVES

To enable the student to determine which types of contracts are covered by the Statute of Frauds to satisfy the element of required form.

CHAPTER CONTENTS

Simple Contracts   Executed Contracts   Executory Contracts   Memorandums   Application of the Statute of Frauds   Glossary   Self Test

The fifth basic element of a contract is required form. As
we learned earlier in the book, there are three basic types
of contracts: (1) *Express* contracts are those where the
mutual assent of the parties is indicated either orally or
in writing. (2) Contracts *implied in fact* arise by the
parties, acting in a manner that indicates their mutual
assent to enter a contract. (3) Contracts implied in law
are those which even though the parties did not intend to
enter a contract the court will create to prevent unjust
enrichment. In the previous chapter, on consideration,
we learned of some types of contracts, known as formal contracts, which depend upon their form alone for validity,
such as checks, notes, and bonds, and in addition sealed
contracts, a type of formal contract at common law. The
seal has effect in only one half of the states today, and
in those only to create a presumption of consideration.
(We will learn later in the course, under the topic
Negotiable Instruments what particular form notes, bonds,
and checks must have to be valid.)

SIMPLE CONTRACTS

All contracts other than formal contracts are called
simple contracts. Simple contracts, as we know, may be
express, or implied in fact, or implied in law. However,
all state legislatures have passed laws, known as the Statute
of Frauds, requiring certain types of simple contracts to
be in writing, because courts discovered long ago that unless certain contracts were required to be written the
possibility and even probability of fraud was high. Even
if the statute does not require a particular contract to
be written, all express contracts should nevertheless be
written if possible. A writing is protection against fraud
and mistake. Also, since it is often several years before
the trial of a disputed contract occurs, and during all this
time memories often become fuzzy and witnesses usually
become unavailable, any express contract which might have
to be enforced against the other party should be in writing.

EXECUTED CONTRACT

A contract which has been fully performed by both sides is
known as an *executed contract*. The Statute of Frauds does
not apply to executed contracts. Thus, if you and I were to

enter an oral contract which the Statute of Frauds would render unenforceable, if we had both performed our duties under the oral agreement, neither one of us could go into court and demand that he be put back into his position before the contract was performed. In other words, if the parties have fully performed an oral contract, even though that contract may have been unenforceable before one or both parties completed performance, the law will not disturb it after it has been fully performed by both.

EXECUTORY CONTRACTS

The other type of contract classified by performance is the *executory contract*—any contract that has not been fully performed by either one or both of the parties. The Statute of Frauds applies to the oral forms of this type of contract. It must be kept in mind through the following discussion, however, that even though the Statute of Frauds may render an executory contract unenforceable, if one party has fully or partially performed but the other has not, so that it would be inequitable to allow the other party to be able to avoid his obligations, the court may imply the contract—either *in fact*, because of the acts of the parties, or, if this is not possible, *in law*.

Thus, if you and I should enter an oral contract which is unenforceable because of the Statute of Frauds, and I fully performed my side of the contract but you refuse to perform your side, the court may imply a contract and require you to perform, if to allow you to avoid performing would be inequitable to me.

This doctrine is known as *part-performance*, and before a court will allow a contract to be implied by part-performance it must be very clear to the court that a contract was intended to be entered by the party. After all, the purpose of the Statute of Frauds is to require a writing so as to better evidence the intent to enter a contract and prevent fraud. So you could not just go out and do some act benefiting me and then claim that I promised to pay you to do it, and expect a court to help you recover.

MEMORANDUMS

Although the Statute of Frauds does not necessarily require the contract itself to be in writing, it requires that

there be some writing or writings, called a memorandum, that:
1. sufficiently identifies the parties;
2. contains the essential terms and conditions; and
3. is signed by the party to be charged.

In closer detail, a memorandum must, first of all, identify the parties. The best way is to name the parties therein, but sufficient identification could occur by *implication*. For example, suppose you and I have written several letters concerning my sale to you of my coin collection. Your acceptance of my terms could be contained in a letter wherein I am not identified by full name but only by first name all through the letter. However, since we have written a series of letters to one another, the court would imply that I was the other party.

Second, the memorandum must contain the essential terms and conditions of the contract. Thus, if our letters to one another regarding the sale of my coin collection to you did not specify which coins you agreed to buy, the Statute of Frauds would not be satisfied. However, under the Uniform Commercial Code, the failure to include a price may not defeat the contract. Thus, if the other requirements of a sufficient memorandum are met, and the court is satisfied that the parties intended to enter a contract, the failure to mention a price will not defeat the contract, and the court will set a reasonable price at the time for delivery as the price under the contract.

Third, a memorandum must be signed by the party sought to be charged (the defendant in the court action). Thus, if under our agreement for me to sell my coin collection to you, you do not sign the letter in which you accept my offer, I cannot force you to perform in court, because you, the party sought to be charged, did not sign. (Under the old Statute of Frauds both parties had to sign the memorandum before it was sufficient, but under the Uniform Commercial Code and the Statute of Frauds of most states today, only the party sought to be charged must sign.)

Of course, the party charging would still have to be sufficiently identified under the contract: Even if you has signed the letter in which you accepted my offer to sell my coin collection to you, if I was not identified in the writings as the other party I could not hold you to the contract, nor could you hold me. Thus we see that the Statute of Frauds requires some writing evidencing the intent of both parties to enter a contract. The purpose of this is to protect us in our business dealings against

faulty memory or intentional misrepresentations that may
occur under oral contracts.

APPLICATION OF THE STATUTE OF FRAUDS

The Statute of Frauds applies to seven types of contracts.
The first type is contracts which cannot be performed within a year from the time the contract was made, contracts
which by their terms *must* extend beyond a year. (It does
not apply to contracts which could be performed within a
year but are not so performed.) For example, assume that
I operate a carpet manufacturing company. You are a carpet
salesman and you orally agree today to work for me as a
carpet salesman for one year starting today. Now since
this contract is to be performed within one year, it is not
within the Statute of Frauds and is, therefore, valid and
enforceable. However, if you were to orally agree with me
today to work for me for two years, this oral contract
would be within the Statute of Frauds and therefore unenforceable, because by its terms it could not be completed
within one year.

Now, suppose you agree to work for me until such time
as you receive a better offer from another carpet manufacturer. This contract would be enforceable. It is not
within the Statute of Frauds because it may be performed
within one year: You could receive a better offer tomorrow
or at any time before the year is up, so the contract does
not by its terms require more than a year for performance.

The fact that you may not receive a better offer within
a year and that you may continue working for me for many
years makes no difference. To determine whether an oral
contract is within this section of the Statute of Frauds we
must look to the agreement itself and not at what might or
might not happen. Therefore, such a contract is within the
Statute of Frauds and thus unenforceable only if by the
terms of the contract itself it is impossible to complete
the contract within one year. Remember also that the year
begins to run from the day the contract is entered.

The second type of contract within the Statute of Frauds
is the contract for the purchase and sale of real property,
or of any part or interest in it. Thus, even the sale of
an easement, of a license, or of crops or fixtures from
land must be in writing. Also, any lease of real property
for over one year must be in writing. Thus, if you were to

go away to college and orally agree to rent an apartment for even a year and a day that agreement would have to be in writing. However, if your lease were for any term less than a year, an oral contract thereon would be enforceable. Thus we see that if you were going to buy or sell any interest in real property, there must be a writing evidencing the agreement, and if you were going to lease some property either to someone or from someone for more than one year, then it also must be in writing. Remember, though, any time you buy any interest in real property, the agreement must be in writing, either the contract itself or a sufficient memorandum.

The third type of contract within the Statute of Frauds is a contract to buy and sell goods over a certain amount of money. The amount is set by statute in each state so you must look to the statute of your state to determine the amount. The Uniform Commercial Code states that a contract for the sale of goods for $500 or more must be written or be evidenced by a memorandum sufficient to indicate that a contract for sale has been made, and must be signed by the party against whom enforcement is sought. Thus, your agreement to buy my car for more than $500 is unenforceable without a writing. There are two exceptions under the Uniform Commercial Code that we should examine: The $500 limitation does not apply if (1) some payment has been made and accepted or if (2) the goods have been received and accepted by the buyer. Actually, these situations would create an implied-in-fact contract. Most states also require a contract with a real estate broker to buy or sell property for you must also be in writing. Thus, if you hire a real estate broker to help you sell your property, agreeing to pay him 5% of the sales price if he finds a buyer, the contract must be in writing to be enforceable.

A fourth type of contract within the Statute of Frauds is the promise to pay the debts of another upon his default. Thus, assuming you were competent to contract and you wanted to buy my stereo set on a time-payment plan, but I would not sell you my stereo unless you obtained a third party to agree to make the payments if you defaulted on them, the third party would not be liable on his promise unless it was in writing. A person who promises to pay another's debts on default is known as a *guarantor*, and the contract he enters is known as a *contract of guarantee*. Guarantee contracts are often confused with *contracts of surety*, while a guarantor promises only to pay a debt if the person who is primarily liable defaults, a surety makes an uncon-

ditional promise to pay. That is, a surety promises to pay
in any event, whether or not the principal party pays.
Only guarantee contracts are included under this section
of the Statute of Frauds.

Guarantee contracts frequently arise when a person who
is incompetent, such as a minor, attempts to enter a contract of purchase. Since we know such contracts are voidable by the incompetent person, the seller will often require
a competent person, such as the minor's father, to guarantee
the contract. In most states, a promise to guarantee a
voidable contract is also within the Statute of Frauds,
and therefore must be in writing.

A fifth type of contract within the Statute of Frauds
is that of an executor or administrator—the person who
handles a deceased person's estate—who agrees to be personally liable for the debts of the deceased person. Thus,
in order for the administrator or executor to be personally
liable for the debts that the decreased person left, his
promise to do so must be in writing.

The sixth type of contract within the Statute of Frauds
is one in which marriage is the consideration for a promise
to pay money to another. For example, if I promise to pay
you $1000 for your promise to marry my sister, my promise
must be in writing in order to be enforceable: Even if
you marry my sister, most states will not allow you to enforce my promise unless it is in writing. We must be sure
not to confuse this situation with mutual promises to
marry, which are not within the Statute of Frauds. Thus if
I promise to marry you in return for your promise to marry
me, even though our promises are oral they are enforceable.

The seventh and final type of contract within the
Statute of Frauds involves agency contracts (we will discuss
agency in greater detail later in this book). An agent is
a person who is authorized to act for another in a particular matter. If an agent is authorized to perform an act
the contract for which must be in writing, the agent's
authorization *itself* must be in writing. If I hire you as
my agent to sell my car for $2000, since under the Statute
of Frauds the contract of sale must be in writing, our
contract of agency must also be in writing. This is known
as the *equal dignity rule*.

To summarize, the seven types of contracts which are
within the Statute of Frauds are:
1. Contracts by their terms not to be performed within
one year;

2.   A contract for the sale of any interest in real property or for a lease over one year in length;

3.   Contracts to buy and sell goods over a certain amount, which is $500 under the Uniform Commercial Code;

4.   A contract to answer for the debts of another upon his default (known as a contract of guarantee);

5.   A contract of an executor or an administrator to be personally liable for the debts of the deceased;

6.   A contract to pay money to another, the consideration for which is marriage; and

7.   Contracts of agency under the equal dignity rule.

GLOSSARY TERMS

Contract of guarantee   Contract a guarantor makes.

Contract of surety   An unconditional contract to pay, whether or not a primary party defaults.

Equal dignity rule   A rule by which if an agent is authorized to perform an act that involves a contract in writing, the agent's authorization to perform that contractual act must itself be in writing.

Executed contract   A contract in which both parties have fully performed its stated terms.

Executory contract   Any contract not yet fully performed by either or both of the parties.

Guarantor   A third party who has promised to pay another's debts on default of that person.

Part-performance   The condition by which an otherwise unenforceable contract is enforced against a party because failure to do so would be inequitable to the party who has fully or partially performed.

Simple contracts   All contracts other than formal contracts.

SELF TEST
CHAPTER 7

NAME_____

DATE_____

7.1　The three basic types of contracts are _____ contracts, contracts implied in _____, and contracts implied in _____.

7.2　_____ contracts are those whereby the mutual assent of the parties is indicated either orally or by a writing.

7.3　Formal contracts depend upon their _____ alone for validity.

7.4　All contracts, other than formal contracts, are called _____ contracts.

7.5　Simple contracts may be _____, implied in _____, or implied in _____.

7.6　The law passed by state legislatures that require certain types of simple contracts to be in writing is known as the Statute of _____.

7.7　Any express contract which you would wish to enforce against the other party should be in writing even though it's not required by the Statute of _____.

7.8　A contract which has been fully performed by both sides is known as a/an _____ contract.

7.9　The Statute of Frauds does not apply to _____ contracts.

7.10　A contract which has not been fully performed by either one or both of the parties is known as a/an _____ contract, and it is to this type of contract, when _____, that the Statute of Fraud applies.

7.11　The doctrine of _____ is the doctrine applied by the courts to situations where it was clear that the parties intended to enter a contract, but it was not in writing as required by the Statute of Frauds, and one of the parties, or both, had performed parts of the contract.

7.12　The purpose of the Statute of Frauds is to require a writing so as better to evidence the _____ to enter a contract and prevent _____.

7.13   The Statute of Frauds does not require the contract
       itself to be in writing, but does require that
       there be some writings sufficiently _____
       the parties; that the writing contain essential
       _____ and conditions; and that it be signed
       by the party to be _____.   Such a writing is
       called a/an _____.

7.14   Under the Uniform Commercial Code, failure to include
       a/an _____ in a memorandum is not sufficient to
       defeat a contract if all the other requirements for
       a memorandum are met.

7.15   Sufficient identification in a memorandum is best
       done by naming the parties, but could occur by
       _____.

7.16   The Statute of Frauds applies to contracts which must
       extend beyond a/an _____ by its terms, but does
       not apply to contracts which could be _____
       within a year, but are not so performed.

7.17   To determine whether or not an oral contract is with-
       in the Statute of Frauds for the one-year requirement
       of its terms, one must look at the _____ it-
       self, and not what might or might not happen.

7.18   Any lease of real property for more than _____
       in length of time must be in writing to be _____.

7.19   The Uniform Commercial Code states that a contract
       for the sale of goods for the price of _____
       or more must be _____, or be evidenced by a
       memorandum sufficient to indicate that a contract
       for sale has been made, and signed by the party
       against whom _____ is sought.

7.20   Two exceptions to #7.19 above are if some _____
       has been made or accepted, or if the _____
       have been received and accepted by the buyer.

7.21   A person who promises to pay another person's debts
       upon default is known as a/an _____, and the
       contract he enters is known as a contract of
       _____.

7.22   A/An _____ promises to pay a debt if the person
       who is primarily liable defaults, whereas a/an _____
       promises to pay in any event, whether or not the
       principal party pays.

7.23   A/An _____ or _____ is the person who
       handles a deceased person's estate, and in order for
       him to be liable for the debts the deceased person
       left, his promise to do so must be in _____.

CHAPTER 7

NAME_____

7.24 _____ promises to marry are not within the Statute of Frauds, but if marriage is to the _____ for a promise to pay money to another, it would have to be in writing to be enforceable.

7.25 A person who is authorized to act for another in a particular matter is known as a/an _____.

7.26 The _____ is the rule that requires a contract of agency be in writing to be enforceable if the agent must perform an act which must be in writing under the Statute of Frauds.

7.27 Most states require that a contract with a/an _____ to buy or sell property for you must be in writing.

7.28 The seven types of contracts which are within the Statute of Frauds are those contracts
a) that are not to be performed within _____;
b) for the sale of any interest in _____;
c) to buy and sell _____ over a certain amount of money;
d) which answer for the debts of another upon his _____, which is known as a contract of _____;
e) of an executor administrator to be personally liable for the _____ of the deceased;
f) to pay money to another, the _____ for which is marriage; and
g) of _____ under the equal _____ rule.

8 Contracts

Parol Evidence Rule

LEARNING OBJECTIVES

To learn the meaning of the parol evidence rule.
To understand its use by the courts.

CHAPTER CONTENTS

Parol Evidence Rule   Limits of the Rule   Court
Use of the Rule   Customs and Usage vs. the Rule   Glossary
Self Test

In the last chapter we saw that under the Statute of Frauds certain contracts must be written. (Of course, all contracts may be written even if not required to be so by the Statute of Frauds.)

A further rule applies to written contracts or to memoranda evidencing contracts—the *parol evidence rule* ("parol" means "oral," so the rule may also be called the oral evidence rule).

PAROL EVIDENCE RULE

The parol evidence rule is to this effect: When the terms of a contract have been written in a complete statement and the parties have assented that the writing is the complete agreement, then prior or present oral statements will not be admitted to vary or contradict the terms of the agreement.

Thus, when the writing appears complete, and it was intended by the parties to be the final expression of their agreement, oral statements made prior to or at the same time as the execution of the writing cannot be used to change the terms contained in the written agreement. For example, suppose you go to a new car dealer and after looking at the various models you choose one and then discuss with the dealer all of the extras and options that you may wish to order with your new car. After discussion and debating with yourself about what to include with this new car, you tell the dealer that you want to order a radio in the car. You have also discussed the price of various options and attempted to get the dealer to discount the price of the car from list price for you.

Now, after you have decided all the extras and options you want to order on the car you and the dealer decide upon the price and enter a written contract for the car at that price including various options. But as the contract is being written up the radio is omitted. However, you overlook that fact and sign the contract anyway. When the car is delivered to you without the radio, you claim that the cost of the radio was included in the price. Do you think the dealer must install a radio at no further cost to you? You can bet your life he doesn't.

The written contract was intended by both parties to be the final expression of their agreement, and prior oral statements about the installation of a radio cannot be admitted to vary the terms of the written agreement under the parol evidence rule. It is absolutely necessary that every written contract be carefully read. Every term and condition which was supposed to be included in the written contract must actually be included therein or it has no legal existence.

LIMITS OF THE RULE

However, if the written agreement is not complete on its face, the entire contract will be deemed oral. Thus, if instead of omitting merely the radio from the written contract, the make and type of car were omitted, then none of the writing would be effective and the whole contract would be deemed oral. Of course, if the Statute of Frauds then requires that this contract be written, there may not be any contract at all. So we see that one must be very careful to make sure that all of the terms and conditions are included in a writing which is intended to be the final written expression of intent.

The parol evidence rule, however, does not prevent the admission of oral evidence that the writing was not intended as the complete agreement. Thus, if the radio was purposely not included in the writing because it was a special radio which was not available from the factory and the dealer orally agreed to obtain the radio somewhere else and install it in your car after it arrived, and you agreed to pay the dealer $100 for doing so, under this exception to the parol evidence rule you could use this separate oral agreement to show that the writing was not intended as the complete agreement.

Also, the parol evidence does not exclude *subsequent* oral agreements which contradict the writing. If, therefore, after the writing has been executed, you and the dealer went on to orally agree to include a radio for so much more, this subsequent oral agreement could be enforced. Nor does the parol evidence exclude oral evidence introduced to prove fraud, mistake, duress, illegality, or undue influence.

Also, oral evidence may be used to explain or interpret the meaning of terms included in the contract. If the contract contains terms which are not clear their meaning may be explained by parol evidence. If, for example, a contract contains the terms that the goods are to be delivered on Friday, oral evidence may be introduced to show which Friday

was intended. The parol evidence rule also does not
exclude evidence of business customs to help interpret the
contract.
    Although the parol evidence rule may work hardship in
certain cases, it's easy to see the reasoning behind it.
The law encourages people to write down their agreements
so as to minimize the danger of fraud, lapse of memory, and
misunderstanding. Therefore, the law presumes that when
people write down their agreements, they have included all
the terms to which they have agreed. Thus, it's wise to always include even the smallest detail in a written contract,
because if it's not there, the parol evidence rule may
prevent you from relying upon it.

COURT USE OF THE RULE

Generally if at all possible courts will construe written
contracts to make them valid. To construe written contracts as valid, courts apply the *Four Corners Doctrine*:
The court will look at the whole writing in order to clarify
or discern the meaning of any unclear or ambiguous terms.
Thus, if the contract states that the goods are to be
delivered on Friday, and if at some earlier or later place
in the document Friday the 13th of March is mentioned as
the delivery date, then the court will construe that date
as the Friday meant in the original term.
    Another rule courts use in construing contracts is that
specific words control general words. If a contract in
one place called for the sale of ten hammers and in another
place described the hammers to be sold, the hammer so
described will be construed as the particular hammers meant.
    Another rule is that handwritten portions will prevail
over typed portions and typed portions will prevail over
printed portions. If a printed portion of a contract
says, "All sales are final," but it is written by hand or
typewriter that the goods may be returned if the buyer is
not satisfied, then the written or typed terms will control
and the goods could be returned.
    Another rule is that words will prevail over figures.
Thus, if you write a check and accidentally put in the
figure "$100.00" but then write out "Ten dollars" under-
neath that, the "Ten Dollars" will control and the check
will only be worth that much.

CUSTOMS AND USAGE VS. THE RULE

Custom and usage of trade known to the parties will be considered, and technical terms will be given their known meaning unless the whole contract indicates a different meaning was intended. Further, interpretation will be preferred to a literal one; thus, if a contract requires that a house be completely built in ten days, the court will overlook the literal meaning of that term and provide a reasonable time for the building of the house.

The subsequent conduct of the parties may also be considered to help determine what their intent was when the writing was executed. If you should enter a contract to work for me but the contract did not indicate in what capacity, if, following the execution of the written contract, you mowed my lawn every week for two months, then the court would construe from your subsequent conduct that the purpose of the contract was for you to mow my lawn. Thus, we see that courts will do everything within their power to construe contracts as valid.

GLOSSARY TERMS

Four corners doctrine   Use of written contract as a
   whole to determine the meaning of unclear or
   ambiguous terms.

Parol evidence rule   The rule that when the terms of a
   contract have been written in complete form and has
   been assented to as such by the parties, no prior or
   present oral statements may vary or contradict its
   terms.

SELF TEST

CHAPTER 8

NAME_____

DATE_____

8.1   The word parol means _____.

8.2   The parol evidence rule states that when the _____
of a contract have been written in a complete
_____ and the parties have assented that the
writing is the complete _____, then prior or
present _____ statements will not be admitted
to vary or _____ the terms of the agreement.

8.3   If a written agreement is not complete on its face,
the entire contract will be deemed _____, and
if the _____ then requires that this contract be
written, then there will not be any contract at all.

8.4   The parol evidence rule does not prevent the admission
of oral evidence that the writing was not intended as
the _____ agreement, nor does it exclude
_____ oral agreements which contradict the
writing.

8.5   The parol evidence rule also does not exclude oral
evidence to prove fraud, _____, _____,
_____, or undue influence.

8.6   _____ evidence or evidence of business
_____ could be used to explain or interpret
the meaning of terms in a contract.

8.7   The general rule is that courts will construe written
contracts to make them _____ at all possible.

8.8   In order to construe written contracts as valid, courts
will apply the _____ Doctrine, which means that
the court will look at the _____ writing in
order to clarify the meaning of any unclear or
ambiguous terms.

8.9   Another rule courts use in construing contracts is that
_____ words control over general words, and
that _____ will prevail over figures.

8.10 Another rule used by the courts in construing contracts
is that _____ portions will prevail over typed
portions and typed portions will prevail over
_____ portions.

8.11 When construing contracts, the courts will prefer a
_____ interpretation to a literal one, and the
_____ conduct of the parties may also be considered to help determine what their _____ was
when the writing was executed.

9 Contracts

Third Parties

LEARNING OBJECTIVES

To learn the rights of a beneficiary to a contract.
To understand the rights of parties when a contract
is assigned.

CHAPTER CONTENTS

We have seen that the rights and duties of two parties who
contract to one another are affected by the contract.
But persons who are not a party to a contract can also be
affected by it.
        Anyone whose rights are affected by a contract to which
he is not a party is a *third party*. There are generally two
ways in which a third party's rights may be affected by a
contract: First, by a *third party beneficiary contract*;
second, by an *assignment*.

THIRD PARTY BENEFICIARY CONTRACTS

A third party beneficiary contract is one made between two
parties with the primary intent to benefit a third party,
who is thus the third party beneficiary.
        There are two types of third party beneficiaries.
The first type is a *creditor beneficiary*, a person who has
given consideration to one of the parties. For example,
you borrow $100 from Jack. You owe it to him, but George
says to you, "If you will work for me for one week, I'll
pay Jack the $100 you owe him." Here Jack is a creditor
beneficiary because he has given consideration to you.
        The second type of third party beneficiary is a *donee
beneficiary*, a person who has given nothing to either of
the contracting parties. For example, George says to
you, "If you work for me for one week, I'll buy your brother
a stereo set." Now since you don't owe your brother any
money, or a stereo set, he's a donee beneficiary if you
accept George's offer.
        This distinction between donee and creditor bene-
ficiary is important because some courts don't allow donee
beneficiaries to enforce the contract for which they
benefit, while all courts allow the creditor beneficiary
to enforce the contract. Thus, in about 7 states, even if
you worked for George your brother would not be able to
force George to give him the stereo set.

ENFORCING CREDITOR BENEFICIARY CONTRACTS

A creditor beneficiary can enforce contracts from which he
benefits by suing either party. Thus if George promised
to pay Jack the $100 that you owe to Jack if you work for
George for a week, Jack may, if need be, sue either George
or you for the $100. However, if you failed to work the

promised week for George and George then refuses to pay
Jack the $100, he would not be able to collect the $100
from George and would have to look to you, since you
breeched your agreement with George, you would not be able
to collect the $100 from him, so why should George have to
pay merely because the money was to be paid to someone else?
   The rule of law to be distilled from this example is
that in a third party beneficiary contract the promisor's
defenses against the promisee are good against the third
party beneficiary. In our earlier example, George, the
person who promised to pay Jack $100 if you worked for him,
was the promisor. You were the promisee, and Jack of
course was the third party beneficiary. So George's defenses against you are good against Jack if Jack sues
George.
   Another way to state this rule is that the third party
beneficiary stands in the same shoes as the promisor, and
has the same defenses against the promisee. Most states
would also allow you as the promisee to collect the $100
from George—assuming of course that you worked the week for
George. But some states would only allow you as the promisee
to sue George, if you yourself had paid Jack the $100 and
now were trying to get it from George.
   Thus, we see that a third party beneficiary contract
is a contract made with the primary intent to benefit a
third party. If the third party is a creditor beneficiary,
or a donee beneficiary under an insurance contract, he may
enforce the contract in all states. All states recognize
the right of a donee beneficiary to enforce an insurance
contract. Say you contract with an insurance company to
pay your brother $50,000 upon your death. Here your
brother would be a donee beneficiary because he has not
given any consideration to either you or the insurance
company. In all states your brother may force the insurance company to pay him the $50,000 upon your death. In
all states but 7, other donee beneficiaries may enforce
the contract also, but always remember that a third party
beneficiary is subject to the defenses that the promisor
has against the promisee.

ASSIGNMENTS

The second type of contract which affects the rights of third
parties is a contract which has been assigned. An assignment is the transferral to a third party of the rights and

benefits one has under a contract. Say you and I have
entered a contract whereby you have agreed to pay me $50
for my record collection; if I transfer my right to collect
the $50 from you to a third party, I have made an assign-
ment.

There are three terms in assignment contracts corres-
ponding to the three parties. The party who assigns his
rights under a contract is known as an *assignor*. When I
transferred my right to collect the $50 from you to a third
party, I was the assignor. The one who receives the right
is known as the *assignee*. The third party who receives
my right to collect the $50 from you is the assignee. The
other party to the original contract, the promisor, is
known as the *obligor*. Since in our example you were the
other party to the contract with me, whereby you obligated
yourself to pay $50 for my record collection, you are the
obligor.

If we should change the facts of our example a little,
so that instead of my assigning my right to collect the
$50 from you, you assigned your right to my record collec-
tion to a third party, then you are the assignor and I am
the obligor. We must be careful to distinguish between
the assignment of *contract rights* and the assignment of
contract duties. In our example, where I assigned my *rights*
to the $50 from you, I am still obligated (by contract *duty*)
to deliver to you my record collection, and if you had
assigned your *right* to my record collection to a third
party, you would still be obligated (by contract *duty*)
to pay me the $50.

Assignment of contract duties is known as *delegation*,
and we will discuss delegation of duties shortly. But for
now, we will only talk about the assignment of contract
rights.

ASSIGNMENT OF CONTRACT RIGHTS

All contract rights are assignable, but some rights are
assignable only by the obligor's consent. The general rule
is that without the consent of the obligor no contract can
be assigned to another if assignment will increase the risk
of breach. Personal rights generally fall within this
category, whereas nonpersonal rights don't. For example,
suppose you and I have entered a contract whereby you agree
to work for me for one week for $50. Assuming you do the
work, you can assign your right to collect the $50 from

me to a third party without my consent because the right
to receive money is a nonpersonal right.

But suppose I try to assign my right to have you work
for me for one week. Here I would have to obtain your
consent to work for the other person, because the right to
personal service is a personal right; you agreed to work for
me, not for somebody else, and you may not wish to work for
the person to whom I want to assign my right. Such an
assignment would increase the risk of your not performing,
and, therefore, increase the risk that the contract would
be breached, because you may not care to work for the
assignee and may refuse to work for him.

However, if you assign your right to collect the $50
from me before you do the work for me, and your having done
so decreases the chances of my getting performance from
you, this assignment may not be valid without my consent.
Thus, if the assignor has fully performed his part of the
contract he may assign his nonpersonal rights without consent
from the obligor; only when the assignor assigns his nonpersonal rights before he has performed his duties does the
problem arise.

Some personal rights which are not assignable unless
the obligor consents are: personal injury damage claims;
claims against the United States; contracts involving confidential relationships; and, as we noted above, rights to
personal services. Generally, *options* are assignable but
offers are not. Thus, if I offered to sell you my record
collection for $50, you can't assign your right to accept
my offer to someone else. However, since options make
offers irrevocable, if you had paid me $5 to hold my offer
open for one week, you could assign your option to accept.
As a general rule, in order to have a valid assignment
there must be the intent to transfer a present interest.
Thus, the future right to something is generally not assignable. For example, if you are the beneficiary of a life
insurance policy on someone else's life, you do not have a
present interest because you do not have a right to the
money unless the insured dies before you do. Therefore,
you have a mere future right, which is not assignable.
However, if the insured dies and you are still living, then
you may assign your right to the money from the insurance
company to another person because at that time it is a
present right to the money.

DELEGATION OF CONTRACT DUTIES

We distinguished briefly, above, between the *assignment* of contract *rights* and the *delegation* of contract *duties*. Nonpersonal contract rights may be assigned without the consent of the obligor, especially if the assignor has completed his performance of the contract, and even personal contract rights can be assigned with the consent of the obligor.

Generally, nonpersonal contract *duties* may be delegated without the consent of the other party. However, the delegating party remains secondarily liable if the party to which he delegated the duties fails to perform. Thus, if you agreed to buy my record collection for $50, and you delegate your *duty* to pay me the $50 to someone else, you would still be liable to pay me the $50 if the other person failed to do so. Only if I agreed to substitute the other party in your place would you be relieved of the duty to pay.

Thus, nonpersonal contract duties may be delegated without the consent of the other party; but if the other party does not agree to relieve the delegating party from all liability, the delegating party will retain *secondary liability*. That is, if you delegated the duty to pay the $50 under the contract, I would first have to look to the person to whom you delegated the duty, and only if he failed to pay could I then look to you.

However, if the contract duty is <u>personal</u>, the other party does not have to accept performance from the third party to whom the duty was delegated. The delegation of personal duties is effective only if the other party consents. For example, if I delegated my duty to sell to you my record collection you would not have to accept the other party's record collection unless you had consented to the delegation.

To briefly summarize, assignment and delegation: Nonpersonal contract *rights* may be assigned without the consent of the other party; personal contract rights may be assigned only with the consent of the other party. Nonpersonal contract *duties* may be delegated without the consent of the other party, but the person who delegates the duty remains secondarily liable to perform unless the other party agrees to substitute the third party; personal contract duties can be delegated only with the consent of the other party.

ASSIGNEE'S RIGHTS OF ENFORCEMENT

About the rights that an assignee has to enforce the contract, the general rule is that the assignee steps into the shoes of the assignor. This means that all the defenses which the obligor has against the assignor are good against the assignee. For example, if I assigned my right to collect the $50 from you to a third party (the assignee), and then you (the obligor) failed to pay the $50, the assignee may sue you for it. But if you have a defense which would be good against me (the assignor), such as my failure to deliver my record collection to you, that defense would be good against the assignee. So if the assignee sued you (the obligor) for the $50, you could defend the action by saying that I (the assignor) failed to perform my part of the contract and therefore you didn't owe $50 to anyone.

If I assigned my right to collect the $50 from you to a third party but didn't tell you about it, and then you paid me the $50 instead of the assignee, since you (the obligor) had no notice of the assignment, your notice to pay the $50 was discharged by paying me. So if the assignee sues you for the $50, he can't collect it from you. However, since no notice to the obligor is necessary to make the assignment valid between the assignor and the assignee, the assignee could sue me (the assignor) for the $50 you paid me and could collect it from me. The obligor must have notice of the assignment before the assignment is valid against him, but after he has notice he must pay the assignee; if he still pays the assignor he may be liable twice because the assignee could still collect it from him.

Now, if the obligor, having notice of the assignment, fails to pay the $50 to anyone the assignee, after unsuccessfully attempting to get the obligor to pay, *cannot* recover from the assignor. The assignor does not guarantee to the assignee that the obligor will pay, but he does guarantee that the obligation is valid, and that he had a right to assign it. Therefore, without a valid contract of sale between you and me, my attempted assignment would be invalid, and the assignee could collect the $50 from me.

Unless statutes provide to the contrary, assignments may be oral, and so may the notice to the obligor.

GLOSSARY TERMS

Assignee   The recipient of the transferred rights in an
   assignment.

Assignment   A transferral to a third party (the beneficiary)
   the rights and benefits of a party to a contract.

Assignor   The contract party who transfers his contract
   rights and benefits to a third party.

Contract duty   The terms of a contract that must be
   fulfilled by contract parties to one another in order
   for a third party to benefit.

Contract right   The benefits of a contract that may be
   transferred by assignment.

Creditor beneficiary   A beneficiary who has given consideration to one of the contracting parties.

Donee beneficiary   A beneficiary who has given no
   consideration to either of the contracting parties.

Obligor   The contract party obligated to fulfill the terms
   of the transferred contract rights to a third party
   beneficiary.

Secondary liability   Liability incurred by the failure of
   the delegated primary party to fulfill contract duty.

Third party   Any person whose rights are affected by a
   contract to which he is not a party.

Third party beneficiary contract   A contract between two
   parties with the primary intent to benefit a third
   party.

SELF TEST
CHAPTER 9

NAME_____

DATE_____

9.1 Generally, the two ways in which a third party's rights may be affected by a contract are by a third party _____ contract and by a/an _____.

9.2 A third party _____ contract is a contract made between two parties with the primary intent to _____ a third party.

9.3 The two types of third party beneficiaries are _____ beneficiaries and _____ beneficiaries.

9.4 The difference between the two types of third party beneficiaries is that a/an _____ beneficiary gives nothing to either of the parties but a/an _____ beneficiary gives consideration to one of the parties.

9.5 Which party may a creditor sue to enforce a contract from which he benefits? _____.

9.6 In a third party beneficiary contract, the promisor's _____ against the promisee are good against the third party beneficiary.

9.7 The third party beneficiary stands in the same shoes as the _____, and has the same defenses against the _____.

9.8 A/An _____ is the transferral to a third party of the rights and benefits one has under a contract.

9.9 The one who assigns his rights under a contract is known as a/an _____, and the one who receives the right is known as the _____. The other party to the original contract, the promisor, is known as the _____.

9.10 Assignment of contract duties is known as _____, and this should be distinguished from the assignment of contract rights.

9.11 All contract rights are assignable, but in order to assign some contract rights, the _____ must consent to the assignment.

9.12 The general rule is that you can not assign a contract to another which will increase the risk of _____, unless you get the _____ of the

obligor. _____ rights generally fall within
this category, whereas _____ rights do not.

9.13 The right to receive money is a (_____—choose
either "personal" or "nonpersonal") right.

9.14 As a general rule, in order to have a valid assignment, there must be the _____ to transfer a
_____ interest.

9.15 The future right to something generally (_____
—choose either "is" or "is not") assignable.

9.16 Generally, nonpersonal contract _____may be
delegated without the consent of the other party;
however, the delegating party remains _____
liable if the party to which he delegated the
_____ fails to perform.

9.17 If a contract duty that is _____ is delegated,
the other party does not have to accept performance
from the third party to whom the duty was delegated.

9.18 The general rule is that all _____ which the
obligor has against the assignor are good against the
_____.

9.19 The obligor must have _____ of the assignment
before the assignment is valid against him, but after
he has _____, he must pay the _____.

9.20 The assignor does not _____ to the assignee
that the obligor will _____, but he does
guarantee that the obligation is _____ and
that he had a/an _____ to assign it.

9.21 Unless statutes provide to the contrary, assignment
or notice to the obligor may be _____, so
would not be considered within the Statute of Frauds.

10 Contracts

Discharge of Contracts

LEARNING OBJECTIVES

To understand each of the five ways in which a contract can be discharged.

CHAPTER CONTENTS

When a contract is *discharged* all the rights and duties of all the parties are terminated. Thus, when a contract is discharged neither party has any rights or duties left under the contract.

There are five principal ways in which a contract or a party to a contract may be discharged: (1) by performance; (2) by the agreement of the party; (3) by performance becoming impossible; (4) by alteration of the contract or its terms; (5) by the acceptance of a breach by one of the parties.

DISCHARGE BY PERFORMANCE

Obviously, if both parties fully performed their duties under a contract, the reason for the contract no longer exists.   In order to discharge a contract by performance, both parties must do what they promised to do.   Thus, if you and I entered a contract whereby I promised to mow your lawn in return for your promise to pay me $2 upon completion, if I had mowed your lawn and you had paid me the $2, the contract is discharged and neither of us has any more rights or duties under the contract.

But since *both* parties must fully perform all their contractual duties, failure of one party to perform as promised is a *breach of contract* by him.   If the breach is material, the other party is allowed to cease performing himself and to seek one of the remedies discussed in the next chapter.   A *material breach* is one that is important and quite damaging; a mere delay in time or a slightly deficient performance is usually not considered material. Thus, if I promised to mow your lawn and you promised to pay me $2, if I had mowed all your lawn except just a very small part of it, this breach would probably not be material, and you would have to pay me the $2.   Although you would have an action for damages against me for the harm caused you by my failure to mow that small part of your lawn, you still could not refuse to pay me the entire $2.

Thus, only if the breach is material is the other party excused from performing.   If the breach is not material, then the other party may sue for the damages he incurred because of the breach, but he is not excused from performing himself and the contract is not discharged.

MATERIAL BREACHES

If one party is to perform by the payment of money, that
person must tender the exact amount due in legal tender.
The party to be paid need not accept any form of property
other than money. If a check is given in place of money,
even though the other party accepts the check there is still
no performance until the check is cleared through the
bank. If I agreed to sell you my radio for $10 and if I
hand you the radio and you hand me a check for $10, I need
not accept the check, and if I do not, then although you
have performed, the contract is not discharged by performance. If I do accept the check in place of the money,
the contract is still not discharged until the bank upon
whom you have written the check pays it. If the check
bounces, the contract has been breached and I can sue you
for the $10.

Often one party fails to perform on time. Many contracts contain a *time of the essence clause*, which makes
failure to perform by the date set in the contract a
material breach rather than the usual nonmaterial breach.
(Remember, if the breach is material then the other party
is excused from performing and he may seek a remedy for
the breach.) Courts will allow time of the essence
clauses to be effective if the party inserting it can show
that there was a good reason for it.

If time is not of the essence, and a reasonable delay
in performance is not a material breach, then even by performing late a party has performed his part of the contract
and the other party is not excused from performance of his
own part. His duty to perform is not discharged, and he
has only an action for the damages caused him by the delay.
Time of the essence may also be implied in a contract,
when to not perform by a due date would defeat the purpose
of the contract.

Another way in which a party may be excused from
further duties under the contract is for him to *tender* his
performance. A tender is an offer to perform one's contract
obligations. Thus, if I am to sell you my radio for $10
tomorrow at noon and at noon I hold out the radio to you
and say, "Where's my ten dollars," if you refused to take
the radio at that time, you have refused my tender and I
need no longer sell you my radio for $10. But there is a
different rule when the tender is of money: If you tendered

the $10 to me at noon and said, "Where's the radio," and I
refuse to make the swap at that time, my refusal to take
your money and give you the radio does not relieve you
of your obligation to pay for the radio if I should tender
it to you later.   (This, of course, assumes that time was
not of the essence of this contract.)   However, if I
should later tender you the radio and you refuse to pay me
the $10, your having tendered the $10 to me previously would
prevent me from being able to collect my court costs from
you if I won the case and from collecting interest from
you.   Thus, the tender of money does not discharge one
from having to pay at a later time, it only prevents the
other party from collecting court costs and interest.
However, the tender of anything other than money discharges
the party from having to perform at a later date at all.

DISCHARGE BY AGREEMENT

Discharge by agreement can be in one of several forms.   In
one type the parties specify in the contract that the
contract shall end by a certain date, or after a certain
time has elapsed.   Thus, if I should pay you $10 now to
work on my lawn until it gets dark, when night falls your
duty to perform further and the entire contract are discharged, because we have both fully performed.
        Another way to discharge a contract by agreement would
be upon the election of either party upon the happening of
a previously specified event, for example, the contract
can state that either party may elect to discharge the
contract if it rains, or in any other previously specified
event.   The contract could also provide for discharge by
either party by the doing of some act, such as giving two
weeks' notice.   For example, if I rent a house from you on
a month-to-month basis with the agreement that either of us
can terminate the rental upon giving two weeks' notice, if
after living in the house for several months I tell you
that I'm going to move out in two weeks, at the end of those
two weeks the contract will be discharged.
        Contracts may also be discharged by the agreement if
both parties agree to terminate it.   This is known as
mutual rescission.   Mutual rescission will work only where
there is a bilateral contract and it is not fully performed
on either side.   In other words, if the contract is unilateral, or if it is bilateral and only one party has fully

performed, the contract cannot be rescinded, because there would be no reconsideration for the agreement of the party who has performed to allow the other party not to perform.

An agreement to modify a contract by substituting new terms, or an entire new agreement in place of the old agreement, is known as an *accord in satisfaction*. If such an accord is made, the old contract is only discharged when the new contract is performed. This is because the bargain is for the performance or satisfaction and not merely for the agreement or accord; and since the accord is a new contract new consideration must also be given. Suppose you and I have a contract by which I am to sell you my rifle for $60. I approach you and say, "I've changed my mind, I don't really want to sell you my rifle, but I will sell you my shotgun for $50 instead." If you agree to substitute the shotgun for the rifle we have an accord.

At this point there are two contracts between us because, as we learned, the original contract does not discharge until the accord is satisfied. So if I fail to deliver you the shotgun—that is, if I fail to perform the accord—you may sue me either on the original contract or on the new contract, the accord. However, if I tendered to you the shotgun then the accord is satisfied and the original contract is discharged as well as the new contract.

A compromise of a disputed claim and a composition of creditors are both also accords in satisfaction. For example, if you and I both agree that I owe you a debt of some money, but I claim that I owe you only $50 and you claim that I owe you $100, if we compromise this disputed claim by my agreeing to pay you $75 for your agreeing to discharge the debt for $75, upon my paying you the $75 the original debt is discharged, as well as our new agreement.

The same is true with a *composition of creditors*, which arises when a debtor owes more debts than he can pay. If all his creditors agreed to accept proportionately less than the full amount owed them, then the debt is discharged when the lesser amount is paid. Since the original debt is not discharged until the new agreement is performed, if the debtor fails to pay the lesser amount the creditors can still sue for the original debt.

Another type of discharge by agreement is a *novation*. We learned about assignments that contract duties could not be delegated so as to relieve the delegating party of his liability unless the other party to the contract agreed to the substitution. A novation is similar: One party to a contract agrees to replace the other party with

a third party so as to relieve the other party from liability. The contract between the two original parties is
thus discharged and a new contract created between the one
original party and the third party. For example, if you
agreed to work for me for one month but then fell ill,
if I agree to substitute someone in your place and to
release you from your duty to work for me our contract has
been discharged and a new contract has arisen between the
substituted party and me by novation.

Finally, contracts may be discharged by an agreement
in which one party releases the other party or contracts
with the other party not to sue him. A *release* is where
one party discharges the other from any further obligation,
usually for a sum of money. A contract not to sue arises
when one party agrees not to sue the other after the other
has breached the contract. Because both the release and
the contract not to sue are new contracts, consideration
is required.

DISCHARGE BY IMPOSSIBILITY

The third way in which contracts may be discharged is by
impossibility, when it has become impossible for one party
to perform the contract because of a change of circumstances.

Generally, one who promises to perform assumes the
risk of loss when it becomes impossible for him to perform
unless the contract provides otherwise. However, *objective
impossibility* is the impossibility of a particular
person's performing the contract; subjective impossibility
does not discharge the contract. Subjective impossibility
would occur if a person contracts to compute and file your
income tax returns for the year but then discovers that because your financial situation is so involved he can't do
it. This does not discharge him from having to perform
because it is merely his own lack of ability which makes it
impossible for him to perform, whereas some other person
can perform the contract. Also, a person's discovery that
it has become economically impossible for him to perform is
subjective impossibility, not objective impossibility.

Various forms of objective impossibility will discharge
a contract. Destruction or unavailability of the subject
matter of the contract is one form. Thus, if I have agreed
to sell you my King Silvertone trumpet but it is stolen
before I can deliver it to you, the contract will be discharged, and I cannot be held for breaching the contract.

However, say I were a dealer in King Silvertone trumpets and
our contract was for me to sell you a new one; if the only
ones I had in the store were stolen I would still have to
obtain a trumpet and sell it to you. Thus, only if the performance of the contract depends on the existence of a
particular thing will its destruction or other unavailability
cause the contract to be discharged. That is, I own only
one trumpet, but a dealer owns or stocks or has access to
more than one.

Also, the destruction or unavailability must not be due
to the fault of the promisor. Therefore, I could not
purposely destroy my trumpet and then claim that I couldn't
perform the contract because it was no longer available.

The second type of objective impossibility occurs when
the purpose of the contract is frustrated. For example,
assume I owned an apartment in London overlooking Buckingham
Square. Also assume that the coronation of Queen Mary is
next week and that the coronation procession passes right
under my apartment window. Say you rent my apartment for
the day of the coronation so that you can see it; if the
coronation is then postponed, the purpose of the contract—
that is, to view the coronation—would be frustrated, and you
would not be liable to pay me the one-day rental.

A contract purpose may also be frustrated by a change
in law. Thus, if you leased a building in which you intended to operate a saloon and then prohibition was enacted,
making it illegal for you to sell alcoholic beverages, the
purpose of the contract would be frustrated by the change
in law and the contract would be discharged.

If in a personal service contract death or inability
occurs, objective impossibility obtains. Thus, if I hired
you to sing in my opera company but you contract laryngitis,
you would be discharged from your duty to perform without
being liable for a breach of contract.

Finally, if some act of the other party makes it impossible for you to perform, the contract is discharged,
and if you tendered performance the other party would then
be liable for breach of contract. So, if you are to
deliver a crate of oranges to me personally at my house
at 5 p.m. on a certain day, and if you show up with
the oranges but I refuse to open the door, I have made it
impossible for you to perform, and since you have tendered
performance you can sue me for breach.

DISCHARGE BY ALTERATION

The fourth way in which contracts may be discharged is by alteration, a change of the contract terms by one party without the consent of the other party. This change in terms must be material, that is, it must materially change the contract itself; it must be done intentionally; and it must be without the consent of the other party. For example, suppose you and I had entered a contract whereby I was to sell you a truckload of peat moss for $40. If I take a pen and alter the sum to make it read $140 I have made an alteration, since I intentionally and without your consent materially changed the contract. This would discharge the entire contract; you would not even have to perform the original contract. That is, you could refuse to accept my performance now and not pay me anything. Such an alteration would actually be fraud and could make the party who committed it liable for damages in court as well as for breach of contract.

DISCHARGE BY ACCEPTANCE OF A BREACH

The fifth way to discharge a contract is by accepting a breach by another party. This kind of discharge will be studied in more detail in the next chapter. Suffice it to say here that if one party materially breaches the contract, and the other party accepts the breach—that is, seizes performance himself and seeks redress from the breaching party—then the contract is discharged.

GLOSSARY TERMS

Accord in satisfaction   An agreement to modify a contract
   by substituting new terms or an entire new agreement.

Breach of contract   Failure of one party to fulfill his
   contractual obligations.

Composition of creditors   An agreement among a party's
   creditors, when that party is unable to fully discharge
   his debts, to accept a proportion of the full amount.

Discharge   Termination of all rights and duties of all
   parties of a contract.

Material breach   An important or damaging breach of
   contract.

Mutual rescission   Termination of a contract by mutual
   agreement of both parties.

Novation   An agreement by one party of a contract to
   replace the other party with a third to relieve the
   second party of liability.

Objective impossibility   The impossibility that anyone
   could perform a given contract.

Release   The discharge by one contract party of the other
   party's obligations.

Subjective impossibility   The impossibility that a particular person could perform a contract.

Tender   An offer to fulfill one's contract obligations.

Time of the essence clause   A contract clause making
   failure to perform by a deadline a material breach.

SELF TEST

CHAPTER 10

NAME_____

DATE_____

10.1   When a contract is discharged, all the rights and
       duties of all the parties are _____.

10.2   The five principal ways to discharge a contract are
       by performance, _____ of the party, perfor-
       mance becoming _____, _____ of the
       contract, or acceptance of a/an _____ by one of
       the parties.

10.3   In order to discharge a contract by _____,
       both parties must do what they promised to do.

10.4   Failure of one party to perform his contract duties
       as promised is a/an _____ of contract on his part,
       and if the _____ is _____, it will
       allow the other party to cease performing himself
       and seek remedy.

10.5   Only a/an _____ breach will allow the other
       party to a contract to be discharged from having to
       perform his _____ under the contract.

10.6   A material breach usually occurs where the breach
       is important and quite _____, whereas a mere
       delay in time or a slightly deficient performance is
       usually not considered material.

10.7   When one party's performance is to be the payment of
       money, in order to perform, that person must
       _____ the exact amount due in _____.

10.8   Many contracts contain a time of the _____
       clause, which is an attempt to make failure to
       perform by a certain time or date set in the contract
       a material breach rather than the usual nonmaterial
       breach.

10.9   A tender is an offer to perform one's contract
       _____.

10.10 The tender of money does not discharge a person
       from having to pay at a later date if the tender is
       rejected, but it does prevent the other party
       from collecting _____ or _____.

10.11 The tender of anything other than _____ dis-
       charges the party from having to perform at a
       later date if the tender is refused.

10.12 A contract may be discharged by both parties
       agreeing to terminate it which would be known as
       _____. In order for this method to be
       effective, the contract would have to be a/an
       _____ contract, which is not performed on
       either side.

10.13 A/An _____ in _____ is an agreement to modify a
       contract by substituting new terms or by substituting
       an entire new agreement in place of the old agreement.

10.14 If a new agreement is substituted for an old agree-
       ment, the old contract is not discharged until the
       new contract is _____.

10.15 A/An _____ of a disputed claim and a/an _____
       of creditors, are both also accords in satisfaction.

10.16 With a composition of creditors, if the debtor
       fails to pay the lesser amount agree upon, the
       creditors can sue for the amount of the _____.

10.17 A/An _____ occurs when one party to a contract
       agrees to replace the other party with a third
       party so as to relieve the other party from
       liability, and thereby discharge the contract be-
       tween the two original parties.

10.18 Contracts may be discharged by agreement where one
       party _____ the other party or contracts
       with the other party not to _____ him, but
       both need _____ to be binding because they
       are new contracts.

10.19 _____ impossibility, which means that it
       would be impossible for _____ to perform the
       contract, may discharge the contract.

10.20 _____ impossibility is where a/an _____
       is unable to perform a contract, and this type of
       impossibility does not discharge contracts, in and
       of itself.

10.21 An example of objective impossibility would be the
       _____ or unavailability of the subject
       matter of the contract, but the unavailability must
       not be due to the fault of the _____.

10.22 Objective impossibility would be construed if the
       purpose of the contract is _____; an example
       of which would be a change in the law.

10.23 _____ or inability of one of the parties in
       a personal contract would be an example of
       _____ impossibility.

10.24 The general rule is that the one who promises to
       perform assumes the _____ of loss when it

CHAPTER 10

NAME_____

       becomes impossible for him to so perform unless
       the contract provides otherwise.

10.25 A/An _____ is a change of the contract terms
       by one party without the consent of the other
       party. This change in terms must be a/an _____
       change and it must be done _____ by the
       party guilty of the alteration.

10.26 If one party materially breaches the contract, and
       the other party accepts the _____, then the
       contract is discharged.

Contracts
Remedies for Breach

LEARNING OBJECTIVES

To learn the remedies available to a party injured by a breach of contract.

CHAPTER CONTENTS

A breach of contract—the failure of one party to perform his contract obligation according to the terms of the contract—is usually the failure to perform when performance is due. But breach can also arise when one party learns in advance that the other party does not intend to perform. This is known as anticipatory breach. Of course, there is no breach of contract by a person who is excused from having to perform under one of the methods we studied in the last chapter.

There are three basic remedies against the party who breaches a contract:
1. rescission and restitution;
2. damages;
3. specific performance.

RESCISSION AND RESTITUTION

In the previous chapter we listed as the fifth way in which a party may discharge his obligations under a contract is to accept the material breach of the other party. A material breach is accepted by the party rescinding the contracts; the party injured by the other party's breach may elect to consider the contract discharged, and himself cease performing. Notification to the other party that you elect to consider the contract discharged rescinds the contract. (Under the Uniform Commercial Code, rescission is known as cancellation.) The entire contract must be rescinded, not just a part of it. To rescind or cancel a contract is in effect to disaffirm it, that is, to declare that the contract is no longer in effect.

But if the person who is cancelling or rescinding the contract has partially or wholly performed himself, merely disaffirming the contract would leave that person in a worse position than he was in before the contract was entered. For example, if I had contracted with you to buy your baseball glove for $10, and I have paid you the $10 but you refuse to give me the glove, if I wish to disaffirm the contract by rescission or cancellation, I'd be out my $10. Could I get it back? The answer is yes.

A person who rescinds or cancels a contract may seek the aid of a court to put him in the same position he was in before the contract was entered. Of course, this is true only if the other party has breached. Since I had $10 more before the contract was entered, the court will order you to pay me $10. This is known as *restitution*. Therefore, in cases where the rescinding party has given to the other party some or all of his consideration, the court may allow him to get it back. The remedy, then, is known as rescission and restitution.

The court will sometimes also allow the rescinding party to retain some of the consideration that the breaching party has paid him. For example, if you were a furniture dealer and I had bought a sofa from you on the installment plan, if after making several payments I failed to make any more, the court may allow you to retain the payments that I have paid to you. Under the Uniform Commercial Code, a seller may keep only 20% of the purchase price or $500, whichever is the smaller amount, unless the parties agree to some other reasonable smaller or larger amount.

Sales contracts often provide that where the buyer breaches the contract the seller is allowed to keep the down payment. A provision in a contract allowing retention by the injured party of an amount paid by the breaching party is known as *liquidated damages*. The Uniform Commercial Code may also allow the injured person to recover damages when a sales contract is cancelled. For example, if the sofa that I agreed to buy from you had been specially made to my specifications and you had incurred special expense in getting it for me, you may be able to recover that expense from me also.

Not just any breach will allow a contract to be rescinded and restitution sought. The breach must be *material* before the court will allow the party to consider the contract as discharged. If the breach is not material, then the party who did not breach the contract must continue to perform, although he may seek damages for the loss caused him by the slight breach. For example, if instead of failing to make any further payments on the contract to buy the sofa, I merely make a late payment, this would be a nonmaterial breach (unless the contract itself provides otherwise), and you would not be able to rescind the contract but could only seek damages from me for the harm caused you by my late payment. Usually the damage is interest on the amount of the payment from the date that it was due.

Rescission and restitution is often used by a party who has given something other than money to the breaching party, and seeks its return. Therefore, if you've delivered

the sofa to me, and I now refuse to make the payments due
on it, you may get the sofa back through restitution,
as well as any liquidated damages that you may be entitled
to.

REMEDY BY DAMAGES

The second remedy for breach of contract is *damages*, the
judgment for money against the breaching party to compensate the injured party for the loss suffered. Recovery of
damages is always in money. A person who seeks damages
affirms, rather than disaffirms, the contract and seeks
to be put in the same financial position that he would
have been in had the contract been performed. Thus, if I
breach the contract to buy the sofa from you, you can, instead
of seeking rescission and restitution, sue me for the total
amount due on the sofa, plus any costs you have incurred
in obtaining judgment. Again, by doing so you affirm the
contract rather than disaffirming it, because you're asking
the court to enforce the contract—that is, to put you in
the position you would have been in had the contract
not been breached. Damages are the most often used remedy
for breach because the injured party would most often
rather be put in the position he would have been in had the
contract been performed instead of the position he was in
before the contract was entered.

REMEDY BY SPECIFIC PERFORMANCE

By *specific performance* the third remedy for breach, the
court will order the party who has breached to perform the
contract exactly as he promised to do. Clearly this also
is an affirmation of the contract, because the injured
party seeks to place himself in the position he would
have been in had the breaching party voluntarily performed.
       Remedy by specific performance is the least used of
remedies, however, because courts are loathe to order a
person to perform certain acts in the future, because it's
very difficult for the court to supervise a person's
future actions. It's much simpler to merely give a
judgment for money against the defendant, so that if the
defendant refuses to pay the plaintiff may attach defendant's property and sell it to cover his judgment. Therefore, courts will only allow specific performance where
damages are inadequate.

About the only kinds of transactions where damages would be inadequate are those for the purchase of real property or of unique personal property. If I had contracted with you to sell you a certain piece of real property, or a unique piece of personal property such as an heirloom or an original painting or something that you could not obtain elsewhere, only then would the court order me to perform exactly as I promised to do.

Specific performance is never allowed in personal service or employment contracts. Courts refuse to order people to work for someone else. Only damages would be allowed in such a case. Thus, we see that specific performance is allowed only when rescission and restitution or damages are inadequate remedies.

To seek rescission and restitution disaffirms the contract, and to seek damages or specific performance affirms the contract; thus rescission and restitution on the one hand, and damages or specific performance on the other hand, are inconsistent remedies. If the injured party in a breach wishes to rescind and seek restitution he must do so immediately after the breach, because if he continues to perform himself he has in effect affirmed the contract and would therefore only be able to seek damages, or, if it were a proper case, specific performance.

Thus, a person who is injured by a breach of contract may elect to either rescind the contract and seek restitution, or affirm the contract and seek damages or specific performance. But if he wishes to rescind and seek restitution, he must do so immediately after the breach.

MEASURE OF DAMAGES

We learned earlier that when one seeks damages, he affirms the contract and asks the aid of the court to put him in the position he would have been in had no breach occurred. Generally, the extent of the plaintiff's injury determines the amount of his recovery. Therefore, the injured party may usually recover: the amount he has already paid; the difference between a contract price and the market price at the time of the breach; and any incidental damages such as interest and court costs. For a typical example, suppose I'm a washing machine dealer and you purchase a particular model of washing machine for $300, paying me $50 as a down payment. Now suppose I refuse to deliver the washing machine to you or to return your $50, and it would

cost you $350 to buy a similar machine elsewhere. Your
measure of recovery would be, first, the $50 that you paid
to me, and probably also another $50, since it will cost
you that much more to obtain the same machine somewhere
else. In addition, you could recover a reasonable interest
value on the $50 that you paid me from the time you paid
it to me up until the time that you recover your judgment
from me. This recovery of interest is granted because,
since I have $50 of yours, you are not able to invest that
$50 and obtain interest on it as you might have if you had
had it in your possession. In most states you could also
recover your court costs.

Thus, the plaintiff can recover an amount sufficient
to put him in the same position he would have been in had
the contract been performed by the other party. However,
the injured party cannot increase his damages by his own
acts; that is, the injured person cannot continue to perform
himself after the other party breaches, thus incurring
more expense. He should do whatever is reasonable to
actively reduce the damages, such as seeking substitutes
right away. This is known as the duty to mitigate damages.

If a party fails to mitigate the damages, his recovery
may be reduced by the additional expense. For example, if
I hire you to work for me for one year but I fire you at
the end of six months, you may not fail to seek work elsewhere and instead just sit around and expect to recover
the last six months' wages. If you do this and I prove
that you could have found another job elsewhere, your
recovery will be reduced by the amount you could have
reasonably earned in that six months. In fact, if you do
seek another job, you may even recover from me your cost in
finding the other employment.

This duty to mitigate damages holds true for the sale
of goods. If I breach my contract to sell you some goods
and you fail to seek similar goods elsewhere at the time I
breached the contract, you will not be able to recover
more than the difference between the contract price and
the market price of similar goods at the time of my breach,
plus whatever consideration you have paid prior to the
breach. That is, you will not recover the difference in
market price between the occurrence of the breach and the
date of the judgment. In unilateral contracts, and in bilateral contracts which are completely performed on one
side, no mitigation is possible because the plaintiff has
already performed. Therefore, he may get the full value

of the defendant's performance. For example, if I had
delivered to you the washing machine you bought from me
but you refused to pay the rest you owe me, since I have
fully performed my part of the contract I may recover the
full amount of the sales price from you.

Sometimes there is really little or no injury to the
plaintiff. For example: If you had bought a washing
machine from me but had not paid me any money yet under
the contract, if I failed to deliver the washing machine to
you and you can obtain one elsewhere for the same price
or less, you are really not damaged; you would be able to
obtain only *nominal damages*.

When damages are named in the contract itself, they
are known as liquidating damages. The rule is that liquidating damages in a contract will be enforced unless they are
clearly unreasonable. If they appear to be an honest
attempt to judge the actual damages incurred, the court will
allow them.

ANTICIPATORY BREACH

Remember, an anticipatory breach occurs when one party
indicates to the other party, either by words or actions,
that he will not perform his promise when it becomes due.
Under this situation, when may the injured sue the repudia-
ting party—when the anticipatory breach occurs, or not
before the time for the contract performance has arrived?
Most courts will allow the injured party to treat the anticipatory breach as a breach of contract, at which time the
injured party may seek to perform himself and seek to
mitigate, but will not allow the injured party to sue until
the time for performance has arrived. For example, if I
hired you to be my guide on a safari six months from now,
but three months from now you go on a world cruise, which
would make it impossible for you to carry out your promise
to be my guide, this would be an anticipatory breach. As
soon as I learn of your inability to perform I could attempt
to find another guide and then sue you for my damages when
the time for you to perform has arrived.

Some courts, however, will allow suit at the time of
the anticipatory breach. And most courts will also allow
rescission and restitution, which would be the best remedy
if in our example I had already paid you to be my guide. In
that event, I would rescind the contract and seek the return
of my money.

However, if the breaching party retracts his repudiation before the other party rescinds the contract, or changes his position by attempting to mitigate, the contract will be reinstated. If before I rescind or hire a guide to take your place you catch a jet from Hong Kong and fly to Africa and inform me that you're ready for me when I get there, then there will have been no breach. As a general rule, and under the Uniform Commercial Code, there is no anticipatory breach merely for the payment of money. If I have delivered merchandise to you under a contract whereby you are not obligated to pay until next month, and if you tell me now that you don't intend to pay for them, I can't sue you now, but I must wait until next month when your payment is due. The reason for this exception is that there is no possibility of mitigation if the payment of money is the performance due.

GLOSSARY TERMS

Cancellation   In the Uniform Commercial Code, rescission.

Damages   Judgment of money against a breaching party to compensate the injured party for losses suffered.

Liquidating damages   A provision in a contract allowing the injured party to keep an amount paid by the breaching party.

Nominal damages   Minor damages obtainable when injury to a contract party is slight.

Restitution   Court-ordered restoration of a party injured by a breach to his condition before the contract was entered, performed by the breaching party.

Specific performance   Court-ordered performance of a contract by a breaching party.

SELF TEST
CHAPTER 11

NAME_____

DATE_____

11.1 Breach of contract usually occurs when one fails to perform when his performance is _____.

11.2 A breach of contract can also arise when one party learns in _____ that the other party does not _____ to perform. This is known as a/an _____ breach.

11.3 The three most common remedies for breach of contract are _____, _____, and _____.

11.4 The party accepting a material breach of contract to discharge his obligations under the contract is _____ the contract.

11.5 The party who is _____ by the other party's breach may elect to consider the contract _____, and cease performing himself. By _____ the other party of this election, the contract is rescinded.

11.6 Under the Uniform Commercial Code, rescission is known as _____.

11.7 In order to rescind a contract, the _____ contract must be rescinded.

11.8 When one rescinds or cancels a contract, he is, in effect, _____ the contract.

11.9 A person who rescinds a contract after a breach by the other party may seek the aid of the _____ to put him in the same position he was in before the contract was entered, and get back any consideration he has paid, which would be known as _____.

11.10 In some cases, the court will allow the _____ party to retain some of the consideration that the breaching party has paid him. Under the Uniform Commercial Code, the seller may keep _____ % or _____, whichever is the smaller amount, unless the parties agree otherwise.

11.11   A provision in a contract allowing the retention
        by the injured party of an amount paid by the
        breaching party is known as _____.

11.12   When one seeks _____, he seeks the judgment
        for money against the breaching party to _____
        him for the loss he has suffered.

11.13   One who seeks damages (_____—choose either
        affirms or disaffirms) the contract and seeks to be
        put in the same position that he would have been in
        had the contract been performed.

11.14   The recovery of damages is always in _____.

11.15   A person by seeking damages is asking the court
        to _____ the contract.

11.16   _____ means that the court will order the
        party who has breached to perform the contract
        exactly as he promised to do.

11.17   The remedy of specific _____ is very limited,
        and the courts will allow this remedy only when
        damages would be _____.

11.18   About the only kinds of contracts where damages
        would be inadequate and necessitate the remedy of
        specific performance would be for those trans-
        actions for the purchase of _____ or of
        _____ property.

11.19   Specific performance is never allowed in _____
        or _____ contracts.

11.20   When one seeks the remedy of rescission and restitu-
        tion, he _____ the contract, but when he
        seeks damages or specific performance, he
        _____ the contract.

11.21   If a person wishes to rescind and seek restitution,
        he must do so immediately after the _____.

11.22   Generally, the extent of the plaintiff's
        _____ determines the amount of his recovery.

11.23   The injured party may usually recover the amount
        he has already paid, the difference between the
        contract price and the _____ price at the
        time of the breach, and any incidental damages such
        as _____ and _____.

11.24   The duty of a party injured by a material breach of
        contract to do whatever is possible to reduce
        further damages is known as the duty to _____
        damages. If the injured party fails to perform this
        duty, the receiver may be _____ (choose either
        increased or decreased) by the additional expense.

CHAPTER 11

NAME_____

11.25   In _____ contracts and _____ con-
        tracts which have been completely performed by the
        plaintiff, the plaintiff may set _____
        value of the defendant's performance.
11.26   _____ damages are awarded to a plaintiff when
        the injury is slight or negligible.
11.27   When damages are set forth in the contract itself,
        they are known as _____ damages, and the
        amounts will be enforced unless they are clearly
        _____.
11.28   An anticipatory breach occurs when one party indi-
        cates to the other party, either by _____
        or _____, that he will not perform his
        promise when it becomes _____.
11.29   Even though most courts allow an injured party to
        treat an anticipatory breach as a breach of contract,
        they will not allow the injured party to sue the
        breaching party until the time for _____ has
        arrived.
11.30   If the breaching party _____ his repudiation
        before the other party _____ the contract,
        or changes his position by attempting to mitigate,
        the contract will be _____.
11.31   The general rule is that there is no anticipatory
        breach merely for the payment of _____.

12 Contracts

Loss of Remedies

LEARNING OBJECTIVES

To learn the various ways in which an injured party may lose his remedies for breach of contract.

CHAPTER CONTENTS

Loss of Remedy by Waiver   Statute of Limitations
Loss of Remedy by Bankruptcy   Quasi Contracts   Remedy
Against Induced Breach   Review of Remedies   Glossary
Self Test

The remedies for breach described in the last chapter are
not always available; a party may lose his remedies for
breach of contract in various ways.

LOSS OF REMEDY BY WAIVER

A party may lose his remedies by waiving his right to sue for
a particular breach. A *waiver* occurs when a party intentionally and voluntarily gives up a right he has under the
contract. For example, if I agree to build a house for
you with redwood siding but instead I use palm siding, and
if you, knowing of the change, fail to say anything to me
about it until after the house is built, you may have
waived your right to sue me for this particular breach of
contract.

Waiver most often occurs when the party who is being
injured knows of the breach but does not notify the other
party that he will consider the contract breached unless
the other party remedies it. Thus, if you are ever involved in a contract in which you know the other party is
committing a breach, it is wise for you to notify the other
party that you will consider the contract breached unless
he remedies it. Otherwise, you may be deemed to have
waived your right to consider the contract breached.

Waiver often occurs when a person buys an automobile
from a dealer under a warranty, something goes wrong on
the car, but the new owner is not sufficiently prompt in
seeking repair under the warranty. The buyer must notify
the seller of a defect within a reasonable time of its
discovery to take advantage of the warranty. As can be seen
from our examples, a waiver needs no consideration to be
binding.

STATUTE OF LIMITATIONS

One may also lose his remedies for breach of contract by
failure to bring suit within the time specified in the
Statute of Limitations, a statute passed by a state
legislature which prohibits suing for a breach after a
certain length of time has elapsed from the occurrence of
the breach.

The periods of time in Statutes of Limitations vary
from state to state. Many states also distinguish among
actions on open account, oral contracts, and written con-

tracts. Most commonly an action on a written contract must be commenced six years from the date of its breach. The Uniform Commercial Code provides that action on a contract for the sale of goods must be commenced within four years from the date of its breach.

Statutes of Limitations do not discharge debts or contracts; they merely prevent the injured party from suing on the debt or breach of contract after a certain period of time from the date of breach or default. Therefore, the breaching party may waive the Statute of Limitations and revive the cause of action in the other party.

Waiver causing revival can occur when a debtor makes a new promise to pay the old debt. This new promise may be either an *express*—which most states require to be in writing—or an *implied* promise. The most frequently implied waiver in revival occurs by part-payment of a debt; such a waiver in revival starts the Statute of Limitations running all over again.

Waiver in revival may also operate when the Statute of Limitations has barred an action for breach of contract. For example, the breaching party may expressly promise to remedy the breach, or attempt to remedy it after the Statute of Limitations has run. Such a promise or attempt would be a waiver of the Statute of Limitations, and the injured party could sue the breaching party for the breach even though the Statute of Limitations had run.

As an example of how the Statute of Limitations operates, suppose you and I entered a contract whereby I delivered to you some goods and you were to pay me $200 for them. If the Statute of Limitations is four years, I must sue you for the $200 within four years from the day that your payment was due. If I fail to sue you within four years, I can never recover the money from you unless you waive the Statute of Limitations by making a new promise to pay me the money after the statute has run.

If more than four years has elapsed and I had not sued you, but you then acknowledge that you owe me the money and agree anew to pay it, or you make a part-payment, the debt has been revived and I have another four years in which to sue you. Since, as we learned before, a waiver requires no consideration, there need be no consideration for this new promise to pay the old debt.

The Statute of Limitations does not operate only on debts for the payment of money. It operates on any cause of action for a breach of contract. Thus, if I contracted to sell you goods for $200 and you paid that sum but I failed to deliver the goods, the Statute of Limitations would limit the time in which you could sue me for my breach of contract.

The Statute of Limitations also makes allowance for a removal of a disability. If a minor has a cause of action for breach of contract by the other party, the Statute of Limitations may not begin to run until the minor becomes competent to contract. For example, if when I contracted to sell you goods, but failed to deliver, you were 18 years old, the Statute of Limitations would not begin to run on you until you reach the age at which you are competent to enter contracts in your state. If 21 were the age of competency in your state you would have seven years to sue me instead of four, since you were 18 at the time the breach arose.

The primary purpose of the Statute of Limitations is to prevent persons from being harassed by actions based on old claims; courts look with disfavor upon a wait of years and years before people decide to enforce their rights. Also, the same considerations which apply to the Statute of Frauds apply to the Statute of Limitations: Because witnesses move and memories fade, records become lost or destroyed and fraud or perjury are likelier after a long period of time, the interest of policy in preventing these occurrences outweighs allowing an individual to keep his rights indefinitely.

There are Statute of Limitations not only for breaches of contract, but for tort actions. Tort Statutes of Limitations are usually shorter because there is no written record on a tort and therefore witnesses and memories become more important in providing evidence.

LOSS OF REMEDY BY BANKRUPTCY

A person may lose his remedies if the breaching party goes into *bankruptcy*. Bankruptcy laws were created to relieve insolvent debtors from their contractual liabilities. A debtor in insolvency is one whose liabilities exceed his assets, or one who is unable to meet his debts as they become due.

Bankruptcy laws are intended to allow persons who have become hopelessly in debt to get back on their feet. Without such a thing as bankruptcy, some debtors would never be able to pay off all the debts they owe and would be destitute the rest of their lives.

There are two forms of bankruptcy: voluntary bankruptcy and involuntary bankruptcy. *Voluntary* bankruptcy occurs when an insolvent person, partnership, or even sometimes a corporation applies to the Federal Court to be declared a bankrupt. When a person does this, he turns over his existing property to the control of the court so that the court may divide it up, subject to some exemptions, and distribute it proportionately among all the creditors.

An insolvent debtor may be forced into *involuntary* bankruptcy by his creditors. Creditors may force an insolvent debtor into involuntary bankruptcy if the debtor has done any of certain acts, known as *acts of bankruptcy*, that are considered harmful to his creditors, such as transferring some of his assets for less than their value, or paying one creditor and not another.

In both voluntary and involuntary bankruptcy, the court first appoints a *receiver* to take and conserve the assets, and then appoints a *trustee* to sell the assets for cash and then distribute the cash to the creditors in proportion to the amount they were owed. Once this is done, and even though the creditors did not receive the total amount due them, the debtor is discharged by the bankruptcy court.

Discharge in bankruptcy is a defense against any further action on the debts that were discharged. That means that even if the debtor should later acquire enough property to pay the debts that were discharged in bankruptcy, the creditors of those debts cannot force the debtor to pay any more on them.

However, as with the Statute of Limitations, the discharge of a debt in bankruptcy may be waived by the debtor's voluntarily assuming to pay it after discharge— either *expressly* by a new promise to pay the old debt, or by *implication*, such as by a part-payment of the old debt after discharge. And, again, since this is a waiver, no new consideration need be given to make the new promise to pay binding.

Although bankruptcy is available to those persons who get into debt beyond their ability to pay, bankruptcy is and should be the last resort of a person in such a situation, because once a person has gone through bankruptcy his credit is forever impaired and he may find it very difficult thereafter to find credit available for his use. Therefore, bankruptcy is a very serious matter and should never be resorted to simply to get out of paying some debts which for one reason or another the debtor does not

want to pay or feels he should not pay. Ours is a credit
economy, and if we are to partake in the material benefits
to which most of us aspire, good credit is an important
asset and should be guarded carefully.

QUASI CONTRACTS

All the remedies for breach of contract we have studied so
far apply to express contracts and contracts implied in
fact. But what about contracts implied in law—that is,
a contract imposed by a court between the parties to prevent
the unjust enrichment of one party at the expense of the
other? There was no <u>real</u> contract between the parties
because there was no mutual assent to form a contract.
Therefore, the three contract remedies we have studied do
not apply to contracts implied in law.

When one seeks to recover the reasonable value of the
services which he provided to another, under a contract
implied in law, he sues in what is known as *quasi contract*:
It is not a real contract because there is no mutual assent;
but it is a quasi contract because the party is asking the
court to imply a contract between the parties. Most often
a quasi contract implies when one person performs services
for another not for a specified sum of money but upon the
indication that at some future time the person performing
the services will be compensated, such as in a will.
Thus, if I gave you the impression that if you were to
work for me I would take care of you at some future time,
such as in my will, and you performed the work but I failed
to provide for you at all, you would sue me, or my estate,
in quasi contract for the reasonable value of the services
you performed for me.

Quasi contract is also often used when one person
pays money to another under a mistake of fact. Thus, if
I were to pay you some money thinking that I owed it to
you when in fact I did not, I would seek its return under
quasi contract.

Finally, quasi contract may be used when a person
provides necessities to a minor who then disaffirms the
contract. Since a minor may be held to pay for necessities
which are furnished to him but he may not be sued on the
contract, because he is not competent to contract, the
person furnishing the necessities would sue in quasi contract.

REMEDY AGAINST INDUCED BREACH

What remedy does an injured party have against a third party who willfully induces a party to the contract to breach it? Willfully inducing one to breach a contract with another is a tort, and damages may be recovered from the person who does the inducing. Willful inducement to breach a contract is a tort because by law a person who enters a contract has a right to be free from interference from third parties with that contract. For example, suppose I contract with you to buy your guitar for $30 but someone else comes along and, knowing of our contract, pays you $30 for your guitar plus another $10 for you to breach your contract with me. Under this situation the third party has willfully induced you to breach your contract with me and I can sue him for damages in tort.

REVIEW OF REMEDIES

For the breach of most contracts, the injured party has a choice of two remedies: either *disaffirm* the contract by rescinding it and seek restitution, or *affirm* the contract and sue for damages. A person may rescind the contract only if it has been breached in a material way; if the breach is not material, the only remedy is for damages.

If there has been a material breach, and you wish to rescind and seek restitution, you may recover whatever you have paid to the other party. If you seek damages, you must be ready to show the court that you actually suffered some loss. In addition, when seeking damages, you must also show that you are able, willing, and ready to perform your part of the agreement. In other words, in order to seek damages, you must tender your performance either before or at the time you file your action with the court, because when you seek damages you affirm the contract, whereas when you rescind the contract and seek restitution you disaffirm the contract.

In order to seek specific performance, you must show that damages or rescission and restitution will not be adequate to compensate you for the loss you have suffered. In other words you must show that your contract was for some unique kind of property. Also, in specific performance, you must tender your performance because, again, as in seeking damages, you are affirming the contract. Remember, that if you have a cause of action against another person for breach of contract, do not delay, both to inform that person of the breach and to bring action on the breach. If you fail to notify the other person of a breach you may waive your right to consider it as such, and if you do not bring the action within the period of the Statute of Limitations you may entirely lose your right to sue on the breach.

GLOSSARY TERMS

Bankruptcy   A legal condition of freedom from contractual liabilities when a debtor is insolvent, that is, in insolvency.

Discharge in bankruptcy   The legal condition of a bankrupt, once his debts have been discharged by bankruptcy in a court, of freedom from any further action on the discharged debts.

Insolvency   The condition of lacking assets to meet liabilities or of being unable to meet debts as they become due.

Involuntary bankruptcy   Bankruptcy forced upon a debtor by his creditors.

Quasi contract   A suit in court seeking to impose an implied-at-law contract on a person.

Receiver   One appointed by a court to take and conserve the assets of a bankrupt.

Statute of Limitations   A statute in each state setting limits on the length of time between a breach and the injured party's attempt at remedy.

Trustee   One who is appointed by a court to sell the assets of a bankrupt and distribute the cash proportionately to the creditors.

Voluntary bankruptcy   Bankruptcy that is applied for in a Federal court by the insolvent party.

Waiver   The voluntary surrender of the right to sue for injury under a contract.

Waiver causing revival   A new promise by a debtor to pay an old debt now made uncollectable by the Statute of Limitations.

Waiver in revival   See "Waiver causing revival."

SELF TEST

CHAPTER 12

NAME_____

DATE_____

12.1 A/An_____ occurs when a party intentionally
and _____ gives up a right he has under a
contract.

12.2 Waiver most often occurs when the party who is being
injured knows of the breach, but does not _____
the other party that he will consider the contract
breached unless the other party _____ it.

12.3 A waiver needs no consideration to be _____.

12.4 A party may lose his remedies for breach of contract by failure to bring _____ within the
time specified in the Statute of _____.

12.5 A Statute of Limitations is a statute passed by the
_____ which prohibits _____ for a
breach after a certain length of time has elapsed
from the occurrence of the breach.

12.6 Statutes of Limitations do not discharge _____
or _____, they merely prevent the injured
party from bringing suit after a certain length of
time.

12.7 The breaching party may waive the Statute of
Limitations and _____ the cause of action in
the other party.

12.8 Waiver causing revival can occur by a debtor making
a/an_____ to pay the old debt. This may be
made expressly, or in most states, be _____.

12.9 The most frequent type of _____ waiver is by
part-payment of an old debt.

12.10 The Statute of Limitations operates on any cause of
_____ for a breach of contract.

12.11 The Statute of Limitations also makes allowance
for removal of a/an_____.

12.12 The purpose of the Statute of Limitations is to
prevent persons being harassed by actions based
on _____.

12.13 In addition to a Statute of Limitations for breaches
of contracts or debts, there is also a Statute of
Limitations for _____ actions.

12.14   Bankruptcy laws were created to relieve _____
        debtors from their contractual _____.

12.15   A debtor is insolvent if his _____ exceed his
        _____, or if he is unable to meet his
        _____ as they become due.

12.16   The two ways a debtor can be declared a bankrupt
        are through _____ bankruptcy by the debtor or
        by being forced into _____ bankruptcy by
        his creditors.

12.17   Creditors may force a debtor into bankruptcy if the
        debtor has committed acts considered harmful to
        creditors which are known as _____.

12.18   _____ (Answer True or False) If a debtor
        later acquires enough assets to pay the debts that
        were discharged by bankruptcy, the creditors of
        those debts can force the debtor to pay more on them.

12.19   The three remedies for breach of contract previously
        studied do not apply to contracts implied in
        _____, so a party seeking remedy under this
        type of contract would sue on a/an _____
        contract. These contracts are not real contracts
        because there is no _____.

12.20   _____ contract may be used in a situation
        where a person provides necessities for a minor,
        and the minor later disaffirms the contract.

12.21   Willfully inducing a party to breach a contract
        with another is a/an _____ and _____ may
        be recovered from the person who does the inducing.

12.22   If a party injured by a material breach sues for
        damages, he must be prepared to show that actual
        damages were incurred, and that he had _____
        performance for his part of the contract.

13 Personal Property

Introduction

LEARNING OBJECTIVES

To understand the concept of the ownership of property.
To discuss various ways of owning property.

CHAPTER CONTENTS

Property   Property Rights   The Importance of
Property Rights   Kinds of Property   Ownership   Forms of
Personal Property Ownership   Glossary   Self Test

Having studied the law of Contracts, we turn our attention
to personal property. We shall learn what personal property
is and the kinds of rights and duties toward it. We'll
also study the means of acquiring ownership of personal
property as well as lesser property interests that one may
have in it.

PROPERTY

The word "property" conjures up in the minds of most people
something tangible or physical—like a car, a dress, or a
house. However, the legal definition of *property* is: the
legally enforceable rights that one has in anything subject
to ownership. *Property rights* include: (1) the right to
possession, use, and enjoyment; (2) the right of disposal
during life and after death; and, (3) the right to inherit.
The word "property" therefore has a double meaning: In its
everyday usage it means something tangible; but in law it
means the rights that one has in anything which is subject
to ownership (a concept we'll study later):   the rights of
possession, use, and enjoyment; the right of disposal
during life and after death; and the right to inherit.
     If you look at your history book and say, "That
property is a book," you mean that the book itself is
something tangible—and in the ordinary sense of the word
it is a piece of property. But if you say, "That book is
my property," then you're speaking in the legal sense—
you're saying, "I have rights in that piece of property."
This may include the right to possess, to use, and to enjoy
the property. It may also include the right to dispose of
that piece of property either while you're alive or upon
your death. Or it may mean that you have the right to
inherit that piece of property.

PROPERTY RIGHTS

Now, property rights may mean all of the rights that we
have mentioned or it may mean only some of them. Property
rights do not always include all of the rights that we
mentioned earlier. Thus, you may have the right to possess,
use, and enjoy a piece of property, but you may not have
the right to sell it, or your heirs may not have the right
to inherit it from you. This will become clearer, but
suffice it to say for now that property may mean all of
those rights or just some of them.

THE IMPORTANCE OF PROPERTY RIGHTS

Property rights are fundamental to our society and system of government. In fact, property rights are the primary difference between our system and pure communism. In our system individuals have personal property rights, whereas under pure communism the State has all property rights in all property. Our Constitution guarantees these private property rights; you can't be deprived of them without due process of law. And, if the state should decide that it needs some of your property rights, it cannot take them from you without fair compensation.

KINDS OF PROPERTY

Property may be classified in one of two ways: It is either *real property* or *personal property*. Real property includes rights in land and all things permanently attached to it, called fixtures. (In a later chapter we'll look more closely at real property. Personal property, on the other hand, includes rights in tangible, that is, physical things which are movable, called *chattels*. For example, trucks, books, animals, telephones, and so on are personal property, or chattels.

But personal property also includes rights in *intangible* things, such as contracts, stocks, and so on. Intangible property, then, is things which cannot physically be taken possession of. That is, although you can take physical possession of a stock certificate or a contract or something like that, the paper that it is written on is not the thing that you actually own; you own the rights which that piece of paper signifies. We will deal in this chapter with personal property, both tangible and intangible.

For an example of the distinction between tangible and intangible personal property, suppose I sell you my tape recorder for $300 and you contract with me to pay me at the end of 30 days. You now have possession and use of my tape recorder, tangible personal property. However, I have possession and use of your promise to pay me the $300 in 30 days. This is an intangible; I may be able to sell and transfer it and otherwise use it, but I cannot feel it

OWNERSHIP

We defined property in its legal sense as the legally
enforceable rights one has in anything subject to *ownership*.
In its strongest sense, *ownership* means all the legally
enforceable rights mentioned: possession, use, and enjoyment, disposal and inheritance. For example, if that history
book mentioned earlier was owned by you, you would ordinarily
have all the legally enforceable rights that we have mentioned in it.

But ownership can mean something less. The general
legal definition of ownership is the right to possession,
superior to all others. You need not actually have
possession but merely a superior right to it over everyone
else. For example, if you own that history book but you
loan it to me you still own it—you have a legally superior
right to possess that book over everyone else, including
me. And if I were to give it to someone else or sell it
you would still have the primary right in that book. So
you don't need to actually have possession of it.

But even though you have ownership in the book—a
superior right to possess it—you may not have the right to
sell it or to otherwise dispose of it. For example, suppose
you acquired that history book from me; only in our sale I
said that the book was yours so long as you did not sell
it to someone else. If you tried to sell it the book would
revert back to me. Now, as long as you have the book and
do not attempt to dispose of it you have the ownership of
it because you have the primary right to possession of the
book over everyone including me. Only if you try to dispose of it would I reacquire ownership in the book. If
this sounds too complicated, just remember that ownership
legally means the right to possession superior to all
others, and the person who has that superior right is
considered the owner.

FORMS OF PERSONAL PROPERTY OWNERSHIP

There are six basic forms of ownership of personal property.
First, property may be owned by one person alone,
who has the superior right to possession over everyone else.
This type of ownership is called *severalty*. For example,
if you purchase a camera from me and pay me cash for it,
you own that camera in severalty—all alone.

The second form of ownership is *joint tenancy*, when
two or more people—joint owners—own an equal share of

the whole. Under joint tenancy, all the joint owners
have an equal right to use the property. No person owns
a separate part of the property; rather each person owns an
equal share of all of it.

Joint tenancy carries with it the right of survivorship, meaning that if one owner dies the remaining owners
take an equal part of his share. For example, if you and
Tom Jones and I own a history book as joint tenants but
then I die, you and Tom Jones would equally get my share
and, therefore, the two of you would be joint owners in the
history book.

Joint tenancy of one joint owner's share terminates
when that owner disposes of his share; the remaining joint
owners continue as joint tenants, but the new owner does
not become a joint tenant. For example, if I sold my
share in the history book, you and Tom would remain as
joint tenants as to one another but the new owner would
not be a joint tenant with you and Tom. For joint
tenancy, three things must happen: (1) there must be equal
shares of interest; (2) the interest of all joint tenants
must have been acquired at the same time; and (3) the
interest must have been acquired from the same person.
You and Tom and I could be joint tenants in that history
book only if we had each paid the same amount for our
interests, and if we had acquired it at the same time,
and if we had all acquired our interest from the same
person.

The third form of personal property ownership is
tenancy in common. Tenants in common do not each own a
share of the whole, but rather each owns an undivided
share of the property, distinct and separate. A tenant
in common has only the right to use the property according
to his share.

Tenancy in common does not carry with it the right of
survivorship; if there are three tenants in common of
a piece of property and if one of the tenants dies, the
other two tenants do not acquire his share. Instead, the
share of the deceased passes to his heirs or under his
will; the person who takes by inheritance would also become
a tenant in common with the others. Shares in tenancy in
common need not be equal; nor must they have been taken
from the same person. Also, a tenant in common can sell
his share without terminating the relationship. If one
tenant in common sells his share, the new owner takes as a
tenant in common with the remaining tenants in common.

For example, if you and I purchase a boat as tenants
in common and you pay one-third of the price and I pay

two-thirds, I can sell my share to Tom and he has a
tenancy in common with you. If Tom then dies, his heirs
or legatees would get his two-thirds share as tenants in
common with you. If there were more than one heir or
legatee, they would split Tom's two-thirds among themselves
as tenants in common. So if Tom dies without a will and
leaves two heirs, each takes a one-third interest in the
boat and you and the heirs are all tenants in common.
This same principle would apply if Tom died with a will or
if he sold his share to more than one person.

In talking about joint tenancy, we stated that a
sale of a share of a joint tenancy terminates the joint
tenancy; the sale of a share of a joint tenancy creates a
tenancy in common. For example, if you and I owned the
history book as joint tenants and I sold my share to Tom,
you and Tom would become tenants in common, each owning
one-half interest in the book. If I sold my share to more
than one person—say if I sold it to Tom and Bill—Tom and
Bill would each take a one-fourth interest in the book,
because I only had a half interest to sell. Then Tom and
Bill and you would all be tenants in common. You owning
one-half share, Tom and Bill each owning one-fourth.

The fourth form of personal property ownership is
tenancy by the entireties, which is like a joint tenancy
except that a husband and wife are the joint owners.
Whenever a husband and wife are owners of a certain piece of
property they are usually owners as tenancy by the entireties.
There is a right of survivorship under tenancy by the
entireties; if the husband dies, the wife receives the
entire share.

(Of course there cannot be more than two tenants by
the entireties.) However, tenancy by the entireties does
differ somewhat from joint tenancy. For one, neither
tenant by the entireties can dispose of his or her interest
without the consent of the other.

Of course, if a husband sells his interest in his
tenancy by the entireties it would dissolve, because the
purchaser would not be the husband of the remaining tenant.
This also would create a tenancy in common. Some states
have abolished joint tenancies; instead, they have
tenancies in common with the right of survivorship, the
fifth form of personal property ownership. In these states,
if a piece of property is sold to a husband and wife in
order to create a tenancy in common with the right of
survivorship, this right to get the property upon the death

of the other must be expressly stated in the instrument transferring ownership. If the right of survivorship is not expressly stated, then the husband and wife would take as tenants in common.

Some states which have abolished tenancy by the entireties have not replaced it with tenancy in common with the right of survivorship, but instead have created by statute a form of ownership called *community property*, the sixth form of ownership of personal property. In eight states, property acquired by either spouse during marriage gives the other spouse a one-half interest in that property. Some of these states provide also for survivorship.

However, community property does not include property which is owned by each spouse at the time of the marriage or property that is acquired by gift or inheritance even during the marriage. For example, if I own a car at the time of my marriage, my wife does not take a half interest in that car under community property; but if I buy a car while married, my wife would have one-half interest in the car, but even if I'm married, if someone gives me a car or I inherit it then my wife would not have a one-half interest in it. Only in community property states does a wife automatically take one-half interest in property that her husband acquires during marriage.

In states which do not have community property, but which have tenancy by the entireties or tenancy in common with the right of survivorship, the husband and wife must take as joint owners. In other words, the sale must be to both husband and wife.

GLOSSARY TERMS

Chattel   Tangible personal property.

Community property   A condition of ownership whereby any property acquired by one partner in a marriage becomes half owned by the other partner.

Joint tenancy   Ownership by two or more persons sharing equal rights to use the property.

Ownership   The right to possession, superior to all others.

Personal property   Rights in all tangible, movable things— all property other than real property—and in all kinds of intangible things.

Property   Any legally enforceable rights that one has in anything subject to ownership.

Property rights   All or any of the rights to possession, use, and enjoyment, to disposal during life and after death, and to inheritance.

Real property   Rights in land and all the things permanently attached to it.

Right of survivorship   The right in joint ownership of all surviving owners to share the portion of ownership left by a deceased owner.

Severalty   Ownership by one person.

Tenancy in common   Ownership by more than one person in which each owner has a distinct and separate, undivided share of the property.

Tenancy in the entireties   Joint tenancy by a husband and wife.

SELF TEST

CHAPTER 13

NAME_____

DATE_____

13.1   The legally enforceable rights that one has in
        anything subject to ownership would be the de-
        finition of _____.

13.2   Property rights include the right to _____,
        use, and enjoyment; the right of _____ during
        life and after _____; and the right to
        _____.

13.3   Property rights (choose "do" or "do not") _____
        always include the three previously mentioned
        rights.

13.4   Property rights are fundamental to our system of
        _____ and _____.

13.5   In the democratic system, _____ have personal
        property rights, whereas in pure communism, the
        _____ has all property rights, in all
        property.

13.6   The _____ guarantees private property
        rights, and a person cannot be deprived of them
        without _____ of law.

13.7   Property is classified as either _____
        property or _____ property.

13.8   _____ property includes rights in land and
        all things permanently attached to it.

13.9   _____ are things in which you may obtain
        rights which are tangible, but _____
        property also includes rights in intangible things.

13.10   _____ property are things of which you
        cannot take physical possession, while _____
        property is something physical.

13.11   The general legal definition of _____ is
        one of who has the right to possession, superior
        to all others, but does not mean that the person
        must have _____, but merely superior
        rights over others.

13.12   _____ is ownership in something by just one
        person.

13.13 _____ is where two or more people own an equal share of the whole.

13.14 _____ carries the right of survivorship.

13.15 _____ means that if one of the owners dies, the remaining owners take a/an _____ part of his share.

13.16 Joint tenancy of one joint owner's share terminates when that owner _____ of his share; the remaining joint owners continue as _____, but the new owner does not become one.

13.17 The three things that must exist or happen in order to become a joint tenant are:
   a) there must be _____ shares of interest;
   b) the interest of all joint tenants must have been acquired at the _____.
   c) and the interest must have been acquired from the _____.

13.18 Tenants in common each own a/an _____ share of the property.

13.19 A tenant in common has the right to use the property according to _____, and does not carry with it, the right of _____.

13.20 If a person who has an interest in property as a tenant in common dies, his share will pass to

_____.

13.21 In a tenant in common relationship, the share of interest need not be _____; the share need not be taken from the _____ nor at the _____; and a tenant in common may sell his share without _____ the relationship.

13.22 Tenancy by the _____ is like joint tenancy, except a/an _____ and _____ are the joint owners.

13.23 There is a right of _____ under tenancy by the entireties, so if one spouse should die, the other would receive the entire share.

13.24 There cannot be more than _____ tenants by the entireties.

13.25 Under tenancy by the entireties, there must be _____ of the other tenant before one tenant's interest may be sold.

13.26 In states recognizing tenancies in common with the right of survivorship, the survivorship right must be _____ stated in the instrument transferring ownership.

13.27 _____ property means that property acquired by either spouse during marriage, gives the other

CHAPTER 13

NAME_____

spouse a one-half interest in the property, except
property acquired by _____ or _____
during the marriage.

13.28 Some of the forms of ownership previously discussed
are:

a) _____ where one person alone has
property rights in something;

b) _____ tenancy which carries with it the
right of _____;

c) tenancy in _____ where two or more
persons are joint owners of an undivided share
of the whole;

d) tenancy by _____ which requires that
both husband and wife be the joint owners;
and

e) _____ property which automatically gives
each spouse a one-half interest in property
acquired during marriage.

14 Personal Property

Social Limits of Ownership. Acquisition Other Than by Sale—I.

LEARNING OBJECTIVES

To learn some of the restrictions on property rights.
To become familiar with some of ways in which property interests can be acquired.

CHAPTER CONTENTS

As we saw in the last chapter, property rights include the possession, use, and enjoyment of property; the right of disposal during life and after death; and the right to inherit. Now suppose someone owns property in severalty and has every property right possible. There are still limits as to what that person may do or how he may use or enjoy his property; an absolute owner—that is, one who has all the property interest in the thing—does not have an unrestricted right of use, enjoyment, or disposal.

SOCIAL RESTRICTIONS ON PROPERTY RIGHTS

Society imposes a number of restrictions on property rights for its own protection and advancement. The first restriction is that a person cannot use property so as to injure others. Suppose you own a gun in severalty and you have all the property interests possible in this gun. Society still imposes restrictions upon your use and enjoyment of that gun: you may not fire it at someone else; you may not fire it certain times of the day or in certain places. And in fact society also imposes restrictions on your right to sell the gun. Society requires a permit or a license for ownership and it may require the person who buys the gun to have obtained a permit or a license.

There are other restrictions that society imposes so as not to injure others. One area of the law is called *nuisance*. Under nuisance law, you may not use your property so as to bother your neighbors or others of the public. For example, there may be laws in your state or city which require you to not play your record player too loudly after certain hours of the night.

A second form of restriction that society imposes upon the use of property is licensing. For example, your city or state may require you to have a license in order to keep a dog or some other animal. You cannot drive your car or even possess it (registration) without obtaining a license. And you must have a license to sell such items as liquor, drugs, and so on.

Third, society taxes the use and enjoyment of many items. In states that have a personal property tax you must pay a tax on the value of personal property that you own. And, of course, in all states there are real property taxes.

Fourth, personal property may be liable for your debts. That is, if you owe money to someone and he obtains a judgment against you, he may attach and sell your personal property to satisfy his judgment.

Finally, the law often will not allow certain dispositions of property; you can't impose a restriction upon a gift or a sale of property that only Caucasians can use the property, or that property is to go to a fund to overthrow the government.

Thus, even though you may have all the rights possible in a certain piece of property, you may still not have absolute ownership of it in the sense that you can do with it as you please, use it as you please, and dispose of it as you please.

ACQUISITION OF PERSONAL PROPERTY

There are nine common ways in which people acquire property interests in things:
1. finding;
2. by gift;
3. by inheritance;
4. by judgment;
5. by original production;
6. by accession;
7. by confusion;
8. by adverse possession;
9. by a contract of purchase, more commonly known as a sale.

MEANING AND LIMITS OF POSSESSION

Before we study the ways of acquiring property, we must have a more thorough understanding of what *possession* is. Possession is comprised of two elements:
1. The mental intent to control, and
2. Actual substantial physical dominion and control.
For example, you may own a piece of property but not have possession of it. If you loan it to someone, then you do not have substantial actual physical control and dominion over it, nor do you have the mental intent to control it at that moment. That does not mean that you are not still the <u>owner</u>, you merely do not have <u>possession.</u> One may also have the mental intent to control something but not have possession of it for lack of substantial actual physical

dominion and control. For example, you may be walking
down the street and see a watch lying underneath the grating
in the gutter. Now, you may have the mental intent to
remove that watch from the grating and control it, but
until you have it in your actual physical dominion and
control you do not have possession of it. On the other
hand, one may have substantial actual dominion and control
and yet not have possession because there is no mental
intent to control. For example, if a bird flies in your
window and you grab it intending to let it back out
through the window, while you hold it you have actual
physical dominion and control, but you do not have possession of it because you do not have the mental intent to
control it.

Now suppose you're walking down the street one day
and you find a can of beans lying in the gutter. You stoop
and pick it up. Now you have actual physical dominion
and control of the can, and you have mental intent to
control the can, therefore you have possession of the can.
But what about the beans that are contained inside it? A
rule of law known as the *container rule* covers this
situation. The container rule states that if you intend
to control a container, you also intend to control what is
normally contained inside that container. Therefore, if
the can you possess contains beans, you also have possession of the beans inside the can.

A famous old case very well points up the container
rule: A little boy was walking down the street and found a
stocking lying in the gutter. He picked it up and threw it
to one of his friends. There were several other boys
along with them, and they threw the stocking back and forth
for some time. Then one of them dropped the stocking and,
low and behold, some money fell out of it. Now, the little
boy who found the stocking claimed that the money was his
because he found the sock, and he had actual physical control and dominion of it, and he mentally intended to control
it. The court held, however, that he did not have possession of the money that was inside the stocking because
normally one would not find money in a stocking and the
container rule states that you have possession of the
contents of a container only if you intend to control what
is normally contained inside. Now, the court said that
since money is not normally contained inside a stocking
the little boy did not intend to control the money inside
that stocking, and it therefore gave the money to the boy who
first picked it (the money) up.

What kinds of rights does mere possession of property give one? As we mentioned in an earlier chapter, an owner has a paramount right to possess property. Therefore, if one finds property and takes possession of it, the owner would still have the right to possess that property if he came along and discovered the property in the hands of the finder.

But what kinds of rights does the finder or the one in possession have if the owner cannot be located? The rule is that a person in possession has a prior right against all subsequent claimants except the true owner; but he does not have the right to possession against *prior possessors*. For example, if you find a diamond ring in the street and you take possession of it and then the real owner comes along, he has the right to take possession of that ring from you. But if you found a ring and a person came along who had found that ring prior to you but had then dropped it, he would also be able to take possession of it from you. You would have the right to possess only over any subsequent person who acquired possession of it—except against the true owner.

SCALE OF POSSESSION

We can set up a scale of possession. First, an owner has the right to possess against everyone. Second, a prior possessor has the next best right. Next, the person presently in possession has the right to possession, And, finally, subsequent possessors have the right to possess.

Another famous old case well illustrates this point: While sweeping out a chimney in old London, a young chimney-sweep came across a pearl necklace in the chimney. He took it to a jeweler to have it appraised and cleaned. The jeweler refused to give the necklace back to the boy claiming that the boy was not the true owner and that therefore since the jeweler had present possession, he had the right to keep it. The court said that, even though the boy was not the true owner, since he had prior possession of it he had the right to possess it against the jeweler, who was a subsequent possessor.

LOST, MISLAID, AND ABANDONED PROPERTY

Another rule is that the first person to possess previously unpossessed property owns it. Therefore, a prospector who discovers a gold mine and takes possession of it becomes the owner. Now, to acquire a property interest by finding something which had been owned by someone, one must possess property which has been lost, mislaid, or abandoned. Property is *lost* when the owner <u>involuntarily</u> parts with it and doesn't know where to find it. The key word, "involuntarily," means that a person must not be aware of parting with the property. *Mislaid property*, on the other hand, is where the owner voluntarily parts with the property but forgets where he left it. For example, if a person staying in a hotel room hides money in the lining of a drawer and later checks out of the hotel, forgetting that he had put the money in the drawer, he has <u>mislaid</u> the money, because he voluntarily parted with it by intentionally putting it in the drawer but then forgot that he did so. When property is mislaid <u>or</u> lost there is no intent to give up ownership.

    Abandoned property, however, is property that the owner voluntarily parts with intending to give up ownership. There must be an overt act to evidence this intent to give up ownership. For example, if a farmer standing in a field sees a man drive an old car intentionally into a ditch, get out of the car and kick it saying, "That's it! I've had it," then the car has been abandoned, because the owner intentionally parted with it intending to give up ownership.

    I'm sure you've all heard the old phrase "finders keepers, losers weepers," but it is not true in most cases. If a person finds property which has been lost—that is, which has been involuntarily parted with and the owner does not know where to find it—the finder need not take possession of it, but if he does take possession, he doesn't immediately become the owner; he becomes the possessor and has the rights of a possessor described above.

    A person who finds lost property and takes possession ot it must do several things: He must make a reasonable effort to find the true owner; he must make a reasonable effort to preserve the property; and he may get reasonable compensation from the owner for preserving the property if the owner is found, but he may not get any compensation for attempting to find the owner. That is a duty put by law upon finders. A person who finds lost property cannot take it home and conceal it in his safe, and he cannot allow the property to deteriorate. If you find a bicycle and take it home, even though you do not attempt to hide it, if you leave it out in the rain and it rusts and the true owner comes along and wants his bicycle back, he may be able to recover damages from you for allowing the bicycle to rust. In most states, statutes describe the duties that must be performed, and for how long, before a finder can become an owner. So you must look to the law of your own state, set by statute, which will tell you how long you have to maintain and keep a piece of lost property before you will become the owner.

We stated earlier that a person who finds lost property may take possession of it and have the rights of a possessor, and if he keeps it for a certain length of time while trying to find the true owner and taking care of the property, he may then become the owner. But there are two exceptions to the rule that a finder may keep possession of property that he finds against all but the true owner: First, if the finder is a servant with a duty to turn the property over to his employer; second, if the property was lost in a ultraprivate part of the premises, such as in a home. The finder would have the duty to turn the goods he found in a home over to the owner of the home. The reason for these exceptions is obvious: If the person who lost the property comes back attempting to find the property, ti will be much easier for him to find it if the owner of the premises, the employer or the owner of the home, has the property than if someone has taken it off the premises. These two cases, of course, are exceptions to the prior possessor rule that we stated earlier, for here the possessor must run the property over to a subsequent possessor.

About possession of mislaid property, the rule is that property which is found in a public place, such as on an airplane, a train, a bus, or in a public building, must be given to the manager if the circumstances indicate that the owner would return there to look for it. Again, the guest in the home must give the property to the owner of the home, for a person who mislays property—even more so than a person who loses it—will probably return to the place where he mislaid it to look for it. Therefore, the finder must give it to the person who has control of the premises. However, if property is mislaid in a place where

there is no person in immediate control, such as in a
vacant lot or in a street, then the finder of mislaid
property has the same rights and duties as the finder of
lost property—that is, he may keep possession of it but he
must hold it for a certain length of time and keep it in
good condition in case the true owner shows up.

Abandoned property, however, is different; the one who
first takes possession becomes the owner. The reason for
this is quite obvious: A person who abandons property has
evidenced his intent to give up his ownership and therefore
the first person to find it and take possession of it becomes
the owner since there is no reason for him to maintain the
property for the original owner.

The abandoned property rule is also applied to *treasure
trove*. Treasure trove is property which has been secreted
somewhere by someone whose intent is to return and reclaim
it, but which has been there for so long that it would be
impossible for the owner to come back to claim it. Another
famous old case illustrates this point: A young boy was
hired by Farmer Jones to clean the farmer's chicken coop.
As the boy was sweeping the floor, he noticed a hard object
just beneath the surface. He dug a little bit and found an
old chest and upon opening it found Spanish pieces of
eight and other jewelry in the chest.

The farmer claimed that the boy should turn the
possession of the goods over to him since they were
obviously mislaid goods and, as we know, a finder of mislaid goods has a duty to turn the goods over to the owner
of the premises so that the true owner can come back and
reclaim it. The court said, however, that since this
property was obviously hundreds of years old the original
owner must be dead and therefore the property was no
longer mislaid property but was treasure trove, and gave
it to the boy.

GLOSSARY TERMS

Abandoned property Voluntary parting with property by the owner with intent to give up ownership.

Container rule A rule that the person who intends to control a container also intends to control what is normally inside that container.

Lost property Involuntary parting with property by the owner but without knowledge of its whereabouts.

Nuisance law The restriction under law that personal property may not be used to disturb neighbors or others of the public.

Possession The mental intent to control a thing and actual substantial physical dominion and control over it.

Prior possessor rule The rule that a person in present possession of something has a prior right against all subsequent possessors, except the true owner.

Treasure trove Property that has been hidden with the posessor's intent to someday return and claim it, but which has remained hidden so long that return of the original owner has become impossible.

SELF TEST

CHAPTER 14

NAME_____

DATE_____

14.1 Society imposes some _____ on property rights for its own protection and advancement.

14.2 A person cannot use property so as to _____ others.

14.3 Under _____ law, you may not use your property so as to bother your neighbors or the public.

14.4 The nine more common ways in which people acquire a property interest in things are by finding, _____, _____, judgment, _____ production, _____, _____, _____ possession, and by a contract of _____, more commonly known as a sale.

14.5 To be a/an _____, one must possess the property that is found.

14.6 Possession is comprised of two elements:
a) The _____ intent to control, and
b) actual, substantial physical dominion and _____.

14.7 The _____ rule states that if you intend to control a container, you also intend to control what is normally inside that container.

14.8 An owner has a paramount right to _____ property; therefore, if one finds property and takes possession of it, the _____ would still have the right to possess that property if he discovered the property in possession of the buyer.

14.9 A person that finds property and possesses it has a/an _____ right against all subsequent claimants except the _____, but he does not have the right to possession against _____ possessors.

14.10 The general rule is that the _____ person to possess previously unpossessed property owns it.

14.11 In order to acquire a property interest in something which has been owned by finding, one must possess property which has been lost, _____, or _____.

14.12   Property is lost when a person _____ parts
with it and doesn't know where to find it.

14.13   _____ property occurs when the owner of the
property voluntarily parts with it, but forgets
where he left it.

14.14   When property is lost or mislaid, there is no
intent to give up _____.

14.15   _____ property is where the owner voluntarily
parts with the property with the intent to give
up _____.

14.16   There must occur a/an_____ act to evidence
the intent to give up ownership.

14.17   A person who finds lost property becomes the
possessor but does not immediately become the
_____.

14.18   A person who finds lost property must do several
things:
a)   he must make a/an_____ to find the owner;
b)   he must make a reasonable effort to _____
the property.

14.19   The two exceptions to the rule that a finder may
keep possession of property that he finds against
all but the true owner are when the finder is a
servant with a duty to turn the property over to
_____, or where the property was lost in a/an
_____ part of the premises, such as the
home.

14.20   If a finder finds mislaid property in a/an_____
place, he has a duty to give the property to the
manager.

14.21   The _____ property rule is also applied to
treasure trove.

15 Personal Property

Acquisition Other Than by Sale—II

LEARNING OBJECTIVES

To learn more of the many ways in which property interest may be acquired.

CHAPTER CONTENTS

Acquisition by Gift   Intent   Delivery   Acceptance
Acquisition by Inheritance   Acquisition by Judgment
Acquisition by Original Production   Acquisition by Accession
Glossary   Self Test

Another common method of acquiring personal property is by *gift*, a voluntary transfer without consideration. The person who gives a gift is known as the *donor* and the person who receives the gift is called the *donee*.

ACQUISITION BY GIFT

In order to make a valid gift, there must be three elements:
1. intent;
2. delivery;
3. acceptance.
If these three elements of intent, delivery, and acceptance are present, then the gift is irrevocable and the donor may not take the property back; he loses all control over the property and the donee becomes the owner. Let's now look more closely at these three elements.

INTENT

Intent means that the donor must presently intend to pass a present interest in the property. A promise to give something in the future or a present gift of a future interest is not an effective gift and may be revoked.
For example, if I say to you, "I'll give you my pencil tomorrow," there is no present gift because I do not have a present intent to pass a present interest. I'm promising you that I'll give you the pencil tomorrow. Since there's no present intent to give a present interest, I may revoke my promise before tomorrow and refuse to give you the pencil.
Also, if I know that I am going to buy a pencil tomorrow and I say to you, "You are now the owner of the pencil that I am going to buy tomorrow," this is not an effective gift either. Although I have the present intent to pass an interest, it is not a present interest but a future interest because I do not yet own the pencil. Therefore I have not made an irrevocable gift, and when I acquire the pencil tomorrow, you have no interest in it.
But if I hand you my pencil and say, "It's yours," I have made a gift, because I have a present intent to pass a present interest. I own the pencil <u>now</u> and I mean for you to have the pencil <u>now</u>. Once the pencil is in your possession I no longer have any interest in it and you have acquired the ownership.

DELIVERY

The second element for an effective gift is delivery,
meaning the transfer by the donor of all control over the
thing that is being given. There must be actual delivery
of possession of a chattel, if possible. So anything
capable of manual delivery must actually be delivered to the
donee—put in his possession. If the chattel is incapable
of physical delivery, then a writing or some other evidence
of the intent to pass a present interest must be given.
For example, since a safe deposit box is not capable of
physical delivery, by giving you the keys to it I have
evidenced my intent to pass all my interest to you presently.
Also, keys to a car might be a similar example.

Intangible things are often evidenced by a writing
when a gift is intended. For example, if I want to give
you my shares of stock in Campbell Soup Company, I would
give to you stock certificates which evidence the ownership that I have in the company, and when I hand you the
stock certificates saying, "They're yours," I have given
up my interest in the company and passed it to you.

If there is actual delivery, there's probably no need
to transfer title also. For example, if I want to give you
my motorcycle and I hand the motorcycle over to you, I
give you control of it, and say "It's yours," then a valid,
irrevocable gift is given at that time even though I have
not yet signed over the title to the motorcycle.

ACCEPTANCE

The third element for a valid gift is acceptance by the
donee. In most cases acceptance by a donee is presumed.
In other words the law assumes that a person accepts a gift
that is being given to him. So if the donee is unaware
of the gift, or if he doesn't want it, he must renounce it
within a reasonable time of his knowledge of it.

If the donee fails to renounce the gift within a
reasonable time of his having knowledge of it, then it
will be his even though he may not want it. For example,
suppose I have been salmon fishing and I've caught more
salmon than I can keep in my freezer, I wrap one up and I
come into your office and while you're on the telephone
I say to you, "Here's a salmon that I've caught and I
want you to have it." I put it on your desk, but you
didn't hear me because you were concentrating on your
telephone conversation. Now when you hang up and you discover

the fish lying on your desk, if you do not want it you
have a duty to notify me within a reasonable time that
you are renouncing the gift. If you fail to do so the
law will presume that you have accepted the gift and it
will be yours.

In a face-to-face transaction, for example, if I came
up to you and handed you my pencil and said, "Here's my
pencil. I want you to have it. It's yours," and you heard
me and took it in your hand, if you don't say right then,
"No. I'm sorry. I don't want your pencil," then there
has been a valid gift and you are now the owner of the
pencil. If you come back up to me an hour later and say,
"Gee, I don't want your pencil after all. Take it back,"
then you are not revoking the gift of the pencil, but
instead you're offering to give it back to me, and the
elements of a valid gift must again occur in order for me
to reacquire ownership.

We learned, too, that to be valid a gift must be
voluntary. If I hold you up on the street and point a gun
at your head and say "Give me your money," and you give me
your money, of course there has not been a gift because
you did not voluntarily part with your property—you had
no present intent to pass a present interest.

In addition, a gift must be without consideration. So
if I approach you and say, "I want you to have my ten-
dollar gold-plated pencil for one penny," and I give you
the pencil and you give me the penny, this is not a gift
but a sale because, as we learned in contracts, the courts do
not generally look into the adequacy of consideration. If
any consideration was passed, it was adequate. Even a
penny is consideration.

ACQUISITION BY INHERITANCE

The third of the common ways mentioned in the last chapter
by which personal property may be acquired is by *inheritance*.
A person dies either *testate*—that is, leaving a will—or
intestate—that is, without leaving a will. (A will, as we
will learn in a later chapter on will and intestacy, is a
formal document executed by a person before death, directing
the distribution of his property upon his death.) When
a person dies intestate, statute directs the distribution
of his property to his heirs. A will may direct the distribution of property to just about anyone (subject to a few
rules that we will learn later). But a person who takes

under the laws of intestacy must be a relative of the
deceased person. So a person may acquire the personal
property of another by taking from a deceased under his
will, or a relative may take some portion of an ancestor's
estate under the rules of intestacy.

ACQUISITION BY JUDGMENT

The fourth way that personal property may be acquired is by
judgment—the judgment of a court. If, for example, there
is a dispute between two persons over the ownership of a
certain chattel, a court may declare who is the owner.
For example, if I am the owner of some land upon which you
find a gold watch, I may claim that the watch was mislaid
by its owner and that therefore you should give me possession of the watch under the rules of finding that we talked
about earlier. You may claim that the watch was not mislaid
but instead lost and that therefore you have the right to
possession of it. If we cannot settle our dispute, we may
go to court and ask the court to declare who is entitled
to possession.

One may also acquire personal property by judgment
through a *judicial sale*. Judicial sales occur primarily
when a creditor has obtained a money judgment against a
debtor and he levies on some of the debtor's property. The
rights and remedies of a creditor over his debtor will be
discussed later in the book; for now we can say that a
creditor who obtains a judgment in court against a debtor
may attach the debtor's property and have it sold by the
sheriff to satisfy the judgment.

For example, suppose you owe me $1000 that was to be
paid to me last month. I have sued you and have obtained
a judgment against you for $1000, but you still refuse to
pay me. How can I collect it? Well, I may ask the sheriff
to attach some of your property and sell it to satisfy the
judgment. Now suppose the sheriff goes out and attaches
your car—takes your car into his custody and then, through
the rules of judicial sales, sells it to someone else for
$1200 and gives me $1000 of it. (Of course, in this case the
other $200 would be paid to you.)

The person who bought the car is now the owner of it;
he has acquired the property by judicial sale. One reservation, however, should be noted: The buyer of property
upon a judicial sale gets only the title to the property
that the debtor had. Now in our example, if you did not yet

own all of the car but were buying it on time and conditional sale by which the seller retained the title to the car until it was fully paid, then the person who purchases the car at the judicial sale will be subject to that conditional sales contract that you had on the car. So he will not become the absolute owner of the car but will only acquire the interest that you had in it.

A third way that property may be acquired by judgment is known as satisfaction of judgment. Satisfaction of judgment occurs when property has been converted by someone— that is, someone takes property that does not belong to him and acts toward it as if he were the owner. If the owner sues the converter and recovers a judgment against him and the converter pays the judgment, the converter becomes the owner of the property. For example, suppose you take off your coat and lay it down and a thief steals it. If you identify the thief you sue him in court for the value of the coat and recover a judgment against him which he pays, the coat is no longer yours but his.

In satisfaction of judgment, the converter gets title only after he pays the judgment, and he gets only the title that the prior owner had.

The thief would not get title to your coat until he paid the judgment, and if, for example, you still owed some money to the store on it, then the thief would not acquire the complete ownership either, only the interest that you had; he would still owe the store for the remainder that you had owed on the coat. Now you can see why satisfaction of judgment is also known as a forced sale—because the court forces the converter to acquire property interest in the goods that he converted, by paying for them.

ACQUISITION BY ORIGINAL PRODUCTION

The fifth means of acquiring personal property is by *original production*, which requires, as it states, something original. A slight variation on something that someone else has produced may not be enough for acquiring a property interest. Acquiring a property interest by original production often occurs when an author writes something new and original or a painter paints an original picture or an inventor invents something new. Such an original producer has an exclusive property right in his own product prior to publication or sale on the market; he owns that thing before it is published or is offered for sale.

If the original producer wants to retain exclusive rights after, say, publication or sale, he must get special authority from the federal government. When an original production is an intellectual production, such as a new book, a painting, a song, its producer (creator) applies for a *copyright*, which gives him the exclusive right to make, publish, sell, or perform his production, or to authorize others to do so. This right lasts for 28 years, with provision for renewal.

If a person invents something new, instead of obtaining a copyright, he applies for a *patent*, which gives the inventor the exclusive right to make, use, sell, or to authorize others to do so for 17 years. A patent is not renewable. For example, suppose you invent a new, faster weaving machine for weaving cloth. If you apply for and obtain a patent on this new machine then only you have the right to make, use, and sell this machine, and, of course, you may authorize others to make it and sell it for you. This right lasts for 17 years. This does not mean that other people cannot also develop a new machine to do the same thing that yours can. It means only that they may not use the same idea that you used, or copy your machine. There's much law on what is a copy of an invention and what is not, and on what is the same idea and what is not, because many people have copied an invention except for just one detail and the court must decide whether the detail is material or not. But, at any rate, you have the exclusive right in that machine and all others exactly like it.

ACQUISITION BY ACCESSION

The sixth method of obtaining personal property is by *accession*, an increase in things one owns, either naturally or by improvement or modification. A simple example of a natural increase is when your cat has kittens; those kittens belong to you by accession. For accession by improvement or modification, the rule is that when goods are added to goods, the owner of the principal goods gets the ownership of the whole where to remove the added goods would cause damage to the whole. For example, an auto mechanic puts a new generator in your car. To remove the generator would damage the car, and, therefore, the generator becomes part of the car, and automatically becomes yours by accession.

Somewhat more complicated would be the purchase of a car on a conditional sales contract—meaning the title, the ownership, stays in the seller until completely paid for. The car did not have a radio when purchased and the buyer wants a radio so he purchases one and drills holes in the dashboard to add it to the car. Now, several months pass and he finds it impossible to continue making payments on the car. The seller then comes and repossesses (take back) the car. The seller would get the radio, since to remove it would damage the car because holes have been drilled in the dashboard for the radio, and to take it out would decrease the value of the car. Therefore the seller of the car would obtain ownership of the radio by accession.

But suppose that for this car the purchaser bought new wheels and snow tires, but also kept the original wheels and tires for summer driving. If the seller repossesses the car, the buyer can keep the snow tires and wheels because, even if they're on the car, removing them and putting on the original wheels and tires would leave the car undamaged. Therefore, the seller could not obtain title to the snow tires and wheels by accession. On the other hand, returning to our earlier example of a newly installed automobile generator, we stated that it would become part of the car and that the owner of the car would obtain the generator by accession. Therefore, a repairman who puts in the generator can't remove it, even if the generator is not paid for, because to do so would damage the car. (However, the repairman has other remedies which are discussed in a later chapter.)

A person who does not own the original or principal goods can also get title to goods by accession. This occurs when a person, in good faith, improves or modifies the original goods to such an extent as to create a new species, or when he improves the value of the original goods manyfold (about six times its original value). For example, suppose we are wheat farmers and after harvest we take our wheat to public elevators for storage side by side. Then I take your grain, thinking it is mine, and make it into whiskey; I may become the owner of the whiskey because I have so improved or modified the original goods that I have created a new species. Although I may be liable to you for the value of your grain, I have become, by accession, the owner of your grain, which is now whiskey.

Another example of acquiring property by accession through improvement of value might occur when a mechanic driving down a country road sees a wrecked car in a ditch and, thinking that it's abandoned completely fixes it up— makes it almost new. In this case, if the value of the

repaired car is about six times or more the value of the
wrecked car lying in the ditch, then the mechanic may
become the owner of the car by accession. Of course, again,
he may be liable to the true owners for the value of the
car as smashed, if the true owner did not abandon the car.

In order to acquire property by such an accession,
the converter must act in good faith, meaning that he
must actually believe that the goods are his or that they
are abandoned; he must not know that the goods belong to
someone else. If he acts in good faith, he may acquire
title to the goods after he has improved or changed them,
but he would be liable to the owner for the original value
as he found it. However, if the converter acts in bad
faith, he would get neither title to the goods nor compensation for the work he put into them. Therefore, if I
intentionally and knowingly took the grain out of your
storage elevator, you would be entitled to the whiskey and
would not have to pay me its value—you wouldn't have to
pay me anything. You would acquire title to the whiskey
by accession; the work that I put into it would now become
yours.

The same thing would hold true if the wrecked car in
the ditch was not abandoned, and the mechanic knew it but
took the car anyway, the owner would get the repaired car
and would not have to pay the mechanic anything for the
repairs that he put into it.

Thus, we have seen that accession occurs under two
circumstances: first, when goods are added to goods,
the owner of the principal goods gets the ownership of the
whole if to remove the added goods would damage the whole;
second, when a nonowner of goods acquires title to the
goods by, in good faith, so changing the goods that they
are no longer the same species, or, by increasing their
value manyfold.

GLOSSARY TERMS

Acceptance   The donee's expressed or implicit willingness to take and keep an offered gift.

Accession   An increase in one's property either naturally or by improvement or modification.

Copyright   Exclusive right to make, publish, sell, perform, or authorize others to do so, of an original intellectual production.

Delivery   Physical passing of an object that is a gift from the donor to the donee, or of a writing signifying such passing when physical transfer is impossible.

Donee   Recipient of a gift.

Donor   A person who gives a gift.

Gift   A voluntary transfer without consideration.

Inheritance   Ownership acquired from a deceased by will or by state disposition to relatives.

Intent   The present intention of a donor to pass a present interest in a property.

Intestate   The condition of not having left a will at death.

Judgment   Disposition of disputed ownership of property by a court.

Judicial sale   A sale of goods directed by a court to cover a person's debts.

Patent   Exclusive right to make, use, sell, or authorize others to do so, of an invention.

Testate   The condition of having left a will at death.

Will   A formal document executed by a person before death, distributing his property upon his death.

SELF TEST

CHAPTER 15

NAME_____

DATE_____

15.1   A voluntary transfer without consideration is known
       as a/an _____.
15.2   The person who gives a gift is known as the _____.
15.3   The person who receives a gift is known as _____.
15.4   The three necessary elements for a valid gift are in-
       tent, _____, and _____, and, if all of these
       requirements are met, the gift is _____ and the
       donor may not take the property back.
15.5   Intent means that the donor must presently intend to
       pass a/an _____ interest in the property; therefore,
       a promise to give something in the _____ or a
       present gift of a/an _____ interest is not an
       effective gift and it may be _____.
15.6   _____ means that the donor must transfer all
       control over the thing that is being given.
15.7   Intangible things are often evidenced by a/an _____
       when a gift is intended.
15.8   If a donee fails to _____ a gift within a reason-
       able time of his having knowledge of it, then it will
       be his even though he may not want it.
15.9   In most cases, _____ by the donee is presumed.
15.10 In order to be valid, a gift must be _____; i.e.,
       the donor must not be forced to make the gift.
15.11 A gift must be without _____; if _____
       was present, the transaction would be a sale.
15.12 When a person dies _____, it means he dies
       with a will.
15.13 When a person dies _____, it means he dies
       without leaving a will, and _____ directs
       the distribution of property to his _____.
15.14 A person who takes property under the laws of intestacy
       must be a/an _____ of the deceased person.
15.15 Acquiring property by judgment means judgment of a/an
       _____.
15.16 Another way in which one may acquire property by
       judgment, is upon a judicial _____, which
       occurs primarily when a creditor obtains a/an _____

against a debtor, and he _____ on some of
the debtor's property.

15.17 The buyer of property upon a judicial sale gets only
the title to the property that the _____ had.

15.18 A third way that property may be acquired by judgment
is known as _____ of judgment.

15.19 In satisfaction of judgment, the _____ only gets
title after he pays the judgment, and then he only
gets the title that the _____ had.

15.20 A satisfaction of judgment is also known as a/an
_____ sale.

15.21 Original production requires something _____;
therefore, a slight _____ on something that someone else has produced may not be enough for acquiring
a property interest by original production.

15.22 Where an original production is an intellectual
production, the producer applies for a/an _____,
which gives the producer the _____ right to
make or sell his production.

15.23 If a person invents something new, he applies for
a/an _____, which gives the inventor the
_____ right to make, use, sell, or authorize
others to do so for _____ years.

15.24 A copyright lasts _____ years, and is renewable,
whereas a patent does not contain a/an _____ right.

15.25 Personal property may be acquired by _____,
which is an increase in things one owns, either
_____, or by improvement or _____.

15.26 The rule for accession by improvement or _____ is
that when goods are added to goods, the owner of the
_____ goods gets the ownership of the _____ where
to remove the added goods would cause _____ to the who

15.27 A person can get title to goods by accession if he,
in good _____, improves or modifies the _____
goods to such an extent as to create a new _____,
or if he improves the _____ of the _____
goods about _____ times their original value.

15.28 If the converter of goods under accession must act
in good _____, he may acquire _____ to
the goods after he has improved, or changed them, but
he would be _____ to the owner for the
original _____ as he found it.

15.29 If a converter acts in bad faith, he would get
neither _____ to the goods converted, nor
_____ for the work he put into them.

15.30 There must be actual _____ of possession of a
chattel if that is possible in order to satisfy the
requirements of the second element for a valid gift.

16 Personal Property

Acquisition Other Than by Sale—III

LEARNING OBJECTIVES

To learn the remaining ways to acquire personal property.

To become familiar with the concept of confusion and adverse possession.

CHAPTER CONTENTS

Acquisition by Confusion   Acquisition by Adverse Possession   Glossary   Self Test

The seventh way in which personal property may be acquired
is by *confusion*. In confusion goods belonging to two or
more parties become intermixed in such a way that none of
the parties are able to identify which is theirs or to
separate the property of the two or more persons. For
example, you and I are wheat farmers who both had bumper
crops. I harvested my wheat first, and placed it in a
public grain elevator. You harvest your crop and place
your grain in the same elevator, not knowing that some
of my grain is already in there. Now, if our grain is the
same type and becomes mixed together it would be impossible
to tell yours from mine, or even if the grains were
different but became mixed together, it would be virtually
impossible to separate the two, and under either of these
conditions confusion would result.

ACQUISITION BY CONFUSION

If the goods that are confused are not of similar value
and can not be separated, the one who did the intermixing forfeits his.

For example, suppose that my wheat was of a much
better quality than yours and we could not separate the
two different wheats; since you are the intermixer I get
all of the wheat. This would be true even if your wheat
were of a much greater value than mine, if you did the
intermixing and we could not separate them. I might get
the benefit of the better wheat that you put in.

But if the goods are of similar value—for example,
if our wheat is exactly the same—then, if the person
did the intermixing in good faith and can prove how much
is his, the parties are tenants in common. If the intermixer
cannot prove how much is his, the other party gets all of
it. So if your wheat was the same quality and grade as
mine and you intermixed them innocently, not knowing that
my wheat was already in the silo, and if you can prove how
much of the total wheat was put in by you, then we are
tenants in common in proportion to the amount of wheat that
we each put into the silo.

So, if you had put in 300 bushels, and there were 450
bushels in total, then we would be tenants in common in the
ratio of two to one. You would own two-thirds of the whole
and I would own one-third. However, if in good faith you
put in wheat of similar value, but you did not know how much
wheat you had put in, then I would own all of it.

Likewise, if the goods are of similar value, but the intermixer acts in bad faith, the intermixer forfeits his goods and the other party gets all.

ACQUISITION BY ADVERSE POSSESSION

The eighth method of acquiring personal property is known as *adverse possession*. Recall that ownership of property gives one a superior right over all others to possess it. But to own something, you need not be in possession of it; nor is a person in possession of property necessarily the owner. In our discussion on finding we saw persons in possession who were not the owners.

You remember that the finder—the possessor—had to give the property up to the real owner if the real owner happened along. But adverse possession means that one has possession of property which is not his, but acts toward it as if he were the owner, adversely to the interests of the true owner. For example, you loan me your stereo for a party but when the party is over I fail to return it to you and I continue to use it as if it were my own; I loan it to friends, I play it all the time, I bought records to use on it, and so on. I act with it as if it were my own. If you came to try to get it but I told you, "You can't have it. It's mine now. It's no longer yours," I would be an adverse possessor, because I am acting toward this stereo as if it were my own. I would be denying ownership in everyone else, including the true owner.

An adverse possessor need not know that he is not the real owner and that someone else is. For example, suppose I find your stereo out in the street and I take it home thinking that it has been abandoned, while in fact it fell off the back of your truck while you were moving and therefore it is really lost property, not abandoned. (I would become the <u>owner</u> of abandoned property by picking it up and taking it home. But I become merely the <u>possessor</u> of lost property and I must hold it for the true owner.) You find out that I picked up your stereo and brought it home. If I've been using this stereo as my very own and claiming it's mine, and you come along and say, "That's my hi-fi. I want it back," but I say, "No, sir. I found this as abandoned property and therefore it's mine," then I am also an adverse possessor.

Thus, a person may be an adverse possessor whether or not he knows that the property he has possession of is not

his. The test is that if that person acts toward the
property as if he were the owner, denying ownership in
everyone else, he is an adverse possessor.

How does an adverse possessor acquire the property
interest—the ownership in something that he adversely
possesses? The rule is that if an adverse possessor openly
and notoriously possesses the property, and does not try to
hide it or remove it from the community without letting the
true owner know, then, after a certain statutory length of
time, in most states at least ten years, the property would
become his.

"Openly and notoriously" means that a reasonable,
prudent owner would know, or should know, that the adverse
possessor had his property and where it was. If an ordinary,
reasonable, and prudent person who lost something valuable
would be able to find out who had it and where it was, if
he were looking for it, then this property would be in
possession, openly and notoriously. "Openly and notoriously"
means that you use it as if it were your own, not trying
to hide it from anybody. It doesn't mean that the true
owner would find it if he were to look for it. It merely
means that you are not trying to prevent him from finding
it.

But say that I found your stereo on the street and
claimed it was mine 8 years ago, and the statutory period
in our state is 10 years. If I continue to adversely
possess the stereo for two more years, I will become the
owner. But you find out that I have the stereo that you
lost 8 years ago, and you come to me and demand the return
of it, but I refuse to give it to you. Now what happens?
If I continue to keep the property for two more years, will
it be mine? No. If the owner demands the return of
property which is being held adversely, and the adverse
possessor refuses to return the property, the statutory
time period starts all over again. So, I would have to hold
the stereo for ten more years now before it would become
mine—in this case, a total of 18 years.

The reason for this rule is that if the true owner finds
property of his which is being held adversely, he then has
the statutory period in which to seek its return through
the courts. For if the owner finds out who has the property
and demands its return but is refused, he has a new cause
of action at that time for conversion. So the statutory
period, which is really a statute of limitations, starts
to run all over again.

As we mentioned before, an adverse possessor may be a person who knows that he is not the true owner and he may even know who the true owner is. So under this rule a thief could actually become the owner of personal property after the statutory period had run, so long as he does not try to hide the fact that he has the property but openly and notoriously displays it as his own. If I had stolen your stereo from you and taken it to my house and acted with it as if it were mine and did not try to hide the fact that I had it, then after the statutory period had elapsed I would become the owner. Once again, the real owner does not have to have actual knowledge of the whereabouts of the property, so long as a reasonable, prudent owner would be able to find out where it is if he looks for it. Adverse possession does not occur very often with personal property, but it does with land, and we'll talk about adverse possession again in our later chapters on real property.

GLOSSARY TERMS

Adverse possession   Possession of property by other than the
    true owner, but acted toward as if the possessor were
    the owner, adversely to the interests of the true owner.

Confusion   An intermixture of the goods of two or more
    parties in such a way that their ownership cannot be
    identified or the goods cannot be separated.

Openly and notoriously   Of property held in adverse
    possession, held in such a manner that a reasonable,
    prudent owner could find his property if he were
    looking for it.

SELF TEST
CHAPTER 16

NAME_____

DATE_____

16.1 _____ is an intermixture of goods belonging to two or more parties forming a composite group where the two parties are unable to _____ which is theirs, or it's impossible to _____ the two.

16.2 If the goods that are confused are not of similar value and can't be separated, then the one who did the intermixing _____ his share.

16.3 If the goods that are confused are of similar value and the person who did the intermixing did so in good _____, then the parties are _____, if the one who intermixed can prove how much is his. If he can't the other party gets _____.

16.4 If the intermixer of goods of similar value did so in bad faith, then he would _____ the goods he had put in.

16.5 _____ of property gives one a superior right over all others to possess it.

16.6 Adverse possession means that one has possession of property which is not his, but _____ toward it as if he were the _____, adversely to the _____ of the true owner.

16.7 It is not necessary for an adverse possessor to know that he is not the _____ and that someone else is.

16.8 The test to see if a person is an adverse possessor is that if that person _____ toward the property as if he were the _____, he denies _____ in everyone else, then he is a/an _____.

16.9 The rule is that if an adverse possessor openly and _____ possesses the property, and does not try to _____ it or _____ it from the community without letting the true _____ know, then after a certain _____ length of time, the _____ would become his.

16.10   If the owner demands the return of the property
        which is being held _____, and the adverse
        possessor refuses to return the property, then the
        _____ starts all over again.

16.11   If the true owner finds property which is being
        held adversely, he then has the _____
        period in which to seek its return through the
        _____.

16.12   (Answer True or False) _____ A thief could
        possibly become the owner of personal property
        through adverse possession.

16.13   The important thing to remember about satisfaction
        of judgment is that the converter obtains
        _____ to the goods only when he _____
        the judgment.

17 Sales

Introduction

The ninth and last method on our list of those for acquiring personal property is the *contract of purchase*, the commonest type of contract. A contract of purchase is better known as a sale, which is the commonest method of acquiring personal property. Since a sale involves a contract the general rules of contract apply—company parties, mutual assent, legal agreement, consideration, and required form. In addition, special rules have developed over the years regarding sales, and different legal jurisdictions have different rules.

But as you know, in recent decades much of our commerce has become nationwide or at least interstate, and the need for uniform rules governing sales became apparent. Therefore, rules governing the buying and selling of goods have been brought together and unified under the Uniform Commercial Code. Most states have adopted the Uniform Commercial Code, but for the states which have not yet adopted it the uniform sales act or the common law still apply. We will base our study of sales on the Uniform Commercial Code because it is the controlling law over most of our commerce today. And even where it has not been adopted many of the rules of the states apply anyway.

SALES

A *sale* is the passage of title to goods from one person to another for the payment of a consideration called the price. Taking a closer look at that definition, passage of *title* means that at the time the contract is entered the title— that is, the ownership, the property interest—passes from the seller who is often called the vendor to the buyer also called the vendee. If our title does not pass immediately upon our entering the contract but is to pass some time in the future, the transaction is not a sale but a contract to sell. To distinguish between a sale and a contract to sell, if I say to you, "I'll buy your ring for $25. Here's the money," and I also say, "I will buy your watch next Tuesday for $30," and you say to me, "Okay, here is the ring and I will sell the watch to you for $30 next Tuesday," the first transaction was a sale because the title passed as the contract was entered—that is, immediately upon my handing you the $25. However, our agreement for me to buy your watch next Tuesday for $30 is a *contract to sell* because the title does not pass until I pay you the $30 and you give me the watch next Tuesday. Of course, the contract

to sell the watch becomes a sale on Tuesday when you give
me the watch and I give you the $30.

The transaction may be a sale, and thus the title is
transferred immediately, even though the entire payment
is not made at the time of the sale—for example, an
installment sale: Suppose I said to you, "I will buy your
ring for $25. You give me the ring and I will give you
$5 now and $5 a month for the next four months." If I
give you the $5 and you give me the ring a sale has occurred
because the title to the ring has transferred; I am now the
owner even though I have not paid you the entire amount. Of
course, my agreement to pay you $5 a month for the next
four months is also a contract and upon my breach of it
you may sue me.

In some cases a sale may also occur even if the seller
retains possession. An example here is a *lay away*: If I
said to you, "Here is $25 for your ring, but keep the ring
for me until tomorrow," the title has passed even though the
seller retains possession. Most of you have used lay away
plans when buying merchandise from retail stores. You
may see an item advertised that you have been wanting for
some time, but you don't have the entire amount to pay for
it now. You go down to the store and pay so much down and
ask them to hold it for you until you have the rest of the
purchase price. A sale occurred when you paid the down
payment on the goods and asked them to hold it for you.

Actually, this transaction is a combination of an
installment sale and a lay away: You have agreed to pay
the purchase price in installment—so much now and the rest
later, either the entire balance at one time or in installment—and you have asked the seller—or the seller has
demanded—to retain possession of the goods until they are
paid for.

We must be careful to distinguish installment sale
from *security agreement* (which will be studied in more detail
in a later chapter). In a security agreement a person buys
goods on an installment plan and takes possession of the
goods but does not become the owner until the goods are
paid for; the seller retains the ownership in the goods
until the total purchase price is paid. This is how most
automobiles are purchased. You pay so much down and get the
car, you drive it, you pay so much per month, but the seller
or the bank remains the legal owner of the car until it is
paid for. In effect, then, a sale on installment in a
security agreement is a contract to sell rather than an
immediate sale, because the title does not pass until the
total purchase price is paid.

OWNERSHIP AND RISK OF LOSS

Both sales and contracts to sell are contracts of purchase
and are governed by the laws of sale. Since both are
contracts they may be breached by either party. But
although both sales and contracts to sell are contracts
of purchase and are therefore governed by the law of sale,
the distinction between them remains important because the
rights and liabilities of buyers and sellers are different
for each.

This distinction is particularly important if the goods
are damaged or destroyed. For the general rule is that risk
of loss follows ownership. Therefore it is important to
determine who had title at the time of the loss. For
example, suppose you go to a jewelry store and see a watch
you like that costs $50, but you have only $25 in your
possession. So you say to the jeweler, "Here's $25, I'll
bring in the other $25 next week. Will you keep that watch
for me until I bring in the rest of the price?" And he
agrees to do so. Suppose that during that week the
jewelry shop burns down and the watch is destroyed. It
becomes important to determine who had ownership of that
watch at the time of its destruction, because generally the
owner will bear the loss. So if this was a lay away plan
and therfore a sale, you would bear the loss because the
title to the watch had passed to you at the time you made
the down payment, even though the seller retained possession. However, if it were a security agreement, by which the
seller kept title to the watch until you had paid for it,
then he would bear the loss. (We will discuss passage of
title and risk of loss in more detail in a later chapter.)

DEFINITION OF GOODS

The distinction between a sale and a contract to sell is
also important for determining the rights of creditors,
insurance companies, and for tax purposes. Therefore, it
often becomes very important to determine whether a particular transaction is a sale or a contract to sell, and if it
is a contract to sell just when it becomes a sale. We
defined a sale as the passage of title to *goods*. Just what
are goods?

Goods are defined by the Uniform Commercial Code as
tangible personal property, that is, physical property which
is movable. Thus a chair, a gallon of gas, a truck, logs,

and a bushel of wheat are all goods within the definition under the Uniform Commercial Code.

Since goods include only tangible personal property, intangible personal property is not goods. The transfers of rights to things like money, insurance, stocks, bonds, copyrights, and patents are not sales as classified under the Uniform Commercial Code. For example, suppose you wish to visit your Aunt Millie in a certain city and you decide to go by train. You purchase a train ticket, but that purchase is not a sale, because a train ticket is intangible personal property and is therefore not a good. True, you get a ticket which you can feel and move, but that ticket is not the thing that you bought; it merely evidences what you did buy. What do you buy when you buy a train ticket? You buy the right to travel on the train from the point of departure to the point of destination.

Is money itself a good and the purchase of it a sale? No, because money is not a thing in and of itself but is merely a right to something such as gold or silver, and is therefore an intangible. So a loan—the purchase of money—is not a sale. (However, rare coins are tangible personal property and are therefore goods, and the purchase of them is a sale.)

Is real property a good? No, although often called a sale, the transfer of land is legally called a conveyance and is not governed by the rules of sales. Nor is the transfer of fixtures (property permanently attached to land). However, growing crops, which are intended to be severed from the land, and the unborn young of animals are both considered personal property rather than fixtures. Therefore, a contract to sell an unborn calf or a bushel of wheat is a contract of purchase, even while it is still growing on the land, because it is intended to be severed from the land and when it is it becomes a good.

The Uniform Commercial Code also says that goods must be both existing and identified before there can be a sale of them. In other words, the thing must be both in existence and pointed out or labeled as the subject of the sale before any title can pass. Goods which are not both existing and identified are called *future goods*, and an attempt to pass a present interest in them is not a sale but a contract to sell. Therefore, only when the thing is both in existence and identified can a sale occur. For example, if you were in the business of selling radios to the public and you order 20 radios from a manufacturer, no sale occurs until the radios are manufactured. Also, those

radios that are manufactured for you must be set aside,
labeled, or identified as yours in the manufacturer's
warehouse before sale occurs.

Although an unborn animal can be a good, to have a sale
of it the unborn animal must be in existence and identified—
it must be in its mother's womb. Thus, a sale of Daisy's
next calf would be a sale if Daisy is pregnant, but will be
a contract to sell if she is not. If Daisy then becomes
pregnant, the contract to sell would turn into a sale at
that moment. Once again the importance of the distinction
between a sale and a contract to sell becomes clear: If
Daisy dies before she gets pregnant the loss would fall on
the seller because no sale had yet occurred; but if Daisy
dies while she is pregnant, or if the calf is born dead, then
the loss would fall on the buyer because the sale had
occurred.

PRICE

The third element in a sale is the payment of consideration,
called the *price*. Now what exactly is a price? The price
can be money or something of value which the buyer gives
or agrees to give in exchange for the transfer of ownership
in the goods. If the buyer is not to give money, he may
give anything else, including goods, the right in
intangible personal property, real property, or even his
personal labor.

The sales law applies to trade or *barters* and the
buyer's agreement to pay the price by his personal work.
For example, suppose I want to buy your tape recorder and
we agree on a price of $100—either in money or in ex-
change for my shotgun which we value at $100. This would
be a trade or a barter, because we would be trading goods
for goods; but my shotgun, paid for your tape recorder,
is nevertheless a price. I might agree to give you certain
stocks that I own worth $100—intangible property. Or I
might have a piece of real property—a lot, for example,
worth $100. Finally, I might agree to work for you for
some specific time for a certain rate of pay until I have
worked off the $100.

If the price is to be paid in goods, then the buyer
is also a seller of the goods he is to transfer, and the
rules of the Uniform Commercial Code apply to him. Thus,
if goods are exchanged for goods, each party is a seller
of the goods he is to transfer, and each party is a buyer—

in effect this is a two-way sale. Now if the price were to
be paid in intangible personal property, such as money, or
in real property, then the buyer would not also be a seller,
because under the Uniform Commercial Code these things are
not goods.

Ordinarily, the seller demands a certain price, or the
parties agree upon a price. Say you agreed to sell me
your tape recorder for $100. In the situation where I
was to transfer intangible personal property or real property
or labor, we valued those things on the basis of $100.
But suppose no price is settled. Suppose I said, "I'll buy
your tape recorder from you," and you said, "Okay, I'll
sell it to you." Can a binding sales contract be entered
when no price is settled in the contract? Yes, if the
parties intend to enter a binding sales contract, then one
may be entered even though the price is not stated.

Binding sales contracts without a stated price can be
entered in various ways. The parties, for example, may
state that the price is to be agreed upon between them at
a later date. For example, I may approach you and say,
"I want to buy your tape recorder," and you say, "Okay,
sold, but let's decide on the price next week." Or instead
we may state that the price is to be the market price of
similar goods, such as at the time and place of delivery.
So we may agree that the price of the tape recorder is to
be the market price of similar tape recorders at the time
and place you are to deliver the tape recorder to me.

Or the parties may provide that the price be fixed by
a third person. This is called a *sale at valuation*. For
example, I tell you that I want to buy your tape recorder
but you say, "All right, sold, but I don't know how much it's
worth, so let's let the owner of the Ace Tape Recorder Shop
set the price on this tape recorder." Finally, the parties
may provide that the price is to be fixed either by the
seller or the buyer. However, if the seller or the buyer
is to fix the price, the Uniform Commercial Code says that
he must do so in good faith, otherwise there is a breach
of contract.

If any of the above methods of fixing the price fail,
or if nothing at all is said about the price in the
contract, the price would then be a reasonable price at the
time of delivery. Courts usually use the market value of
similar goods at that time as a reasonable price, but if there
is no market price, such as when the goods in question are
unique—there are no others on the market like them—then
the court would set a reasonable price under all the

circumstances at the time. Of course, if nothing at all
is said about the price in the contract, there is only a
valid and binding sales contract if the parties intended
to enter one anyway.

GLOSSARY TERMS

Barter   An exchange in value of goods for goods.

Contract of purchase   A sale, a passage of title for consideration.

Contract to sell   An agreement to a sale at a later date.

Conveyance   The transfer of title to real property.

Down payment   A portion of the purchase price given for consideration to pass title or to reserve title to the payer.

Future goods   Goods that are not both in existence and identified.

Goods   Tangible personal property.

Installment sale   A sale by which for part payment the purchaser takes possession of both the goods and title to the goods.

Lay away plan   A plan by which title passes to the purchaser for part payment but possession remains with the seller.

Price   Money or something of value that the purchaser gives or agrees to give for transfer of ownership in goods.

Sale   Passage of title to goods from one person to another for a consideration.

Sale at valuation   A sale in which the price is fixed by a third person.

Security agreement   A form of installment sale by which for part payment the purchaser takes possession of the goods but the seller, or a bank, retains title until payment is complete.

Title   Ownership, property interest.

Trade   Barter.

SELF TEST

CHAPTER 17

NAME_____

DATE_____

17.1   The most common type of contract is a contract of
        _____ and _____ are the most common
        method of acquiring personal property.

17.2   We will base our study of sales on the _____
        Code because it is the _____ law over most of
        our commerce today.

17.3   A sale is the passage of _____ to goods from
        one person to another for the payment of a/an
        _____ called the _____.

17.4   _____ of title means that at the time the
        contract is entered, the title, or property
        _____, passes from the seller, who is often
        called the _____, to the buyer, also called
        the _____.

17.5   If title to goods is not to pass when the contract
        is entered, but is to pass sometime in the future,
        the transaction is not a sale, but a/an _____.

17.6   A contract to sell becomes a sale when title is
        _____.

17.7   A/An _____ sale is an example of a sale that
        has title transferred immediately even though the
        entire _____ is not made at the time of sale.

17.8   A sale may occur if the seller retains _____
        in some cases.

17.9   A/An _____ is where a person buys goods on an
        installment plan and takes possession of the goods
        but does not become the _____ until the
        goods are paid for.

17.10   A sale on installment in a security agreement is in
        effect a contract to _____ rather than an
        immediate _____.

17.11   A security agreement is also known as a/an
        _____ sale.

17.12   The general rule is risk of loss follows _____.

17.13   Goods are defined by the Uniform Commercial Code as
        _____ personal property.

17.14   Money, insurance, and stocks are examples of
        _____ personal property and not included in
        the law of sales.

17.15   Land, or real property, is not transferred by a
        sale, but by _____.

17.16   The Uniform Commercial Code says that goods must
        be both _____ and identified before there
        can be a sale of them.

17.17   Goods which are not both existing and identified
        are called _____ goods, and an attempt to
        pass a present interest in them is not a sale but
        a/an _____.

17.18   The _____ can be something of value which
        the buyer gives or agrees to give in exchange
        for the transfer of _____ in the goods.

17.19   If goods are exchanged for goods, each party is
        a/an _____ of the goods he is to transfer,
        but if the price were to be paid in _____
        personal property or real property, then the
        buyer would not also be a seller.

17.20   If there is a/an _____ to enter a binding
        sales contract then one may be entered even though
        the _____ is not stated.

17.21   A binding sales contract may be entered without a
        price being stated, and the parties may provide
        that the price be fixed by a third person, which
        is known as a sale at _____.

17.22   If a sales contract states that the buyer or seller
        is to fix a price for the sale of goods at a later
        date, the Uniform Commercial Code says that he must
        do so in _____, otherwise there is a/an
        _____ contract.

17.23   If a sales contract provides no mention of price or
        no provision was made for the price, then the price
        would be a/an _____ price at the time of
        _____. Courts usually consider this price
        to be the _____ value of similar goods at
        that time.

18 Sales

Competent Parties. Mutual Assent—I.

LEARNING OBJECTIVES

To learn the rules of passage of title.
To learn the rules of ownership in sold goods.
To compare contract law with sales law.

CHAPTER CONTENTS

Competency to Contract to Sell   Competency to Sell
Passing Better Title Than the Seller's   Mutual Assent in
Sales Contracts   Glossary   Self Test

Remember that in the last chapter we said that all sales
and, of course, contracts to sell are based on a contract,
and therefore the general rules of contracts apply. But
the Uniform Commercial Code contains some rules that are
somewhat different from the rules of general contract law,
and it contains some additional rules to cover special
situations which are created by sales.

COMPETENCY TO CONTRACT TO SELL

The first element of a valid contract, you will recall, is
that the parties who enter into it are competent to contract. Generally, anyone competent to enter an ordinary
contract is competent to enter a sales contract—either as
the buyer or the seller. You will recall that minors and
other incapacitated persons are not competent to enter
binding valid contracts enforceable by both parties.
Minors and other incapacitated persons enter voidable
contracts, meaning that they may enforce the contract
against the other party but the other party may not enforce
the contract against them.

A person is competent to enter a contract to sell
something that is not yet in existence. For example, a
manufacturer of bicycles can contract to sell bicycles that
he has not yet made. He will be bound to deliver the bicycles
on the date specified in the contract and if he does not
do so he will be in breach. But he may require of himself
to sell something that he has not yet acquired. Of course,
as we learned earlier, no title can pass to the buyer until
the goods are in existence.

One need not own the thing that he contracts to sell.
A person can contract to sell something he does not yet own.
Of course, failure to obtain ownership by the time the
contract is to be performed will be a breach. For example,
suppose I contract to sell you a Stradivarius violin. Now,
I don't own one, but I believe I know where I can get one
for the price less than the contract price that we agreed
upon. Now if I was to deliver this violin to you within
two weeks and I do not do so, then I am in breach of contract and you have a cause of action against me.

Just as a person can contract to sell something of
which he is not the owner, he can contract to sell something
he owns but does not have possession of. But again, if he
contracts to do so and does not obtain possession of it by
the time the contract is to be performed, then there is a

breach. For example, suppose I own a typewriter but it is in the repair shop. You and I agree that you will buy my typewriter and I am to deliver it to you in two days. If I don't acquire possession of it so that I can deliver it to you within the time specified in the contract, then I will be in breach of contract.

COMPETENCY TO SELL

The above situations all involve a contract to sell, that is, a seller is competent to contract to sell—that is, to pass title in the future—something which is not yet in existence, which he does not presently own, or which he does not have possession of. But as we have learned, no title can pass to something which is not in existence, so there could not be such a sale. It must be a contract to sell or else there is an immediate breach, in fact a fraud.

However, an owner can pass title to something not in his possession. If that occurs, the new owner, then, is entitled to possession. For example, if I sell my typewriter to you even though I do not have possession of it because it is in a repair shop, then as the new owner you are entitled to possession and you may go to the shop and pick it up. (Of course, as the new owner you are required to pay the cost of the repair now.) Thus, there can be a sale of a good which is presently owned but not in the seller's possession.

PASSING BETTER TITLE THAN THE SELLER'S

About the competency to sell something one doesn't own, the general rule is that a buyer ordinarily acquires no better title than the seller has. Thus, one must generally own something in order to be able to sell it—that is, to pass ownership in it. For example, I may say to you, "See that book on the table? I'll sell it to you." Now, if it's not my book, then you acquire no ownership in it even if you pay me for it. In the same way a thief or one who attempts to sell a lost article he found can pass no valid ownership, and if the true owner comes along he may take it back from the buyer. Thus, one who does not have ownership of something generally cannot pass the immediate title to it. He can contract to sell it in the future, but he cannot pass the present interest.

There are, however, several situations in which a nonowner
can pass good title. First, the person selling the goods
can be the agent of the owner. (Agency will be more
closely studied in a later chapter.) An agent is generally
one who is authorized by the owner to sell the goods for
him. A common example is a salesclerk in a store; the
salesclerk has the authority to pass the store owner's title
to the goods to the purchaser.

Sometimes an agent who is not authorized by the owner
to pass the owner's title may effectively do so. If an
owner does not authorize his agent to sell a good, but he
allows circumstances in which others believe that the agent
has such authority, then an innocent buyer may get the
owner's title. For example, suppose you own a shop near
a park where you rent bicycles to people who want to ride
in the park, and you hire me as your agent to run the
store and to rent out your bicycles. But suppose someone
comes in and says, "I don't want to rent a bike, I want to
buy one." I'm running a store where there are many bicycles
around and there's no indication that I am not the owner
of the store. If I purport to sell a bicycle to this person,
he may obtain good title to it—your title—even though
you did not authorize me to sell these bicycles for you,
but merely to rent them. In such a situation, even though
you cannot get your bicycle back from the purchaser, you do
have a cause of action against me for breach of our agency
contract.

An innocent buyer also may obtain good title, when
the owner clothes another with apparent ownership. For
example, suppose you rent me your lawn mower and you allow
me to use it in my job of mowing lawns—that is, I go
around and mow people's lawns for a living and the lawn
mower I use I'm renting from you. Suppose one of my
customers wants to buy the lawn mower and I sell it to him.
He can get good title even though I'm not an agent of yours,
because you the true owner have clothed me with apparent
ownership of this lawn mower. There is nothing to indicate
to the purchaser that I am not the owner.

A person may pass a better title than he has when he
perpetrates fraud upon the seller and resells the goods to
an innocent third person before the seller learns of the
fraud. Generally, a buyer who buys goods by practicing
fraud upon the seller acquires only a voidable title—that
is, the seller can rescind the sale upon discovering the
fraud and reacquire the ownership. But if the buyer sells
the goods to an innocent third party—that is, a person who
does not know of the fraud that the buyer practiced on

the seller—before the seller rescinds, then the third
person gets the title.

For example, suppose I play electric guitar in a
band and I have lost or broken my guitar, and I tell you
that I need a guitar in order to play the date that my band
has arranged coming up tomorrow, and I'll pay you the money
for the guitar after I get paid for the date. Suppose
also that I don't have any date arranged to play, but you
sell me your guitar upon my representation. Upon discovering
that I do not have the date that I told you I had, you could
rescind the transaction and get your guitar back. But
suppose that before you find this out, I sell the guitar
to another person who believes that I am the owner. That
person would acquire the ownership of the guitar and all
you would have is a cause of action against me for fraud
and breach of contract.

A person may pass a better title than he has when he
sells the same goods twice, such as if a buyer allows the
seller to retain possession of the goods and the seller
sells again to an innocent third party, the *second buyer*.
The second buyer would become the owner and would cut off
the rights of the first buyer.

Finally, a person may pass better title than he has
when he purchases goods on an installment contract—that is,
he has possession of the goods but does not obtain title
until the goods are paid for in full—and sells the goods in
his possession to an innocent third party. Most states
require a seller who sells goods on an installment contract
to record that contract in a public record book. That
recording gives notice to all persons that the buyer—the
one who is in possession and is buying the goods on the
installment sales contract—does not have title to those
goods until he has paid for them in full. If the seller
omits recording the contract, third persons have no way
of knowing that the installment buyer does not own the
goods, since he is in possession of them, and they may
acquire the full ownership to the goods when they buy them
from the installment buyer. But if there is a recorded
installment sales contract in the public records, the
third party will not obtain title.

The innocent third party is known as a *good faith
purchaser for value*. He must have no knowledge of the
defect in his seller's title and he must give that seller
valuable consideration. If he knows of the defect, or he
does not give value, he will not acquire better title than
his seller had. Of course, as we mentioned before, where

fraud or wrongdoing is involved between the original seller and buyer, the original owner has a cause of action against the wrongdoer even though he may not get his goods back from the innocent third purchaser.

MUTUAL ASSENT IN SALES CONTRACTS

You will recall that the second basic element of a contract is mutual assent. Since sales and contracts to sell are contracts (contracts of purchase), they must also have mutual assent as evidenced by an offer and acceptance. In our study of contracts we said that if no time is stated in the offer itself the offer stays open for a reasonable time, and if the duration of the offer is stated the offerer could revoke the offer prior to the expiration time if he did so before the offeree accepted. To make an offer irrevocable for a stated time there had to be a separate contract, called an option.

These same rules, with one exception, apply to sales contracts. The exception is that a merchant—a person who regularly deals in goods of the kind under consideration—who promises in writing to keep an offer open for a certain period of time (up to three months) must do so even though there was no consideration, no option. This rule applies only if the offerer is a merchant, and his promise to keep the offer open must be in writing. If these requirements are not met, there must be a separate option contract.

As an example of how this exception might apply, suppose you get an offer in the mail from a retailer of coats stating that for two months from the date of receiving the offer you may purchase a fur coat for a 25% discount. Since that offer is from a merchant and is in writing, it will be open to you for the two months and cannot be rescinded by the offerer. Thus, if a week later you receive from the offerer a notice that the offer is no longer open, you can disregard this notice and require him to sell you a coat for the 25% discount.

Under general contract law, if an offer does not expressly state the mode of acceptance, acceptance must generally be made in the same way as the offer—if an offer was made by mail, the acceptance should be returned by mail, and so on. But in a sales contract, any reasonable manner of acceptance is authorized unless the mode is clearly stated in the offer or the circumstances would dictate otherwise. Thus, if an offer is made by telegram, unless

the offer itself states that the acceptance is to be made
in a certain manner, or it is apparent from the circumstances that the acceptance must be returned immediately,
you could accept by letter, or telephone, or any other
reasonable manner.

Also remember that additional terms in an acceptance
were construed under general contract law as a counteroffer
and, thus, no valid contract was entered until the original
offerer accepted the counteroffer. But in a sales contract,
an acceptance which contains additional terms is construed
as an acceptance and the additional terms are construed as
proposals for addition to the contract. Thus, even though
an acceptance contains additional terms, it is an acceptance
of the original offer, and if the original offerer does
not accept the additional terms, the offeree will be bound
to the original offer. For example, suppose I offer to sell
you my car for $1000 and you say, "Alright, I'll buy it if
you will guarantee it for one year." Now, if I do not
accept your additional terms—that is, the guarantee—you
will be bound to buy my car for $1000. However, if both
the buyer and the seller are merchants, and the acceptance
contains additional terms, then those additional terms will
become part of the contract automatically, unless one of
three things occurs: (1) the additional terms materially
alter the contract; (2) notification of objection is given
by the original offerer to the offeree within a reasonable
time; or (3) the offer itself expressly limited the
acceptance to the terms of the offer. Let's suppose, for
example, that we are both automobile dealers and I offer
to sell you a car for $1000. If you then say, "I'll buy
it if you add a radio to it," that additional term will
become part of the contract because: It does not
materially alter it; I did not notify you of objection to
the additional term within a reasonable time; and because
my offer did not expressly limit acceptance to the terms
of the offer. If, however, one of those three situations
had occurred, you would be bound to buy the car for $1000
without the radio.

We learned also under regular contract law that once
a contract is entered it cannot be modified or rescinded
without further consideration being given. But in a sales
contract, an agreement modifying or rescinding the contract
needs no consideration to be binding. For example, suppose
you contract to buy from me a car with a certain type of
radio, and then you decide that you want another kind of
radio in the car. Now if I agree to put in the other type

of radio for the same price, then you will be able to
force me to do so, and if you should later come in and
tell me that you don't want the car at all, if I agree to
tear up the contract, and no consideration is given, then
I cannot enforce the contract against you any longer.

GLOSSARY TERMS

Good faith purchaser for value   An innocent purchaser of
goods from an installment purchaser who has possession
but no title.

Second buyer   An innocent third party who purchases goods
from a seller who has already sold them to another
party but has kept possession.

SELF TEST
CHAPTER 18

NAME_____

DATE_____

18.1   Anyone competent to enter into _____ contract
       is competent to enter a sales contract.
18.2   A person is _____ to enter a contract to
       sell something that is not yet in existence, but no
       _____ can pass to the buyer until the goods
       are in existence.
18.3   A person can contract to sell something he does not
       yet own, but failure to obtain ownership by the time
       the contract is to be performed will be a/an_____.
       The same situation occurs when one owns something
       but does not have _____.
18.4   There cannot be a sale of something not yet in
       existence and identified; it must be a contract to
       _____ or else there would be a/an_____
       breach.
18.5   If one owns something he can pass title to it even
       though he is not in _____, and then the new
       owner would be entitled to _____.
18.6   The general rule is that a buyer acquires no better
       title than the _____ has.
18.7   One of the situations in which a nonowner can pass
       good title is where the person who is selling the
       goods is the _____ of the owner.
18.8   A/An_____ is one who is authorized by the
       owner to sell goods for the owner; i.e., to pass the
       owner's _____.
18.9   Sometimes an agent who is not authorized by the
       owner to pass the owner's title may _____
       do so and give an innocent buyer good title.
       This usually occurs when the owner clothes another
       with _____ ownership.
18.10 Generally, a buyer who buys goods by practicing
       fraud upon the seller acquires only a/an_____
       title and the seller can _____ the sale
       upon discovering the fraud and reacquire _____.

18.11   Another situation where a person may pass a better
        title than he has, is where a seller _____
        the same goods _____. This situation may
        occur when the first buyer allows the seller to
        retain _____ of the goods.

18.12   Most states require a seller who sells goods on an
        installment contract to _____ that contract
        in a/an _____; thereby giving _____ to
        all persons that the person in possession of the
        goods is paying for them on the installment plan,
        and will not have title to the goods until they
        are _____ for in full.

18.13   If a seller omits recording an installment contract,
        and the buyer sells the goods to an innocent third
        party, then the innocent third party would acquire
        _____ ownership of the goods. The innocent
        third purchaser would have to be a/an _____
        purchaser for _____; i.e., he must not know
        of any defect in the seller's title.

18.14   Since sales and contracts to sell are _____,
        there must also be mutual _____ in them as
        evidenced by a/an _____ and _____.

18.15   The exception to the rules of options, when they
        pertain to a sales contract, is where a/an _____
        promises in writing to keep an offer open a certain
        period of time, up to three months, and must do so
        even though there is no _____.

18.16   In a sales contract, any _____ manner of
        acceptance is authorized unless the mode is clearly
        stated in the offer.

18.17   In a sales contract, an acceptance which contains
        additional terms is construed as a/an _____
        and the additional terms are construed as _____
        for additions to the contract. If the two parties
        are merchants the additional terms in the acceptance
        become part of the contract automatically unless
        the additional terms _____ alter the con-
        tract, or _____ of objection is given by
        the original offerer to the offeree within a
        reasonable time.

18.18   If the contract in question is a sales contract, an
        agreement modifying or rescinding the contract
        needs no _____ to be binding.

19 Sales

Mutual Assent—II. Legal Agreement.
Consideration. Required Form—Uniform
Commercial Code. Statute of Frauds.

LEARNING OBJECTIVES

To learn to differentiate between how law applies
to ordinary contracts and Statute of Frauds, and how law
applies to sales contracts.

CHAPTER CONTENTS

Enforcement of Sales Contracts   Legality of Purpose
in Sales Contract   Consideration in Sales Contracts
Required Form in Sales Contracts   Glossary   Self Test

In this chapter we'll continue to examine rules which
apply to mutual assent in the formation of a sales contract.
Under ordinary contract law, if one of the material terms
of the contract is omitted the contract will not be enforceable. This does not necessarily apply under sales law.
Earlier in our discussion on sales we mentioned that the
price need not be stated in a contract as long as the
parties intended to enter a contract anyway. So when the
ordinary contract would fail for the lack of such a
material term, a sales contract is still enforceable.

ENFORCEMENT OF SALES CONTRACTS

Sales contracts may be enforceable even if they leave a
particular of performance—the assortment of the items
ordered, or the delivery schedule, and so on—to be determined by one or the other party. Thus, if the contract
states that one or even all of the particulars of performance are to be determined by one of the parties, the contract will be enforceable so long as that party specifies
such performance in good faith. For example, suppose I
am a small retail bicycle dealer, and I order 1000 bicycles
from you, but I don't have the capacity to store that many
bicycles at once. Therefore, we may state in the contract
that I am to specify the delivery dates as I need the goods.
Now, if I do so in good faith the contract will be enforceable for the entire 1000 bicycles by both parties.
    There must be mutual assent before a valid sales con-
tract can be entered, but what about the situation where a
person receives, usually by mail, goods that he did not
offer to buy—that is, unordered goods? Must he pay for
the goods? For example, suppose you get a book in the mail
and a letter accompanying it which says, "Send us $1."
Must you pay for the book? A closer look at that situation
will answer it. Since you did not send an offer or an order
to the sender of the book, he is the offerer and you are
the offeree. Therefore, to have a binding contract you
would have to indicate your acceptance. You could, of
course, do this by sending a dollar. Or you may indicate
your acceptance by reading the book, if you take the book,
open it, and read it, that will be deemed acceptance by a
court. If you don't want the book you must not indicate
any intent to become the owner.
    What do you do if you receive some goods in the mail
or otherwise that you don't want? First, you may refuse to

accept them—you may tell the mailman, "I will not accept these goods," and have him take them back. Second, you may take receipt of the goods but return them to the owner without opening them. Finally, you may keep the goods subject to the sender's order, but without using them or in any way exerting any dominion over them which could be evidence that you intended to keep them.

In most states there is no obligation to notify the owner that you are holding the goods per his order, and if the owner demands their return he must pay for returning them. An exception to the general rule is that if you have previously purchased goods under similar circumstances from this particular sender, then you may be obliged to notify him of your refusal. For example, if this person had been sending you books in the past and you have been accepting them and paying for them, then if you don't wish to keep this particular book you would have to notify him of your refusal to accept the book and keep the book subject to his order.

LEGALITY OF PURPOSE OF SALES CONTRACT

The third element of a valid contract was that the agreement must be legal; a contract with illegal subject matter, such as gambling, is void and cannot be enforced by either party. The same general rule applies to sales contracts; the subject matter of a sale must be legal or else the contract will be void and the court will leave the parties in the position in which it found them. Thus, the sale or a contract to sell something prohibited by the law of your state is void. For example, if it is illegal to sell liquor to minors in your state, but a minor contracts to purchase a bottle of bourbon, the contract cannot be enforced by either party—and of course there may be criminal laws which apply to these situations also.

CONSIDERATION IN SALES CONTRACTS

The fourth element of a valid contract is consideration. As we have learned, in order for there to be a sale, some consideration, known as the price, must be paid by the buyer. Of course, the consideration the buyer receives is

the title to the goods in a sale, or a promise by the
seller to transfer the title to the goods in the future,
in a contract to sell.

Generally, title to goods is transferred—that is, a
sale occurs—at the time the goods are delivered to the
buyer's possession by the seller and the buyer pays the
price. There is generally no duty on the seller to deliver
the goods to the buyer's possession until payment in full
is offered by the buyer, and likewise there is generally
no duty on the buyer to pay for the goods until delivery
into his possession is offered by the seller. Thus, in an
ordinary sale delivery and payment often occur simultan-
eously. For example, suppose you come into my store and
order a vacuum cleaner to be delivered to your house
tomorrow and you agree to pay the price of $100. At this
point there is no sale. We have a contract to sell because
no title has transferred from me to you. Tomorrow, if I
bring the vacuum cleaner out to your house, I do not have
the duty to hand it over to you—in other words, deliver
it to your possession—until you tender to me the price of
$100, and likewise you do not have the duty to pay me the
$100 until I tender to you possession of the vacuum
cleaner. In this situation the sale, that is the transfer
of title then, occurs when I hand you the vacuum cleaner
and you hand me the price.

But in some sales agreements the parties may agree to
have payment made before delivery—such as in the lay away
plan. For example, you may have come into my store and
said, "I want to buy that vacuum cleaner, but I don't have
the $100. So you keep it, and I'll pay you $20 a week.
Then when it's paid off, I will get it." Or the parties
may agree to delivery before payment. I may agree to let
you have the vacuum cleaner on your promise to pay me $20
a week. It is in these situations that the transfer of
title becomes important, and we will examine in more detail
in a later chapter the transfer of title in situations such
as these.

As in general contract law, the courts will not look
into the adequacy of the consideration and therefore if
there is any price at all there will be a valid contract.

REQUIRED FORM IN SALES CONTRACTS

The final element of a valid contract is required form.
Under general contract law, you will remember, certain

contracts had to be in writing, or at least be evidenced by a written memorandum. The Statute of Frauds requires this of some contracts before they could be enforced. The Uniform Commercial Code also contains a Statute of Frauds. It provides that a contract for the sale of goods for the price of $500 or more is not enforceable unless: (1) The party to be charged, that is the one against whom enforcement is sought, has signed a contract of sale or a written memorandum; or (2) the buyer has received and accepted the goods; or (3) the buyer has paid the price for the goods; or (4) the goods are specially manufactured for the buyer; or (5) the party to be charged admits in court that a contract was made. If none of these five requirements is present, a contract for the sale of goods for the price of $500 or more is not enforceable by either party. So, if you orally agree to buy, and I orally agree to sell you, my boat for $600, neither one of us can enforce that contract against the other. That does not mean, of course, that we can't perform the contract anyway. Thus, if you tender the $600 to me and I tender the boat to you, a sale has occurred, you are now the owner, and the contract has been performed.

Now let's take a closer look at these five methods of getting around the sales Statute of Frauds. The first method was, if the party to be charged—that is the one against whom enforcement is sought—has signed a contract of sale or a written memorandum, then the contract may be enforced against him. Thus, if you agreed to buy my boat for $600 and if we had both signed a contract of sale for the boat, it could be enforced by either of us against the other. However, if only one of us had signed the contract, then the contract could only be enforced against that person who signed. The person who did not sign could not be held to the contract. It is obvious from what we have said also that even if there is a written contract, it will not be enforceable by either party unless the party to be charged has signed it.

Now what happens if we don't enter a formal contract, but instead I hand you a piece of paper which reads, "Sold to you, 1 boat, $600," and then I sign it but you don't? I cannot enforce it against you because you did not sign it. But I did sign it, so you can enforce it against me. This was a sufficient memorandum of sale, and since I signed it you can enforce it against me.

The requirements of a memorandum are first of all,
it need <u>not</u> be a formal document or contain all the terms
of the agreement. For example, the price may be omitted, and
we learned that the court will construe a reasonable price.
But there is one thing that must be <u>in</u> the memorandum: The
quantity must be stated.   If it is not, no contract can
be enforced, and if the quantity is incorrect the contract
will not be enforceable beyond that quantity stated.

The memorandum can be written on just about anything
and need not even be a single document as long as it
indicates that there is an actual sales agreement existing
between the parties, is signed by the party to be charged,
and contains the quantity.

The memorandum need not even indicate which party is
the buyer and which the seller.   If it is otherwise
sufficient—that is, it indicates that there was an actual
sales agreement, is signed by the party to be charged,
and contains the quantity—then oral evidence can be used
in court to fill in the omitted term.   For example, suppose
you orally agree to buy 100 widgets from me for $1000 for
delivery next week.   This agreement was over the telephone.
Now I send you a memorandum which reads, "Sold, 100 widgets,"
that I have signed.   You then write to me and say, "Send
the widgets next week."   If I refuse to send the widgets
to you, you can enforce this contract against me because
that memorandum I sent to you indicated that there was
an actual sales agreement, it was signed by me, and it
contained the quantity.   If you refuse to go through with
the agreement, though—you refuse to pay for the widgets—
I can enforce it against you because even though that note
you sent back to me did not contain the quantity, it was
sufficient as a memorandum in conjunction with the note
that I sent to you, which did contain the quantity.   It
evidenced the fact that an actual sales agreement was in
existence between us, and you signed it.   Therefore, this
contract could be enforced by either of us against the
other.

The fact that we did not mention the price, $1000, in
our written correspondence will not defeat the contract.
The one attempting to enforce the contract against the other
could admit into evidence that it was orally agreed that
the price would be $1000, and if that figure were reason-
able under the existing market conditions the court would
enforce it.   If it were not reasonable under the existing
conditions the courts would still enforce the contract
and use a reasonable price, usually the market price at that
time.

There is an exception to the rule that the party to be charged must sign the contract or memorandum in order to have it enforced against him. If the contract is between merchants, it can be enforced if one of the merchants sends a written confirmation within a reasonable time and the other merchant does not object to the confirmation within ten days. For example, suppose we were both merchants in the widget example, and I had sent to you the note, "Sold, 100 widgets." If you don't object to that memorandum within ten days, then I can enforce that contract against you even though you did not sign it or send back any memorandum to me with your signature on it.

The parol evidence rule, you will remember, prevents the introduction of evidence tending to contradict the terms of a contract. Under the Uniform Commercial Code, the parol evidence rule states that you cannot contradict the terms of a writing by evidence of a prior or contemporaneous outside agreement. Thus, suppose you were trying to enforce the contract for widgets against me, in other words, you were trying to get me to send you the 100 widgets. I cannot bring in evidence that either prior to or at the time of our entering the contract we agreed to some other amount of widgets. The amount stated in the writing will control. However, after we enter the contract we could agree on a different amount and this could be brought into court as evidence, since it was a subsequent agreement and, you'll remember, under sales law a contract can be varied after it is entered without consideration so long as the parties agree.

A contract for the sale of goods for $500 or more can also be enforced if the buyer has received and accepted the goods—the second method of enforcement. In order for this to work, there must be both elements—*receipt* and *acceptance*. Receipt of goods is possession and control. Thus, if I send you the widgets and you take them into your possession—you put them in your warehouse or whatever—then you have received them because they are in your possession and control.

Acceptance can occur in one of three ways: First, the buyer signifies to the seller that he accepts the goods; or second, the buyer fails to notify the seller of his rejection after he has had a reasonable opportunity to inspect them; or third, the buyer does any act inconsistent with the seller's ownership—such as treating the goods as his

(the buyer's) own. For example, if all we had was an
oral agreement between us and no memorandums were sent by
either of us, and I send you the 100 widgets and you take
them into your possession and control—in other words, you
receive them—if you then notify me that you accept them
or you fail to notify me that you are rejecting them after
you have had a reasonable opportunity to inspect them, or
you do some act inconsistent with my ownership such as
change the widgets in any way or sell some or all of them
to a third party, then I may enforce this contract against
you for the price.

But what would happen if I sent you only part of the
widgets? Say, for example, I send you 50 of them. If
you receive and accept those 50 widgets, then I can enforce
the contract against you only for those 50 widgets. So
I would only be able to recover from you $500. I would
not be able to force you to accept the other 50 widgets,
and if I sent those to you, you would have to receive and
accept those the same as you did the first 50.

The third method of satisfying the Statute of Frauds
is for the buyer to pay the price. If the seller accepts
all of the price, the whole contract can be enforced.
For example, you send me a $1000 check for the widgets
and I accept the check, but I haven't sent the widgets
to you yet. Even if there's no writing evidencing our
intent and signed by either of us, you may force me to send
those widgets to you because I have accepted your payment.
If you paid me only part—say $500 instead of $1000—you
would be able to enforce against me only that proportion
of the contract—50 widgets. Now, if you had sent me this
check and I had sent it back to you uncashed, there would
have been no acceptance by me, the seller, of your tender
of the price and therefore there would have been no contract. Thus, for the contract to be enforceable by the
payment of the price by the buyer, the seller must accept
the tender of the price.

The fourth method of enforcing the contract under
the Statute of Frauds was if the goods were specially
manufactured for the buyer. Then the contract could be
enforced, even though it was not in writing. Specially
manufactured goods are those which are made to the buyer's
specifications and which are not suitable for resale in the
seller's ordinary course of business. Once the seller had
made commitments for the procurement of the goods or has
substantially begun their manufacture, the contract will be
enforceable. For example, suppose you orally order from me

a stove of special dimensions so that it will fit into your homemade camper. As soon as I either have made contracts with my suppliers for necessary equipment to make the stove or I have actually substantially begun to manufacture it, you cannot rely on the Statute of Frauds to get out of paying for it and I can enforce the contract.

The fifth and final method of satisfying the Statute of Frauds for the sale of goods over the price of $500 is if the party to be charged admits in court that a contract is in existence. This can be done in the pleadings, which are the special legal documents filed in a lawsuit to identify the issues—for example, the plaintiff alleges in his complaint that the defendant entered a contract to buy, and if in his answer the defendant doesn't allege that it is not true, then the making of the contract is proved. (Of course, the plaintiff must still prove its terms.) Also, of course, the defendant could admit in his testimony orally in court that there was a contract. If the defendant admits the contract, but admits only that it was for a certain amount of goods, then the plaintiff can enforce the contract only as to that amount.

To summarize enforcement by the Statute of Frauds of the Uniform Commercial Code, a contract for the sale of goods for the price of $500 or more is not enforceable unless the party to be charged has signed a contract of sale or a written memorandum, or the buyer has received and accepted the goods, or the buyer has paid the price for the goods and the seller has accepted that price, or the goods are specially manufactured for the buyer and the seller has substantially begun performing the contract or has made commitments for doing so, or the party to be charged admits the contract in court.

GLOSSARY TERMS

Acceptance   Any one of three acts by a buyer: (1) express-
    ing to the seller acceptance of the goods; (2)
    failures of the buyer to notify of rejection; (3)
    treatment of the goods as if ownership were the
    buyer's.

Particular of performance   A material detail in a sales
    contract, such as quantity, delivery date(s), and
    so on.

Receipt   Possession and control of tendered or shipped
    goods.

SELF TEST
CHAPTER 19

NAME_____

DATE_____

19.1 Sales contracts may be enforceable even if they leave a particular of _____ to be determined by one or the other parties.

19.2 A particular of _____ is something such as the assortment of the items ordered, delivery schedule, etc.

19.3 If goods were received in the mail that a person did not order, or _____ to buy, to have a binding contract, he would have to indicate his _____.

19.4 If a person receives goods in the mail that he does not want, he may _____ to accept them; he may take _____ of the goods but return them to the owner without opening them; or he may keep the goods subject to the sender's _____, but without using them or in any way exerting any _____ over them which would be _____ that he intends to keep them.

19.5 In most states, if unordered goods are received, there is no obligation to _____ the owner that the goods are being held, but if the owner demands their return, the _____ (choose either owner or receiver) must pay for returning them.

19.6 Unless the circumstances would indicate otherwise by a course of _____ in the _____, a person who receives goods in the mail is not bound to _____ for them, but he had better be careful not to exert any _____ or _____ over them which would indicate his intent to become the _____.

19.7 The _____ matter of a sale must be legal or else the contract will be _____, and the court will leave the parties in the _____ in which it found them.

19.8 In order for there to be a sale, some consideration, known as a/an _____, must be paid by the _____.

19.9 The consideration that a buyer receives in a sale is _____ to the goods, and in a contract to sell the con-

sideration the buyer receives is a/an _____
by the seller to transfer the title to the goods
in the _____.

19.10   In an ordinary sale, title is transferred when
the seller _____ the goods to the buyer's
_____, and the buyer pays the _____.

19.11   In an ordinary sale _____ and payment often
occur _____.

19.12   As in general contract law, the courts will not look
to the _____ of the consideration and there-
fore, if there is any _____ at all, there
will be a/an _____ contract.

19.13   The Statute of Frauds of the Uniform Commercial Code
provides that a contract for the sale of goods for the
price of _____ or more is not enforceable unless:
  a)   the party to be _____ has signed a contract
       of sale or a written _____; or
  b)   the buyer has received and _____ the
       goods; or
  c)   the buyer has _____ the price for the
       goods; or
  d)   the goods are _____ manufactured for
       the buyer; or
  e)   the party to be charged _____ in court
       that a contract was made.

19.14   Under the Statute of Frauds, if only one of the parties
had signed the contract, then the contract could only
be _____ against that person who signed.

19.15   Unless there is a written contract, it will not be
_____ by either party unless the party to be
_____ has signed it.

19.16   One thing that must be stated in a memorandum is
the _____.

19.17   All that a memorandum must contain is an indication
that there is an actual _____; that it be
signed by the party to be _____; and contains
the _____. If these items are present, then
_____ evidence can be used in court to fill
in the _____ terms.

19.18   An exception to the rule that a contract or memorandum must be signed by the person who is to be
_____ is where the contract is between
_____.

19.19   If the contract is between merchants, then it can
be enforced if one of the merchants sends a written
_____ within a reasonable time and the other
merchant does not _____ to the confirmation
within _____ days.

CHAPTER 19

NAME_____

19.20 Under the Uniform Commercial Code, the _____ Rule states that you cannot contradict the terms of a writing by evidence of a/an _____ or contemporaneous outside agreement.

19.21 Under sales law, a contract can be varied after it is entered without _____ so long as the parties agree.

19.22 _____ of goods is possession and control.

19.23 Acceptance can occur in the following three ways:
a) if the buyer _____ to the seller that he accepts the goods; or
b) if the buyer fails to notify the seller of his _____ after he has had a reasonable opportunity to _____ them; or
c) if the buyer does any act _____ with the seller's ownership, such as treating the goods as _____ .

19.24 In order for a contract to be enforceable by the payment of the price by the buyer, the seller must accept the _____ of the price before the contract is _____ .

19.25 Specially manufactured goods are those goods which are made to the buyer's _____ and which are not suitable for _____ in the seller's ordinary _____ of business.

19.26 Once the seller has made commitments for the _____ of the goods or has _____ begun their manufacture, the contract for goods made specially for the buyer would be _____ .

19.27 The Statute of Frauds can be satisfied for the sale of goods over the price of $500 if the party to be charged admits in court that a contract is in existence. This admission can be made either in the _____, which are the special legal documents filed in a lawsuit to _____ the issues, or by _____ testimony in court.

19.28 If a defendant admits that a contract was in existence, but only for a certain amount of goods, then the plaintiff can enforce the contract only as to that _____ .

20 Sales

Passage of Title

LEARNING OBJECTIVES

To learn the role of the Uniform Commercial Code in the laws concerning passage of title and risk of loss.

CHAPTER CONTENTS

You will remember that the difference between a sale and a
contract to sell is that in a sale title passes immediately, whereas in a contract to sell it is to pass at some
future time. The distinction is important because the
general rule is that risk of loss generally follows ownership; the owner of goods generally suffers the loss when the
goods are destroyed, stolen, lost, or damaged without fault
of someone, and the owner also is usually responsible if the
goods are misused and hurt someone else. Thus, if your dog
bites a neighbor, as the dog's owner you are generally
responsible for the tort.

        Also, although one who owns something has the right to
possess, use, enjoy, and dispose of it, in some special
situations one who does not own goods can pass title to
them. But generally one must own what he sells in order to
pass ownership. In addition, the owner of goods is usually
liable for paying the taxes upon them, and generally his
creditors can take the goods for his debts. The Uniform
Commercial Code states several rules for the passage of
title (which is the same as the transfer of ownership to
goods).

IDENTIFICATION OF GOODS

Title cannot pass to goods unless they are both **existing**
and identified. Goods are in existence when they are
physically in existence somewhere and ownership is in the
seller.

        Basically, they are identified when they are selected,
and this may occur at any time and in any manner explicitly
agreed upon by the parties. For example, suppose you order
a sailboat from me that I have not yet constructed. We
may expressly provide in our agreement that identification
can occur anytime—even as late as when I have all the parts
but not yet assembled, or later than that, when the sailboat is completed.

        It may also be agreed that either party is to make the
identification. For example, if you are to order a carload
of fruit from me, we may agree that either you or I shall
select which fruits are to make up the carload.

RULES OF IDENTIFICATION

Now if there is no explicit agreement about when identification occurs and by whom, then identification occurs in one

of two ways: First, when the contract is made—if the contract is for the sale of goods already existing and pointed
out as the goods to which the contract refers. For example,
suppose you come to my store to buy two specific records.
If I have only one of the records that you want, when I pick
it up and hand it to you it is identified, but if I have to
order the other record for you it is not yet identified.

The second rule of identification is that if the contract is for the sale of future goods, then identification
occurs when the goods are shipped, marked, or otherwise
designated by the seller as the goods to which the contract
refers. For example, the record I had in the store was
identified when we picked it from the rack and agreed that
this was the record I would sell to you. However, the record
I had to order is not identified until either I get it in
the store and set it aside for you, or I send it to you.
Only then is it identified. It is not identified the
moment it reaches my store. I must take it and mark it or
set it aside as your record.

Now not only can title pass to goods once they have
been identified, but even if it does not, under the rules
we will study next, identification creates a special property
interest in favor of the buyer.

Once identification occurs, the buyer may do one of
several things: He may insure the goods; he may inspect
the goods; he may compel delivery if the seller wrongfully
withholds them (for example, if the goods are to be
delivered upon identification and the seller refuses to
deliver them the buyer can force the seller to do so); and,
finally, the buyer may sue third persons who take the goods
or damage them. All this is true even though title has not
yet passed.

Identification gives the buyer these rights, but it
does not automatically pass title, although identification
must occur before title passes. As long as the goods have
already been identified, title may pass from the seller to
the buyer in any manner and on any conditions explicitly
agreed upon by the parties. For example, suppose I agree
to sell and you agree to buy my tape recorder; you pay the
money but we state that the machine is not to become yours
until tomorrow. Therefore, even though you've paid the
money, title will not pass to the tape recorder until
tomorrow.

RULES FOR PASSAGE OF TITLE

Parties do not usually specify when title is to pass.   In
that event, any one of four rules apply: First, title
passes from seller to buyer at the time and place at which
the seller physically delivers the goods as per the agreement.   For example, if we did not specify when title for
the tape recorder was to pass, and under the contract I was
supposed to deliver the recorder to you tomorrow, title
would pass to you upon my delivering it to you.

Second, if the contract requires or authorizes the
seller to send the goods to the buyer but does not require
him to deliver the goods at any particular destination,
then title passes to the buyer at the time and place of
the shipment by the seller.   For example, suppose you
order 100 dozen plastic flowers from me, and I live in a
different city.   If you order these flowers to be shipped
by rail you are going to specify to the shipper where to
ship them.   When I deliver the flowers to the railroad,
title has passed to you and they are now yours.

Third, if the contract requires the seller to ship the
goods to a particular destination, the title passes at that
destination when the goods are tendered there to the buyer.
For example, suppose that I am to ship the plastic flowers
to you at the destination of the railway depot in your
city.   When the goods arrive at that destination and are
tendered to you, the title passes to you at that time.
(*Tender* of delivery means that when I the seller get the
flowers to their destination, I must hold them for you and
notify you of the fact that they are there awaiting your
disposition.   As soon as you receive notification that
the goods are at the destination and awaiting your disposition, title passes to you.)

Generally, if the buyer is to pay the transportation
cost (called a *shipment contract*), title passes when the
seller delivers to the carrier.   But if the seller pays the
transportation cost (called a *destination contract*), title
generally passes when the goods are tendered at the destination point.   This is usually the easiest way to determine
whether it is a shipment contract (the type of the second
rule), or a destination contract (the type of the third
rule).

The fourth rule is that if delivery is to be made
without moving the goods—for example, at the seller's
place of business or residence—or if both parties know
that the goods are at a third place, then no matter where

the goods are title passes at the time and place the contract is entered.

Thus, title will generally pass at the time and
place the contract is entered, unless the seller is to
deliver or ship the goods. For example, if no mention is
made in our contract as to where the plastic flowers are
to be delivered, then delivery is to be made at my factory.
So the title passes to the flowers to you at the time and
place we enter the contract—as long as the flowers were
identified and we did not expressly provide for title to
pass at some other time or place.

RULES OF RISK OF LOSS

As we stated before, risk of loss generally follows ownership, and before the Uniform Commercial Code was codified,
in almost all states the person in whom title rested at
the moment of the loss of the goods bore the loss. Even
under the Uniform Commercial Code this is usually true.
For example, if you lose your watch or it is accidentally
destroyed or stolen, you would bear the loss. But what
about if goods are damaged, destroyed, or stolen, or even
lost, while in transit from the seller to the buyer? Or
when a prospective buyer is trying out the goods for a
limited period? Or when the goods are identified but
stored in the seller's warehouse? Must the buyer pay the
seller the price even though he doesn't get the goods?

If the contract requires or authorizes the seller to
ship the goods by carrier (a shipment contract), then the
contract requires the seller only to deliver the goods to
a shipper, not to a particular destination, so the risk of
loss passes to the buyer when the goods are delivered to
the carrier. But if the contract requires the seller to
ship the goods to a particular destination (a destination
contract), then the risk of loss passes to the buyer when
the seller tenders delivery there.

You will notice that these rules are the same as for
passage of title. Thus, in a shipment contract—where
the seller is to merely deliver the goods to a shipper—if
the goods are lost or destroyed or stolen while in transit
to the buyer, the buyer will bear the risk of loss and must
pay the seller for the goods anyway. But if the seller
is to deliver the goods at a particular destination and
they are lost in transit—before they arrive at destination

and therefore before tender could be made to the buyer,
then the seller suffers the loss and the buyer need not pay
for the goods.

The Uniform Commercial Code presumes in a contract
where the seller is to ship that unless the seller had
specifically agreed to ship to a particular destination, it
was a shipment contract and risk of loss passed to the buyer
upon the shipment. Thus, if the seller is to ship, but no
specification is made as to whether or not it is a shipment
or a destination contract, then the Uniform Commercial Code
sets up the presumption that it is a shipment contract
and that the risk of loss passes to the buyer at the time
the seller delivers the goods to the shipper. For example,
in our contract for plastic flowers, if the contract
merely says, "Goods to be shipped by truck," then when I
deliver the flowers to the trucker, the risk of loss is
passed to you, and if the truck gets in an accident on the
way to your warehouse you will bear the loss.

If it is not a contract where the goods are to be
shipped, then the risk of loss generally passes to the buyer
when the seller tenders delivery. Compare this rule to the
fourth rule of passage of title, in which the goods are
not to be moved. Title passes when the contract is entered—
but not risk of loss. Risk of loss passes when the seller
tenders delivery.

Also, compare this risk of loss rule with the rule of
passage of title that if the seller is to deliver the
goods to the buyer, title passes when the seller physically
delivers the goods to the buyer—but risk of loss passes
when the seller tenders delivery to the buyer, that is,
when the seller notifies the buyer that the goods are at
the place that the contract designated for delivery and
are at the buyer's disposition. For example, if delivery of
the plastic flowers were to be made by me, the seller, at
my place of business, then the title passed when the contract
was entered, but risk of loss did not pass to you, the
buyer, until I tendered delivery to you at my place of
business. There is one exception to this rule: If the
seller is a merchant, then the risk of loss does not pass to
the buyer until he is in actual receipt of the goods. If
instead of being a manufacturer I am a dealer in plastic
flowers—that is, a merchant—no risk of loss would pass to
you until you actually had possession of the flowers—not
merely on my tender of delivery.

In all of the above cases, however, the parties may
explicitly specify when the risk of loss is to pass, and this

specified time will control. Also, none of the above
rules are effective if one of the parties is in breach of
the contract. In the event of breach by one of the parties,
risk of loss is on the party that caused the breach. For
example, if I were to ship the 300 plastic flowers to
you by rail but not to a particular destination, ordinarily
risk of loss would be on you when I delivered the flowers
to the carrier. But if the flowers are not conforming to
those that you ordered under the contract—that is I am in
breach—risk of loss would remain on me all the time unless
and until you should decide to accept the flowers anyway.

GLOSSARY TERMS

Destination contract   A sales contract agreement whereby
the seller pays transportation costs of goods and title
passes to the buyer when the seller tenders delivery.

Shipment contract   A sales contract agreement whereby the
buyer pays transportation costs for the goods and
title passes to the buyer at the time of delivery
by the seller to the carrier.

Tender   To pass title by notification from seller to
buyer that the goods have arrived at the shipment
destination stipulated by the buyer.

SELF TEST

CHAPTER 20

NAME_____

DATE_____

20.1 The owner of goods generally suffers the _____ when the goods are destroyed, stolen, lost, or damaged without _____ of someone, and the _____ usually is responsible if the goods are misused or hurt someone else.

20.2 The passage of _____ is the same thing as the transfer of _____ to goods.

20.3 Title cannot pass to goods unless they are both _____ and _____.

20.4 Goods are in existence when they are _____ in existence somewhere and _____ is in the seller.

20.5 Identification may be likened to _____ and may occur at _____ and in any manner _____ agreed upon by the parties.

20.6 If there's no explicit agreement about identification, then it occurs when the contract is _____ if the contract is for the sale of goods already _____ and pointed out as the goods to which the contract _____.

20.7 If the contract is for the sale of _____ goods, then identification occurs when the goods are shipped, marked, or otherwise _____ as the goods to which the contract refers.

20.8 _____ creates a special property interest in favor of the buyer.

20.9 Once identification occurs, the buyer may _____ the goods, _____ the goods, or compel _____ if the seller wrongfully witholds them, or _____ third persons who take the goods or damage them.

20.10 The mere act of identification does not _____ pass title.

20.11 The first rule about passage of title when the parties do not specify when title is to pass is that title passes from seller to buyer when the seller physically _____ the goods as per the _____.

20.12   If the contract requires the seller to send the
         goods to the buyer, but does not require him to
         deliver the goods to any particular destination,
         then title passes to the buyer at the _____
         and place of _____ by the seller.

20.13   If a contract requires the seller to ship the goods
         to a particular destination, then title passes at
         the _____ when the goods are _____
         there to the buyer.

20.14   _____ of _____ means that when the
         shipper gets the goods to the destination, he must
         hold them for the buyer, and _____ the buyer
         of the fact that the goods are awaiting his
         _____.

20.15   Generally, if the buyer pays the transporation costs,
         it is a/an _____ contract, and title passes when
         the seller delivers the goods to the _____.

20.16   Generally, if the seller pays the transportation
         costs, it is a/an _____ contract, and the title
         passes upon tender of delivery at the _____.

20.17   If delivery is to be made without moving the goods,
         title passes at the time and place the _____
         is entered.

20.18   If the contract is a shipment contract, and the
         seller is only required to deliver the goods to the
         shipper, then risk of loss passes from the buyer
         when the goods are delivered to the _____.

20.19   If the contract requires the seller to ship the
         goods to a particular destination, then the risk of
         loss passes to the buyer when the seller _____
         there.

20.20   Under the Uniform Commercial Code, if the contract
         is silent about whether the seller is merely to ship,
         or to ship to a specific destination, the contract
         will be construed as one for _____.

20.21   If it is not a contract where the goods are to be
         shipped, then the risk of loss generally passes to
         the buyer when the seller _____. An ex-
         ception to this rule is that if the seller is a
         merchant, then the risk of loss does not pass to
         the buyer until the buyer is in actual _____
         of the goods.

20.22   If the time of the passage of risk of loss is
         _____ in the contract—that will control.

20.23   In the event of breach of contract by one of the
         parties, risk of loss is on the party that
         _____.

21 Sales

Risk of Loss. Warranties—I.

LEARNING OBJECTIVES

To gain thorough knowledge of passage of title and risk of loss.

To acquire a basic understanding of express and implied warranties.

CHAPTER CONTENTS

Title and Risk During Trial Periods   Title and Risk in C.O.D.   Title and Risk at Auction   Warranties Express Warranties   Implied Warranties   Glossary Self Test

In the last chapter we discussed some of the rules for
passage of title and risk of loss under the Uniform Commercial Code. There are still more specifications in the
Uniform Commercial Code for when title and risk of loss
are to pass.

TITLE AND RISK DURING TRIAL PERIODS

What happens when goods are delivered to the buyer upon
the agreement that the buyer may return them, or some of
them, if he is not satisfied, and they are destroyed while
he's trying them out? The Uniform Commercial Code states
that unless it is otherwise specified in the contract, such
a sale to a consumer—that is, to a person who is going to
use the goods—is called a *sale on approval*, and both the
title and the risk of loss remain in the seller until the
buyer accepts the goods.

Of course, use of the goods consistent with the purpose
of trial is not acceptance, but the buyer's failure to
notify the seller of his election to return the goods
within the time specified in the contract or, if no time
is specified, within a reasonable time is acceptance. For
example, suppose that on a used car lot you see a car that
you think you might like but you're not quite sure of its
condition. The owner of the lot tells you, "Go ahead and
use the car for ten days, and if you don't like it you can
return it to me." If the car is stolen during that ten-day
free trial period when you have possession of the car, the
seller would bear the loss because this is a sale on
approval and the risk of loss remains in the seller until
the buyer accepts the goods. This is because you are a
consumer; you are buying the goods for your own use.

But if a merchant is buying the goods for resale;
then, unless the contract specifies otherwise, both the
title and risk of loss pass to the buyer (the merchant)
until he returns the goods. A sale to a person who has
bought the goods for resale purposes is called a *sale or*
return, and it passes both title and risk of loss to the
buyer until return.

Title and risk of loss do not revest in the seller
unless the buyer returns the goods in substantially their
original condition within the time set in the contract or,
if no time is set in the contract, within a reasonable
time. For example, suppose you own a clothing store and
you order from me, a clothing manufacturer, a number of

styles and sizes of men's suits, with the right to return
those suits you do not sell within six months. Until
you return to me, within six months, those clothes you did
not sell, in good condition, the risk of loss remains on
you. If in that six-month period a fire occurs in your
store and consumes all of the suits, those you would have
sold within the six months and those you would have returned, the entire loss is upon you.

TITLE AND RISK IN C.O.D.

When a seller ships goods to the buyer *C.O.D.*—"collect on
delivery"—the seller instructs the carrier not to deliver
the goods to the buyer until the buyer pays the price and
the cost of shipping to the carrier. However, title and
risk of loss pass to the buyer at the time the seller
delivered the goods to the shipper. (This provision is
similar to the shipment contract, described in the last
chapter.)

     Thus, under C.O.D., even though the buyer gets the
title and the risk of loss at the time the seller delivers
the goods to the shipper, he does not get the right to
possession until he pays the shipper the price and the
cost of shipment. In an earlier chapter on personal
property, we used the example of wheat in a grain elevator
in our discussion of confusion. *Fungible goods* are
goods each unit of which is similar to every other unit in
the mass. Oil, grain, and seed are common examples of
fungible goods. Since every unit is similar to every
other unit, identification need not occur before title and
risk of loss can pass, because if every unit is similar to
every other unit in the mass, then it doesn't matter which
part of that mass you have agreed to buy. Thus, if you buy
200 gallons of oil out of a tank containing 1000 gallons,
title and risk of loss pass when the contract is made.
So, if, through no fault of the owner's, the tank explodes
before you can get your oil out, you must pay the seller
the purchase price of the oil even though it was still in
his tank at the time of the destruction.

TITLE AND RISK AT AUCTION

At an auction, title and risk of loss pass to the bidder
whose bid was the last one made before the hammer falls.

If a bid is made while the hammer is falling, the auctioneer
has one of two choices: He can either sell to the person
upon whose bid the hammer was falling, or he can reopen
the bidding. For example, you bid $32 for a sofa at an
auction and the auctioneer was lowering the hammer on
your bid, but at that very moment I yelled, "Thirty-three
dollars." Well in this event, the auctioneer can either
sell to you for $32, or he can reopen the bidding starting
at $33. Therefore, my bid would stand at $33, and if he
reopened bidding and there was no higher bid after that, I
would get it for $33.

WARRANTIES

A *warranty* is a statement of fact about the goods made by
the seller which induces the buyer to buy the goods. The
word "warranty" can be likened to the word "guarantee."
Warranties may be expressed by the seller in the contract
or orally. Such an expression is called an *express
warranty*. Even if the seller does not state any warranties
expressly, the law implies certain warranties; that is, the
law holds the seller to certain promises about the goods
even though he does not expressly state them to the buyer.
These are called *implied warranties*.

EXPRESS WARRANTIES

Any promise or statement of fact relating to the goods
made by the seller to the buyer which induces the buyer to
buy creates an express warranty that the goods will
conform to the promise. For example, suppose you want to
buy my boat, and I say to you, "This boat is almost new,
it's been run only ten hours." This statement that the
boat has been run only ten hours is an express warranty
if you rely upon it in buying the boat. Or suppose I want
to sell you my football and I tell you that it is the same
as the one used in NFL games. Or suppose you want to buy a
used car and the dealer tells you that the brakes on the car
have just been relined—or even says, "You buy this car and
we will repair it free for one year." These are all express
warranties.
     So far they have been oral, but any one of them could
have been written into the contract itself. The contract
for the boat could read: "warranted to have been run only

ten hours;" your contract for the purchase of a used car
could state that the car has new brakes, "Free repairs for
one year."

When a sale is made based on a description of the
goods there is a warranty that the goods will conform to
the description. For example, suppose you agree to buy and
I agree to sell to you two dozen #10, 3/4 inch, steel-plated
nails. There is an express warranty that the nails I send
to you will conform to this description. When a sale is
based on a sample or model, there is also a warranty that
the goods will conform to the sample or model. For
example, suppose a salesman shows you a vacuum cleaner, and
you sign an order for one. Well, the vacuum cleaner sent
to you must conform and be exactly similar to the one showed
to you by the salesman.

To create an express warranty the seller need not say
"I warrant" or "I guarantee." In fact, the seller need not
even have the specific intent to create a warranty. If he
merely makes a statement of fact about the goods upon which
the buyer relies for his purchase of them, an express
warranty is created.

But we must be careful to distinguish between express
warranties and mere statements by the seller as to the
value of the goods or as to his opinion or commendation
of the goods. Such statements are not warranties because
they are not statements of fact about the goods. They are
merely the seller's opinion, and the law does not allow a
buyer to rely upon the mere opinion of the seller.

Such statements are often called seller's "puffing"
because they are an attempt by the seller to inflate or
puff the value of the goods in the eyes of the buyer to
entice him to buy. Anyone purchasing something, especially
from a merchant or a person who deals in goods of the kind
being looked at, must be careful to distinguish between
mere statements of opinion as to value or worth of the
goods and statements of fact about the goods. For example,
suppose a seller says to you, "This radio which I am
offering to you for $35 is worth at least $50. You just
can't afford to pass it up." "This is the best radio for
the price you'll find in town." Or even, "This radio is
in top condition." That is still a statement of _opinion_,
not of fact. He's stating his opinion that the radio is
in top condition.

You can see from these examples that it is sometimes
quite difficult to distinguish between statements of fact
and statements of opinion. In general, the way to dis-

tinguish one kind of statement from the other is that
general statements about the goods—"good condition,"
"best in town," "good value for the money," "worth so
much"—are not statements upon which you can rely.
However, if the seller says to you, "This radio regularly
sells for $50, but I'm selling it to you for $35," that is
a warranty because it is a statement of fact. He is stating that, as a matter of fact, he usually sells that radio
for $50. He isn't saying it's worth that much, he's telling
you that that is the regular price on it. So that would be
a warranty.

   If you went to buy a used car and you signed a sales
contract for that car, for a value of $500 or more—
remember, the contract would have to be in writing—and
the seller had told you that he will warrant the car for
one year for all parts and labor that may be necessary for
repairs, but it is not written in the contract, you could
not hold him to this express oral warranty. Express
warranties made at or before the sale must be in the same
form as the sales contract. Therefore, if the contract
is in writing, all warranties made before and at the time
of signing the contract must be in writing. Of course if
the contract is oral, and is enforceable, oral warranties
would be enforceable. However, warranties made after the
contract has been entered may be oral even though the
contract is in writing. So if you had signed the contract
for the used car, and then the dealer said to you, "Oh, by
the way, we'll warrant this car for all parts and labor for
one year," and you did not write it in the contract, you
could still enforce it against him, because the contract
had already been entered.

IMPLIED WARRANTIES

As we mentioned earlier in the chapter, the law implies
certain warranties in a sale. In this chapter we will look
at two kinds of such warranties: the *warranty of good title*
and the *warranty against encumbrances*.

   The warranty of good title. The law implies that the
seller warrants that he will convey good title to the buyer,
and that its transfer is rightful. That is, the seller
warrants he has good title to transfer, and that he is not
wrongfully transferring it. For example, suppose I sell you
four hubcaps that had been stolen. If you are required to
turn them over to the true owner, I have breached the warranty

of title and you have a cause of action against me. The
reason is, of course, that as a thief I do not have title
to the goods and therefore I cannot transfer the ownership to you. Thus, I have breached the warranty of good
title.

In a contract to sell future goods, the seller
warrants that he will have good title to transfer at the
future time that he is to transfer it. For example,
suppose I am working on a model ship and you have contracted
to buy it from me when I complete it. If you find out that
I have sold the ship since the time you contracted to buy
it and before the time it was completed, then I have
breached the warranty of good title at the time that you
learned that I had transferred it to someone else. So
you need not wait until the time for delivery was supposed
to occur; you can sue me for breach of this warranty at any
time after you find out that I have sold it to someone else.

A seller who is a merchant further warrants that the
goods are free from the claims of third persons for patent,
copyright, or trademark infringement. However, if the
buyer furnished specifications to the seller, then the buyer
warrants that the seller will not be held liable for any of
these infringement claims. For example, I order from you a
coffee machine for my office, you deliver it, and later I
get sued by the inventor of the machine because you used
his patent without his permission. I would have a cause of
action against the seller for breach of the warranty of
good title. However, if this were a machine that the
seller had made to my specifications and a patent had been
infringed, then if the seller got sued by the patent holder,
the seller could recover from me for breach of this warranty,
because I had specified how the machine was to be made.

The warranty against encumbrances. The seller warrants
that even though he has good title and transfer is rightful, no encumbrances exist at the time of delivery. An
encumbrance is a right in a third party to repossess the
goods or sell them for a debt owed by the seller. For
example, I sell you a camera which I am buying on credit
from a camera store. If I then stop making payments and the
store repossesses the camera from you, I have breached the
warranty against encumbrances.

This warranty is not breached even if the encumbrance
exists at the time of the sale, as long as it is removed by
the time of delivery: If I had paid off my credit account
after the sale of the camera but before its delivery to you,
then there would be no breach of the warranty against

encumbrances. This warranty exists only at the time of
delivery, not at the time of sale. Because the seller
promises that he will give you the goods free from the right
of any third party to regain possession of the goods, it
therefore can't be breached until you gain possession.
This warranty extends only to encumbrances that the buyer
does not know about. So if you knew that I was buying
the camera on time, and you contracted to buy it from me,
then there would be no warranty against encumbrances.

We shall continue the subject of warranties in the
next chapter.

GLOSSARY TERMS

C.O.D.   Collect on delivery: instructions to the carrier
   to give possession of goods to the buyer only in
   exchange for the price and the cost of shipping.

Encumbrance   A right in a third party to repossess goods
   or sell them to recover a debt owed by the seller.

Express warranty   A warranty expressed by a seller either
   in a contract or orally.

Fungible goods   Goods of which each unit is similar to
   every other unit in the mass.

Implied warranty   A warranty on goods that is implied
   by the law.

Sale on approval   Transfer of possession of goods for
   the buyer's approval, without passage of title or
   risk of loss from the seller until the buyer's
   acceptance of the goods.

Sale or return   A sale to a merchant which allows return
   of the goods but which passes both title and risk of
   loss to the merchant until he returns the goods.

Warranty   A statement of fact about the goods by a seller
   which induces the buyer to buy the goods.

Warranty against encumbrances   An implied warranty by a
   seller that no encumbrances exist at the time of
   delivery.

Warranty of good title   An implied warranty by the
   seller that he will convey good title to the buyer,
   and that its transfer is rightful.

SELF TEST
CHAPTER 21

NAME_____

DATE_____

21.1 The Uniform Commercial Code states that if the sale
is a sale on _____ to a consumer, title and
risk of loss are with the _____ until the
_____ _____ the goods.

21.2 With a sale on approval, use of the goods by the
consumer _____ with the purpose of the trial
is not _____, but failure to _____
the seller of the buyer's election to _____
the goods within a reasonable time is _____.

21.3 A sale on approval to a person who has bought the
goods for resale purposes is called a/an_____
or _____, and both title and risk of loss
are with the _____ until the goods are
returned.

21.4 Title and risk of loss do not _____ in the
seller unless the buyer returns the goods in substantially their _____ condition within the
appropriate time.

21.5 The initials C.O.D. mean "_____ on _____."

21.6 Under C.O.D., even though the buyer gets the
_____ and _____ at the time the
seller delivers the goods to the shipper, he does
not get the right to _____ until he pays the
shipper.

21.7 _____ goods are goods, each unit of which is
similar to every other unit in the mass, and since
every unit is similar to every other unit,
_____ does not need to occur before title
and risk of loss can pass.

21.8 At an auction, title and risk of loss pass to the
bidder whose bid was the _____ made before
the _____ falls.

21.9 A/An_____ is a statement of fact about the goods
made by the seller which _____ the buyer to
buy the goods.

21.10 Any _____ or statement of fact relating to
the goods made by the seller to the buyer, which

_____ the buyer to buy, creates a/an_____
warranty that the goods will _____ to the
promise.

21.11   An express warranty may be created even if the seller
        does not have the specific _____ to create a
        warranty.

21.12   Statements by the seller as to the _____ of
        the goods or the seller's _____ or commenda-
        tion of the goods is not a/an_____ warranty.
        These types of statements are often called seller's
        _____.

21.13   Express warranties made at or before the sale must
        be in the same _____ as the sales contract.

21.14   Warranties made after the contract has been entered
        may be _____ even though the contract is in
        writing.

21.15   The law _____ that the seller warrants that
        he will convey good _____ to the buyer, and
        that its _____ is rightful.

21.16   A seller who is a merchant further warrants that the
        goods are _____ from the _____ of
        third persons, for patent, copyright, or trade
        infringements.

21.17   The seller also warrants that even though he has
        goods title and transfer is rightful, no _____
        exist at the time of _____.

21.18   A/An_____ is a right in a third party to
        repossess the goods or sell them for a debt owed
        by the seller.

21.19   The warranty against encumbrances is not breached
        if an encumbrance exists at the time of the sale,
        but is removed by the time of _____.

22 Sales

Warranties—II. Rights and Remedies.

LEARNING OBJECTIVES

To further understand the law on warranties.
To become informed of the rights of buyers and
sellers when they are injured by breach of a sales contract.

CHAPTER CONTENTS

Warranty of Merchantability   Exclusion of Warranties
Caveat Emptor and the Uniform Commercial Code   Rights of
the Buyer in a Sales Contract   Rights of the Seller in a
Sales Contract   Remedies of the Buyer in a Sales Contract
Remedies of the Seller in a Sales Contract   Glossary
Self Test

In the last chapter we looked at the implied warranties of
title and encumbrances. The third implied warranty in a
sale is that of *fitness for a particular purpose*. This
warranty arises when the seller knows, or should know, at
the time of the sale the particular purpose for which the
buyer is buying the goods, and knows, or should know, that
the buyer is relying upon the seller's skill or judgment
to select and furnish suitable goods to that purpose.

   If a buyer is relying upon the seller's skill or
judgment and the seller knows, or should know, of the buyer's
particular purpose and that the buyer is relying upon his
judgment, then the law will imply the warranty that the
goods that the seller chooses for the buyer will be fit
for that purpose. For example, suppose you come into my
sporting goods store and you want a salmon fishing pole,
but knowing nothing about fishing poles you say to me,
"I'm going salmon fishing tomorrow and I would like a good
pole," and I take a fishing rod off the rack and say, "This
is an excellent salmon fishing pole." Well if you buy it
from me relying upon my commendation of it as a good
fishing pole for salmon and go fishing with it the next
day and find that it is a trout pole and not a salmon pole,
I have breached the warranty of fitness for particular
purpose.

   The basis of the warranty is the buyer's reliance on
the seller's skill or judgment; thus, no warranty arises—
even if the seller knows the use for which the buyer is
buying—when the buyer selects the goods himself, or when
he gives the seller specifications for the goods that he
wants. There must be reliance by the buyer on the seller's
skill or judgment.

WARRANTY OF MERCHANTABILITY

The fourth implied warranty that may arise under the law is
that of merchantability. This warranty arises only when the
seller is a merchant who deals in the goods that are the
subject of the sale. The *warranty of merchantability* says
that the goods are fit for the ordinary purposes for which
such goods are ordinarily used. For example, suppose you
buy new tires for your car from a dealer, and he puts them
on your car and pumps them up with air and you drive out of
his store and five minutes later all four of the tires go
flat—they won't hold air. The seller has breached the
warranty of merchantability because the tires are not fit
for the ordinary use given to tires, that is, to hold air.

This warranty extends to food and drug sales. The seller warrants that the product is fit for human consumption: If you go into a grocery store and buy a banana, take it outside and peel it and discover that it's rotten inside, the seller has breached the warranty of merchantability because the banana is not fit for human consumption. This warranty applies whether the food is sold packaged or is eaten on the premises. So if you go into a restaurant and order a hamburger, and it turns out that the hamburger is spoiled, the seller has breached the warranty of merchantability.

A merchant seller also warrants that the goods conform to any promises made on the container or label. If you buy a bottle of hair dye which says on the label, "Not harmful for human consumption," and you happen to get some in your mouth and it poisons you, again the warranty of merchantability has been breached.

EXCLUSION OF WARRANTIES

Sellers can make express warranties and the law implies certain other warranties under certain conditions, but a seller can sometimes exclude these warranties from the sales transaction. For example, suppose you buy a car and in the contract is written, "Engine guaranteed for one year," but at the end of the contract these words are printed, "No warranties." Now, after you have the car six months the engine blows up. In this case the disclaimer of the express warranty—that is, the words "No warranties"—is not effective against the other warranty that was written in there that the engine was guaranteed for one year. Words tending to negate or limit express warranties which have been made are inoperative to the extent that to give them effect would be inconsistent with the express warranties made. If, for example, the contract is written, and the seller also tells you, "We'll guarantee the radio in that car for one year," then the written disclaimer on the contract, "No warranties," would be effective, and, of course, this is because of the Statute of Frauds and the parol evidence rule. However, of course, if there is an effective oral warranty, then an oral disclaimer would not be effective.

About the exclusion of implied warranties, the Uniform Commercial Code says that all of them may be excluded by expressions like "as is" or "with all faults" if they are conspicuously placed on the contract so that they would draw the buyer's attention to the fact that there were no warranties. If, for example, the words were printed in the contract in small type and were not conspicuous, they would probably not exclude the implied warranties under the contract since to give the words such effect would be unfair and unreasonable. However, if the words were printed in large type right above where the buyer was to sign, then the words may exclude all implied warranties.

If there is no such effective general disclaimer excluding all implied warranties, then to exclude the warranty of merchantability the language of the disclaimer must use the word "merchantability" and, if in writing, be conspicuous. On the other hand, to exclude the warranty of fitness for a particular purpose the exclusion must be in writing and be conspicuous, but there need not be mention that this particular warranty is being excluded.

CAVEAT EMPTOR AND THE UNIFORM COMMERCIAL CODE

Caveat emptor—in Latin, "Let the buyer beware"—is an old common law rule which meant that if the buyer did not examine the goods before he entered the contract, then there is no implied warranty of merchantability. The assumption behind the old common law was that if the buyer did not take the trouble to examine the goods that he was buying, he deserved any defects of merchantability that might be present in the goods. However, the Uniform Commercial Code limits this old rule by saying that the mere failure to inspect the goods will not remove the warranty of merchantability. Only if the buyer does inspect the goods before entering the contract as fully as he desired, or if he refuses to examine the goods after the seller demands that he inspect them, is there no warranty as to the defects which an examination should have revealed. For example, suppose you buy a car without driving it— always, of course, a very foolish thing to do—there would initially be a warranty that, say, the car would run, but if you tried to start the car without success and bought it anyway, then the warranty that the car would run would disappear. And if the seller demanded you to inspect the car—that is, try to drive it—but you refused to do so, there is also no such warranty.

About the extent of warranties, the Uniform Commercial Code says that warranties extend to anyone in the buyer's family or household or to a guest in the home of the buyer if it is reasonable to expect that the guest might use or be affected by the goods.

RIGHTS OF THE BUYER IN A SALES CONTRACT

The rights of a buyer under a sales contract are basically to get good title and delivery of the goods from the seller, to enforce all terms of the contract as to the duties that the seller is to perform which are not contrary to public policy, to inspect the goods before accepting them to see that they conform to the contract.

However, a buyer cannot keep a deliveryman waiting while he inspects the goods. He must accept delivery of them and then inspect them before accepting them. If defective goods are delivered to the buyer and he has not accepted them, he can reship them to the seller at the seller's expense, or he can sell the goods and send the proceeds to the seller. If defects in the goods are not known to the buyer at the time that he accepts them, and he could not have discovered the defects at reasonable inspection, then he can revoke his acceptance within a reasonable time by giving notice to the seller.

We said above that the buyer has the basic rights of getting good title to the goods and delivery of the goods. We understand title and the implied warranty of good title, but what is *delivery*? Delivery means that the seller must put the goods at the disposal of the buyer according to the terms of the contract. If the contract requires the seller to ship the goods to the buyer, then only upon shipping them to him has he made delivery. If the contract requires the seller to personally bring the goods to the buyer, then he must do so before there is delivery.

If the contract is silent, the the seller need not physically take the goods to the buyer but must merely hold them for the buyer at his disposal. So, unless otherwise agreed that the seller delivers the goods to the buyer's home or place of business or anywhere else, he only needs to put the goods at the buyer's disposal at his (the seller's) place of business or, if the seller has no place of business, his residence, or somewhere else if the goods are known by both parties to be there. However, the seller must notify the buyer that the goods are now at his disposal before there is proper delivery.

The buyer also has the right to the delivery of the proper quantity of goods. If the seller tenders too little of the goods under the contract terms, then the buyer may refuse to accept any of them. But if the seller tenders more goods than the contract requires, the buyer must accept the correct amount and may reject the rest if he can separate the goods without unreasonable expense or trouble. If it would require an unreasonable amount of trouble or expense for the buyer to separate the proper amount from the total amount tendered, then he may reject the complete tender. However, if the buyer accepts either a larger or a smaller amount—which he may do—then he must pay, at the contract rate, for the amount that he accepted. Thus, if too few goods are tendered, the buyer may either reject all of the goods or accept the lesser amount at only a proportionate price under the contract; and if the seller tenders too great an amount, the buyer may separate the proper amount out of the whole and pay according to the contract, or he may accept the total amount, and pay proportionately more than the contract price. Furthermore, unless the contract specifies that delivery is to be made in installments, the buyer need not accept delivery by installments. The final right of the buyer is to choose the assortment of the goods, unless it is otherwise agreed.

RIGHTS OF THE SELLER IN A SALES CONTRACT

The seller has various rights in sales contracts. First, he has the right to get the buyer's acceptance and payment for conforming goods, and, unless the contract specifies otherwise, the seller has the right to arrange for shipment to the buyer if it is to be a shipment contract. The seller may identify conforming goods to the contract if the buyer breaches the contract before identification has occurred. That is, if the buyer breaches the contract before the seller has prepared the goods or manufactured them, he can finish manufacturing them and need not let them stay in their useless state. Another right of the seller is to retain possession of goods not paid for according to the contract terms—even if the title has passed. Furthermore, a seller may stop a carrier's delivery to the buyer and get return of the goods if the buyer becomes insolvent before he gets the goods or if he refuses to pay when payment is due before delivery. Finally, under certain conditions, a seller may cure a defective tender of delivery. That is, after he tenders defective products, or products not according to the contract, he may—before he can be held to breach of contract—substitute the proper goods to the buyer.

REMEDIES OF THE BUYER IN A SALES CONTRACT

When the seller fails to deliver and to transfer title to goods conforming to the contract—that is, he delivers nonconforming goods—the buyer has several remedies. First, the buyer may reject the goods and sue the seller for damages. In a sales contract the measure of damages is the difference between the market price at the time the buyer learns of the breach and the contract price.

Second, a buyer may cancel the contract and recover any amount that he has already paid, or he may recover damages for the losses he has sustained, including expenses of holding the goods, shipping them back, and so on.

Third, the buyer may seek the remedy of *cover*: Within a reasonable time, if the buyer acts in good faith, he may purchase substitute goods elsewhere and sue the seller for the difference between price and the contract price.

Fourth, when the title has passed to the buyer under the rules of passage of title, the buyer may recover the goods themselves or their value. A buyer's suit for the possession of the goods themselves is called *replevin*.

Fifth, a buyer might seek the remedy of specific performance; if the goods must be unique, so that the buyer could not buy them elsewhere, the buyer can force the seller to perform the contract.

Sixth, a buyer might seek the remedy of a *lien*. When the buyer rightfully refuses to accept nonconforming goods, or has rightfully revoked acceptance that he has already given, but he keeps possession of the goods, he may hold on to the goods until the seller returns any amount that the buyer had paid to him plus his expenses in keeping them, or he may resell the goods and deduct the amount that he paid to the seller and his reasonable expenses.

Finally, the buyer may accept the goods anyway, even if nonconforming, and sue for the loss in their value, or his damages, which would be the difference between the value that they would have had if they had conformed and the value that they have as nonconforming goods.

The buyer also has remedies for breach of warranty by the seller. Since a warranty is basically part of the contract, a breach of a warranty is a breach of contract, and, ordinarily, the buyer has all the appropriate remedies that we have already discussed when the seller breaches contract. However, when a warranty is breached, if the buyer does not notify the seller of the breach within a reasonable time after discovering it, or after he should have discovered it, then he may waive his right to sue for the breach. Therefore, under a breach of warranty, the buyer must use even more care than when the contract itself has been breached by, say, delivery of nonconforming goods, because the buyer must notify the seller of the breach of warranty within a reasonable time.

REMEDIES OF THE SELLER IN A SALES CONTRACT

The seller also has remedies when the buyer refuses to accept or pay for conforming goods. First, the seller may sue for the purchase price. He can do this if the buyer has accepted the goods and not paid for them on time, or he may do so if the risk of loss has passed to the buyer and the goods are lost or damaged. He may also sue for the purchase price if he, the seller, is unable after a reasonable effort to resell identified goods still in his possession for a reasonable price, or the circumstances indicate that such effort would be useless. If the seller recovers the price from the buyer, he must hold the goods for the buyer, and when the buyer demands them, give them to him.

Second, a seller may also seek the remedy of a lien. As in the seller's first remedy, the seller can resell identified goods still in his possession even if they are owned by the buyer, and he can sue the buyer for the difference between the sale price and the contract price plus his expenses. Of course, the sale must be made in good faith.

Third, when the buyer refuses to accept conforming goods, or wrongfully repudiates the contract after acceptance, then the seller can sue for damages, and here his amount of recovery would be the difference between the contract price and the market price at the time for delivery plus his expenses.

When the buyer breaches, the fourth remedy of the seller is to cancel the contract.

GLOSSARY TERMS

Caveat emptor   An old common law rule that unless the buyer examines the goods before entering the contract there is no warranty of merchantability.

Cover   A buyer's remedy for breach, whereby he buys substitute goods and sues the breaching seller for the difference between their price and the contract price.

Delivery   The seller's putting the goods at the disposal of the buyer according to the terms of the contract.

Fitness for a particular purpose   An implied warranty that arises when the seller knows, or should know, at the time of sale the particular purpose for which the buyer is buying the goods, and knows, or should know, that the buyer is relying upon the seller's skill and judgment to select and furnish goods suitable to that purpose.

Lien   A remedy by which the injured party in a breach retains possession of the goods until his costs have been restored by the breaching party.

Replevin   Suit by a buyer against a breach by a seller, in which the buyer sues for possession of the goods to which he already has title.

Warranty of merchantability   An implied warranty that the goods are fit for the ordinary purposes for which such goods are ordinarily used.

SELF TEST

CHAPTER 22

NAME_____

DATE_____

22.1   The warranty of _____ for a particular purpose arises when the seller knows or should know at the time of the sale the particular purpose for which the buyer is buying the goods and that the buyer is relying upon the seller's _____ or _____ to select or furnish suitable goods for that purpose.

22.2   Since the basis of warranty for fitness for a particular purpose is the buyer's _____ on the seller's skill or judgment, no warranty arises if the buyer _____ the goods for himself, or gives the seller _____ for the goods that he wants.

22.3   The warranty of merchantability only arises where the seller is a/an_____ who deals in the goods that are the _____ of the sale. The seller warrants that the goods are _____ for the ordinary _____ for which the goods are ordinarily _____.

22.4   The warranty of merchantability extends to food and drug sales, whereby the seller warrants that the product is fit for _____.

22.5   Words tending to _____ or limit warranties which have been made are _____ to the extent that to give them effect would be _____ with the express warranties made.

22.6   The Uniform Commercial Code says that all _____ warranties may be excluded by the use of expressions such as "_____," or "with all faults," if they are _____ placed on the contract so that they would draw the buyer's attention to the fact that there were no _____.

22.7   If there is no effective general disclaimer excluding all implied warranties, then to exclude the warranty or merchantability the language of the disclaimer must use the word _____ and be _____ in writing.

22.8   _____ in Latin, means "Let the Buyer Beware."

22.9   The Uniform Commercial Code states that the mere _____ of the buyer to _____ the goods will not remove the warranty of _____.

22.10   A buyer in a sales contract has a right to get good
        _____ and _____ of the goods from the
        seller.

22.11   A buyer in a sales contract has the right to
        _____ the goods before accepting them to see
        that they conform to the contract.

22.12   Delivery means that the seller must put the goods
        at the _____ of the buyer according to the
        terms of the contract.

22.13   The seller must _____ the buyer that the goods
        are now at his disposal before there is proper
        delivery.

22.14   The buyer in a sales contract has the right to the
        delivery of the proper _____ of the goods.

22.15   If the seller _____ a larger or smaller amount
        of goods than was ordered by the buyer, the buyer
        may accept the larger or smaller amount, and then
        pay for the goods at the contract _____, for
        the amount that he _____.

22.16   The final right of the buyer is to choose the
        _____ of the goods, unless it is otherwise
        agreed.

22.17   The seller has the right to get the buyer's
        _____ and _____ for conforming goods,
        and unless the contract specifies otherwise, the
        seller has the right to arrange for shipment to the
        buyer if it's to be a/an _____ contract.

22.18   The seller may identify conforming goods to the con-
        tract if the buyer breaches the contract before
        _____ has occurred.

22.19   A seller may stop delivery to the buyer from a
        carrier and get the goods back if the buyer becomes
        _____ before he gets the goods, or if he re-
        fuses to pay if payment is due before _____.

22.20   A seller may cure a/an _____ tender of delivery.

22.21   If the seller delivers nonconforming goods, the
        buyer could _____ the goods and sue the seller
        for damages; or he could _____ the contract, or
        he could _____ the goods; or he could _____
        the goods themselves or their value; or demand
        specific _____ of the seller; or attach a/an
        _____ on goods in his possession; or sue for
        the loss in _____ or damages of the nonconfor-
        ming goods.

22.22   If the buyer refuses to accept or pay for conforming
        goods, the seller may sue for the _____.

23 Real Property

Distinction from Personal Property.
Ownership of Things upon or under Real
Property.

LEARNING OBJECTIVES

To gain thorough knowledge of what constitutes
real property.

CHAPTER CONTENTS

Real and Personal Property Reviewed   Extent of Real
Property Ownership   Fixtures   Glossary   Self Test

To begin our study of real property—the interest one
may have in it, how one may buy, sell, lease, and dispose
of one's interest in it—we should review our earlier
distinction between real and personal property. Objects
that can be owned are divided into two broad categories:
real estate, called real property or realty, and personal
property, sometimes called personalty. The law deals with
these two types of property differently.

REAL AND PERSONAL PROPERTY REVIEWED

Real property is, you remember, land and objects attached
to and used in connection with land in such a way as to
be part of it. For example, a farm house would be part of
the real property, just as the barn and the fences and the
well.

Fences are not always real property, however, if the
fence is temporary, one that can be removed easily without
being dug out of the ground, then it might be personal
property, while most farm fence posts, which are dug into
the ground and placed permanently, are real property. But
fence posts stacked beside the barn for repairs or
additional fencing are personal property until they are
placed in the ground permanently as part of a fence.

Likewise the large tractor with its disk, or the combine
for harvesting hay or alfalfa, or the large, specialized
truck used for spraying the orchard, although used only
on the farm and only in connection with growing crops on
the real property, all are personal property because they
are not attached permanently to the land. Personal
property, then, includes movable objects not attached to the
land.

EXTENT OF REAL PROPERTY OWNERSHIP

What do we own when we own real property? If you own
your home or a farm the ownership includes ownership of
the minerals and everything beneath the land—unless there
has been a restriction or reservation in the deed. The
ordinary deed that conveys real property or title to real
property includes all the rights to the minerals and everything beneath the surface of the land within the boundaries
of the property—unless, again, there is an express reservation of mineral rights.

This is very important in the parts of our country where there are valuable mineral rights under the surface of the land. For example, in Oklahoma and the Midwest many people took title to property not knowing that there was oil beneath the surface, and when oil was discovered their property values rose tremendously, because their title to the surface of the land included ownership rights in the minerals and valuable wealth beneath its surface. Later, land in this oil-rich country was sold with reservations— that is, exceptions were made, and a person bought the surface of the land but the seller reserved the mineral rights beneath the land.

Who owns the crops that are growing upon a farm when you take title? I own a farm that grows wheat and desire to sell the farm to you, and at the time that we arrive at an agreement and I pass title to you by a deed, the crop is half grown upon the land. We pass title and you go into possession of the farm, but then I realize that the crop has now matured and that it should belong to me. To whom does the crop belong after you have gone into possession? The law says that while the crops are growing upon the land, they are part of the real property and pass to you when the title to the real property itself passed to you. So unless we had thought about this problem and in the deed I reserved the growing crops upon the land for that crop year, you own them.

However, the rule is different for crops that I have stored in the barn. If I sell the farm to you in winter and I have the full winter's hay requirements of my farm stored in my barn, upon the sale of the property to you and you're going into possession I would have the right to come upon the land and remove the severed or stored crops from the barn, unless we had thought about this problem and in the contract of sale or deed there had been a specific mention that the sale included the severed crops and crops stored in the barn. This is simply because severed crops are personal property, whereas growing crops are real property.

FIXTURES

Fixtures are personal property that are permanently fixed to the real property or so tightly to the land that to remove them might damage the real property. Fixtures become part of the real property when they are placed upon the land

or buildings in a permanent fashion. Remember that while
fence posts were stacked next to the barn they were
personal property. But once put into the ground and made
part of the fence they became real property.

To see how this concept works in the city instead of
in the earth of a farm, say I purchase a home that had a
new furnace installed. The seller of the home made no
mention of the new furnace and he just sold the real
property—the house—but with no reference to the new
furnace. I move in with my family and find there is no
furnace. I call the seller of the house: "Say, we don't
seem to have a furnace in this house, but when I looked
at it before the purchase there was a furnace. Now where
is it?" The seller tells me, "Well, I didn't include the
furnace in the sale to you of the house." I say, "Oh yes
you did, because you gave me a deed to all of the real
property, and the furnace became a fixture because it was
permanently affixed to the premises, including the house."
Now, who would be right? Is this a permanent or a temporary
fixture? The law would conclude in this case—where the
parties have been silent in the deed or the contract of
sale—that the furnace was a necessary and permanent fixture
to the house and passed when title passed to me upon the
purchase. Consequently, I would be entitled to have the
furnace replaced in the home and not have to pay additionally for it.

But what if the house that I purchased had a new
range in the kitchen that was not a built-in range but a
free-standing range that plugged into an electrical outlet
in the wall? Moving into the house I found the range had
been removed and I asked the owner who had sold the house
to me about that, and he said, "Well certainly you didn't
expect me to sell the range as well as the house and
furnace. Certainly that belongs to me because that is not
a fixture and can be removed without doing damage to the
house itself." And I said, "Oh no. I thought I was getting the range when I bought the house." Who would be
right? Is this a permanent or a movable fixture? In most
states the law would say that the stove was not a permanent
fixture to the house and I was not entitled to it unless I
had contracted separately to buy it as part of the house in
question. So I would not be entitled to have the seller
of the house return the range without my paying something
for it or contracting to buy it.

There are numerous such examples and you have to be
careful in purchasing a house to make absolutely sure that

you're getting all that you're entitled to as fixtures, and
if you have a doubt about it you should make mention of
the other furnishings in the house that may or may not be
fixtures, depending upon the unique situation. If you desire
to buy something and the owner desires to sell it as part
of the real estate, it should be included in the deed or
the contract of sale.

What about wall-to-wall carpeting or drapery rods?
Are those considered fixtures or personal property that
we must buy separately? About drapery rods that are
screwed or permanently affixed to the wall, and wall-to-wall
carpeting that is tacked down around the entire room or
several rooms of the house, the law has neither a clear yes
or no answer in every case. If the rods are affixed in
such a way that to remove them would damage the wall
extensively, most courts in this country would view the
curtain rods to be fixtures, and therefore, passing with
the real property upon sale if there had been no other
expression in the deed or contract of sale. If the wall-to-
wall carpeting is laid over rough or plywood flooring, as in
some homes in which carpeting is laid instead of hardwood
or linoleum, then it is considered to be a fixture and
passes with the deed or contract in the absence of language
to the contrary in the deed or contract. But if the rugs
merely cover hardwood floors, the law is not quite as clear
and it's always a good idea to mention specifically in the
deed or contract of sale or purchase whether the rugs are
included as part of the real estate or whether they are
not going to pass with the real estate.

GLOSSARY TERMS

Fixtures   Personal property so affixed to real property
    that their removal without damage to the real property
    is impossible and thus have become part of the real
    property.

SELF TEST

CHAPTER 23

NAME_____

DATE_____

23.1 Real property is _____, and objects which are
_____ to, and used in connection with
_____ in such a way as to be regarded as a/an
_____ of it.

23.2 All property that is not attached _____ to
land is _____ property.

23.3 Those _____ on the land which become part of
the land _____ are part of the real property.

23.4 Generally, when someone takes title to the _____
of the land, they also take ownership _____ in
the minerals and valuable wealth _____ the
_____ of the land. This may not be true
if there are restrictions or _____ in the _____.

23.5 The law states that when crops are growing upon the
land, they are part of the _____ property,
and ownership (choose either "passes to the buyer" or
"remains with the seller") _____ when the title
to the real property is transferred.

23.6 Severed crops are _____ property whereas
growing crops are _____ property.

23.7 The difference between permanently affixed to the
land and movable makes clear that personal property
is _____ and not _____ to the land, and
real property includes all those things which are
affixed to the land and _____.

23.8 __ _____ are personal property that are fixed
to the real property permanently or so tightly to
the land, if you will, that to remove it might
_____ the _____ property.

23.9 Fixtures become part of the _____ property when
they are placed upon the land or buildings in a
_____ fashion.

23.10 Generally, when purchasing real property, it's always
a good idea, when in doubt, to _____ mention
whether these sort of _____ pass with the
_____ or are not included.

24 Real Property

Easements. Profits. Licenses. Passage of Title.

LEARNING OBJECTIVES

To acquire an understanding of rights and interests in real property.

To understand how such rights and interests are conveyed.

CHAPTER CONTENTS

Easements   Buying and Selling Title to Real Property   Fee Simple   Life Estate   Estate for Years Conditional Interest   Methods of Sale and Purchase Glossary   Self Test

Simply defined, an *easement* is the right to use property
belonging to another—generally a right to cross the land of
another at a particular place and within particular
boundaries, sometimes a right to erect power poles or put
pipelines across property. By a power line easement, a
public utility company or the federal government buys
the right from the owner to cross his land, either above
the land or beneath the land with powerlines or pipelines.
The natural gas runs from Oklahoma all the way to New York
City generally under easements across private property.

EASEMENTS

An easement, created by conveyance in a deed or a recorded
contract, gives a right to a person to make use of the
property belonging to another. For example, Mr. Jones
sold one acre of land to Mr. Smith, but retained title to
all the land surrounding Mr. Smith's purchase, and Mr. Jones
did not sell an easement across the land that he still
owned to the acre that Mr. Smith purchased. The court
would imply an easement of necessity because Mr. Smith's
land was land-locked by Mr. Jones' land, and it would therefore be valueless because he couldn't get to it without
the right of access. When absolutely necessary, therefore,
an easement may be implied in law, but generally easements
are created by a written document which grants to the
holder of the easement the right to cross the land of the
dominant estate, the land upon which the easement is
located. Mr. Smith had an easement across Mr. Jones'
dominant estate.
　　An easement may be terminated by its holder's
deeding it back to the owner of the dominant estate. Or,
say, Mr. Jones, the owner of all the land surrounding
Mr. Smith's acre, bought Mr. Smith's property back from
him, the easement would be extinguished by operation of law
because there would be no necessity for the easement.
Mr. Jones would own all the property again and would not
need a private right to go across the land that he owned
himself.
　　Another interest in land that is not possessory but
is merely a user right is called a *profit*, a right to take
something from the land (the real property) of another.
Often a farm has a reservoir on it and the owner of the
farm, Farmer Brown, agrees to let Farmer Jones use some
water from his reservoir for a given fee a year. Farmer

Jones would then run his pipeline up to Farmer Brown's reservoir and pipe the water to his own property. The pipeline across Farmer Brown's property would be an easement (a pipeline easement), but the right to take the water from the reservoir would be called a profit. The distinction should be clear: An easement is the right to use a person's property, generally to cross it, while a profit is the right to take something from another person's property, such as water, minerals, or other crops or things that grow or are found on the property.

Another small interest which is not an ownership interest but a user interest that we can have in real property is called a *license*. Signs painted on barns or silos or even nailed on fenceposts often are generally permitted by license, the right to do something on the land of another that would otherwise be unlawful. You and I have no right to go upon a farmer's ground and paint a sign on his barn, but if we have an agreement that gives us a right to paint a certain type of sign for a given fee and for a given number of years, this would be called a license. Neither the right to use the property nor a right to take something from the property, it is the right to do something on the property. There are numerous types of licenses, easements, and profits, and they are very technical instruments. The method of creation, the use of these rights, and their extinguishment or termination, both by implication and operation of law, and by express termination, are extremely complex subjects, and for dealing with these subjects, the aid of a person's lawyer or attorney is usually necessary.

BUYING AND SELLING TITLE TO REAL PROPERTY

We studied title earlier, in relation to personal property. Now we will relate it to real property. All land in the United States is owned by somebody or some state; public lands are held by the United States government or by a state, county, or city government. All other land is owned by private parties—people like you and me—or corporations owned by people like you and me. Some land is owned by Indian tribes. Reservation lands were those lands deeded by treaty to Indian tribes during the great Indian wars and peace settlements.

All the land is owned by someone or something. In fact, you've probably read in the newspapers of a growing

concern by many nations as to how much land they own
beneath the ocean surrounding them. Chile, for example,
claims title to the ocean bed 100 miles off its shore.
The United States claims title to land running 6 marine
leagues out to sea, and will probably claim title farther
from shore than that in the next several years. Even
Antarctica has been claimed and boundaries have been
established among the nations who first explored and
claimed title to the Antarctic.

FEE SIMPLE

Title, therefore, means ownership and the right to free
and uninterrupted use of the property for the extent of
ownership. The best or greatest title in real property
is title to the *fee simple* estate; that is, the deed to a
piece of property in fee simple will say, "to you and to
your heirs." In feudal England the king granted all title
to property to the lords, knights, and feudal barons for
their life, and upon their death the property would go back
to the king who could then give the property to his
favorites and people who would help him. The king had this
method of paying for armies and money and support—a wonderful
patronage system.

But after its use for many hundreds of years, the king
began to give title to the lord and his son, so that the
title would pass to the oldest son of the lord, duke, or
whoever had gotten title. Slowly this grew into a fee
simple—the fee of the land simply given to the family.
And the deeds would then be enrolled on the king's charter
as "to Lord So-and-so and to his heirs," Lord So-and-so
would own the property and upon his death it would pass
to his eldest son and then from his eldest son to his son
and down we'd go through the generations of ownership.

This was the beginning of fee simple, which means that
if you own property in fee simple, upon your death it does
not revert to the state or the government, but belongs to
your heirs or to any other person that you may have willed
your property to in your will, upon your death.

LIFE ESTATE

A smaller interest in land is a possessory interest or
ownership interest, and title passes to the person holding

this interest, but is limited to the life of the holder.
This interest in real property is called a *life estate*.
Upon the owner's death the property reverts to the donor or
grantor of the property or goes to another person. It is
created by a conveyance, by a deed, just as the fee simple
was created, but the deed says "to X for his life and then
to Y." If the deed used the words "To X and his heirs,"
the deed would be a fee simple, but a deed that says, "To
X and upon X's death, then to Y," is a life estate. If you
own property by life estate, you do not have the right to
sell that property for more than the length of your life,
nor can you will it, because the deed automatically transfers title upon your death to a third person.

ESTATE FOR YEARS

The third type of major estate or interest or title that
we have in land is *estate for years*—an ownership interest
in land that is created for a term of years. Mr. Jones, by
deed, transfers his interest in real property to Mr. Brown
for a period of 25 years, and upon the expiration of 25
years, then the land is to be vested in Mr. White. The
owner for a term of years could lease the property only
for that term of years because his interest terminates
upon the expiration of the time in the deed. This, then,
is an estate for years.

CONDITIONAL INTEREST

Another type of estate or ownership interest that we have
in land can be created on a fee simple interest, a life
estate, or an estate for years—a *conditional interest* in
land; the grantor, or seller, can put a condition in the
deed. There are many different types of conditions. For
example, a deed could say, "Mr. Jones deeds his interest
and all of his right and title to the land in question to
Mr. Brown, conditioned upon Mr. Brown's never using the
property for an ice-skating rink; and in the event
Mr. Brown uses the land for an ice-skating rink, then the
land shall automatically revert to Mr. Jones." This is an
estate on condition, and if the owner of the estate violates
the condition, the grantor of the estate or land can
reenter and retake the land automatically by law. This
is an estate upon condition with a right of reverter.

There is another type of conditional estate in which
Mr. Jones grants the property to Mr. Brown upon condition,
and if Mr. Brown violates the condition then the property
interest shall terminate and Mr. White shall take possession and be entitled to the property. Mr. White, the party
who would take after the condition was breached would have
an interest in the land, but it would be a conditional
interest in the land or an expectancy in the land; Mr. White
is known in the law as a remainderman, because he would
have the remainder of the property if the condition came
to pass but he would not know if the condition was going
to come to pass, because a condition has to be something
that is not predictable. But the remainderman does have
an interest in land and it may be of value, because some
conditions in the deed may come into existence which will
vest title in Mr. White and he will no longer be a
remainderman, but will own fee simple title to the land.

Rights in land and title to land is a very complex
and difficult subject—so difficult that many companies
and many lawyers work exclusively in real estate and land.
In fact, in every state there are companies which insure
title—that is, check out the title of all real property
being purchased or sold to insure that the title is not
subject to some condition that the purchaser doesn't know
about—and issue a policy of title insurance. For example,
in the purchase of a home, the seller can be required to
have a title search made of the property, and the company
issues to the buyer a policy of title insurance which
insures that the estate taken by deed was a fee simple
estate. If some remainderman or some person with a
right of reverter came upon the scene and said, "In an
old, old deed, the land that you hold has been subject to
a condition, and the condition has come to pass. Consequently, we now own this land," and if it was found that
the deed had been recorded but the title company had
missed it, and the new owner no longer had a right to the
property, then the title company would pay the owner his
purchase price for the home.

If the law is so complicated that it requires
insurance on titles, then you need all of the expert
help you can have in the purchase and sale of property
so that you're sure that the title you purchase or sell
is exactly as it appears on the face of your deed.

METHODS OF SALE AND PURCHASE

Most property today is bought and sold through real estate
brokers, who make their business of selling property by
listing it for purchasers who desire to sell and attempting
to find buyers who want to buy. Generally a real estate
broker or realtor is the <u>agent</u> of the seller or vendor, and
not the purchaser.

        Generally, if you are purchasing property through a real
estate agent, and you desire a particular property, the
real estate agent will have a form called an earnest money
receipt in which you will make an offer to purchase the
property for a given price and accompany the written offer
of the purchase with a down payment or earnest money to
show that you're serious in the offer. And generally the
offer is open for a number of months or weeks or days, 10
days, 15 days, 30 days, and if the seller accepts the offer
and accepts the earnest money then you have a binding
agreement. Be very careful in the preparation and signing
of an earnest money receipt because it contains many of
the terms of the sale or purchase by which you will be
bound if the offer is accepted.

        After the earnest money and the offer is accepted, then,
as we learned in contracts, there is a binding agreement.
Sometimes, thereafter, in large purchases, a contract of
sale or a land-sale contract is entered into upon which all
of the terms of the agreement—the payment, the terms of
payment, the length of time for the payment, the interest,
the type of property and legal description, the obligation
of the seller to furnish title insurance, the mortgaging of
the property to obtain the financing for the purchase
or sale—are all set forth. A land-sale contract is an
extremely technical and precise instrument if drawn correct-
ly, and requires the services of an attorney to adequately
protect both sides to the agreement.

        But a land-sale contract does not pass title upon
its signing. In the United States, title is passed only
when the deed has been properly executed, or signed, and
delivered into the possession of the purchasers of the real
property. In most states in the U.S. it is required that
all deeds to real property be <u>recorded</u>. In every county
there is a book in which all deeds are entered, and sometimes copies are made of those deeds, so that title can
always be searched and there is a record of who owns each
piece of land in the United States.

But recording does not pass title; <u>delivery</u> of the deed
passes title. Consequently, many, many land-sale contracts
are *closed in escrow.* You, the purchaser, pay your money
to a third person—a company, generally—and the seller
deposits his deed with that third person when the purchase
price has been paid to him. When the deed has been
recorded it is finally delivered to the owner, but in the
event of someone's death before the delivery, the property
does pass to the purchaser of the property. This is
called closing a real property sale in escrow, and it's
a good protection for both parties. But keep in mind that
title passes with the transfer of possession of the deed
itself.

I look at the deed now in my possession on the
purchase of property, and I find that it is a warranty
deed, a deed warranting certain things by the seller to
the purchaser. A warranty deed conveys the title from
the grantor to the grantee (the seller to the purchaser),
and the warranties are that the seller·is the owner of
the land and has the right to convey it; that the land has
no mortgages or other liens unless specifically stated;
that the purchaser shall have quiet, uninterrupted enjoyment of the property and will not be evicted by anyone
else; and that the seller will defend the right of the
purchaser to enjoy the property, and further, that the
seller or grantor will execute any other deeds or instruments required to perfect or remedy any defect in title.

Another ·less valuable type of deed, called a quit-
claim deed, does not warrant these things; the seller
merely passes any title he owns but does not state what
type of title it is and does not warrant that he will
defend that title.

GLOSSARY TERMS

Closing in escrow   A sale of title to real property in which buyer and seller respectively deposit the purchase price and the deed with a third party for holding until the deed is recorded.

Conditional interest   Ownership that lasts as long as stated conditions are not violated.

Dominant estate   The land on which an easement is located.

Easement   The right of a person to use property belonging to another.

Estate for years   Ownership created for a term of years.

Fee simple   Ownership that is passed to heirs rather than reverting to a state.

Land-sale contract   A contract for sale of real property which sets forth all the terms of the agreement.

License   The right to do something on the land of another that would otherwise be unlawful.

Life estate   Ownership for life that reverts to the donor or grantor or someone else on the owner's death.

Profit   The right to take something from another person's property.

Remainderman   In a conditional interest, a third party who will receive title to property if the conditions are violated.

Title   Ownership and the right to free uninterrupted use of real property.

SELF TEST
CHAPTER 24

NAME_____

DATE_____

24.1 A/An _____ is the right to use property belonging to another. Generally, it is a/an _____
to cross the land of another at a particular place
or within particular _____.

24.2 An easement is created by _____ in a deed or
in a contract that is _____ and it gives a
right to a person to make use of the _____
belonging to another.

24.3 An easement may be _____ in law, when it's
absolutely necessary, but generally, easements are
created by a/an _____ document which grants the
_____ of the easement, the right to cross
the land of the _____ estate.

24.4 The _____ estate is the land upon which the
easement is located.

24.5 An easement may be terminated by the holder of the
easement _____ it back to the owner of the
_____, or by operation of _____ if
there is not a/an _____ for the easement.

24.6 There is another interest in land that is not
_____ but is merely a user right, and that
is called a/an _____.

24.7 A profit, when we use it relating to real property,
is a right to _____ something from the land
of another.

24.8 A/An _____ is the right to use a person's
property, whereas a/an _____ is the right to
take something from another person's property.

24.9 The right to do something on the land of another
that would otherwise be unlawful is granted by a/an
_____.

24.10 Title means _____ and the right to
_____ and _____ use of the property
to the extent of _____ that a person has in
property.

24.11   The best, or largest, or greatest title that a
        person can have in real property is title to the
        _____. This type of deed would read "to
        you and to your _____." This type of
        interest started in the _____ times in
        England.

24.12   An interest in real property that is limited to
        the life of the owner and upon his death the
        property reverts back to the _____ or
        grantor of the property is known as a/an_____
        estate.

24.13   A life estate is created by a/an_____ or
        deed, just as the fee simple was created.

24.14   If a deed uses the words "To X and his heirs," the
        deed would be a/an_____ simple, but if the
        deed says, "To X and upon X's death, to the . . .,"
        then the deed would be a/an_____ estate.

24.15   If property is owned by life estate, the owner
        wouldn't have the right to _____ the property,
        nor would he have a right to _____ it
        because the deed automatically transfers title upon
        the owner's death to a third person.

24.16   An ownership interest that is created for a term
        of years is known as a/an_____.

24.17   An estate that is granted with conditions in the
        deed, and upon violation of these conditions,
        allows the grantor of the estate to reenter and
        _____ the land automatically is known as an
        estate upon _____ with a/an_____ of
        _____ _____.

24.18   A remainderman does have a/an_____ in land
        and it may be of _____, because some
        conditions in the deed may come into _____
        which would vest a/an_____ title to him.

24.19   The types of interest that a person or corporation
        can own in real property are _____,
        _____, estate for _____, a/an_____
        right, or an estate on _____.

24.20   In every state in the union, there are companies
        that insure _____, that is, they check out
        the title of all real property that is being pur-
        chased or sold to insure that the _____
        is not _____ to some _____ that the
        purchaser doesn't know about and the company
        issues a policy of _____.

24.21   Generally, a real estate broker is the agent of the
        _____, or _____, and not the
        _____.

CHAPTER 24

NAME_____

24.22 The real estate agent will have a form called an
earnest money _____ in which the prospective
purchaser will make a/an _____ to purchase
the property for a/an _____ and accompanying
the written _____ of the purchase is a down
payment or _____ to show the serious intent
of the prospective purchaser.
24.23 After the seller accepts the offer and earnest
money, there is a/an _____ agreement.
24.24 (Answer True or False) _____ A land-sale contract upon signing does not pass title.
24.25 Title is only passed when the _____ has been
properly _____, or signed, and _____
into the _____ of the purchasers of the real
property.
24.26 Many land-sale contracts are closed in _____.
24.27 But keep in mind that title passes with the
transfer of _____ of the _____
itself.
24.28 A/An _____ deed conveys the _____
from the seller to the purchaser, and the warranties
are that the seller is the _____ of the land
and he has a/an _____ to convey it; that the
land has no mortgages or other _____ unless
it is otherwise specifically stated; that the
purchaser shall have quiet, uninterrupted enjoyment
of the property; that he will _____ the
right of the purchaser to enjoy the property; and
that the seller will execute any other deeds or
instruments required to _____ or remedy any
_____ in title. A/An _____ claim deed
does not make these warranties.

25 Real Property

Warranty Deeds. Quit-Claim Deeds. Mortgages. Tenancy by the Entirety. Tenancy in Common. Ownership Rights and Restrictions.

LEARNING OBJECTIVES

To learn more about deeds.
To learn the procedures for mortgage foreclosure.
To learn the method of jointly taking title to real property.
To become acquainted with the rights and duties in owning real property.

CHAPTER CONTENTS

Warranty Deeds   Quit-Claim Deeds   Foreclosure
Satisfaction of Mortgage   Tenancy by the Entirety
Tenancy in Common   Ownership Rights and Restrictions
Glossary   Self Test

In the previous chapter we discussed briefly the differences between a quit-claim deed and a warranty deed. If we look at them in more detail their differences will be clearer.

WARRANTY DEEDS

A warranty deed for the transaction of sale of real property basically reads as follows: "Know all men by these presents." This document is thus notice to the world that a transfer of property has occurred. The grantor then puts in his signature, "in consideration of" so many dollars "to me in hand pay by"—the purchaser then signs his name and the grantor then says, "I do hereby grant, bargain, sell, and convey unto the grantee, his heirs and assigns all of the following real property, with the tenements, herediments, and the pertenances situated in the County of _____ and State of _____ bounded and described as follows . . . ." Description of the property follows.

        The warranties then begin: "The grantee to have and to hold the above described granted premises unto the grantee and his heirs and assigns forever." The grantor then further warrants that "the grantor does convenant that he is lawfully seized in fee simple of the above granted premises, free from all encumbrances except . . . ." Any encumbrances like mortgages or other liens against the property are then inserted. The grantor further says, "I will, and my heirs, executors and administrators shall warrant and forever defend, the above granted premises and every part and parcel thereof against the lawful claims and demands of all persons whomsoever." Thus, there are specific promises as to the type of property interest that is being passed. A fee simple is being passed in the deed of our example, and the grantor warrants that he holds a fee simple and that he will forever defend the title of the granted premises and every part and parcel thereof against the lawful claims of all persons. The promises are part of a warranty deed and are enforceable, and the grantor may be held liable for any defect in the title that he has warranted.

QUIT-CLAIM DEEDS

A quit-claim deed used in the passage of title reads basically as follows: "Know all men by these presents that I . . . ." The grantor inserts his name, "in consideration of" so many dollars

"to me in hand pay by"—The grantee or purchaser signs his
name and the grantor says, "release and quit claim to the
grantee all of my right, title, and interest, if any, in
that real property situated in the County of _____,
State of _____, described as . . . ." Here the
property is described, the quit-claim deed ends. The
grantor then merely signs the quit-claim deed making no
promises as to his title and no warranties that he will
defend his title. He merely transfers whatever title he
held.

Thus, if you received a deed for property that you
had purchased, you would look for the promises and warranties in the deed to make sure that you had a warranty
deed and were getting good and sufficient title to the
property that you were purchasing.

Basically then, the distinction between the warranty
deed and the quit-claim deed is that a warranty deed
warrants good title in the seller and promises to defend that
good title, whereas a quit-claim deed merely releases or
quits the seller's interest, whatever it may be, in the
land that he is selling.

Assume that we have purchased the property and we have
the deed in our possession. We would next want to record
the deed at the County Courthouse in the Deed Record book
so that all the world would know that we owned the
property. But how did we pay for this property? Usually
no one has cash to pay for real property. Almost all the
purchases of real property are done through lending
institutions: We borrow the money to pay for the property
in cash and then repay the loan. Lending institutions that
loan on the purchase of real property take *mortgages* on
the property.

Two documents are required by the lending institution
or bank before they will make a loan on real property.
One, you must sign a promissory note to repay the loan to
the bank; second, you must mortgage your property as
security for repayment of the loan. A mortgage, a document
recorded after it has been signed in the mortgage record
books of the county, gives to the bank or lender the right
to have the property seized and sold if the mortgage loan
is unpaid within the time set forth in the promissory note.

If you or your parents have a mortgage on the property
you live in, then the mortgage on the property secures the
loan. Assume that there is a default on the promissory note,

on the payment of taxes, or interest, or principal on the
note, then the mortgage—that is, the lender or bank—has
a right to foreclose the mortgage. A *foreclosure* is a
proceeding by which a court establishes that the loan has
been defaulted upon and the real property may be sold to
the highest bidder. If a third party comes in on the
mortgage sale and bids the property in (pays money on the
property), that money is first applied to the mortgage, any
balance that is left over after expenses of the sheriff's
sale have been paid is then paid to the mortgagor, or owner
of the property-— in our case, you or your parents. Thus,
any surplus over and above the mortgage balance you would
receive. But if the bid on the property upon the sheriff's
sale is inadequate to repay the mortgage—in other words,
there is still a debt due from you to the lending bank—
then you will have some personal liability on this deficiency
and you might have to repay that balance still owing to the
bank.

FORECLOSURE

You probably have all read books and seen movies about the
terrible banker who comes in and evicts the widow from her
home into a blizzard. That hasn't occurred for 75 years
in this country. In a mortgage foreclosure the sale is made
by and through a court, the balance owed on the mortgage is
judicially determined, and the payment on the mortgage
after the sheriff's sale is supervised by the court. After
the court foreclosure becomes final, and you are out of your
property and the new owner is in the property, you still
have, in most states, one year in which you may redeem the
property, and that is called a *right of redemption*. Most
states allow one full year for you to tell the court that
you want to repurchase the property for the amount that the
mortgage sale sold the property for. Say the mortage lender
has sold the property on sheriff's sale for $10,000. There
is a balance due on the property of $2,000. You pay off the
$2,000 on the promissory note and within one year after the
sale of land by sheriff's deed you have a right to petition
the court to have the property returned to you upon the
payment of $10,000 plus the statutory interest fee. So,
even though you are foreclosed in the first sale, you have
a right to redeem your interest in the property within one
year after the foreclosure sale.

SATISFACTION OF MORTGAGE

Recall that the mortgage was recorded in the mortgage
records. Assume that over a period of years you paid off
the mortgage on the property that you purchased. It's very
important that you obtain from the lending institution
which loaned the money a document called a satisfaction of
mortgage. You then take the satisfaction of the mortgage
over to the County Courthouse and have the satisfaction
recorded just as the mortgage was recorded. This will show
all people who are interested in the property that the
mortgage has been fully paid and it is not a lien on the
property. Consequently, you own the property now, free and
clear from all liens and encumbrances.

TENANCY BY THE ENTIRETY

Another point to discuss briefly is how title is taken
jointly. Assume that your mother and father have purchased
a property that they live in. The deed grants to each of
them, Jane Jones and Joe Jones, husband and wife, the
property in question. The law states that this is a
tenancy by the entirety: Both husband and wife take a
joint interest, an undivided interest in the property, and
neither the husband nor the wife can singly transfer the
property without the consent of the other, and that consent
must be by deed. If either spouse were to sell the property
he or she would have to have the other spouse sign the deed
in granting the property to another person. In a tenancy by
the entirety (a tenancy between man and wife), if one spouse
dies the other spouse inherits his or her interest in the
land unless some other provision has been made by law.

TENANCY IN COMMON

When two women or men who are not related buy property together a tenancy in common is created, unless some other
provision is made clearly in the deed. In a tenancy
by the entirety if either spouse dies before the other, the
other inherits the deceased's half. In a tenancy in common
if one owner dies before the other dies, his half of the
property goes to his heirs. In other words, the joint tenants

or his concurrent tenants do not inherit the other tenant's rights to the property; it passes directly to his heirs.

OWNERSHIP RIGHTS AND RESTRICTIONS

Remember that a warranty deed guarantees the right to free and unobstructed enjoyment of the premises. What does that mean? Now that we own a piece of property, what rights do we have to use that property? First, what kind of building can we construct on our property? You might assume you can construct any type of building you wanted to, but that may not be true. There are various and, sometimes, numerous restrictions upon the use of real property, and these restrictions are valid and enforceable. Assume that the lot you purchased to build your home on is 70 ft. by 100 ft. and is on a city street. When you looked at the land you thought that your lot went right up to the pavement of the street, but upon looking at the title insurance policy you found that there was a setback of 10 feet on the front of your property which was called road right-of-way. Although this road right-of-way is unpaved, with no sidewalk, it belongs to the city or municipality; they own it for expansion of the streets or placement of sewer lines, gas lines, water lines, and underground electric lines. You do not own that piece of property and you cannot build your house upon it; if the city wants to, it can take that property and put a gas line or other utility in or it can widen the street. That's the first restriction upon your property.

You go to an architect or builder and have your house designed. You take the plans down to City Hall, to the building inspector, who advises you that you cannot obtain a building permit because the house is within 10 feet of each side of the property, and the building restrictions in the city require a 10-foot setback on either side of the house. So you must redraw the plans of your house to comply with the building and zoning restrictions of the city.

In addition, you are advised that the house must set back 25 feet from the roadway in front, so another design change must be made in the house. In cities across the country there are numerous zoning and building restrictions that must be carefully examined before you purchase a piece of land in which to build your dream house. Also, zoning restrictions in most counties and cities provide that in residental zones factories cannot be built, and in factory zones apartment houses may not be built, and put many other restrictions on land use.

Assume that the property you have in mind is adequately zoned for your particular use and you begin
excavation of the land for a basement; the contractor advises
you several days after excavation has begun that there is
some caving in, and to such an extent that property on the
other side of your property line—your neighbor's property—
is beginning to cave in. If you're wise you will stop
excavating immediately because your neighbor, like any owner,
has a right to have his land supported in the position and
to the grade that it was before you began excavating.

Thus, the unrestricted right to enjoy the property,
the surface as well as the mineral rights below, should be
qualified: so long as you did not disrupt or dislocate the
land of adjacent owners or your neighbor's property. He
has a right to support of property; you have a right of
support and this is called a *reciprocal support easement*.
Neither you nor your neighbor can dig into your property so
as to cause the other's to cave in.

Another very valuable property right that goes with
the land, and is subject to a tremendous amount of dispute
and litigation in this country, is the water rights. In
the arid states without adequate water supply, there
isn't enough water to go with the land so water rights are
sold and purchased separately. But assume that a stream
runs through your property. What are your rights to the
water in that stream? In most states you would have the
right to make reasonable use of the stream and its water
for a beneficial and reasonable purpose to the land, to
such an extent that it did not materially diminish the
flow of this stream or damage the quality of the water.
For example, if you put in a large factory upon your
property and took all of the water from the stream so that
downstream users had none, you would probably be stopped by
a court of law, just as you probably would be if you took
water from the stream and put pollutants or trash into the
stream so that the quality of the water downstream was
damaged. In some of the arid western states a *prior
appropriation* law is in effect: The first person to make
beneficial use of the stream has a fixed right to a continuing use of that water for the purpose that he made the
prior appropriation on. The right to the stream and the
water from the stream is known as a *riparian right*.

Assume that the lot you purchased was for the construction of an all-night commercial laundry; and that you

had a large number of lights and boilers and other equipment; and it created noise and odor; and people were
coming and going from the property during the night and
in the day, and the neighbors began to complain. You
respond by saying, "This is alright with the zoning
authority and is in accordance with the building code, so
you have nothing to complain about. I have a perfect
right to make use of this property in any way I see fit,
because it is legal and city, county, and state officials
have told me so." You may be wrong, because there is a
common law right that anyone may use his property as long
as he does not interfere with the other people's beneficial
enjoyment of their property—that is, so long as he is not
guilty of a *nuisance*. Your neighbors may be able to bring
suit in court for damages to their property and the lack
of full enjoyment of it. Or they may be able to obtain a
court injunction ordering you to stop using your property
to such an extent that it damages your neighbors' private
use and enjoyment of their property. Here, then, is a
restriction of your unrestricted use of land, and that
is you may not make use of your land so that it unreasonably interferes with the interest in and the use and
enjoyment of others' land. Now you have the same right to
your property.

Another right every owner has in real property is the
right to be free from trespass. As you know, a trespasser
is someone who comes upon property without invitation and
without right, but a trespasser is not necessarily the
robber who comes in the night. A trespass can be created
by a tree, a fence, by smoke, by insecticide spray, and so
on.

For example, several years ago an orchardist sprayed
his orchard, and the spray traveled 10 miles to another
man's property damaging the very valuable flowers in his
greenhouse. The person brought suit in the courts against
the orchardist on the theory that his spray had trespassed
upon the plaintiff's land. The court agreed with the
plaintiff and gave damages, even though the orchardist
didn't know the plaintiff, didn't know where his property
was and had never anticipated that his spray would be blown
by the wind some 10 miles across the valley to this plaintiff's property. If you put your fence 6 inches over your
line onto your neighbor's property line, that is a trespass
and he has a right to have it stopped or to obtain damages
for your taking of his property, even though it's only 6
inches in width. If by your actions on your property you

may not trespass upon the property of another, why can
the city, the state, or the federal government build free-
ways and other buildings right across private land? Isn't
this a nuisance, or at least a trespass? It would be,
except for the law that a public or government agency has
the right of eminent domain, also known as the right of
condemnation. This right grants to a government agency
the power to use property and take it upon payment of fair
market value to you for the taking and use of your property,
as long as it is not for private use or for resale, but only
for a public use.

GLOSSARY TERMS

Eminent domain   Government right to private property, upon
    fair market value reimbursement, for public use.

Foreclosure   A processing by which a court determines that
    a loan has been defaulted upon and the property is
    sold to the highest bidder.

Mortgage   A recorded document giving a lender the right to
    seize property for default of payment on a promissory
    note.

Nuisance   Any use of property that materially destroys
    or diminishes other people's beneficial use of their
    property.

Prior appropriation   The fixed right to continued use of
    a stream by the first person to make beneficial use
    of it.

Reciprocal support easement   The right of owners of real
    property to have their land free of disruptions or
    dislocations by adjacent neighbors.

Right of redemption   A period during which property that
    has been foreclosed can be redeemed by the person
    upon whom it was foreclosed.

Riparian right   Right to use of a stream running across
    one's property.

Satisfaction of mortgage   A document signifying that a
    mortgage has been paid in full.

SELF TEST
CHAPTER 25

NAME_____

DATE_____

25.1 A person signing a quit-claim deed makes no promises
as to his _____, and makes no _____
that he will defend his title.

25.2 Basically then, the distinction between the warranty
deed and the quit-claim deed is that a warranty
deed warrants good _____ in the _____
and promises to _____ that good _____,
whereas a quit-claim deed merely _____ or
_____ the seller's interest in the land he
is selling.

25.3 After the property is purchased and the deed is in
the buyer's possession, the next thing to do would
be to _____ the deed at the county courthouse
in the _____ book, thereby telling the world
who owns the property.

25.4 The two requirements that are required by the lending
institution before they will make a loan on real
property are that the borrower must sign a/an
_____ note to repay the loan, and he must
_____ the property as _____ for
repayment of the loan.

25.5 A/An _____ gives the bank or lender the right
to have the property seized and sold if the
_____ is unpaid within the time specified
in the _____ note.

25.6 A/An _____ is a proceeding in court where the
court establishes that the loan has been defaulted
upon, and that the real property may be sold to the
_____.

25.7 If the bid on the property upon the sheriff's sale
in inadequate to repay the mortgage, then the party
foreclosed upon will have a personal _____
on the deficiency.

25.8   After a court foreclosure becomes final, the party
       upon whom foreclosure was made still has, in most
       states, one _____ in which he may redeem the
       property. This is known as the right of
       _____.

25.9   After repayment of a mortgage on property, it's
       very important to obtain from the _____
       a document called a/an_____ of mortgage. This
       document would then be _____ at the county
       courthouse to show anyone that there is not a/an
       _____ on the property.

25.10 Tenancy by the _____ means that both husband
       and wife take a/an _____ interest, a/an
       _____ interest in the property, and neither
       the husband or wife can singly _____ the
       property without the _____ of the other, and
       that _____ must be by _____.

25.11 In a tenancy by the entirety, if either spouse dies
       the other spouse _____ the deceased spouse's
       _____ in the property.

25.12 If two people, not related, buy property together,
       a tenancy in _____ is created.

25.13 With tenants in common, the joint tenants or his
       _____ tenants do not inherit the other
       tenant's right to the property, it passes directly
       to his _____.

25.14 There are numerous _____ and _____
       restrictions in cities across the country which
       place a limit on what can be built on real property.

25.15 Both the owner and his neighbor have a right to
       support of property which is called a/an_____
       support _____.

25.16 The right to a stream and the water from the stream
       that is located on a person's property is known
       as a/an _____ right.

25.17 The law states that a public or governmental agency
       has the right of _____ domain or right of
       _____. The government cannot take property
       for _____ use or resale, it must take the
       property for public use.

26 Real Property

Review. Leases.

LEARNING OBJECTIVES

To become thoroughly familiar with leases.

CHAPTER CONTENTS

Tenancy for Years   Periodic Tenancy   Obligations of
Lessor and Lessee   Eviction   Rights of the Tenant
Glossary   Self Test

A very important right of a person who owns real property, and a very troublesome part of real property law, is the leasing of property. As you know, one who owns property and leases it for a period of time at an agreed rental is called a *lessor*, or landlord, and the person who goes into possession of the property for an agreed rental is called a *lessee*, or tenant. Generally the words *lessor* and *lessee* are used in commercial leases, and in apartment rentals or home rentals the words <u>landlord</u> and <u>tenant</u> are used, but there is no real distinction between them; lessor and landlord are the same, and lessee and tenant are the same.

TENANCY FOR YEARS

There are two basic types of lease, known as *tenancy for years* and *periodic tenancy*. A tenancy for years may be a lease that runs for one year, 10 years, 90 years, or for one week, one month, or 6 months. In other words, a tenancy for years does not actually have to run for a year. The lease clearly states that it shall run for a fixed time and terminates at a fixed time. Any lease is a tenancy for years that expires on a given date or a given time that can be computed.

PERIODIC TENANCY

A periodic tenancy may also be for a week or a month or years, but it merely provides for rental for that length of time without providing for automatic termination or expiration of the lease. There is no way to tell that such a weekly tenancy could not go on for up to 99 years, for there is no writing that says when it will terminate. A weekly rental is known as a tenancy by the week. Any lease, whether it is a tenancy by the week or is month-to-month tenancy or a tenancy for years, may be made orally if it is going to expire before one year is up. Any other lease that extends beyond a year must be in writing. But to have leases in writing is always a good idea, as we'll see below. The distinction between a tenancy for years and a periodic tenancy is important. Here is a written lease: "I, John Jones, agree to rent Sam Smith's house and pay $1,000 a year." This lease, you can see, does not state when it will terminate. It is a periodic tenancy, and at the end of the lease period, the year,

John Jones may have an obligation to continue to rent the
house for another whole year for $1,000. Had the lease
provided that "I, John Jones, agree to rent San Smith's
house for one year at a rental of $1,000 for that year,"
it would be a tenancy for years and the obligation would
terminate at the end of the year. But if the termination
was not stated in the lease and if there is a holding over,
or possession, after the termination of one year, the year-
to-year tenancy continues and in most states John Jones is
responsible for another year's rental.

OBLIGATIONS OF LESSOR AND LESSEE

The basic obligation of the landlord or lessor is to give
the tenant possession and continued occupancy of the
premises free from interference and annoyances. Also,
there is an implied obligation that the premises are suitable for habitation. In other words, that the floor will
not cave in under ordinary weight, that the ceiling will
not crash down, and that there is suitable plumbing and
heating to allow for normal living. That is an implied
obligation although it may be expressly waived in a lease.

The tenant or lessee has the obligation to pay the
rental agreed upon and to keep the property that he owns
during this period of lease in reasonable condition, and to
repair all damages that he may cause. In the normal
apartment or home lease, the landlord has the responsibility
of maintaining the stairways and halls and sidewalks that
are owned in common by all of the tenants. But the tenant
has the responsibility of keeping his own premises in
reasonable repair and condition and he implicitly, and in
most leases, expressly, agrees to return the premises to the
landlord in the same condition as he took them from the
landlord, ordinary wear and tear being excluded.

Now, if the lease is not in writing, or if the lease is
in writing but with no prohibition of subletting, the tenant
may sublet, or rent a portion of the leased premises to a
third party. If you are a tenant and you desire to sublet
a portion of your premises to a third party, you become a
landlord to the *subtenant*, but the true landlord still has a
right to look to you and enforce all of the obligations of
his lease against you. You do not replace your obligations
by subletting to another third party, you are still
responsible for all of the leased premises that you took
from the head lessor. You may not tell the landlord that
damage was caused by the subtenant or that the subtenant

didn't pay his rent on time. In most written leases, subletting the premises is prohibited without the express,
written consent of the landlord.

EVICTION

Eviction means that the landlord or lessor may remove the
tenant or lessee from the premises. There are two types of
eviction: *constructive eviction* and *actual eviction*.
Assume that your family has an apartment house on the fifth
floor of an apartment building and the landlord, without good
reason, removed the elevator or the stairs from the building,
and you can get to your apartment only by means of the fire
escape. This is constructive eviction, because the landlord
has interfered with your right to unobstructed possession
of the premises and your duty to pay rent at that time would
be ended. This happens very rarely.

In most states eviction must be preceded by written
notice of default by the tenant or lessee of one of the
terms of the lease. If the default, whether nonpayment of
rent, or damage to the property, or the noisy condition
of the premises, is not repaired within the period of time
granted in the notice, then the landlord has the right to
come in and remove the tenant from the premises and re-let or
re-lease the premises. This is actual eviction.

RIGHTS OF THE TENANT

Remember that the landlord agreed in his lease to give you
continued occupancy free from interference. Assume that
the landlord, by mistake or on purpose, lets or rents the
apartment to a third party even though you are not in default under your lease. You have two rights: You may
bring the landlord into court and ask the court to make the
landlord specifically perform the lease, that is, allow you
the continued occupancy of the premises free from interference, or you may treat a lease as terminated and breached
and sue the landlord for the damages—your moving expense
and the actual damages you suffered as a result of his
breach of the rental contract.

But assume that you have your apartment and your rent
is paid and your landlord has kept his warranties. Assume
also that you have the most common form of lease, a month-
to-month periodic lease—in other words, it does not state

when the lease will terminate. What are your rights in
giving notice to the landlord that you are moving out?
Generally in every state the law requires that you give
notice to your landlord equal to the rental period for which
you pay rent. For example, if your rent is due on the
first of each month on a month-to-month tenancy, then you
must give notice 30 days or one month in advance of the
termination of your rental contract. If you are on a week-
to-week periodic tenancy, then you must give notice of
your termination of the lease one week in advance of your
removal from the premises.

Assume that you have a month-to-month tenancy that is
a tenancy for years—that is, the lease will terminate on
a fixed date—and the rental period is one year after the
date of its execution. But say that 6 months after you have
gone into possession of the premises you want to move. What
type of notice must you give to your landlord to terminate
the lease? Now this is why earlier we mentioned the
importance of having a written release. If you had been
careful, you would have a provision of termination in the
lease which provided that you could give 30 days notice of
earlier cancellation than the normal expiration of the
lease. But if you hadn't gone into such a written release
with your landlord and carefully reviewed it and had it
written out the way you wanted it, then you would be
obligated to continue your rental payments for the full term
of the lease—that is, for the entire year. Now in most
states there are statutes that change this rule, but you
would want to know that before you entered into such a
lease. It is important in a tenancy for years to have a
clause allowing for earlier termination.

Now what happens if the property is destroyed by fire,
tornado, or earthquake and the landlord does not rebuild
the premises? What are your duties with respect to continuing to pay the rent? Under the common law you had a
duty to continue to pay the rent because the risk of loss
was on you, but in virtually every state a destruction by
fire that makes the premises untenantable releases you and
the landlord from all obligations under the lease. In other
words, the lease is terminated by operation of law.

What are the tenant's or lessee's rights to remove
fixtures from the premises? For example, you have an apartment and you have affixed curtain rods to the wall. You
have also placed your television antenna on the roof of the
apartment house because there is no common antenna, and you
have also placed wall-to-wall carpeting in the front room and
down the hallway. What are your rights of removal of these

fixtures? Again, it is extremely important for you to
have in mind the distinction between personal property and
fixtures which become part of the real property, and your
lease should provide explicitly that wall-to-wall carpeting,
the television antenna, and curtain rods shall be the
property of the tenant and may be removed at the expiration
of the lease or earlier termination. In general, you'll
remember that if the fixtures become so attached and firmly
affixed to the premises that to remove them would damage
the premises, then the property will probably belong to the
landlord upon the termination of the tenancy. Why? Because
they are fixtures and have become part of the real property
that you rented.

GLOSSARY TERMS

Actual eviction   Legal, physical removal of a tenant from the premises for default of some term in the lease and failure to repair.

Constructive eviction   Obstruction of the tenant's use of rented property by an unreasonable act of the landlord.

Eviction   The landlord's right to remove a tenant from the premises.

Landlord   A lessor.

Lease   A document giving occupancy of premises for a rent.

Lessee   The person to whom property is leased.

Lessor   The owner of property who leases it.

Periodic tenancy   A lease with no termination date.

Rent   The consideration for a lease on property.

Sublet   The renting, by a tenant, of rented property to a third party.

Subtenant   A tenant who is subletting from a tenant.

Tenancy for years   A lease that runs for a fixed, stated time and terminates on a fixed date.

Tenant   A lessee.

SELF TEST

CHAPTER 26

NAME_____

DATE_____

26.1   One who owns property and leases it for a period of
        time at an agreed rental is called a/an_____
        or _____, and the person who goes into
        possession of the property for an agreed rental is
        called a/an_____ or _____.

26.2   The two basic types of leases are known as a tenancy
        for _____ and a/an_____ tenancy.

26.3   Tenancy for _____ means that the lease
        terminates at a/an_____ time and it is clearly
        stated in the lease that it shall run for a/an
        _____ time.

26.4   A/An_____ tenancy does not provide for an
        automatic termination or _____ of the lease.

26.5   A lease that is going to expire before one _____
        is up may be made _____, but a lease that
        extends beyond this period of time must be in
        _____.

26.6   The basic obligation of the landlord is to give the
        tenant _____ and _____ occupancy of the
        premises free from _____ or _____.

26.7   The implied obligation of the landlord is that the
        premises are suitable for _____, but this
        obligation may be expressly _____ in a lease.

26.8   The tenant has the obligation to _____ the
        rental agreed upon and to keep the property that is
        being leased in _____ condition, and to repair
        all damages that are caused by the _____.

27 Real Property

Steps in Purchase of a Home

LEARNING OBJECTIVES

To study in detail the steps in buying a home, as a review of acquiring and holding real property.

CHAPTER CONTENTS

Earnest Money Receipts   Conditions of Purchase
Land-Sale Contracts   Mortgages   Satisfaction of Mortgage
Self Test

In this chapter, to review the concepts, the acquisition and ownership of real property, we are going to go step by step through what you do when you become a purchaser of real property—in our example, a home.

EARNEST MONEY RECEIPTS

My wife and I have found a four-bedroom home with a lot that is 70 feet by 102 feet. Let us say the price is $10,000. I've talked with the real estate agent and my wife and I have examined the home. The real estate agent puts before me a document called an earnest money receipt and says, "Mr. Jones, if you will put a deposit down, I'm sure that the seller will be willing to sell this home for $10,000, if you will make a bonafide offer upon the property." My wife and I are anxious to own the property, so I read the earnest money receipt, and it provides that I offer to buy the property and pay $500 down upon the property for 30 days; if the seller accepts my offer within 30 days the $500 will be applied to the purchase price. If the seller accepts my offer to purchase the property for $10,000 and for any reason he does not deliver title to the property for the $10,000, I get my $500 back. But if the seller is able to give me good title to the property for the purchase price and for any reason, I refuse to go ahead with the deal, then I lose my $500.

CONDITIONS OF PURCHASE

Thus, I look at the earnest money receipt with some care because I don't want to lose my $500. I notice that the earnest money receipt prepared by the real estate agent provides that I unconditionally offer to purchase the real property for $10,000. I tell the real estate agent, "We will have to change this because I will offer to purchase the real property on three conditions: First, that the seller can furnish good title to all of the real property without any liens or encumbrances upon the property; second, that I am able to get a bank loan for the purchase of the property, and am able to mortgage the property to the bank for the amount of the loan that I have obtained from the bank; third, that certain fixtures are specifically mentioned in the deed as being transferred with the property." (These fixtures could include the wall-to-wall carpeting, the TV

antenna, and any other fixtures about which we doubted the
seller's willingness to transfer with the real property.)

In addition, I place in the earnest money receipt a
provision that all real estate commissions shall be paid by
the seller, and that the real property taxes upon the real
property shall be prorated as of the time that the property
is transferred to my possession. For example, if one-half
of the tax year has expired, then the seller is responsible
for one-half of the real estate taxes on the property and
I'm responsible for the other half. With my $500 and the
earnest money receipt signed by me, I give the real estate
salesman a letter advising him to look to the seller for all
of his commission on this particular sale. The salesman
then takes the earnest money receipt and offer to the seller.
If the seller agrees to the terms of my offer, he writes
his acceptance upon the earnest money receipt—exactly as
the contract law requires: an offer accepted upon the terms
of the offer. I receive a copy of the earnest money receipt
accepted by the seller and I go to the bank and request
financing for the purchase of the home. If the bank is
willing to loan the money, they will require, first, a
title report showing that good title rests in the seller
and second, that my wife and I sign a promissory note and
a mortgage once title has been transferred to my possession.

LAND-SALE CONTRACTS

After I have obtained a written commitment from the bank
for the necessary funds, I enter into a land-sale contract
with the purchaser: I agree to purchase the property
upon the terms that I have already agreed to in the conditional offer of purchase, and we provide for such things
as closing the sale in escrow so that the bank can send its
loan funds to an escrow, or third party agent, to hold,
and the seller shall give his deed and his wife's deed to
the escrow agents.

Once the escrow agents have received the funds, they
will make the necessary distribution. They will pay part
of the taxes; they will pay for the title insurance policy
which I have demanded; and they will pay the real estate
agent his commission, and the remainder of the funds will
go to the seller. After the funds are distributed, the
deed is then given to my possession and I and my wife are
the owners of the property. If the escrow agent has not
recorded the deed I immediately do so.

MORTGAGES

Thereafter, the bank and I enter into a mortgage in which
I pledge the property to secure the loan that they have
made to me and my wife. My wife joins in the mortgage as
well because, as you remember, she and I both hold title to
this property, and a mortgage by one person who holds title
is not binding upon the other person's title to the property.
Thus, the bank insists that we both sign the mortgage and
promissory note. After the mortgage is signed, the bank
immediately records it to give notice to the world that the
property has a lien upon it to the extent of the mortgage
loan.

We go into possession of the property and we find that
all of the fixtures that we have contracted to purchase, and
which were included in the deed to my wife and me, are
in place on the property. We are happy that we were careful in preparing the land-sale contract and in looking over
the deed, which was a full warranty deed. Our title insurance policy, paid for by the seller, insures that we have
fee simple title to the property in my wife's and my name,
and, of course, when my wife and I hold property we hold as
tenants by the entirety.

SATISFACTION OF MORTGAGE

After 20 years of payments upon our mortgage and note, we
have finally paid off our promissory note and mortgage.
The bank returns the original mortgage to us together with
a document called a satisfaction of mortgage. I immediately
take the satisfaction of mortgage over to the County Courthouse and have it recorded so that all the world will know
that at last my wife and I, as tenants by the entirety,
own our home and real property free and clear of all liens
and encumbrances.

SELF TEST
CHAPTER 27

NAME_____

DATE_____

27.1 When a husband and wife purchase property jointly,
both must join in the mortgage because _____
to the property is held by both, and a mortgage by
one person who holds title is not _____
upon the other person's _____ to the property.

28 Real Property

Duties of Owners and Occupiers. Duty of Seller to Buyer for Condition of Property.

LEARNING OBJECTIVES

To learn the duties owed to others by owners and occupiers of real property.

CHAPTER CONTENTS

Duties Owed to Persons Off the Premises   Duties Owed to Trespassers   Duties Owed to Licensees   Duties Owed to Invitees   Duties of Sellers to Buyers of Real Property   Glossary   Self Test

In this chapter we will look at the rights and duties that
owners and occupiers of land have once they occupy the
premises. *Occupiers* of land, of course, are those people
that do not own the fee simple in the land but have
possession of the real property by legal right, such
as by an easement or a lease.

There are four different categories of legal duties
that an owner or occupier owes to others upon and outside
the premises.

DUTIES OWED TO PERSONS OFF THE PREMISES

What is the duty of a land owner or occupier to someone
passing in front of his property—passing on a thoroughfare, or street, or upon a neighbor's property, but
not upon the owner's or occupier's property? The general
rule throughout the country is: A possessor of land is
required to make reasonable use of his premises which
causes no unreasonable harm to those in the vicinity,
either through the character of the use itself, or
through the manner in which it is conducted. An
occupier's liability may be based upon intent, upon
negligence, or upon a condition or activity for which
strict liability may be imposed. In particular, he is
required to exercise reasonable care for the protection
of those using the public highway. Throughout this
country there is no liability for conditions of purely
natural origin existing on the land, but there are
indications that a different rule is developing for city
or urban land, as we will see further below.

You just read that if you use reasonable care in
the activities upon your premises, you have no liability
for injury to another occurring off your premises.
However, we saw in earlier chapters that if we have a
smoky, odorous, or noisy factory, we may be guilty of a
private nuisance and be enjoined from that activity by
a court of law if it substantially damages other users
of the property. But there are restrictions on this
liability; we are not liable for injuries occurring to
someone off our premises arising from the natural condition of the land. Say I own a piece of land that fronts
a road, and on its corner stands an old, majestic oak
tree. I am unaware that the oak is rotten in the middle,
but during a windstorm the oak tree topples over upon the
street. A car later crashes into the oak tree. Am I

liable for that condition upon my premises which caused
the tree to go across my property line and upon the
public road? Generally, no. However, if the oak tree
had been allowed to remain in the public thoroughfare for
an unreasonable length of time, and a car crashed into it,
I could be liable for the resultant damage to the automobile or personal injury to its occupants. The rule
about natural conditions upon the property cover only
natural conditions to property. For example, if my
property fronts upon a public road and I cut away the
bank of my property and thus make the ground unstable, and
if the ground caves in upon the public road and someone
is injured or property damage occurs, I may be liable
for my conduct on the property, because the instability
of the property was not its natural condition.

We mentioned above that the rule on natural conditions is changing for city lands. Many times courts
have held that although property in its natural condition
in the country would not invoke liability upon the
owner for damage that had occurred, in the city a
different rule is imposed. By statute, sometimes, and
city ordinances it is incumbent upon property owners to
shovel away the snow that falls upon the sidewalk in
front of their property, so that passers-by will not be
injured by the slipperiness of the sidewalk. These
ordinances have been held constitutional and enforcable
against the property owner, and if someone is injured
and the property owner has not removed the snow within
a reasonable time, liability may be imposed even though
the condition of the property was natural.

For another example, say Mr. Black built a bakery
and upon its front he had a sign company erect a large
neon sign saying, "Black's Bakery." Mr. Black could
not climb the wall of his building and inspect the sign
each day to make sure that the bolts holding it to the
building were sound, but some 80 days after the sign
was installed it came crashing down upon the sidewalk,
very seriously injuring Mr. Brown. Mr. Brown went to
court, suing Mr. Black for the negligent installation
of the sign which caused it to come loose from the
building and hurt Mr. Brown. Mr. Black, through his
attorney, contended that he wasn't negligent; he had had
a sign company put the sign up and he thought it was
adequately attached to the building, but he certainly
hadn't been guilty of negligence.

As a matter of law, should Mr. Brown recover for the negligent installation of the sign which allowed it to fall 80 days after it had been installed? Or should Mr. Black be allowed a defendant's verdict because he proved that he didn't put the sign up and wasn't negligent in its construction? The answer is not clear in this case, but probably Mr. Brown, the injured party, has a better chance of winning before most judges. For although the law states generally that you are not liable for damage to people who are not on your premises if you've used reasonable care, another rule of law says that, in the ordinary course of events, signs do not fall down 80 days after they are constructed if they have been constructed and attached to a building with reasonable care. So in this case, Mr. Black would be liable to Mr. Brown, because it could be presumed that the sign was not carefully attached to the building. In all likelihood, Mr. Black could recover from the sign company, the damages and court costs that he had to pay.

DUTIES OWED TO TRESPASSERS

The second category of owner's and occupier's duties to others is the duty to trespassers upon our land. Now here you might think that if someone trespasses upon your land you don't owe him a duty. But you do. Although not much of a duty, it is a legal duty. Although a general rule applies to trespassers—"No affirmative duty is owed to a trespasser by a landowner"—there are two exceptions to this rule. Although we have no *affirmative duty* to prospective trespassers—we need neither fence our land to keep them out nor award damages to, say, a trespasser who climbs a rotten limb on our tree and falls and is injured—the two exceptions are (1) that if the trespasser is discovered upon the premises, the possessor generally must exercise reasonable care for his safety, as to any active operation the possessor may be carrying on, and as to any highly dangerous condition on the land; and (2) if the owner or occupier of land knows that trespassers frequently intrude upon a particular place or limited area of his land, he is required to exercise reasonable care as to any activities carried on, and probably as to dangerous conditions.

For an example, a large construction company is building a 20-story building downtown. An old man is

seen to walk upon the construction site. The contractor
cannot lower a large crane directly over the old man's
head. That's highly dangerous and he has a duty not to
increase this trespasser's chance of injury. Also, he
sees the old man walking toward a large excavation in the
ground that has just been dug and is still not stable and
may cave in. The contractor has an affirmative duty to
warn the old man to stay away from that excavation even
though he's a trespasser. It's a humanitarian instinct.
Even though the old man has no right to be upon the
property, we don't want to increase his hazard by a
dangerous condition or a highly dangerous operation. So,
the exception to the rule is, if you know a trespasser
is upon your property, you do have an affirmative duty
to warn him of your hazardous activity and of an extremely
hazardous condition upon the property.
     For an example of the second exception, say Mr.
Jones owned a lumberyard and he knew that workers in a
nearby factory walked from their parking lot across his
lumberyard to get to the factory. He gave them no easement or license to go upon his premises, but he knew that
they did trespass. He also knew of a large, unstable
stack of old rotten lumber that had been on the property
many years in the vicinity of the trespassing. One day
the stack of lumber came crashing down upon one of the
trespassing workmen, seriously injuring him. The owner of
the property was held liable because he knew of the frequent
trespassing next to this pile of lumber and he knew of
its dangerous condition. The court held him liable, for
he had an affirmative duty either to stop the trespassers
from coming upon the dangerous area of his land or to
remedy the dangerous condition.
     This rule about dangerous conditions holds especially
for children, who are always curious about things that
are high and wobbly and things that are dangerous—
swimming pools and unguarded wells and all such things.
If an owner or occupier knows, or should know, that
children trespass upon his property, he has an affirmative
duty to guard this condition from the inquisitive hands
and eyes of small children, and he may be held liable if
he did know of the trespassing children and did not
guard against this dangerous condition.

DUTIES OWED TO LICENSEES

A *licensee*, as we learned in an earlier chapter, is a person
who has the owner's or occupier's consent to enter upon
the land of another. They may be, for example, people
who are taking shortcuts across property. If your front
yard is a shortcut for neighborhood children and you
don't keep them off the premises, they're licensees—you
allow them to use the front yard. A licensee can also
be the garbage man, the milkman, or the mailman.
Sometimes spectators, who are not invited upon the premises for profit, come to look at something that is occurring on the property. Or someone who comes over to your
house to borrow tools may be a licensee.

What duty do we owe such a person, one who has our
consent to come upon the property but not our express
invitation? First, although as owner or occupier we
do not have an affirmative duty of making the property
safe for him, we must use reasonable care to avoid injuring him by our activities upon the land. For example,
I can't back my car out of my garage and run over the
mailman. I must use care as I drive out of my driveway as
he comes to deliver the mail.

Second, I must use reasonable care to warn him of
any concealed dangerous conditions or activities which
are known to me but which are hidden to him. For
example, when the garbageman comes to our premises, we
have a duty of warning him if we have a dangerous dog
upon the premises, and we have a duty of exercising
reasonable care to see that the dog does not bite the
garbageman. Or if one of my children has dug a hole in
the yard and put a cover over it—a trap, in effect—we
have a duty of warning the garbagemen not to step into
that trap. We have, then, a duty to avoid injuring
him by our activities and to use reasonable care in
warning him of any hazard or condition that we know of
but that he might not know of.

DUTIES OWED TO INVITEES

An *invitee* is a person who is invited or permitted to
enter or remain on land for the purpose of the occupier.
Anyone I invite upon my land for my profit or pleasure
is an invitee, and as an owner or occupier of land, I
am required to exercise reasonable care to warn the

invitee of any danger coming from the condition of the property or my activities on it. I also have an affirmative duty to make the premises safe for the invitee, and to remedy any dangerous condition that I know of, or should reasonably know of, so that the invitee will not be injured.

Say I own a small store and I invite, by my advertising, the public to come in and make purchases in my store. Mrs. Jones comes in and as she is walking up to the counter to make a purchase, she stumbles over a broom left in the aisle by one of my employees. She falls and is seriously injured. I am liable for that injury to Mrs. Jones, for I had a duty to warn her of the dangerous condition, the broom left in the aisle, and I also had the affirmative duty of not leaving it in the aisle.

But say that Mrs. Jones has come into my store to make a purchase, and not finding what she wants in the front part of the store, where the public is invited, she goes, without my invitation or knowledge, down into the basement stockroom of my store. It is not well lit, and as she is rummaging around through our stock in the basement, she stumbles and falls over a broom in the aisle of the stockroom. I am not liable because I did not invite her to go into the stockroom. She was, in fact, a trespasser into the stockroom, even though she was an invitee to the public area of the premises.

Quite frequently a woman comes into a grocery store and goes over to the vegetable counter. While walking along the vegetable counter, she steps on a banana peel or a lettuce leaf, slips, falls, and is injured. Is the store liable, as a matter of law, for her injuries? No, for not every momentary condition imposes liability. The injured party must prove that the banana peel or lettuce leaf had lain on the floor an unreasonable length of time, and therefore, that the store owner either didn't inspect sufficiently, which is one of his duties, or when he did inspect, failed to see the banana peel or lettuce leaf and pick it up so that someone would not be injured. But if a lettuce leaf falls to the floor and immediately thereafter a person comes and steps on it, there is no liability. There must be some proof that the lettuce leaf or banana peel was there for a sufficient period of time so that the duty of inspection, if followed by the owner or occupier of the store, would have noted the banana peel and removed it.

DUTIES OF SELLERS TO BUYERS OF REAL PROPERTY

Before we leave real property we shall discuss very
briefly the duty that a vendor, or seller, of real
property owes to a vendee, or purchaser, of property—
that is, to what extend the vendor is liable for the
condition of property that he sells to a vendee. In
most jurisdictions of this country, the vendor of real
property is not liable to the vendee or to a third person
for the defective or dangerous condition of the property.
However, the vendor is required to disclose to the vendee
any concealed defects or danger in the property of which
he has knowledge, and which creates an unreasonable risk
of harm to the vendee or a third party. For example,
Mr. Brown is selling his home to Mr. Smith. Mr. Brown
knows that a large marble slab that makes up the mantle-
piece above the fireplace is very loose, is poorly held
in place by its cement, but he does not tell Mr. Smith
of this dangerous condition. Mr. Smith goes into
possession of the property, and one evening while he is
lighting a fire in the fireplace, the mantle slab comes
loose, falls, and injures him. Mr. Brown, the vendor,
would be liable for those injuries for a reasonable period
of time, because he knew of the dangerous condition in
the premises and did not advise the vendee. In most
jurisdictions this rule is also extended to the vendor
for conditions upon the property which the vendor knew had
a large potential for creating damage or injury to
people outside of the premises.

Therefore, a vendor has reasonable responsibilities
of calling hidden defects to the attention of a vendee,
provided the vendor himself knows of the hidden defects,
and if the vendor does not call known hidden defects to
the attention of the vendee, he may be liable for subsequent damage and injury to the vendee or third party.
Keep in mind that this duty arises only with respect to
hidden defects. Normally, defects that are open to view
and inspection are purchased by the vendee, and the
liability of the vendor terminates upon the transfer of
title. In other words, you buy real property as is, and
the vendor is liable for only those hidden defects of which he
had knowledge but didn't advise you.

GLOSSARY TERMS

Affirmative duty A duty to protect trespassers from hazards on property or to mitigate or correct hazards in areas of frequent trespassing.

Invitee A person invited or permitted to enter or remain on property for the purpose of the occupier.

Licensee A person who has the owner's or occupant's consent to enter or cross the property of another.

SELF TEST

CHAPTER 28

NAME_____

DATE_____

28.1 A possessor of land is required to make _____ use of his premises which causes no unreasonable _____ to those in the vicinity, either by reason of the _____ of the use itself, or because of the manner in which it is conducted.

28.2 An occupier's liability may be based upon _____, upon _____, or upon a condition or activity upon which strict liability may be _____.

28.3 It is a general rule throughout the country that there is no _____ for conditions of purely _____ _____ existing on the land.

28.4 The general rule concerning the duties that an owner or occupier owes trespassers is: "No _____ duty is owed to a trespasser by a/an _____."

28.5 If a trespasser is discovered upon the premises, the possessor generally must exercise _____ care for his _____, as to any active operation the possessor may be carrying on, and as to any highly _____ condition on the land.

28.6 If the owner or occupier of land knows that trespassers _____ intrude upon a/an _____ place or limited area of his land, he is required to exercise _____ care as to any activities carried on, and probably as to dangerous conditions. This rule, with respect to dangerous condition, is especially true when _____ are the trespassers.

28.7 A/An _____ is a person who is privileged to enter upon the land of another by virtue of the owner or occupier's _____.

28.8 An owner or occupier does not have a/an _____ duty of making the property _____ for a licensee, but does have a duty to use reasonable

care to avoid _____ him by activities upon
the land. Also, the owner or occupier must warn
a licensee of a dangerous _____ condition.

28.9   A/An_____ is a person who is explicitly
invited upon or allowed to remain upon the
premises for the purposes of the owner or
occupier.

28.10 The owner or occupier is under an affirmative
duty to make the premises safe for a/an_____,
and to _____ any known dangerous condition
so that injury will be avoided.

28.11 An owner or occupier has an affirmative duty to
make a/an_____ of the public portion of the
premises to make sure no dangerous or hidden
conditions exist.

28.12 It is not every _____ condition that
imposes liability on an owner/occupier.

28.13 The vendor, or seller of property, is required
to disclose to the _____, or buyer of
property, any _____ defects or danger in
the property of which he has _____, and
which creates an unreasonable _____ of
harm to the vendee or a third party.

28.14 Normally, defects that are open to view and
_____ are purchased by the vendee, and the
liability of the vendor _____ upon the
transfer of title.

29 Employment

Legal Relationship

LEARNING OBJECTIVES

To learn the definitions of an employer and an employee.

To learn the types of employment contracts.

To learn the implied duties of an employee to an employer.

CHAPTER CONTENTS

In this and the next chapter we will discuss employer-employee relationships—the law of employment. A legal relationship exists between employer and employee.

EMPLOYERS AND EMPLOYEES

The law describes an *employer* as a person who hires another to work for him for an agreed consideration. An *employee* is any person who agrees to do work subject to the direction and control of another for consideration.

Say Mr. Jones owns a grocery store and he agrees to hire Tom Smith to work Saturdays as a carry-out boy and to pay him $7 a Saturday. Tom Smith says, "Yes. I'll come to work for you for $7 a day for each Saturday I work and I'll show up at 9 o'clock in the morning and leave at 5:30." An employment contract has been created because Mr. Jones has agreed to hire the services of another to work for him for an agreed consideration, and the employee has agreed to work for another for an agreed consideration.

The consideration for the employment need not be in the form of a salary or wage. Many times young people will approach an employer and say, "May I come to work for you and be bound by your instructions for the experience?" and sometimes an employer will be willing to train a young person on the job without payment of salary for the work performed. But this system of employment—which used to be called apprenticeship—is rapidly being replaced in our society by the education that students receive in school, and most people today receive a monetary compensation for their employment. An *employment contract* is, therefore, an agreement between the employer and the employee that the employee will work for the employer and be subject to the employer's direction and control for an agreed consideration.

EMPLOYMENT CONTRACTS

The employment contract may be in writing, it may be oral or it may be implied, because it is a contract, and you'll remember from our earlier chapters that a contract may be in writing, or oral, or implied in fact or in law. An employment contract requires all of the legal elements of any other type of contract: offer, acceptance, consideration, and lawful object.

When Mr. Jones hired Tom Smith for Saturday work in his grocery store, they made an oral contract of employment. Mr. Jones hired Tom Smith for one day a week, but *not* for one day a week for the next five years. If he had entered into a five-year contract in which Tom Smith would be expected to work on Saturdays for five years, the contract would have to be in writing. For you'll remember that a contract that cannot be performed within one year must be put in writing. But this oral contract could be performed within one year, that is, each Saturday. It might extend beyond one year but it could be terminated at any time prior to the expiration of one year.

DIRECT WRITTEN CONTRACTS

A direct written contract involves an offer and an acceptance of the offer, and the terms of the contract are clear. For example, say Mr. Jones owns a shoe store and he agrees to hire Mr. Smith as a salesman, and they enter into a letter agreement. Mr. Jones writes a letter to Mr. Smith stating, "I want you to come to work for me, and you will be paid $200 a week plus 3% commission on the gross sales that you make." Mr. Smith writes back and says, "I accept your offer of employment, and I will begin work on Monday of next week."

COLLECTIVE BARGAINING—UNION CONTRACTS

Often the employee does not deal directly with the employer, but his interests and rights are represented by his union, and the union has a right to bargain for the employees. This is known as *collective bargaining*; the union representative meets with the representative of the employer and sets the terms and conditions of the employment for all of the members of the union working for that employer.

The laws of employment between unions and management are very complex; there are literally thousands of lawyers, judges, and representatives of labor and management dealing every day with them. But briefly the

union contract comes about when a majority of the
employees of a given employer hold an election, supervised by the federal government, and determine that a
specific union will represent their interests with their
employer. After the election has been certified as being
accurate and honest, the elected union is the bargaining
agent for the employees and has the exclusive right to
determine and bargain for the rights of the employees
with the employer.

Various U.S. states have passed laws of their own
relating to the types of contract that a union may hold
with an employer. Briefly, there are four types of
union contracts that can be entered into in the various
50 states: the closed shop; the union shop; the
agency shop; and the open shop.

A *closed shop* is a company in which the union has
the right to have employed in that shop only union
members; prospective employees must become union members
before they can be employed by the employer. In many
states, the closed shop union contract is illegal.

A *union shop* is a company or employer that agrees
with the union to require new employees to join the
union within a specified period of time—normally 30
days. For example, John Smith applied for employment
at the Ajax factory; they accepted his application for
employment and he reported to work. Immediately after
he came to work, a union agent contacted him and told him
that he must make application for the union and become
a union member within 30 days.

In an *agency shop* a union represents the employees
or a portion of them, and the union has entered into
an agreement with the employer that although no employee
is required to join the union, all employees must pay
dues to the union, to be deducted by the employer from
wages. The argument for the agency shop is that many of
the good working conditions were provided to meet the
demands of the union and that therefore the employees
who do not belong to the union should help support the
union that made those working conditions possible for them
also to benefit from. Agency shops are very rare.

An *open shop* is one in which there is no agreement
or contract between the employer and any union regarding
union membership of employees or requirement that they
be union members. Similarly, the employer by law may
not fire an employee merely because he happens to belong
to a union.

IMPLIED CONTRACTS

Since by the law of contracts a contract may be implied,
an employment contract may also be implied. Allen
Andrews, a senior at Central High went down to Mr. Bill
Bates' taxicab company and said, "Mr. Bates, is there
anything I can do down here for you after school that
might be helpful to you? I want some part-time employment." Mr. Bates said, "Yes. If you'll come down after
school Mondays through Fridays and wash two of my taxis
each day, that would be very helpful. I'll agree to
have you as an employee." So Allen came down for a month
each day after school and washed two cabs a day for
Mr. Bates, and into the second month he hadn't been paid
anything and he went into Mr. Bates and said, "Mr. Bates,
I wondered if I could get paid for the work I've done for
you for the last 30 days. I've come down each day after
school and washed cabs." And Mr. Bates said, "Well,
son, I don't owe you anything. You wanted to come to
work down here to be helpful to me and I said 'Yes, you
sure could be helpful by coming down and washing these
cars for me,' but I didn't agree to pay you anything."
But obviously the law implies a promise by Mr. Bates to
pay reasonable compensation to Allen, his employee. So
Allen would receive reasonable compensation for the work
that he had performed.

This can also serve as a precaution in another
respect. If Allen had brought his own buckets, hoses,
and detergent to use on the taxicabs, he might be viewed
as an *independent contractor* and not an employee. He
would still be entitled to the reasonable value for his
services, but he might not be considered an employee.
But if Allen used all of Mr. Bates' equipment and took
direction from his foreman as to how to wash the taxicabs
and which cabs to wash and when to do them, then he would
be under the direction and control of Mr. Bates and be
considered an employee.

EMPLOYEE'S DUTIES—EMPLOYER'S RIGHTS

As you know from earlier chapters, every right has a
reciprocal duty. The employee has certain duties that the
employer has a right to expect. The employee's first
duty to his employer is to <u>follow reasonable instructions</u>;
an employment contract requires that the employee subject

himself to the reasonable direction and control of the
employer. When I go to work for another person there
will be certain rules and directions that the employer
will have for the employee, and it is implied in the law
that, as an employee, I must follow these reasonable
rules and instructions. I am not required to follow
every direction or rule that the employer has—it must be
reasonable. For example, an employer cannot ask or
force me to climb a telephone pole to secure a wire or
a banner to it for the employer's purpose unless I was
hired specifically to do that job and am competent to
do it. But if I were hired as an office employee,
obviously that would not be a reasonable instruction and
I would not have to follow it.

Another duty that an employee has which is implied
in law, is the duty of loyalty to the employer. Loyalty
is a negative duty; that is, an employee is not required
to do anything affirmative or positive to advertise or
promote his employer's business. But he is under a
duty not to do anything which positively damages or
injures it. For example, a man who owns a grocery store
and has three employees has no right to demand that his
employees buy their groceries from his store, nor does
he have a right to demand that in their off hours the
employees go around telling their friends and neighbors
that their employer's grocery store is the best in town,
with the best products and service. The employee has no
affirmative duty of promoting the employer's business
unless the employee is specifically hired to do so.

But the employer does have a right that the employees
do not by their acts and statements damage the employer.
The grocery store employer has a right to terminate the
employment of an employee who goes about town saying, "My
employer's grocery store has terrible products and
merchandise and gives terrible service and is over-
priced."

Every job that you and I take as an employee implies
a duty upon us that we will be reasonably competent to
fulfill the tasks that the job requires of us. We may
not have to be experts or geniuses at the particular
job, but we have to be reasonably competent to fulfill the
obligations of our employment. For example, an employer
desires to hire Miss Jones as a secretary. He looks at
her typing speed and stenographic ability, he asks her
about her experience, and is satisfied with her basic

qualifications. He employs Miss Jones as a secretary
and after she has been on the job several weeks the
employer finds that Miss Jones can type well, take
dictation well, and do other stenographic chores—but she
cannot spell. Now obviously a secretary sending business
mail out must be able to spell words that have been
dictated to her. This is an implied basis of her
employment—that she is reasonably competent in spelling
words in the English language. But you would be surprised
how many secretaries are not basically competent in
spelling skills and, therefore, are not retained as
employees of business firms.

The final implied duty of an employee is to perform
tasks assigned. How does performance of tasks assigned
differ from competence and following reasonable instructions? It differs in this way: As an employee you must
come to work to do the job you are assigned to do. You
cannot go drink coffee or be absent from your place of
employment. You must perform the job that you are hired
to perform (this includes, of course, following reasonable
instructions as well as basic competence).

GLOSSARY TERMS

Agency shop   An employer-union arrangement whereby
    although no one must join the union that represents
    some of the employees, everyone must pay union
    dues.

Closed shop   An employer with a union contract by which
    all employees must become union members before
    being hired by the employer.

Collective bargaining   Union representation of the
    employees and their rights.

Employee   Any person who agrees to do work for another,
    subject to his direction and control, for an agreed
    consideration.

Employer   A person who hires another to work for him for
    an agreed consideration.

Employment contract   An agreement between employer and
    employee that the employee will work for the
    employer and be subject to his direction and control
    for an agreed consideration.

Open shop   A place of employment in which there is no
    agreement or contract between employer and union
    about union membership of employees or requirement
    of membership.

Union shop   An employer that has agreed with the union
    representing its employees that all new employees must
    join the union within a specified period.

SELF TEST

CHAPTER 29

NAME_____

DATE_____

29.1   An employment relationship consists of two parties,
       the _____ and _____.

29.2   The _____ describes a/an _____ as a
       person who hires another to work for him for an
       agreed consideration.

29.3   A person would not be an employer of his son
       because his son is expected to participate in the
       _____ of his own home.

29.4   It is not always necessary that the consideration
       for the employment be in the form of a/an_____
       or _____.

29.5   A/An_____ is an agreement between the
       employer and the employee that the employee will
       _____ for the employer, and be subject to
       the employer's direction and _____ for an
       agreed _____.

29.6   An employment contract requires the legal elements
       of _____, _____, _____, and
       _____ object.

29.7   An employment contract that cannot be performed
       within one year must be put in _____ to be
       enforceable.

29.8   A/An_____ is any person who agrees to do
       work subject to the direction and control of
       another for agreed consideration.

29.9   The main types of employment contracts are
       _____ and _____ contracts.

29.10 Collective bargaining is where the representative
       of the _____ meets with the representa-
       tive of the _____ and sets the terms and
       conditions of the employment for _____ of
       the _____ of the union that work for the
       employer.

29.11 A closed shop is a/an_____ in which the union
       has the right to have employed in that shop

only _____, and they must become union
members _____ they can be employed by the
employer. In many states, closed shop union
contracts are _____.

29.12   The most typical type of union contract entered
today is that of a/an_____ shop.

29.13   A/An_____ shop is a company that agrees
with the union that, within a specified period of
time, any new employee that comes to work will
join the union that represents the current
employees.

29.14   An agency shop is one wherein the union represents
the employees, or a/an_____ of the employees,
and they have entered into an agreement with the
employer in which they agree that _____ must
belong to the union, but that _____
employees will pay union _____ to the
union.

29.15   A/An_____ shop is one in which there is no
agreement between the employer and the union
regarding union _____ of employees or
requirement that they be _____; however,
the employer by _____ may not fire an
employee merely because he belongs to a/an_____.

29.16   As previously discussed, the four different types
of employment relationships which relate to
unions are: closed shop, _____ shop,
_____ shop, and _____ shop.

29.17   In addition to _____ and written,
employment contracts may be _____.

29.18   A person might be considered an independent
_____ and not an employee if he is not
subject to the _____ and control of the
person who hired him.

29.19   Every right has a/an_____ duty.

29.20   The first duty that an employee has to his
employer is the duty of following reasonable
_____.

29.21   Another duty that an employee has which is
implied in _____ is the duty of _____
to the employer.

29.22   Loyalty of an employee to an employer really
means a/an_____ duty. An employee is not
required to do anything affirmative or _____
to advertise or _____ his employer's
business; but he is under a duty not to do

CHAPTER 29

NAME_____

      anything which positively _____ or
      _____ the employer's business.

29.23 The employee also has a duty of reasonable
      _____ to fulfill the _____ of his
      employment.

29.24 The final implied duty of an employee is perfor-
      mance of _____ _____.

29.25 In conclusion, then, there are four _____
      obligations of an employee in every employment
      contract: _____ reasonable instructions,
      _____ to the employer, reasonable
      _____, and _____ of tasks
      assigned.

30 Employment

Employer's Duties—Employee's Rights.
Labor Laws.

LEARNING OBJECTIVES

To learn the rights of the employee and duties of the employer under employment contracts.

To learn the state and federal laws regulating employment and the safety of employees.

CHAPTER CONTENTS

Employer's Duties—Employee's Rights   Workmen's Compensation Laws   Unemployment Compensation Laws   Workers' Safety Laws   Child Labor Laws and Women's Working Laws   Laws on Wages and Hours and Fair Employment Laws   Social Security   Self Test

In the previous chapter we discussed the employee's duties and the rights of the employer; in this chapter we will look at the employer's duties and the employee's rights.

EMPLOYER'S DUTIES—EMPLOYEE'S RIGHTS

Since an employer is a person who hired another to do work for him for an agreed consideration, the first duty that the law imposes upon an employer is the duty to pay the consideration agreed upon. While consideration is usually money, it can be something else. For example, Mr. Jones owes Mr. Brown $100. Mr. Jones offers to work for Mr. Brown for one week if Mr. Brown will cancel the debt at the end of that week. Mr. Brown agrees, and at the end of the week's work, Mr. Jones and Mr. Brown agree that the debt is canceled. No money was turned over from Mr. Brown to Mr. Jones for the week's work but good consideration was given by Mr. Brown's cancellation of the $100 debt.

The duty of the employer is to make payment of the consideration agreed upon, otherwise the employee has a right to abandon the job and the employment relationship. If the employment relationship consists of an agreed upon weekly, two-week, or monthly payment and if the employer fails to make the payment upon the terms and at the times agreed upon, then the employee has the right to terminate and abandon the employment relationship. And if back salary is owed to the employee, he has a right to bring suit for the collection of his wages.

In the majority of states, statutes protect employees in recovering their wages. If an employer has willfully and wrongfully withheld wages from an employee, many states provide that the employee may recover double his wages that he would otherwise be entitled to plus his court costs and attorney's fees. So there is protection in many states for an employee who is unfortunate enough to work for an unscrupulous employer.

The second implied duty of an employer in the employment relationship is to provide a reasonably safe place for the employee to work in; whether the place of employment is an office, a factory, a farm, or whatever. There are different standards for the different types of employment. Obviously standards for an iron foundry would not

be applicable to an office. Water on an office floor
might be unreasonably hazardous, while water on the floor
of iron foundry many times is a necessary part of the
work itself and is reasonable so long as the water is not
an ultrahazardous condition.

Similarly, whether a condition of employment is
reasonably safe or not depends upon the location; what
may be reasonable in Portland, Oregon, may not be
reasonable in New York City, or Galveston, Texas. The
standard of the community governs what is reasonable and
what is not reasonable. But the duty remains the same—
that is, reasonable care must be taken by the employer
to furnish a safe place to work for all employees.

The employer also must furnish to his workers reasonably safe tools and equipment with which to do their jobs.
If an employer furnishes to an employee defective equipment and the employee is injured by the equipment, then
the employer has breached his contract of employment and
the employee may recover compensation for his injuries.
In addition, if the employer has not furnished his
employees with reasonably safe tools and equipment, the
employees may walk off the job and abandon the employment
relationship and not be liable to the employer for any
damages occurring because the job was not completed on
time. This seems a fair rule: As employees we have
agreed to follow the directions and control of the
employer and to exercise our best competence to get the
job done; we should not be asked to risk our lives, health,
or welfare. So we have these reciprocal duties and
reciprocal rights.

The employer also has the duty to furnish reasonably
competent workmen. Just as he must provide a safe
working place and safe tools he must provide reasonably
competent co-workers if the job requires two or more
people to work on it. If I and a co-worker are on a
construction project that requires the lifting and carrying of heavy objects, then my co-worker should be able
to carry heavy objects. Or if we are doing welding work,
my co-worker should be reasonably competent as a welder
so that I can proceed with the job and he can help me
with it reasonably competently, and vice versa.

The fifth duty of an employer implied in an employment contract is the duty to protect from wrongful
assault. It is imperative that the employer protect each
employee from the assault of any other of his employees.

For example, say an employee of the Ajax Company is told
by the employer's foreman, "Go run and get a hammer
for me so that I can finish the construction of this
particular building." The employee begins to walk to the
tool shed and the foreman shouts at him, "Get a move on"
and picks up a rock and throws it at the employee to get
him moving faster. The rock strikes the employee. At
that point the foreman has been guilty of a wrongful assault
upon the employee and the employee is within his rights
to abandon his employment. And if he is injured, the
employer is responsible for compensation to the employee
for that injury. The employer must refrain from wrongful
assaults upon employees even to get the employee to
exercise his duties of competence and performance of
tasks.

But to change the example somewhat, say Mr. Huggins
works for the Ajax Company as a carpenter, and on the
job one of his fellow carpenters, Mr. Brown, loses his
temper while he is talking with Mr. Huggins and strikes
him. Mr. Huggins reports this to the foreman and the
foreman immediately fires Mr. Brown for losing his temper
and striking Mr. Huggins. Mr. Huggins remains on the
job but later discovers a further injury or complication
from the beating he took from Mr. Brown. Mr. Huggins then
brings suit against the employer, Ajax Construction
Company, for the beating he received from Mr. Brown. Ajax
Construction Company says, "We're not liable for the
assault of Mr. Brown as we did not know that he was given
to violent outbursts of temper, and immediately upon
discovering that characteristic of him, we fired Mr.
Brown." The courts would probably not hold the employer
liable for the beating that Mr. Huggins received, because
Ajax Construction Company, using reasonable care in hiring
a competent carpenter to work with Mr. Huggins, did not
know that Mr. Brown was given to violent fits of temper,
and immediately upon discovering so, it fired Mr. Brown
so as not to expose any other employee to Mr. Brown's
violent temper.

But had the employer known through past experience
that Mr. Brown had a violent temper and occasionally
struck other employees but nevertheless kept him on the
job, Ajax Construction Company would very likely be
liable to Mr. Huggins for the injuries he received at
Mr. Brown's hands. (We will discuss the employer's
liability for the acts of his employees in greater detail
in the chapters on agency.)

WORKMEN'S COMPENSATION LAWS

One hundred years ago if an employee was injured while working for an employer, he would have to depend upon the employer to continue his salary during his hospital or medical care and recuperation. Or he would have to rely upon his own family for medical and hospital expenses, and the family would have to live upon savings while the workman was unable to work. In every state, and for all employees of the United States federal government, these circumstances have been changed by the adoption of Workmen's Compensation Laws. Under such laws, if an employee is injured or incurs an illness on the job or connected with the job, the employee has a right to medical and hospital care paid for out of a Workmen's Compensation Fund, which the employer makes available either through private insurance or through a State Industrial Accident Commission or state agency. For each employee he has on the job, the employer makes a contribution to the insurance company or to the State Industrial Accident Commission. If an employee is injured or incurs an illness from his work and is required to miss work, losing time from the job (each state has different requirements for how many days the employee must lose work to be entitled to benefits), then he is entitled to have his necessary hospital and medical expenses paid, as well as a percentage of his salary or wage for the time he was off work as a result of his injury. An injured employee is entitled to a certain percentage of his wages based upon the length of time he was off work and the severity of the injury. (Compensation for loss of a leg or serious back injury is much greater than for injury to a thumb.)

The employer covers the cost of this workmen's compensation insurance coverage by increasing the price of his product, so we all participate in bearing the risk of injury to ourselves and other employees, rather than having each employee bear the risk of loss to himself, which might be catastrophic and wipe out all of his savings and prevent him from ever working again.

UNEMPLOYMENT COMPENSATION LAWS

Another law that affects the employee is one that provides for compensation to him if he is out of work for no fault

of his own—if for example, business in the country may
be bad and goods are not being sold and it is impossible
for a family to find work. Each state has a system of
unemployment compensation. It works in concert with the
Social Security Act, which also provides money for the
state for unemployment compensation. But the compensation
is run by each of the states, and each state has its own
rules regarding eligibility for unemployment compensation
and regarding the length of time that unemployment benefits will be paid to an unemployed worker. Each state
also has general rules disqualifying certain workmen
from benefits; generally a person is not entitled to
unemployment benefits if he refuses suitable work without
cause. A person is not paid for not working unless he
will take work and is actively seeking employment; nor is
a workman entitled to benefits if he has been discharged
or fired from a job for misconduct, or, in most states,
if he has voluntarily quit a job without good cause.

WORKERS' SAFETY LAWS

Each state also has laws relating to working conditions and
to the health, welfare, and protection of employees on
the job. Some states have safety appliance acts; others
have general safety laws relating to hazardous occupations.
The federal government also has a Safety Appliance Act
and a Federal Employer's Liability Act, covering the
safety of workmen on the job and the employer's responsibility to furnish reasonably safe places to work,
reasonably safe tools, and reasonably competent fellow
workmen. In your state, the safety acts may apply to
all employees in the state, or only to minors or
children, or only to extra-hazardous industries such as
mining, or steelworking, or logging, or longshore jobs.

CHILD LABOR LAWS AND WOMEN'S WORKING LAWS

Some occupations are prohibited to minors under 18 years
of age because they are ultra-hazardous. In addition,
the laws strictly regulate the number of hours a person
under 18 years of age may work in a day and the times that
such a minor may go to work—generally not before 8 a.m.
and not after 10 p.m. These laws generally limit themselves to factory or production work and do not cover
agricultural employment. These laws generally require a

work permit for all minors less than 16 years of age,
although some states have the work permit as low as 14
years of age.

There is also federal legislation with respect to
child labor. Generally, a business operating in interstate commerce—that is, selling its products across a
state line—may not employ a minor under 16 years of age,
except minors who work for their parents in non-hazardous
work such as motion pictures, radio, and television.
However, children between the ages of 14 and 16 may be
employed at occupations other than mining and manufacture
if the employment is confined to periods that will not
interfere with their schooling, health, or well-being.
Federal law prohibits minors under the age of 16 from
operating power-driven machinery or working in mines or
in certain classified hazardous occupations such as
transportation, warehousing and storage, communication,
public utilities, and certain specified manufacturing
industries.

Most states have laws governing wages and hours and
types of occupation which women may enter into. Again,
these laws vary from state to state and generally regulate
the number of hours a woman may work, the type of labor
she may do, and the conditions which the employer must
make available to women in their employment.

LAWS ON WAGES AND HOURS AND FAIR EMPLOYMENT LAWS

In the late 1930s the Congress passed the Air Labor
Standards Act, which stated that in certain occupations
and industries and interstate commerce a minimum hourly
wage must be paid and work done in excess of 40 hours a
week must receive time-and-a-half compensation. From
time to time the Congress increases the minimum hourly
wage to be paid an employee who works for an industry in
interstate commerce. Similarly, many states have passed
minimum wage and hour laws governing employees who work
for industries not in interstate commerce.

Eighteen states and the federal government have
passed laws that in hiring employees no employer may
discriminate on the basis of race, religion, or national
origin. Some states have enacted legislation to prohibit
discrimination between men and women in employment and in
payment of wages. And some states have passed legislation

to prohibit an employer from refusing a job to a man or
woman solely by reason of that person's age.

SOCIAL SECURITY

The Social Security Act passed by the Congress in 1935
has been amended many times to increase its coverage of
workers in this country and to provide additional benefits for workmen. How does it work? Briefly, the employer
and the employee, during the employee's working years,
make a contribution of a percentage of the employee's
wage to the federal government. This is held in the
federal government's Social Security Retirement Fund.
When the employee reaches the age of 65, or in some cases
62, the employee is then entitled to a retirement income
for the rest of his life, and his wife is entitled to a
percentage of that retirement income upon his death, for
the rest of her life. This system of social security
also is an insurance policy against death or disability
of a worker. For example, if Mr. Jones was disabled or
killed before age 65, his family would be entitled to
certain payments from the federal government for the life
of the wife and until the children reached 18 years or
left the home and were self-supporting. Benefits are
changed by the Congress to meet the needs of this country.

SELF TEST

CHAPTER 30

NAME_____

DATE_____

30.1 The first duty that the _____ imposes upon an employer is the duty of _____ of the _____ agreed upon.

30.2 If this first duty is not met by the employer, the employee has a right to terminate and _____ the employment relationship.

30.3 The second implied duty of an employer in the employment relationship is to furnish the employee a/an_____ place to _____.

30.4 The employer must also furnish safe _____ and _____ to his workmen.

30.5 The next duty implied in an employment contract is for the employer to furnish reasonably _____ _____ for fellow employees to work with.

30.6 The employer also has an implied duty to protect the employee from wrongful _____.

30.7 The employer must refrain from wrongful assaults upon employees even if it's to get the employee to exercise his duties of _____ and _____ of tasks.

30.8 (Answer True or False) _____ If a company continued to employ an employee who had, in the past, assaulted numerous employees, the company could possibly be held liable for any future wrongful assault on fellow employees by the employee in question.

30.9 If an employee incurs an illness or is injured on the _____ and connected with the _____, the employee has a right to _____ and _____ care paid for out of the _____ _____ Fund which the _____ makes available either through _____ insurance or through a state _____ of some sort.

30.10   The employer covers the costs of this workmen's
        compensation insurance coverage by _____
        the _____ of his product so that we all bear
        the risk of injury to ourselves or other employees.

30.11   The law that provides for compensation to an
        employee who is out of work due to no fault of his
        own is _____ compensation. It works in
        concert with the _____ _____ Act
        which provides money for the various states
        compensation systems, but the _____ runs
        the compensation system.

30.12   The rules are, generally, that a person will not
        be entitled to unemployment benefits if he:
        a) refuses _____ work without _____; or
        b) has been discharged or fired from a job for
           _____; or
        c) has voluntarily quit a job without good
           _____.

30.13   All states have some _____ acts that protect
        the employee and require the employer to furnish
        a safe place to work.

30.14   The child labor laws prohibit minors from working
        in certain occupations because of their _____
        nature.

30.15   In addition, child labor laws strictly regulate
        the number of _____ a person under 18 may
        work.

30.16   Child labor laws generally limit themselves to
        _____ or production work and not
        _____ employment.

30.17   The Fair _____ Act states that in certain
        occupations, work done in excess of _____
        hours a week must receive time-and-a-_____
        and a minimum standard of _____ was set.

30.18   Under the Social Security Act, a person, when
        reaching a certain age, is entitled to a/an
        _____ income for the rest of his life, and
        is an insurance policy against _____ or
        _____ of a worker.

31 Business Organizations

Sole Proprietorship. Partnership.

LEARNING OBJECTIVES

To become acquainted with the advantages and disadvantages of a sole proprietorship and of a partnership.

CHAPTER CONTENTS

Now that we have discussed how the law of the land covers
employee/employer relationships, let's take a brief look
and discuss the law generally, as it relates to the type
of business organization that may be an employer. In
this chapter we will discuss business organizations—how
they are created, their duties, their liabilities, how
they operate, and how they may be terminated.

Most business organizations in this country are
begun and operated by one person. These businesses are
not partnerships or corporations; they are known in the
law as *sole proprietorships*. Most businesses in this
country are owned by a single person who engages in the
business privately, invests his own capital, and is
personally liable for any debts that he incurs in his
business. Many small businesses that you have in your
town or city such as the drugstore perhaps, the shoe store,
the barber shop, and most farms are owned and operated
by one man—the individual proprietor.

LIABILITIES UNDER SOLE PROPRIETORSHIPS

A sole proprietor has complete control of the capital
invested in the business and the operational management
of the firm. He is also able at any time to discontinue
his business upon payment of all creditors and sale of the
assets of the business itself. But several obligations
are implicit in a sole proprietorship: The sole
proprietor or individual owner of the business is
personally liable for all debts that he incurs in the
business. For example, Mr. Jones owns a grocery store
and he incurs $1000 liability in purchasing goods and
produce. But he lacks sufficient capital in the grocery
store to pay for the goods when the bill comes due, his
creditors advise him that they are seizing his personal
bank account—not the grocery company's bank account but
his personal bank account—and that they are also going
to sue him and his wife jointly for the payment of the
$1000. The grocery store owner advises the supplier that
his wife works as a secretary in an office and has nothing
to do with the grocery business, but the supplier replies
that since he is the sole proprietor the income of his
entire family may be held liable for debts incurred by the
business. From this you can see that the sole proprietor
or individual owner has unlimited liability for all debts
incurred.

On the other hand, the sole proprietorship business
may be liable for debts incurred by the individual.
That is, say Mr. Jones, who owns the grocery store in
our example above, and his wife purchase a new automobile and agree to pay over a period of time $3000
for the automobile. Business turns bad and Mr. Jones
has difficulty meeting his obligations in the grocery
store, and his wife loses her job. They experience real
difficulty in meeting their car payments. One day the
car dealer comes into his grocery store and tells Mr.
Jones that he is going to sue him and attach the income
of the grocery store to pay for the car on the contract
of purchase. Mr. Jones says that the business was not
made liable for the debt, only himself and his wife.
But the car dealer says, "No, your personal expenses
and obligations may also be paid for out of the company
income that you own as a sole proprietor."

Consequently you can see that a sole proprietor may
be held personally liable for the debts of his business
and his business may be held liable for his personal
debts. In other words, a sole proprietorship has *unrestricted personal liability.*

PARTNERSHIPS

Although most small businesses are individually owned,
sole proprietorships, another widely used form of organization is known as a *partnership*. A partnership is a
combination of two or more people who agree to join
efforts in a lawful business purpose. The partnership
may be oral or written, and may be either of two types—
a *special partnership* and a *general partnership*.

A special partnership is an agreement by two or more
people to form a partnership for a limited and special
purpose only. For example, two businessmen decide that
they are going to purchase together a piece of property
for a mountain cabin. They draw up a partnership agreement wherein each of them agrees to contribute one-half
the capital necessary to acquire the cabin, that each
partner will have equal access to the cabin, and that the
partnership is limited to the acquisition and use of the
cabin. This is a special partnership, because it does
not bind either partner to do anything more than contribute equally for the acquisition and maintenance of the
cabin and for its subsequent operation for their joint use.

A special partnership may also be created for commercial or business purposes, but it limits the partnership to a specific undertaking and both partners are limited in their rights and duties to that specific purpose.

The general partnership is the more common of the two. This is a partnership between two or more people to engage in a commercial purpose of a rather broad nature. And either partner can act for the other in pursuing and promoting the interests of the partnership itself. For example, Mr. Jones and Mr. Brown decide to go into the used car business—the purchase and sale of used cars. They agree that each will have an obligation to supply one-half the capital necessary for the business and each will be entitled to one-half the profits. The partnership is general because it undertakes that each partner will have the right to involve their partnership in indebtedness on the purchase of cars, to sign contracts and loans, to sell automobiles, and to do all things necessary for the protection of the partnership business and for the earning of profit or income for each of the partners.

GENERAL PARTNER

A *general partner* is one who participates in the company either by expending his time or investing capital with a right to profits from the partnership. He has a right to a vote equal to his percentage of the partnership assets or equal to whatever agreement he has made with his other partners, and he is active and liable for the debts of the business. If Mr. Jones and Mr. Brown decide to open a grocery store, and both are going to work at the store, are going to contribute an equal amount of capital, and are going to draw equally from the income of the store, Mr. Jones and Mr. Brown are general partners.

APPARENT PARTNERS

An *apparent partner* is in fact not a partner at all, but he holds himself out to the world or to people dealing with the partnership as a partner, and he may be liable for all the acts of the partnership. For example,

Mr. Jones and Mr. Brown, partners in a grocery store,
hire Mr. Smith to help them run the store. Mr. Smith
is only an employee and not a partner, but both Mr. Jones
and Mr. Brown soon allow him to sign contracts and checks
for the partnership, they allow him to sign receipts for
produce and goods delivered to the store, to hold himself
out as a partner. And soon suppliers and creditors of
the partnership come to rely upon Mr. Smith, all with
Mr. Jones' and Mr. Brown's acceptance.

One day Mr. Smith signs a large contract for $4000
to have some new shelving put in the grocery store.
Mr. Jones and Mr. Brown refuse to pay for this shelving
after it is delivered. The court would hold that Mr. Jones
and Mr. Brown were liable for the shelving because they
allowed Mr. Smith to appear as partner in the company
and are bound by his decisions. The court would say,
"Mr. Smith was an apparent or ostensible partner and,
Mr. Jones and Mr. Brown, you are stopped from denying
liability because you allowed Mr. Smith to act as a
partner in the past."

SILENT PARTNER

Say that in the partnership between Mr. Jones and
Mr. Brown, our grocery store partners, they find that they
need an additional $3000 as working capital. They ask
Mr. Young if they can borrow $3000 from him and he
agrees to loan them $3000 if they will agree to take
him into the partnership, allow him to approve any and
all expenditures they are going to make, and allow
him one-third of the profits of the partnership until the
$3000 with interest is paid. Mr. Jones and Mr. Brown
agree, but Mr. Young says, "But I don't want anyone to
know that I am a partner with you in this venture because
I am merely using this partnership interest as security
for my loan." Mr. Jones and Mr. Brown agree. Mr. Young
would therefore become a silent partner—he would not have
an active management of the company, he would merely be
allowed to approve any large expenditures they were going
to make. But if the partnership became involved in a
lawsuit, Mr. Young would be liable along with Mr. Jones
and Mr. Brown for the partnership's debts because he
invited himself in for the partnership interest of one-third.
Consequently, he might very well be held liable for all
of the partnership's debt even though he was a silent
partner.

LIMITED PARTNER

A *limited partner* is allowed in approximately two-thirds
of our states. A limited partner is one whose liability
to the partnership and to any third party creditors is
limited to the amount of his investment in the partnership itself. In most states that allow a limited partnership they require the partnership have the words "limited"
in it, so that those people who deal with the partnership
know that perhaps one or more of the partners has
limited liability.

      As an example of a limited partnership, say Mr. Jones
and Mr. Brown are again in need of further operating
funds for their grocery store. This time they ask a
Mr. Black if they can borrow $3000 from him for use in
their grocery store. Mr. Black agrees but sends them
to his attorney to draw up a limited partnership agreement wherein Mr. Jones and Mr. Brown agree to take
Mr. Black as a limited partner in which his liability to
the partnership will be limited to $3000 and his liability
to any creditors of the partnership will be limited to
$3000.

      The partnership agreement is signed and the assumed
business name in the city and state is changed to Jones
and Brown Limited, and Mr. Black's interest as a limited
partner is shown in that document so that anyone dealing
with the partnership will know of the limited nature of
Mr. Black's participation. Mr. Black—unlike Mr. Young who
as a silent partner was held liable for other debts of
the partnership—will be held liable only for his investment in the partnership.

RIGHTS AND DUTIES OF GENERAL PARTNERS

General partners, partners active in the contribution of
capital and management of a partnership, have the duty of
exercising their best efforts for the protection and promotion of the partnership interest. They also have a
duty to act in good faith for the interest of the partners
and the partnership. They have a right to a share in the
profits and to participate in the management of the business,
and to be reimbursed any monies they have paid out on
behalf of the partnership so that the indebtedness of each
for the partnership will be equalized by the indebtedness

. of all. Each partner has a right to continue as a partner
without being subjected to expulsion, and has the right
to a full accounting of all the partnership's business,
expenses, and income. Now, a partnership agreement may
provide that unequal shares of profits go to the
partners, or that only one of the partners shall have
the management of the business. But in the absence of
such an agreement, partners are presumed to be equal
in their rights to manage and to collect partnership
profits.

A partner may incur debts for the partnership in
the course of doing business. For example, Mr. Jones
is looking for a truck to use as the grocery store
delivery van. He goes into the used car lot and buys
a truck and has it painted "Jones and Brown Grocery."
He also sees a flashy convertible that he wants to buy
for his wife. He writes a check for both cars on the
partnership account. When Mr. Brown sees the amount of
the check, he says to Mr. Jones, "You had no right to
incur this indebtedness for your flashy convertible. The
partnership is responsible to pay for the truck but not
for your personal car."

Of course, Mr. Brown is right. He has the responsibility of paying one-half the cost of the truck to be
used in the partnership business, but he has no responsibility to pay for Mr. Jones' personal car. This is an
important distinction, for it is sometimes very difficult
to tell the difference between a debt that is incurred
in the course of a partnership business and a debt that
is personally incurred. If the partner had bought two
pickup trucks for the grocery store even though only
one was actually needed, it would be a very close question
whether the partnership would be liable for both trucks.
Probably a court would hold that the partnership was
liable on the basis that the dealer in the truck had a
right to rely on the partnership liability because
Mr. Jones had the ostensible authority to incur the debt
on behalf of the partnership.

Similarly, if Mr. Jones had gone downtown to buy
an extensive amount of office equipment for the partnership without Mr. Brown's permission, the office supplier
would probably be entitled to recover against both Mr.
Jones and Mr. Brown or either of them. The rule is that
a partner may be liable individually or jointly with his
co-partners for all debts that are incurred in the course

of the partnership's business. Remember, the debt must
be incurred in the course of the partnership's business
and for the benefit of the partnership.

     But keep in mind that an individual partner can be
held <u>individually or jointly</u> liable with his co-partners
for all debts that are incurred in the prosecution of
the partnership business or for its benefit. For example,
Mr. Jones and Mr. Brown are partners in the grocery
business. Mr. Jones goes downtown and buys very expensive
meat handling equipment—saws and knives and all of the
meat department facilities that are required, and the
bill comes to $10,000. The partnership income is not
sufficient to pay this bill and the company that sold
the material brings suit against both Mr. Jones and
Mr. Brown. As it turns out, the court determines that the
partnership has insufficient assets to pay for the
equipment and it also turns out that Mr. Jones, who
purchased the equipment, does not have personal assets
to pay the bill, but Mr. Brown has a nice home and other
investments in some land that he owns on the other side
of town. The court finds judgment against the partnership, and the creditor levies execution upon the property
of Mr. Brown, forcing Mr. Brown to sell some of his
investments and the property across town to satisfy
the $10,000 judgment. So then, Mr. Brown was held
individually liable for the debts of the partnership
which were incurred by Mr. Jones. This is what we mean
by individual and joint liability.

TERMINATION OF PARTNERSHIPS

Obviously if such a situation that we just described had
come to pass, the partnership between Mr. Jones and
Mr. Brown would have been terminated. There are various
methods by which a partnership can be terminated. A
partnership may be terminated by the agreement of the
partners to go their separate ways. Or a partnership may
be terminated by the withdrawal of one partner from the
partnership, either by being bought out by the other
partner or selling his interest to a third person who then
becomes a general partner with the remaining partner.
Additionally, a partnership may be dissolved by a decree
of court. In the situation we talked about before where
Mr. Brown was held personally liable for the debts
incurred by the partnership, Mr. Brown could have gone into

court and asked the court to dissolve the partnership
and distribute half of the assets to Mr. Brown and half
to Mr. Jones but also asking the court to hold Mr. Jones
liable for one-half the $10,000 debt that Mr. Brown
had to pay off.

In addition, if one of the partners is insane or
physically incapable of continuing the partnership
obligation, a court will decree that a partnership is
dissolved and once the creditors and bills of the partnership have been paid, distribute the assets equally between
the partners. In addition, a decree may be granted
terminating a partnership when one of the partners has
failed to carry out his obligations undertaken in the
partnership agreement.

A partnership may also be terminated by operation
of law, and this occurs automatically if the partnership
is, say, bankrupt, or if one of the partners dies, or
if the partnership business is declared illegal. Three
examples will show how each of these legal dissolutions of
a partnership works. When Jones and Brown had the debt
of $10,000, if either the partnership of Jones and Brown
took bankruptcy, or if Mr. Jones had taken bankruptcy
for himself, the partnership would have been decreed
dissolved. Or if either Mr. Jones or Mr. Brown dies, the
law automatically dissolves the partnership. In addition,
if Mr. Jones and Mr. Brown were involved in a business
which the city, state, or federal government declared
illegal, then the partnership is dissolved by an operation of law.

Whenever a partnership is terminated or dissolved,
all of its debts must be paid before the partners are
entitled to any of the assets. First paid are secured
creditors, that is, creditors who have mortgages or conditional sale contracts which are recorded, then all
other creditors of the partnership are paid, and
only after all the debts are paid are the partners
entitled to their respective shares of the assets which
remain. This concludes our very brief and sketchy review of partnerships.

GLOSSARY TERMS

Apparent partner   A person who is not a partner but who
    with the consent of the partners assumes some of
    the powers and obligations of a partner.

General partner   A partner who participates equally, or
    in proportion to his investment, in the duties and
    income of a general partnership.

General partnership   A partnership engaged for a broad
    commercial purpose.

Limited partner   A partner who limits his liability to
    the partnership or to third parties by the amount
    of his investment.

Partnership   The joining of two or more people for a
    lawful business purpose.

Silent partner   A partner who assumes partial, and usually
    temporary, activeness in a partnership.

Sole proprietorship   A business owned by one person.

Special partnership   A partnership formed for a limited
    and special purpose.

Unrestricted personal liability   A liability of the
    individual for debts incurred by a sole proprietorship
    and of the sole proprietorship for debts incurred by
    the individual.

SELF TEST
CHAPTER 31

NAME_____

DATE_____

31.1 The most common form of business organization in
this country is the sole _____, which
means _____ ownership.

31.2 A sole proprietor has complete control of the
_____ invested in the business and the
operational _____ of the firm.

31.3 A sole proprietor is able at any time to discontinue his business upon payment of all
_____ and sale of the _____ of the
business itself.

31.4 The sole proprietor is personally _____
for all _____ that he incurs in the business.

31.5 The sole proprietorship _____ may be liable
for all debts incurred by the _____.

31.6 A sole proprietorship has _____
liability.

31.7 Partnership is a/an_____ of two or more
people who agree to join _____ in a
_____ business _____.

31.8 The two types of partnerships are a/an_____
partnership and a/an_____ partnership.

31.9 A special partnership is an agreement by two or
more people to form a partnership for a/an_____
and special purpose only.

31.10 A special partnership can be created for _____
or business purposes, but it limits the partnership to a specific undertaking and both partners
are limited in their _____ and duties to
that specific purpose.

31.11 A/An_____ partnership is more common, and
it is a partnership between two or more people
to engage in a commercial purpose of a rather
_____ nature.

31.12 In a/an_____ partnership either partner can
act for the _____ in pursuing and promoting
the _____ of the partnership itself.

31.13   A/An_____ partner is a partner who participates in the company either by expending his
_____ or investing _____ with a
right to profits from the partnership.

31.14   A general partner has a right to vote equal to
his _____ of the partnership _____
or equal to whatever agreement he has made with
the other partners and he is active and _____
for the debts of the business.

31.15   An apparent or _____ partner may, in fact,
not be a partner at all, but holds himself forth
to the world or to people dealing with the
partnership to be a partner.

31.16   A/An_____ partner does not have an active
_____ role in the company, but is still
considered liable for partnership _____.

31.17   A/An _____ partner is a partner who limits
his _____ to the partnership and to any
third party creditors to the amount of his
_____ in the partnership itself.

31.18   The two basic types of partnerships are _____
partnerships and _____ partnerships.

31.19   The four basic types of partners are general
partners, _____ or ostensible partners,
_____ partners, and _____
partners.

31.20   Generally speaking, it is the duty of each
general partner to exercise his best efforts for
the _____ and promotion of the partnership
interest. He also has a duty of acting in good
_____ for the interests of the partners
and partnership.

31.21   A general partner has a right to share in the
_____ and to participate in the _____
of the business. He also has the right to continue
as a partner without being subject to _____,
and he has the right to a full _____ of
all the partnership's business, expenses and
income.

31.22   In the absence of an agreement otherwise, partners
are presumed to be _____ in the management
rights and rights to partnership profits.

31.23   A partner may be liable individually or _____
with his co-partners for all debts that are
incurred in the course of the partnership's
_____.

CHAPTER 31

NAME_____

31.24 Most states that allow a limited partnership to exist also by _____ make it necessary that the partnership have the word "_____" in its title.

31.25 It is important to distinguish between a debt that is incurred in the _____ of a partnership business and a debt that is _____ incurred.

31.26 A partnership may be terminated by the _____ of the partners to go their separate ways, and the partnership may be terminated by such a/an_____.

31.27 A partnership may be terminated by the _____ of one _____ from the partnership, either by being _____ out by the other partner, or by selling his _____ to a third person who then becomes a/an_____ partner with the _____ partner.

31.28 A partnership may be dissolved by a/an_____ of a court.

31.29 A decree may be granted terminating a partnership when one of the partners has failed to carry out his _____ undertaken in the partnership _____.

31.30 A partnership may be terminated by operation of _____, and this occurs automatically if the partnership is, say, _____, or if one of the partners dies, or if the partnership business is declared _____.

31.31 Whenever a partnership is terminated or dissolved, all of the debts of the partnership must be paid before the partners are entitled to any of the _____. First, _____ creditors, that is, creditors who have mortgages or _____ sales contracts which are _____ are paid, then all other creditors of the partnership are paid.

32 Business Organizations

Corporations

LEARNING OBJECTIVES

To gain extensive knowledge of the features of a corporation.

To be able to compare and contrast the three main forms of business organization.

CHAPTER CONTENTS

Corporations   Types of Corporations   Private Corporations   Funding of Corporations   Limited Liability Disadvantages of Corporations   Dissolution of Corporations Glossary   Self Test

Although sole proprietorships are the commonest form, and
partnerships are the second commonest form of business
organization, *corporations* are the largest of the businesses
in this country. Virtually everything you buy and most
of the services you receive come through corporations.
Indeed, the corporations that nationally advertise on
television and radio and in your newspapers are generally
large. General Motors is a corporation, American Telephone and Telegraph Company, and most of the business
enterprises of great size are corporations. But you don't
have to have a large business enterprise to form a
corporation.

CORPORATIONS

A corporation is an artificial, legal entity created by
government grant. Throughout these chapters the law has
always been defined as it relates to people—the landlord
and tenant, the employer and employee, the buyer, the
seller, the vendor, the purchaser, the mortgagor and the
mortgagee and all of the examples that you've had to
date have dealt with people. But the concept of the
corporation creates a legal entity that is not a real
person, but is a legal, artificial person.
    A corporation has all of the rights and obligations
of a person, depending upon the particular legal situation;
it is dealt with in the law as a legal separate person
or entity. How does a person go about creating such a
legal entity? Each state has various rules and regulations enforced by the corporation department of the state
government for the creation and control of corporations
who do business or are created within the state.
    Most states provide that three persons may file
articles of incorporation, which advise the state of
the names of the officers of the corporation, the amount
of stock that the corporation will issue, the purpose
for which the corporation is formed, and the names of its
original incorporators and officers of the corporation.
After these articles of incorporation have been filed
with and reviewed by the state, a *charter* is issued by
the state and the corporation from that point has life or
is then an artificial, legal entity separate from its
incorporators or promotors and from its stockholders.
It is for all purposes in the law, a separate, legal
entity.

The corporation is bound by its original charter or articles of incorporation. It can do only those things that are expressly authorized in the original charter or articles of incorporation and, in addition, those things that are implied in the grants of the specific powers. For example, if Mr. Jones and Mr. Brown, our perennial grocers, decided to incorporate their business, they would file with the Secretary of State or the Director of Commerce of their state a petition or articles of incorporation for review by the state. They would set forth the name, Jones and Brown Grocery, Incorporated (or Inc., or Company); the powers of the corporation to buy and own land and to buy and sell foodstuffs and all things that are connected with a grocery store; the total amount of stock that the corporation was to be allowed to sell; the names of the incorporators or promoters—in this case, Mr. Jones and Mr. Brown—and the address of the corporation. They would also forward to the state the corporation's *bylaws*—the rules of conduct of the official business of the corporation, calling for a Board of Directors and Stockholders' meetings, setting forth the corporation officers' titles and the types of stock that would be issued.

After the charter is issued, the corporation would have the express power to enter into the grocery business. Mr. Brown and Mr. Jones would sell their partnership interest to the corporation in return for shares of stock; and after it did all the things required by the state, the corporation would be free to enter into the business of running a grocery store and would have certain implied powers, such as to borrow money, to enter into contracts, to issue bonds or mortgages, to purchase its own stock. But unless it was expressly authorized by statute or in its charter, it would not have the power to consolidate with another corporation or to enter into a partnership or to make donations or gifts for civic or charitable purposes.

TYPES OF CORPORATIONS

There are two broad categories of corporations: <u>public</u> corporations and <u>private</u> corporations. Because we are studying business law we will concentrate on private

corporations, but let us look briefly at *public corporations*. A public corporation is one which is owned by
all of the public; for example, all cities in this country
are corporations and they have their life by reason of
a statutory or legislative grant of a corporate charter—
the City of Detroit, the City of New York. All have
charters and they are all corporations; they do not have
stockholders—all of the citizens of a city are its
members and have a right to vote in corporate matters
in the government of the city—the election of the mayor
and the duty of supporting the corporation by taxes and
other revenue measures. In addition, school districts,
water districts, lighting districts, and villages are
public corporations. Sometimes public corporations are
formed by states to enter into the development of land
or electric power. All of these are called municipal
or quasi-municipal corporations.

PRIVATE CORPORATIONS

Private corporations may be one of two types: corporations
for profit, the business corporation we will be most
interested in, and nonprofit corporations. Nonprofit
corporations are such things as private schools, fraterni-
ties, churches, lodges, libraries, historical societies,
social clubs, and private hospitals. They are not formed
to enter into the business of making a profit for their
shareholders, but rather to give service to members of
the society, or lodge, or fraternity, or church, or to
the public at large.

How does a private corporation for profit operate?
Remember that in partnerships the partners ran the
company and had a duty to each other to operate the
company for the gain of the partnership. A corporation
does not operate in that fashion. A corporation is owned
by *stockholders*, who purchase shares of stock in the
corporation. For example, if a corporation has five
shares of stock and sells each share to a different
person, there are five stockholders in the corporation.

In large corporations there are many millions of
shares of stock and they are held by many thousands of
people. Generally, each of these common shareholders has
the right to one vote in the government of the corporation, although there are corporations that have different
classes of stock, such as <u>preferred stock</u>, in which the

shareholders do not have a right to vote. But generally,
a shareholder has one vote for each share of stock, and
also has the privilege of receiving dividends from the
corporation when profits are declared distributable
to the shareholders.

The shareholders, then, own the company, but do not
manage it. The shareholders elect at their annual
meeting a Board of Directors, and the Board of Directors
has the direct responsibility of setting the policy of
the corporation and governing its overall business
enterprise. But the directors of a corporation do not
have the responsibility of the day-to-day management
of the corporate affairs. The day-to-day management of
a corporation is passed to the officers of the corporation—generally its president, vice president, secretary,
and treasurer. The bylaws of the corporation set forth
the duties of each of these officers. These officers
may be shareholders, and they also may be members of the
Board of Directors, but they do not have to be. Thus,
we see the bare skeleton of our corporation. It is owned
by the shareholders, who elect a Board of Directors, who
hire officers to run the company.

The officers of the corporation, the president, vice
president, secretary, and treasurer have the day-to-day
management of the corporate affairs; they are the real
managers of the company. The Board of Directors has
an important duty as well, though. The directors have
a duty to the stockholders to see that the corporate
affairs are run well so that the corporation has a
reasonable expectation of making profit; they also have
the responsibility of declaring what percentage, if
any, of the profits of a corporation are going to be
distributed to the shareholders in the form of a dividend.
In a given year all of the profits may be distributed
to the shareholders or none of them may be, but instead
may be reinvested in the corporate business. The directors, then, manage the policy of the corporation and
determine the amount of return that the shareholders will
receive from their investment in the corporation.

FUNDING OF CORPORATIONS

All of you are aware of the stock markets in New York,
Chicago, and San Francisco, and are aware of the fluctua-
tions of corporate stock prices. The stock price

represents investor's confidence in the corporation and
its management and also in the amount of return that the
investor will receive from his investment in the stock
of a corporation. The sale of stock by a corporation
and its brochures about its own stock are very carefully
regulated by federal law, known as the Securities and
Exchange Act. Also, sales of stock within each state
but not beyond its boundaries are regulated by its state
securities acts. These laws are to protect the investor
in corporations, to prevent the making of untrue statements about the well-being of a corporation and the
value of stock. The Securities Exchange Commission
oversees and controls the interstate sale of stock on the
New York Stock Exchange, the Chicago Stock Exchange,
and the San Francisco Stock Exchange.

   If you wanted to buy a share of stock in a corporation
you would contact a broker, or sometimes a small corporation in your state directly and upon your payment of
the value of the stock you would be entitled to a
certificate of stock with your name upon it, guaranteeing
you the same rights as every other stockholder of that
class in the corporation. But why would you want to
invest in a grocery store in your town that was a
corporation when you had no rights of management over
that corporation except the right to elect a Board of
Directors whom you may or may not know? Indeed, most
people don't want to invest in a new, small corporation
because they don't know how well it has done as a
corporation and whether it's a sound investment. But
if a corporation survives and gets more and more experienced
and becomes more profitable, there are many people in
this country who desire to invest in the securities of
that company for a good return on their investment.
This is one of the advantages of a corporation—its life
is perpetual. If the president dies or becomes incapacitated a new president is hired. (Remember, that in a
partnership if one partner becomes incapacitated the
partnership is dissolved.) Also, when many people invest
in one corporation it has much more capital than the
old Jones and Brown partnership, which was always
borrowing funds. More stock is issued and more investment capital comes into the corporation allowing Jones'
and Brown's company to hire a professional grocery
manager as an employee, or even as president, of the
company. Keep in mind that a president of a large corporation or even a small corporation is still an employee of
the corporation itself.

LIMITED LIABILITY

There are two advantages, then, to a private corporation
for profit: one, large accumulations of capital for
the corporate business; and two, perpetual existence of
the corporation. There is another very important feature
of a corporation. You'll remember when Jones and Brown
were partners, each was personally liable for the debts
of the company. But if Jones and Brown incorporated and
own stock in the corporation, the corporation is liable
for its own debts and the stockholders are not personally
liable for the debts of the corporation. This is known as
limited liability. If Mr. Jones went downtown and bought
two trucks for the company and signed the company's
name as president, the car dealer could look only to the
corporation to satisfy that debt. He could not look to
Mr. Brown or Mr. Jones as their liability is limited to
the amount of their investment in the corporation; although
the car dealer would have a right to sue the corporation
and take all of its assets including the investments that
Mr. Jones and Mr. Brown had made in their stock, he could
not hold either Mr. Jones or Mr. Brown personally liable
for the purchase.
  There is another very basic advantage of having a
corporate form of business organization—the ease by
which a corporation can transfer ownership. For example,
the partnership of Jones and Brown is dissolved when one
of the partners withdraws and a new partnership is formed
with the entering partner. But as a corporation, the
Jones and Brown Grocery Company may be sold entirely
or in part to a third person and still retain its
corporate name and existence by Jones and/or Brown's sale
of their stock to the new owners; the corporation would
continue as an artificial legal entity.
  In large corporations this is especially important
because the stock of large corporations is sold many,
many times during the course of a year, and the owners of
the company therefore change because, as you'll remember,
the shareholders own the company. Sometimes you hear of
big stock fights that occur in corporations. One stockholder has enough shares or a group of stockholders have
enough shares which they vote as a bloc to remove someone
from the Board of Directors or replace the entire Board
of Directors so new policies can be established for the
corporation. This can work to the advantage or the
disadvantage of a corporation. For example, a few years

ago a large chain of drugstores was owned by three men.
They sold more stock in their company and bit by bit
their major competitor bought up this stock and finally
was able to remove two of the stockholders from the
Board of Directors and take their place. You can imagine
the original owner's state of mind when he found his major
competitor on the Board of Directors. Ultimately, things
worked out fine for the remaining original owner because
the two corporations merged, with the approval of the
state, into one large corporation and they put all of
their operations together and it turned out very well for
the consumers as well as the owners of the corporation.

DISADVANTAGES OF CORPORATIONS

The most important disadvantage of a corporation is that
it is taxed separately from its shareholders on the
profits it makes. (Remember, it is a separate legal
entity for all purposes.) Its earnings are taxed
separately just as if it were a sole proprietorship.
In effect, this is double taxation, because the profits
of a corporation are taxed both <u>before</u> they are distributed
to the shareholders and <u>after</u>: When the shareholders
receive dividends they are taxed upon that dividend
income. In some cases perhaps another disadvantage is
that the corporation has only those powers that are
expressly and impliedly set forth in its charter. For
example, Jones and Brown Grocery Company has a charter
to engage in the grocery business and cannot manufacture
and sell airplanes or automobiles or real estate but must
limit its activities to the grocery business and all
things related to it. That disadvantage might be termed
limitations of charter powers.

We can see that the advantages in some cases far
outweigh the disadvantages. Each form of business
organization has its own set of advantages: The sole
proprietor has the advantage of personal management of
the company by the owner, the partnership form of
organization has great advantages in many situations,
not just in taxation but in the business organization
of the company and in the ability to change its purposes;
and the corporate form of organization has many advantages,
such as limited liability and flexible sources of capital
through stock sales. In each case, the form of organization
is a very difficult decision and requires good business
judgment and good legal analysis.

DISSOLUTION OF CORPORATIONS

Although a corporation has perpetual life or continuous
existence, all things can be changed and terminated.
How, then, is a corporation terminated? In some states
the corporate charter or articles of incorporation are
given for a fixed number of years and at the expiration
of those years the charter terminates or expires, and if
the articles are not renewed the owners hold the stock as
trustees and all of the assets are distributed to the
owners after the bills are paid. Or the owners can
voluntarily surrender their charter to the state after
they have paid all of the bills and distributed all of
the assets of the corporation.

Another method of termination is *merger*: A large
corporation takes over the assets of a smaller corporation.
The stockholders of the small corporation take stock in
the new corporation, or larger corporation, and the smaller
corporation that was merged into the larger corporation
ends and its charter is surrendered. The last method is
consolidation: Two corporations of approximately equal
size agree to set up a third corporation and both of
these corporations transfer their stock into the new
third corporation. The two transferring corporations
terminate their existence and their stockholders each
receive stock in the third corporation.

GLOSSARY TERMS

Articles of incorporation   A document listing officers, amount of stock to be issued, and purpose of formation, submitted to a state for purposes of being incorporated; also a document granting the organization the legal status of a corporation.

Bylaws   The constitution of a corporation; the rules of conduct of official business.

Charter   Articles of incorporation issued by a state creating a corporation.

Consolidation   Establishment of a third corporation by two corporations of equal size which then dissolve and enter into the new corporation.

Corporation   An artificial, legal entity created by government grant to have the rights and obligations of a person.

Limited liability   Confinement of liabilities incurred by a corporation to the corporation itself.

Merger   Purchase of the assets of one corporation by a larger corporation.

Private corporation   A corporation owned by stockholders.

Public corporation   A corporation owned by the public by virtue of their residence within its boundaries, as, say, an incorporated city.

Stockholders   Persons who own a portion of a corporation by purchase of shares in its interest.

SELF TEST

CHAPTER 32

NAME_____

DATE_____

32.1 The _____ form of business organization
      accounts for the _____ of the businesses
      in this country.

32.2 A corporation is a/an_____, _____
      entity created by _____ grant.

32.3 A corporation could also be referred to as an
      artificial _____ created by _____

32.4 The governmental grants giving corporations
      existence or identity are called, either
      _____ of incorporation or original
      _____.

32.5 A corporation can only do those things which are
      _____ authorized or _____ in the
      grants of specific powers.

32.6 The rules of conduct of the official business of
      the corporation are called _____, and are
      the _____ of the corporate organization.

32.7 Some implied powers of a corporation would be
      the power to borrow money, to enter into
      _____, and to issue _____ or
      mortgages.

32.8 Generally speaking, the two broad categories of
      corporations are _____ corporations and
      _____ corporations.

32.9 A public corporation is one which is owned by all
      of the _____.

32.10 City governments, water districts, etc. are
      examples of municipal or _____ municipal
      corporations.

32.11 Private corporations may be one of two types:
      corporations for _____ or _____
      corporations.

32.12 The duties of nonprofit corporations are to give
      _____ to people.

32.13 A corporation is owned by _____, who
       purchase shares of _____ in the corporation.

32.14 Generally speaking a shareholder has _____
       vote(s) for each share of stock owned.

32.15 The shareholder has the privilege of receiving
       _____ from the corporation when _____
       are declared distributable to the shareholders.

32.16 Shareholders _____ the company, but the
       shareholders do not _____ the company.

32.17 The _____ of _____, who are elected
       by the _____, has the direct _____
       of setting the _____ of the corporation
       and _____ its overall business enterprise,
       but they do not have the responsibility of the
       day-to-day _____ of the corporate affairs.

32.18 The day-to-day _____ of a corporation
       is passed along to the _____ of the
       corporation.

32.19 The _____ of a corporation, because they
       perform the day-to-day management of the corpora-
       tion, are most like the general partners we have
       previously discussed.

32.20 The _____ have the responsibility of
       declaring what percentage, if any, of the profits
       of a corporation are going to be distributed to
       shareholders, which, in effect, determines the
       amount of _____ the shareholders will
       receive from their _____ in the corporation.

32.21 The price of corporate stock in the stock
       _____ represents investor's _____
       in the corporation and its _____.

32.22 The federal law controlling and regulating the
       sale of corporate stock is the _____ and
       _____ Act.

32.23 One of the advantages of a corporation is that its
       life is _____.

32.24 The president of a corporation is still a/an
       _____ of the corporation, so death of an
       officer will not dissolve the corporation.

32.25 Another advantage of the corporate form of
       organization is the ability to accumulate large
       amounts of _____.

32.26 A corporation is liable for its own _____
       and the stockholders are not _____ liable
       for the debts of the corporation. This is known
       as _____ liability.

CHAPTER 32

NAME_____

32.27 Another basic advantage of having a corporate form
of business organization is the _____ by
which a corporation can transfer _____.

32.28 Another advantage that can be gained by incorpora-
ting is _____ and sometimes more ____ ___
management of the company.

32.29 Perhaps the most important advantage of the corporate
form of business organization is the _____
of stockholders for the _____ of the
corporation.

32.30 The most important disadvantage of a corporate
form of organization is that it is _____
separately from the _____ on the _____
it makes. This is often referred to as _____
taxation.

32.31 Another disadvantage is that the corporation has
only those powers that are expressly and
_____ set forth in its _____. This
disadvantage is often termed _____ of
_____ powers.

32.32 A/An _____ occurs when a large corporation
takes over the assets of a smaller corporation.

32.33 A/An _____ occurs when two corporations of
approximately equal size agree to set up a/an
_____ corporation, and both of these
corporations transfer their stock into the new
corporation.

32.34 The four basic methods by which a corporation
can be terminated are:
a) by _____ of its charter; or
b) by _____ of its charter; or
c) by a/an _____; or
d) by a/an _____.

32.35 The (choose either State or Federal) _____
governments are the governmental bodies that grant
corporate charters.

33 Negotiable Instruments

Introduction. Money. Credit.

LEARNING OBJECTIVES

To gain a basic understanding of the basis of negotiable instruments.

CHAPTER CONTENTS

In the next five chapters we will discuss negotiable
instruments, which include checks, drafts, and promissory
notes. Negotiable instruments are really credit instruments, that is, a method of obtaining credit for goods
and services that we receive now. They are a means of
deferring payment in money for services presently rendered or goods presently received. Before we discuss in
detail these credit instruments known as negotiable
instruments, we should look in detail at money itself:
what it is, why we value it, and how we use it—and how
in some cases it uses us. Credit and negotiable instruments cannot be fully understood as a part of the credit
structure of our society unless we understand money and
its part in our society and every society in recorded
history.

MONEY AND EXCHANGE

Before there was money or a *medium of exchange*, people
had to *barter* their goods or their services for the goods
and services of other people. For example, a candlemaker
would exchange his candles for the goods and services
he needed—say wheat from a miller or meat or vegetables
from a farmer—if he were lucky enough to run upon a
person who has some meat or some wheat that he needs for
his family. But sometimes that candlemaker might have
difficulty finding a person who wishes to exchange food
or services for candles. Thus, the barter system is of
limited usefulness because each person within a barter
system must spend all of his time producing his goods
and services and then going out and finding another
person who has what he, the first person, wants and wants
in return what he, the first person, can offer.

You can see that the barter system is very rudi-
mentary and cannot survive after the society reaches a
certain number of people. Thus, a system is developed
in every society by which there is some acceptable standard
of value; it may be beads, or cattle, or gold, or even
rocks—and in some emerging societies it was slaves.
It has also been paper money.

Money is used in part as a medium of exchange; it
is used in the place of goods or services to exchange
goods and services. For example, if I have a boat that
I no longer use and am interested in selling so that I
can buy a record player which I want, instead of going out

and trying to barter the boat for a record player, I put
it on the market for $50 and finally receive an offer for
$35. I accept the offer of $35 and sell the boat to the
purchaser. With the $35 I go down and shop for a record
player that I can buy with this money. The value of the
boat was established at $35 because that's what I received
for it, and the value of the record player that I ultimately purchase is $35, for that's what I purchased it for.
The medium of exchange was dollars—not the goods or
services that we exchange for them. The boat really
resulted in my getting a record player, but the person who
sold the record player received money, the medium of
exchange.

Money is defined as an article which serves as a
standard of value, and which because of general acceptability is used primarily as a medium of exchange.

What do we mean by the words "standard of value"?
Well, money is the common denominator of what a product
or service is worth. Recall that I had a boat that I
desired to sell for $50; to me the boat was worth $50.
I used money as a standard of value: I don't say it was
worth a record player, or a record library, or an automobile. I used the most acceptable standard of value there
is—the medium of exchange—money. Assume that I had
found a person with a record player that I desired, and
its owner said the record player is worth $50, and I had
said the boat is worth $50, and we exchanged.

Really we would have bartered our two commodities
in agreement but we had still used the standard of value
of money for that exchange. But if the record player
owner had said, "This record player is worth $60, and
your boat is worth only $50. Do you still want to trade?"
I would say at that point yes or no depending upon my
intent, "Yes. I will give you my boat which is worth
$50 plus $10 and you give me your record player." Now
here the standard of value has been established by money,
but the exchange has been accomplished both by barter and
money as a medium of exchange, to the extent of $10.
Now the standard of value and the medium of exchange which
we discussed as a part of the definition of money depend
equally upon the third part of the definition—the acceptability of money to furnish the standard of value and the
medium of exchange.

Dealing in this country with our fellow Americans, we
accept the American dollar as the standard of value and
medium of exchange because we know its value and have

confidence in its value.   But if we go abroad to a foreign
country, we may be very leery about accepting pounds, or
francs, or pesos, or the medium of exchange of that country
because we do not know its standard of value.   In fact when
we do go abroad, rates of exchange tell us the dollar is
worth so many pesos, or francs, or marks, and we can
exchange our dollars for francs or marks or pesos in that
country on an equitable exchange.   Therefore the definition
of money is composed of three parts; each part depends on the
other: The medium of exchange depends upon the standard
of value, and the standard of value must be known if
the money is to be acceptable as a barter instrument.

MONEY AND STANDARD OF VALUE

We will have to go back into our recent history to find out
how we established the standard of value of our money.
Prior to 1933 and 1935, the money in circulation in this
country was backed by gold.   That is to say, for each
dollar in paper money in circulation, there was a dollar's
worth of gold in the Federal Treasury.   This money was
known as gold certificates.   If you took a dollar into a
Federal Reserve Bank, or any bank for that matter, the
bank was obligated to give you one dollar's worth of gold.
But in 1933 and 1935 this country went through a very
severe depression and gold certificates were no longer
issued because the government needed more money in circulation to pull this country out of the depression.   Silver
certificates were issued for some period after this.
Silver certificates were backed by silver, and $1 in paper
money was redeemable at a bank by one dollar's worth of
silver.   Again this policy was changed in 1935 and paper
money was issued based upon the credit of the United States
government.   Today you cannot use gold as a medium of
exchange.   We cannot go to the bank and redeem a dollar
for gold or silver; it is based upon the credit of the
United States government.   That credit is backed up by the
U.S. government's gold supply, which equals approximately
20% of the money in circulation.   But more important, it
is backed up by the government's promise to buy gold from
anyone who wishes to sell it to the United States government
for $35 an ounce.   In addition, the federal government
promises to pay to anyone outside of this country—that is,
anyone who is not a citizen—$35 worth of gold for the
return of 35 American dollars.   In this way, you see, the

credibility or acceptability of our country's credit and its
money is maintained. You have noted in the last several
years, several foreign governments have exchanged $35 in
our American paper money for gold. In this way, they are
attempting to build up their gold reserves and also testing
the acceptability of American money—paper money as a medium
of exchange. When the dollar is doubted, abroad as well
as in this country, there is a demand for gold in exchange
for dollars, and as long as the U.S. federal government
pays one ounce of gold for each 35 American dollars that
are redeemed by a foreign country, then the American paper
dollar is sound. But if our government refuses to pay one
ounce of gold for each 35 American paper dollars, then the
acceptability of the paper dollar will be diminished and a
new value for the paper dollar will have to be established,
that is, less gold for each $35.

But remember, we can't redeem these dollars for gold
within the United States. Only a foreign country can do so
to test the acceptability of the American dollar as a
medium of payment, and to establish its standard of value.
If a U.S. citizen cannot test the value of a dollar by
attempting to redeem it in gold, how do we establish the
standard of value of a dollar in the United States? The
value of the Federal Reserve notes (which is what our
dollars are) that you and I use as a medium of exchange
is established by the prosperity of the country. In other
words, the standard of value of the American currency is
fluctuating with the standard of value of the economy.
How does this come about?

Our currency in the United States is controlled by
the Federal Treasury and Federal Reserve Banks across the
country. Now the bank that you and your family do your
banking at has on its window, "Member of the Federal
Deposit Insurance Corporation" (F.D.I.C.). That bank
belongs to the Federal Reserve system and has a national or
state charter. Each of our banks must keep a certain percentage of its money available so that every person who has
deposits in the bank can withdraw all of his or her money
at any given time. In addition, the bank in your community
loans money to businesses, to your parents, to yourself—to
all types of people for all types of purposes.

When they loan up to their reserve—that is, when they
have no more funds available to loan—they will discount
or send one of the long-range mortgages or promissory notes
of a company to the Federal Reserve Bank. If the local bank
has not exceeded its quota, the Federal Reserve Bank will

credit that local bank with some more funds or paper currency. It says in effect, "We will hold this mortgage or note that you have sent to us and replace it with 50% or 75% or 95% of the value of that note with some more paper currency." So the local bank has the power to loan more money to people or to use it as a medium of exchange for the economy of the town that it's located in. Now, as the demand for money increases, the value of the money increases—just like everything else—and when the value of money increases, it inflates the value of the money, so we must pay higher interest rates to have the use of the money on a loan and if we go too far, we have serious inflation to a point where $10 is really only worth $1 in purchasing power. That is, $10 will buy no more than what $1 bought at some given past date.

Inflation has to be checked by the Federal Reserve system, and the method used is to say to the local bank, "We will pay you only 40% on all negotiable or commercial paper that you send to us." This dries up or limits the amount of money that is available for circulation, fewer people borrow money and in time there is a redress of the inflationary spiral because the demand on the money is smaller and the economy cools off (as some economists call it). The Federal Reserve then allows a less restrictive policy on the borrowing of money—that is, it says to the local bank, "Now we will give you a paper money credit of 60% or 90%, even, of the commercial paper that you trans-fer to us." (These percentages are only for illustration, because the actual percentages are quarters and halves of percents.)

By this manipulation of banks' credit, the credit of the money and the credit of the economy are affected. The more restrictive the Federal Reserve Banks are in granting loans to their member banks, the more restrictive the money supply is. Conversely, the more liberal the Federal Reserve Banks are with the local banks, the more money there is in circulation because the local banks have more money to lend and put in circulation. In this way the federal government through the control of money not only establishes the standard of value of money, but attempts to keep the American economy in balance—that is, attempts to keep the supply of money equal to the productive need of the people for money, so that we do not have runaway infla-tion or serious deflation or depression. Therefore, the standard of value of our money in America is based upon the vitality and economic growth of the country.

MONEY AND CREDIT

You can now see that the paper money we use in this country
is credit itself: We have confidence in the U.S. federal
government and in our economy. Therefore, we accept money
as the standard of value and as the medium of exchange even
though that standard of value fluctuates, and some times
buys more goods and services than at other times. You
well know that in any period of 10 years a dollar will
sometimes buy more and sometimes buy less, depending upon
the level of the economy. But the money that we use is a
note, and it is based upon the credit of the economy and
our confidence in the economy. That's how the standard
of value is accomplished and that is why our money is
acceptable throughout the world on various rates of
exchange—because the credit of the United States economy
backs our paper money.

The money we've been talking about, or currency,
really accounts for less than 10% of the monetary transactions that individuals, families, and business engage
in. There simply is not enough money to run our economy
in an orderly fashion. For example, if the wage earners
in your family were each paid in cash, or hard currency,
every payday, and they had to make all of their purchases
in cash or hard currency—think what a trouble and bother
that would be. You would have to carry with you at all
times suitable cash to pay your rent or your mortgage, and
for every purchase you made, no matter how big or how small—
and it would be virtually impossible to make some of your
purchases. For example, if you or any company wanted to buy
something in a neighboring state or neighboring town, you
would have to take to that neighboring town the actual cash
amount that was needed for the purchase.

Most transactions occur over long distances—
especially in business: Cars are made in one part of the
country; timber is grown in another part of the country;
steel is produced in another part of the country; oil is
produced in still another part of the country or far from
our shores. If we had to pay cash for the purchase of these
items, commerce would slow to a dead halt. Each individual
and business would have to have many hundreds or thousands
of dollars on tap for the purchase of goods and services.
A simple example should suffice: You want to buy an automobile, and the car you want is in stock in a neighboring
town. You go over and negotiate on the purchase price and
you're ready for delivery when the dealer says, "I want the pay-

ment in cash." You have to come home and go to your bank
(or reach under your bed or dig up in your backyard) for
the cash, which they hold in deposit for you, then you must
drive or walk to the agency and pay the agent in cash.
Well, imagine the risk you're taking in the loss or theft
of that cash plus the inordinate amount of time you've
wasted in negotiating on the price, then obtaining the
actual cash amount required and making payment of it.
Business could not operate that way, either. If an automobile factory needed steel but couldn't receive it until
it paid cash, it would have its messenger run to the steel
factory with the correct amount of cash for the steel and
then accept delivery; and each order would also be held up
until the cash was paid. Business would come to a stand-
still—even if there were enough hard currency in supply
to furnish all of our daily needs and all business needs.
But actually, as we said above, the hard currency of this
country accounts for less than 10% of the total monetary
transactions: The rest of the monetary transactions are by
private credit instruments.

PRIVATE CREDIT INSTRUMENTS

Private credit instruments include checks, promissory notes,
drafts, and letters of credit. Note that these are <u>private</u>
credit instruments; these are documents of credit issued by
private parties—corporations or individuals. (Municipal,
state, or federal bonds are also credit instruments,
investments made by the people of America for an interest
return. But these will not be considered under the title
of negotiable instruments.)

  While private credit instruments are based upon the
individual credit of the issuer or drawer, they still
will be based upon the monetary standard of the country
in which they're issued or drawn. In other words, hard
currency—money—is the foundation upon which all private
credit is based. Money establishes the <u>standard of value</u>
upon which credit instruments are drawn, and it is the
<u>acceptable</u> standard of value, but in private credit
instruments, money, or hard currency, is <u>not</u> the <u>medium</u>
<u>of exchange</u>. The credit instrument itself is the medium
of exchange. That is, returning to the example of the rowboat
and the record player, you'll remember that the record
player owner and I agreed that his record player was worth
$60 and my rowboat was worth $50. Instead of giving him a

$10 bill to make up the difference, I could give him my
personal check made out in the face amount of $10. Now,
if he knows me well, he will accept that credit instrument
in payment of the debt. However, if he does not know me
or if we deal at long distances, he might prefer to be
paid in cash or hard currency. Thus, if he accepts my
check that is the medium of exchange—but he is perfectly
within his rights to withhold the record player until the
check is honored or cashed at the bank and he has received
$10 for that check, because my check was not as acceptable
as a medium of exchange as the dollars that he demanded
as the medium of exchange. Our currency, therefore, is
the standard of value accepted as the medium of exchange.
It is a credit instrument of the government to be used in
the place of barter.

GLOSSARY TERMS

Barter   Exchange of goods or services for goods or services.

Medium of exchange   An object or set of objects, such as pieces of gold, or beads, etc., that have an accepted standard of value, and by which goods and services can be exchanged for each other.

Money   A medium of exchange.

Negotiable instrument   An instrument of credit based upon money as the acceptable standard of value.

SELF TEST
CHAPTER 33

NAME_____

DATE_____

33.1   Negotiable instruments are really _____
instruments, that is, a method of obtaining
_____ for goods and services that we receive
now.

33.2   Negotiable instruments are a means of _____
payment in _____ for services presently
rendered or goods presently received.

33.3   Before there was money or a medium of exchange, a
society and the people in the society had to
_____ their goods.

33.4   In exchange of the barter of goods and services, a
system is developed in every society where there is
some acceptable _____ of _____.

33.5   Money is used in part as a/an_____ of
_____, where in it is used in the _____
of goods or services to exchange goods and services.

33.6   Money is defined as a/an_____ which serves as
a/an_____ of _____, and which, because
of its general _____, is used primarily as a/an
_____ of _____.

33.7   Money is the common _____ of what a product
or service is _____.

33.8   In order for a medium of exchange to be acceptable,
people must have _____ in its value.

33.9   Prior to 1933 and 1935, the money in circulation in
this country was backed by _____, and the
money was known as _____ certificates.

33.10   After 1935, paper money was issued based upon the
_____ of the United States. Also, the
federal government promised to buy _____
from anyone and pay _____ per ounce for it.

33.11   The value of the Federal Reserve Notes that are
used as a medium of exchange is established by the
_____ of the country. In other words, the
standard of value of the American _____ is
fluctuating with the standard of value of the
_____.

33.12 The currency of the United States is controlled
       by the Federal _____ and Federal _____
       Banks across the country.
33.13 As the demand for more money increases, the value
       of money _____, which _____ the value
       of money, so people have to pay _____
       interest rates to have the use of money on a loan.
33.14 The more restrictive the Federal Reserve Banks
       are in granting loans to their _____, the
       more restrictive the _____ is.
33.15 Currency, or paper money, accounts for less than
       ____% of the monetary transactions engaged in in
       the United States.
33.16 There is simply not enough money in circulation to
       run the country in a/an_____ fashion.
33.17 Actually, the hard currency of this country
       accounts for less than _____% of the <u>total</u>
       monetary transactions, the remainder being accounted
       for by _____ credit instruments.
33.18 Private credit instruments are those documents of
       credit which are issued by _____ parties,
       such as _____ or individuals.
33.19 Hard _____, or money, is the foundation upon
       which all private _____ is based.

34 Negotiable Instruments

Checks. Letters of Credit.

LEARNING OBJECTIVES

To acquire a thorough knowledge of the check as a negotiable instrument.

CHAPTER CONTENTS

Importance of Checks   Checks as a Medium of Exchange
Insufficient Funds   Stop Payments   Nonpersonal Checks
Glossary   Self Test

In this chapter instead of first giving general definitions and the rules of law that relate to negotiable instruments, we will examine a very familiar form of negotiable instrument. Only after we have examined the instrument itself and how it works will we discuss the rules that make it operate as a system of credit. This negotiable instrument is the ordinary check—the bank check that individuals and businesses use for the commerce that is necessary in this country.

IMPORTANCE OF CHECKS

Remember from our last chapter that the supply of hard currency is inadequate to furnish a medium of exchange for all of our transactions; in addition, it would be impractical to require the use of hard currency in these transactions. In the United States more than 14.5 billion checks are transferred each year, aggregating in total dollar volume over four trillion dollars a year (a four followed by 12 zeroes). It is estimated that by 1980, 20 billion checks will be issued annually, and that these transactions will exceed 10 trillion dollars a year. The common, ordinary household check and business check are the most important medium of exchange in our economy.

CHECKS AS A MEDIUM OF EXCHANGE

The ordinary bank check carries the name of the bank and generally an identification number. The check also has the city or town, and state, and the date of its issuance. Then the check says, "Pay to the order of _____." Following this is the amount being made payable to a given person. On most checks there is also a place to write this amount in longhand ("Fifty-four dollars") and a place to put the amount in figures or numbers ("$54"). Then at the bottom of the check, in the right-hand corner, there is a place for the signature of the person making the check.
    What is a *check*? A check is merely an order upon a bank to pay a specific sum of money to a specific person. The person who orders the bank to make the payment is known as the *drawer*. The bank that is instructed to make payment is known as the *drawee*.
    The person who is to receive the payment on the check is called the *payee*. For example, I owe Mr. James $25 for

books that he sold to me.   I take one of my checks, which
is issued by the First State Bank, and upon that check
I fill in the date.   Then I order the First State Bank, the
drawee, to pay Mr. James the sum of $25:   I put in the
figures and the words for $25 in the appropriate places.
Then I sign my name as drawer.   Mr. James is the payee, the
person to whom payment is to be made; my bank, the First
State Bank, is the drawee; and I am the drawer of the check.

Upon receipt of this check, Mr. James can take the check
to the bank and submit it to the cashier for payment.   The
bank will check my account to see that I have $25 in my
checking account, and if I do the bank will then ask
Mr. James to indorse (to sign) the back of the check to
establish that he is the person to whom the check is to be
paid.   Once they are satisfied by his indorsement that he
is the person to whom payment has been ordered, they will
pay him the cash from my account in satisfaction of the
check.

When Mr. James signed the check to establish his
identity, he became an *indorser* of the check.   The check
is then given to the bank, which authorizes it to withdraw
$25 from my account, and the transaction is completed.
Mr. James has become both the payee and indorser—transferring the check to the bank or negotiating by indorsement
of the check to the bank.   The bank withdraws the funds,
$25, from my account and submits that cancelled check in
my bank statement at the end of the month to establish their
right of withdrawal of $25 from my account based upon my
drawing the check authorizing payment to Mr. James.   I have
the cancelled check as proof of my payment and Mr. James
has received actual payment for $25 as I have instructed
the bank to make payment upon.

Assume that Mr. James has his business bank account in
the Community Bank, a different bank from mine.   After
Mr. James receives my check in which I have ordered paid
from my account $25, Mr. James endorses that check on the
back as an indorser and instead of taking it to my bank
deposits it in his account with the Community Bank.   Upon
the indorsement of that check to the Community Bank and its
deposit, Mr. James' account is provisionally credited with
$25.   The Community Bank then acts as a collecting bank
and submits my check endorsed by Mr. James to the First
State Bank.   The First State Bank is the *depository bank*
because that's where my funds are deposited.   Upon the
receipt of that check, the First State Bank then examines
my account to make sure that I have a $25 balance in it.

If my account has $25 in it, the bank accepts the check and
removes $25 from my account by a ledger entry and the
credit to Mr. James' account done by the Community Bank
is allowed to stand. Consequently, my bank account is
depleted by $25 and Mr. James' account is increased by
$25 even though no actual dollars have been transferred,
or changed hands.

How can people keep changing balances in their
various accounts when there are no real dollars behind it?
In every city there is a bank called a clearing house,
and each bank in the city, or even in the state, that is
a member of the clearing house has credits and debits against
every other bank in the clearing house, and these debits
and credits are made and they pretty much equal each other
out at the end of the year—so many dollars have been
transferred from bank to bank in the clearing house—and
that's how Mr. James' account is increased by $25 and
my account has been depleted by $25. There is actually less
money in my account and if I wanted to withdraw all of my
account from the bank it would be shy $25 by reason of
the check that I have drawn on Mr. James.

INSUFFICIENT FUNDS

If I had made a mistake and my account was not large enough
to cover (to pay) the check that I have ordered my bank
to pay by drawing my check upon my account, when my bank
receives the check from the Community Bank, it checks my
account and finds that it is inadequate. Within 24 hours
of receipt of that check, my bank returns it to the
Community Bank, noting on it or on a card with it,
"insufficient funds." Mr. James' bank removes the provi-
sional credit to his account of $25 and returns my check
to Mr. James and on it or on a card notes that Mr. Mack's
account has insufficient funds to honor this check.

At this point Mr. James does not have a right to claim
payment from his bank or my bank. But he does have a
right to bring suit against me or to make claim in any way
possible upon me to make good my check—either by cash
payment or by certifying the check (we'll talk about
certification of checks a little later). Mr. James' claim
against me is valid. In fact, if I have a history of
drawing checks on insufficient funds or if there is some
question as to my honesty, Mr. James can turn the checks
over to the District Attorney or state officials and have

me prosecuted for breaking the law, because in every state the drawing of a check against a nonexistent account or against insufficient funds is a crime and is punishable, it is really obtaining credit—from Mr. James in this case—upon false pretenses. If I knew that my bank account was not sufficient to cover that check I could be indicted and tried for the crime of obtaining money under false pretenses or of issuing a fraudulent check.

Thus, it's a very good idea to keep track of your bank balances and to make sure that your checks will be adequately covered by your bank. The bank also has a duty to make sure that if you do have an adequate supply of money in your account to honor those checks that are drawn against the account. If the bank negligently fails to honor a check upon your account when there is sufficient funds in the account, the bank is liable to you as the drawer of the check, for any loss of credit or for any damages that you might have suffered upon the dishonor of the check by the bank. But, generally speaking, the bank and its procedures are such that it has a daily accounting of the status of a bank account.

When the collecting bank submits the check for payment upon the depository bank, the bank that has my account in it, when it has honored the check, the depository bank then becomes the *payor* bank. Finally, after the check has been honored, or paid, by the depository payor bank, the check is returned to the drawer as a cancelled check— proof that payment has been made. This is one reason why checks are so widely used in business as well as personal affairs. A cancelled check is very good evidence of payment. We shall look at several features of a check with respect to payment. You will remember that it is a crime to issue a check when you knew that there were insufficient funds in your account to honor or pay the check, because a check is a promise to pay from present funds upon presentation of the check to the depository bank. One method, sometimes used to avoid the difficulty of having a fund overdrawn, is to postdate a check. For example, I have an obligation to Mr. James for $25 for books he has sold to me; I advise Mr. James that at present my bank account is not sufficient to honor this particular check for $25. Mr. James says, "Well, when will it be?" and I tell him, "Well, just as soon as I can get to the bank and make a deposit." He says, "Why don't you *postdate* the check?" That is, I will date the check several days from today so that the check cannot be cashed for several days—or until there are sufficient funds in the account to cover or honor the check. No bank can cash a check until it is due—that is until upon or after the date written on the check. Many businesses will sometimes postdate a check for presentation to a bank, giving the business or person time to deposit funds sufficient to cover the check.

STOP PAYMENT

You've heard about stopping payment on a check. Let's assume that Mr. James tells me that the books that I am purchasing cover certain subjects, and I give him my check payable to him and date the check for $25, and that day I review the books carefully and find that the subjects Mr. James said were covered are in fact not covered; the books are not of any use to me whatsoever. If I call the bank and tell them the check number, the payee's name, and the date of the check, and I instruct the bank not to cash the check, they will not do so, and if the bank negligently does so, the bank, and not my account, is liable for that amount. An oral stop-payment order upon a bank is valid for 14 days and a written stop-payment order is valid for six months after which time the check becomes stale and will not be honored by the bank and Mr. James will have to obtain a new check from me if he wants to be paid on this particular transaction.

Stop-payment orders upon a check will be honored by a bank, but merely by stopping payment on a check because you've changed your mind about the purchase of services or goods will not relieve anyone of liability un- less he has good cause to rescind the contract. You will remember in our earlier chapters on contracts that I have certain rights to rescind a contract, in this case my agreement to purchase books from Mr. James, and if one of those rights is available to me, then Mr. James may come and pick up his books and there is no more contract. But if I am mistaken and I have a duty to purchase those books based upon our contract, then Mr. James has a right to sue me for the $25. In any event, due to my stop- payment order upon the check the bank will not honor the order upon the bank to pay out of my funds the $25. If the bank has honored the check and paid the funds to Mr. James before receiving my order to stop payment, then my only remedy is to sue Mr. James to recover the purchase price for the books based upon misrepresentation of the seller, Mr. James, in the contract. The bank has no liability to recredit my account with $25 because it had acted in justifiable reliance upon my check before receiving notification to stop payment on that check.

NONPERSONAL CHECKS

The checks that we've been talking about are personal checks or commercial checks. There are other kinds of checks that we should briefly review. A *bank check* is a check written by a bank; the bank is the drawer and it withdraws funds from another bank in another city. It works the same way as the personal check, but it is a transaction between two banks.

A *cashier's check* is one in which a bank withdraws funds from my account—or any other private person's account, including corporations—and on my request the head cashier of the bank will draw a check upon the bank itself made payable to the person whom I direct. For example, if Mr. James is not satisfied to receive my personal check but would like a cashier's check just to make sure that the check will be honored, I instruct the bank to please draw a cashier's check, dated, made payable to the payee, Mr. James, in the amount of $25. Upon receiving said written instruction the First State Bank will withdraw from my account $25 and the cashier will draw a check against the bank itself made payable to Mr. James. In this case the bank is both the drawer and the drawee and Mr. James is the payee. This guarantees that payment will be made upon the cashier's check.

A *certified check* is one that is drawn upon my bank account but has been certified by the head cashier or officer of the bank to be matched by sufficient funds with which to pay this particular draw. When the check is certified the bank will withdraw those funds from my account so that the check will be honored.

A *money order* is nothing more than a check written by a bank or lending institution on funds paid to them. That is, you pay the bank a cash amount, requesting a money order for that amount, and they draw a money order which you, as the drawee, have a right to give to whomever you please, with the guarantee that it will be paid. The money order is very frequently used in the form of

traveler's checks, checks that you have purchased
guaranteeing that, when presented, they will be paid by
the travel agency or bank that has issued the check.
In purchasing a traveler's check, you deposit money with
the agency or bank and you endorse your name upon the check
and when you use the check in payment for services or
goods you sign it and become a drawer against that
account. This is a substitute for money—it's a safer
substitute because the traveler's check has no validity
unless it is signed by you as a drawer. Once you have
signed it, it replaces money—it is acceptable, it sets
forth upon its face the standard of value, and it is
used as a medium of exchange.

In addition, there are *letters of credit* that are
used generally in commercial transactions. If I were
going to a foreign country or a distant city, I would
deposit funds with my bank; the bank would hold the funds
and issue to me a letter of credit in which the bank
promises, to whom it may concern, that it will pay up to
the amount of money I have in the bank upon any check I
draw upon that bank. This is a guarantee, in effect, that
I have sufficient funds to engage in my intended business
in a foreign country or distant city or state where my
credit is not established. Rather than take traveler's
checks or personal funds, I ask my bank to assure the
person who is going to sell me goods on credit that my
credit is good up to a given amount.

In the next chapter we will discuss other forms
of negotiable instruments.

GLOSSARY TERMS

Bank check   A check written by a bank, in which the bank is the drawer.

Cashier's check   A check drawn by the cashier of a bank on the bank after the covered amount has been drawn from a private account to the bank.

Certified check   A check drawn on a private account but certified by the bank's cashier to be matched with sufficient funds for payment, which funds are then set aside for covering that check.

Check   An order upon a bank to pay a specific sum of money to a specific person.

Depository bank   The bank in which funds to be drawn upon by a check are deposited.

Drawee   The bank instructed by a check to make a payment to a specific person.

Drawer   The person who orders a payment to be made on a check.

Indorser   The person who signs a check enabling deposit or transfer of funds to his account or hard currency to his possession.

Letters of credit   A document issued by a bank guaranteeing to pay on checks drawn on a certain account up to a certain amount.

Money order   A check written by a bank to the amount of cash funds tendered them, and payable to whomever the purchaser designates.

Payee   The person instructed to be paid by a check.

Payor   The depository bank making payment on a check.

Postdate   To write on the face of a check a date sometime in the future before which the check cannot be drawn upon or cashed.

Traveler's check   A form of money order but cashable only to the person predesignated as the drawer.

SELF TEST
CHAPTER 34

NAME_____

DATE_____

34.1 It was noted in prior chapters that the supply
of currency was _____ to furnish a medium of
_____ for all of our transactions, and it
would be impractical to require the use of hard
_____ in these transactions.

34.2 In the United States more than 14.5 _____
checks are transferred each year aggregating in
total dollar volume, in excess of four _____
dollars a year.

34.3 It is estimated that by 1980, _____ checks
will be issued annually, and that these transactions
will exceed _____ dollars per year.

34.4 The common, ordinary, household _____ and
business _____ that you're familiar with is,
therefore, the most important _____ in our
economy.

34.5 The ordinary bank check has the name of the _____
upon the check at the top, generally it has an
_____ number.

34.6 The check also has the place and date of its
_____.

34.7 On a check will be the words, "Pay to the
_____ of . . . "

34.8 A check is merely a/an_____ upon a/an_____
to pay a/an_____ sum of money to a specific
_____.

34.9 If you draw a check upon your bank, you are the
_____ and the bank which is instructed to
make payment to a specified person of a specified
amount is the _____.

34.10 The person who is to receive the _____ on
the check is called the _____.

34.11 When the person to whom the check is made payable
_____ the check to establish his _____, he
becomes a/an_____ of the check.

34.12   If the person to whom the check was made payable
        deposits the check in his personal checking account
        at his bank instead of the drawee's bank, his bank
        will become the _____ bank, which will give
        him _____ credit for the deposited check
        until it is collected. The drawer bank, in this
        case, would also be known as the _____
        bank, because that is where the drawer's funds are
        kept.

34.13   In every city there is a bank called a/an_____
        house which is used by member banks to transfer
        funds between banks.

34.14   The person or firm instructed to make the payment
        that a drawer of a check has made is known as the

        _____.

34.15   If a drawee or depository bank receives a check
        from a collecting bank, and the drawer's funds are
        inadequate to pay the check, the depository bank
        has (how long?) _____ from the time the check
        is received to return the check to the _____,
        noting that the check was returned because of
        _____ funds.

34.16   The payee of a check returned because of insufficient
        funds has a claim for the funds against the
        (choose either the "bank" or the "drawer") _____.

34.17   In every state, the drawing of a check against a/an
        _____ account, or an account with _____
        funds, is a crime, because it is really obtaining
        _____ under false _____.

34.18   The bank has a/an _____ to make sure that if
        you do have an adequate supply of money in your
        account, to _____ those checks that are
        drawn against the account.

34.19   If the bank _____ fails to honor a check
        upon an account with sufficient funds, it will be
        liable to the _____ of the check for any
        loss of _____ or other _____ suffered
        because of the bank dishonoring the check.

34.20   A depository bank becomes, when it honors a check
        against an account, a/an _____ bank.

34.21   After a check has been honored, or paid, it is
        returned to the drawer as a/an_____ check,
        which is _____ that payment has been made.

34.22   One method to avoid the difficulty of having a fund
        overdrawn is to _____ a check.

34.23   No bank can cash a check until it becomes

        _____.

CHAPTER 34

NAME_____

34.24 An oral stop-payment order upon a bank is valid
for _____ days, and a/an_____ stop-payment
order upon a bank is valid for _____ months,
after which time a check becomes _____.

34.25 Merely stopping payment of a check will not
_____ the drawer of liability unless he has
good cause to _____ the contract.

34.26 A check written by a bank where the bank is the
drawer and it withdraws funds from another bank in
another city, is known as a/an_____ check.

34.27 A/An_____ check is a check in which a bank
withdraws funds from a private person's account,
and upon his request, the head cashier of the bank
will draw a check upon the _____ made payable
to another person as directed. In this case the
bank is both the _____ and the drawee.

34.28 If the check is a/an_____ check, the head
cashier has certified that adequate funds exist in
the account upon which the check was drawn.

34.29 A/An_____ of _____ is a document issued
by a bank that guarantees a sufficient amount of
funds as stated on the document and is very useful
in conducting business in a foreign country where a
person may not have _____.

34.30 Traveler's checks are a safe substitute for money,
because a traveler's check has no _____
unless it is signed by the drawer.

35 Negotiable Instruments

Drafts. Promissory Notes. What Makes an Instrument Negotiable.

LEARNING OBJECTIVES

To become acquainted with the legal aspects of drafts and promissory notes.

To learn the rules of negotiability.

CHAPTER CONTENTS

We will begin this chapter with a brief discussion of the
form of negotiable instrument known as the draft. Many
people use the word draft when they really mean check.
You'll remember that a check is an order by the drawer
upon the drawee to pay money to a third person—the
payee; the drawer orders the drawee to pay money to the
payee.

DRAFTS

In a *draft* the drawer requests—not orders—that the drawee
pay a third person a specified sum, the amount of the draft.
While a check is a means of obtaining credit, a promise to
pay, a draft is a document used to collect payment from a
debtor. For example, returning to my transaction, from
the previous chapter, with Mr. James for books, after I
have agreed to purchase the books from him I have undertaken to pay him the $25. He returns to his office and
prepares a draft somewhat as follows: He dates it in the
upper right hand corner and then draws it, "To Mr. Gary
P. Mack, pay upon sight the sum of $25 to the Community
Bank." He then signs his name to the draft and sends
it to the Community Bank, requesting that it obtain
collection of the draft. His bank, the Community Bank,
then presents the draft to me and I write "accepted"
on it and pay the bank the draft amount with a certified
check, cashier's check, or cash. The draft, marked
"paid," is left with me. You have seen how a draft works:
The drawer draws money against me and asks a third person
to collect it.
        Mr. James could also have drawn the draft and
indorsed it to a third party. That third party, whom
I've never met and had no prior obligation to, could
present the draft to me and say, "Please pay me directly
for the debt that you owe Mr. James." If Mr. James had
endorsed the draft to the third person, I would be
obligated to make the payment to the third person, or
indorsee.
        Thus, a draft is a collecting instrument, not a paying
instrument; a check is used to pay, a draft to collect.
There are two types of drafts—sight drafts and time
drafts. *Sight drafts* are payable immediately upon presentation to the drawee, while *time drafts* indicate that they
are payable a specific time after presentation—say, 10,
15, or 30 days later. These are, in effect, postdated
collection documents—sight drafts and time drafts.

PROMISSORY NOTES

A *promissory note* is a written promise to pay money to a
specific person. Not all promissory notes are negotiable
instruments; some are merely written contracts to pay
money, or contracts of indebtedness, and are not
negotiable. So before we study negotiable promissory
notes, we will look first at promissory notes themselves.
While the person who draws a check is called a <u>drawer</u>, a
person who signs a promissory note as an *obligor*, or
debtor, is called the *maker of the note*. Just as with a
check, the person to whom the promissory note is payable
is called the payee. Once the promissory note is
delivered, the payee is called the *holder*—and a promissory
note has validity only when it is transferred or held by
the payee or someone who takes after him.

Thus, we have initially two parties to a promissory
note—a maker and a payee. Just like a check, a promissory
note is enforceable only when it is held by someone other
than the maker or drawee. A promissory note may or may
not be a <u>negotiable</u> promissory note, depending upon certain
facts. If the note is <u>not</u> negotiable it is a mere contract to pay. As you'll remember, a person who has the
transfer of a contract or is the assignee of a contract
has no better right to enforce the contract than the
person who was the original contracting party. But when
a person takes a negotiable instrument this rule is
different.

We will discuss in greater detail the rights of a
negotiable instrument holder who takes it from a party
who has a right of collection, but first we will investi-
gate what makes a credit instrument (check, draft, or
promissory note) a negotiable instrument.

NEGOTIABLE CREDIT INSTRUMENTS

Any written credit instrument must have four things on
its face if it is to be negotiable: First, the credit
instrument must be signed by the maker or drawer. Second,
it must contain an unconditional promise or order to pay
a sum certain in money (the promise to pay a sum certain
in money is a promissory note); third, it must be payable
on demand or at a definite time; fourth, it must be payable
to the order of the person named in the instrument, or to
the *bearer*. A bearer is anyone who holds possession of a
document.

Thus, again, the elements of negotiability of any credit instrument is that it must be signed by the maker or drawer, contain an unconditional promise or order to pay a sum certain in money, payable on demand or at a certain time, and be payable to the order of the person named in the instrument, or to any bearer of the instrument.

As to the first element of a negotiable instrument, if I draw a promissory note in which I say, "I, Sam Smith, promise to pay Abe Schwartz $4," and my wife signs the note, it is not a negotiable note because the person who promised to make the payment was not the person who signed the instrument. Or if it is unsigned it is not a negotiable instrument. Only the person who signs the note as a promisor or maker may be held liable on the contract and it is not clear whether I or my wife promised to pay the money. Or if an employee of mine draws a note in which Ajax Construction Company agrees to pay $20 to Sam Brown and the note is signed by Tim Brown, foreman of Ajax Construction Company, Ajax Construction Company will not be bound by the note, for the name of the construction company does not appear on the note and only the person who signs the note may be held liable.

The second element of negotiability is an unconditional promise or order to pay a sum certain in money. An unconditional promise is just what it seems to be—a promise that is based upon no condition, it is unqualified. For example, "I, Sam Jones, agree to pay Tim Brown $3500 if he quits smoking." Obviously, this contract of payment is not a negotiable instrument because the promise of payment is not a negotiable instrument because the promise of payment is not unconditioned. It is expressly conditioned upon Mr. Brown's discontinuing his filthy habit of smoking, and no person who holds that note will take any better right than Mr. Brown had, and if Mr. Brown does not discontinue smoking, the person who holds the note subsequent to Mr. Brown will not be able to recover payment—even though the holder of the note never smoked a day in his life. This is the meaning of an unconditional promise. And many, many cases have been tried and won or lost on the question of whether or not a promise in a promissory note was conditioned or unconditioned.

The second element is an unconditional promise or order to pay a sum certain in money. Just like a check, a promissory note very often has the amount in both words and figures. For example, in my check to Mr. James for the purchase of books I could have mistakenly written $30 in figures and $25 in writing. That mistake in a check will not make the check unnegotiable because the written part of the check controls over the figures in the amount payable. But in cases of ambiguity, where two written parts of the instrument, either check or promissory note, are conflicting, then the instrument is not negotiable. For example, if I write, "I, Tim Brown, agree to pay to Don Watson $4500 or 7 cattle ten days after the date of this note," clearly $4500 or 7 cattle are inconsistent. We don't know which will be paid, the 7 cattle or the $4500. Therefore, the promise to pay is not an unconditioned promise to pay a sum certain, it may be cattle or it may be $4500. Consequently this particular promissory note is not in a sum certain and is, therefore, not a negotiable instrument.

The third element of negotiability is that it is payable on demand or at a definite time—that is, stated as on or before a specified date, or at a fixed period after a stated date, or at a fixed period after presentation. For example, a note saying, "Tim Watson agrees to pay $3500 to Tom Brown upon Tom's marriage," is not a negotiable instrument. While it is a contract to make a payment, it is not a negotiable promissory note because the certainty of Tom Brown's marriage is not apparent upon the face of the instrument itself. Tom may be married in two days or in 25 years, and anyone looking at the promissory note would not know whether he was entitled to payment or not, unless he was, in fact, Tom Brown.

The fourth and last element of negotiability is that the words of the note or check must be payable to a specific person and order or to the bearer. All of the notes described so far are nonnegotiable for this reason alone, aside from the other reasons that we've talked about. All negotiable instruments are payable to the order of the named person, and some negotiable promissory notes are payable to the bearer—the person who has possession of the promissory note. If you write a contract of payment in which you say, "I, Sally Brown, agree to pay to Sharon Olsen, $25." and you sign it and date it, it is a contract of payment but it is not a negotiable promissory note, because only Sharon Olsen may collect the amount owed to her and no other person. If you had said, "I, Sally Brown, agree to pay to Sharon Olsen, or her order, $25," or if you had said, "I, Sally Brown, agree to pay to the bearer of this note" whatever money that was involved, then there would be a negotiable promissory note and Sharon Olsen could negotiate that note by endorsing it and any person who took from her could collect the note amount from you, either as the bearer or as the holder in due course from Sharon Olsen.

   If you make a note or a check payable to "cash," then any person who holds that check or note will be able to redeem it from you, because a check made payable to cash is a check made payable to bearer. It's very important that if you draw a check made payable to cash, you take it directly to the bank and redeem it from your own account for the cash. In a later chapter we will discuss why we should be careful about negotiable instruments, including checks and promissory notes, but if you draw a promissory note payable to bearer, or if you draw a check payable to cash (that is, to bearer), then you should make sure that when you receive the cash from the check it is payable to a bank, or that when you pay off a note payable to bearer you get the note back marked "paid" and destroy it.

GLOSSARY TERMS

Bearer The possessor of a document.

Debtor A maker of a promissory note.

Draft A document requesting that a drawee pay a specified sum to a third person.

Holder A payee of a promissory note who is in possession of the note.

Maker of the note A person who signs a promissory note.

Obligor A maker of a promissory note.

Promissory note A written promise to pay money to a specific person.

Sight draft A draft payable immediately on presentation.

Time draft A draft payable some indicated length of time after presentation.

SELF TEST

CHAPTER 35

NAME_____

DATE_____

35.1 In a draft, the drawer _____, not orders, that the _____ pay to a third person a specified sum.

35.2 A check is used as a means of obtaining _____ —a/an _____ to pay; whereas, a draft is a document used to _____ payment from a/an_____.

35.3 The two types of drafts are _____ drafts and _____ drafts.

35.4 A/An_____ is a written promise to pay money to a specific person, not all of these promises are considered _____ instruments.

35.5 A person who signs a promissory note as a/an_____, or debtor, is called a/an_____.

35.6 The person to whom a promissory note is made payable is called the _____.

35.7 Once a promissory note is delivered or transfer- red, the person in possession of the promissory note is known as the _____.

35.8 A promissory note only has _____ when it is transferred or held by the payee, or someone who _____ after him.

35.9 If a promissory note is not negotiable, it is a mere _____ to pay.

35.10 The four attributes of every written credit instru- ment which must be apparent on the _____ of the credit instrument to make that credit instrument negotiable are:

a) the credit instrument must be _____ by the maker or drawer;

b) the credit instrument must contain a/an_____ promise or order to pay a sum _____ in money;

c) the instrument must be payable on _____ or at a certain time;

d) it must be payable to the _____ of the person named in the instrument, or to the _____.

35.11   Only the person who signs a promissory note may
        be held _____ on the note.

35.12   An unconditional promise is based upon no condition,
        it is _____.

35.13   The _____ part of a check controls over the
        figures in the amount payable.

35.14   In cases of _____ where it is not really
        clear, or where two written parts of the instru-
        ment are conflicting, then the instrument (choose
        either "is" or "is not") _____ negotiable.

35.15   Definite time means that the time is stated
        _____ or before a/an _____ date.

35.16   A check made payable to "cash" is a check made
        payable to _____.

35.17   The reasons for the rules for negotiable instruments
        is that negotiable instruments are substitutes for
        _____.

35.18   Credit instruments must be in _____ form,
        or they will not be acceptable as _____.

36 Negotiable Instruments

Transfer–Negotiation. Liability of Indorser.

LEARNING OBJECTIVES

To learn how negotiable instruments are transferred.

CHAPTER CONTENTS

In this chapter we will discuss how a person takes a transfer of a negotiable instrument from the original payee. Contracts are assigned; negotiable instruments are negotiated; all documents may be transferred. Remember that when a contract is assigned it gives to the assignee the same rights and the same obligations as the original party to the contract. Thus, if I have a defense to enforcement of the contract, or if I have a right to rescind a contract, that right remains with me against any trans- feree or assignee of the contract. The party that assumes a contract by assignment stands in no better position than the party who originally contracted with me.

But this is not true in negotiable instruments, for certain parties who take possession of the negotiable instrument may have rights superior to the original payee. That is, a holder in due course from a payee may not be subject to the same defenses that I have against the original payee. But before we examine the rights and duties between a holder in due course and the original maker or drawer of the negotiable instrument, let's find out how a negotiable instrument is transferred.

TRANSFER OF NEGOTIABLE INSTRUMENTS

We already know that a negotiable instrument is <u>negotiated</u> in its transfer. If it is truly a negotiable instrument it is not assigned, it is negotiated. A negotiable instrument is negotiated by <u>indorsement</u> and hence transferred from one payee to a subsequent holder who has the right to payment. Because indorsements can take many forms we must discuss briefly the forms that are possible in a negotiable instrument, and their effects. The effects of the indorsements are extremely important because the method of indorsement will create or limit the liability of the indorser of the instrument.

Let's first look at the negotiable instrument that is payable to bearer. Remember that a check left blank where the name of the party or to his order is supposed to be inserted is a bearer instrument, as is a check made payable to cash, and as is a promissory note with a promise to pay to bearer. Transfer of any of these instruments may be made merely by delivery because there is no payee named on that instrument. Such transfer is *indorsement by delivery*. Consequently, the instrument can pass from hand to hand with no one signing his or her name as an indorser

of the check or promissory note. This form of negotiation
is not by indorsement, for as a matter of law no indorsement is required.

As a matter of practice, most bearer notes and bearer
checks are indorsed by the people who hold them, simply
because the person who takes the bearer note would like
to have additional names on that bearer note as additional
security. For example, if a check passes from the third
to the fifth to the seventh hand pretty soon the person
who receives the check doesn't know the original drawer
of the check and would like to have the credit of his
indorser attached to the check so that if the check is not
honored he will have a ready remedy against the indorser.
You can see that indorsement is very important because it
puts you on the hook for payment of the document that
you have indorsed. Let's, then, be careful in understanding
the methods of indorsement.

METHODS OF INDORSEMENT

One form of indorsement of a negotiable instrument is by
blank indorsement. Blank indorsement is not the same as
not signing the instrument, as happens in delivery of
bearer instruments that we discussed above. A blank
indorsement is instead the signing of the promissory note
or check, generally on the back, with your name only.
For example, a note says, "I, John Jones, promise to pay
to the order of Sam Smith $25." On the back of the note
Sam Smith indorses his name with no other words and
transfers the note to Mr. Joe Black. Mr. Black takes the
note by blank indorsement because Sam Smith has passed
the note by delivery and indorsement. Remember, the note
was to Sam Smith or his order (to the order of Sam Smith).
By blank indorsement Sam Smith has given full title to
Joe Black.

A third form of indorsement is a *special indorsement*.
A special indorsement makes the promissory note or check
payable to a specific person. For example, John Jones
writes a check for cash for $25. That check is bearer
paper; but he gives the check to Mr. Sam Smith, who gives
him $25 for it. Sam Smith then indorses on the back of
the check, "Sam Smith, pay to the order of Joe Black."
The bearer paper has become order paper—that is, payable
to the order of a specific person; now only Joe Black
can negotiate that check, and anyone else who got hold

of that check could not negotiate the check further, nor
could they cash it without the indorsement of Joe Black
upon it.

Our fourth type of indorsement is a *qualified indorsement*, which qualifies the indorser's responsibility to
stand behind the negotiable instrument that he is
indorsing. That is, Joe Jones writes a check for $25
payable to the order of Sam Smith. Sam Smith has given
Joe Jones the $25, but he indorses upon the check,
"Without recourse, Sam Smith." and transfers or negotiates
the paper to Joe Black. By the words "Without recourse"
Sam Smith has told Joe Black that he will not stand behind
this check: If Joe Jones dishonors the check or cannot
pay for it upon presentation at the bank, Joe Black may
look only to Joe Jones, not to Sam Smith.

An indorsement can be a combination special and
qualified. For example, when he had Joe Jones' check
Sam Smith could write, "Pay to the order of Joe Black
without recourse," and indorse it "Sam Smith." The paper
becomes order paper held solely by Joe Black, and Sam Smith
has no responsibility to make the paper good, because
he has said to Joe Black, "You cannot have recourse
against me if that rascal Joe Jones doesn't pay the
check." A qualified indorsement does not make the
negotiable instrument nonnegotiable, it merely removes
the indorser from liability upon the face amount of the
negotiable instrument—whether it is a draft, a check, or
a promissory note.

Our fifth type of indorsement is a *restrictive
indorsement*, which limits the negotiation of the note
beyond the indorsee. The person who receives the note
after the restrictive indorsement may collect the note
from anybody prior to the restrictive indorser—the
maker or drawer of the instrument or any one who indorsed
the note prior to the restrictive indorser's signature.
However, any person who takes after such a restrictive
indorsement still has all of the rights of any other
indorser or holder against the maker or drawer of the
check and against any indorser who preceded the restrictive indorsement upon the negotiable instrument.

The most common form of restrictive indorsement is
found on checks and reads, "For collection only," and bears
the name of the indorser. Many times checks are received
by a person or a company in satisfaction of services or
goods sold and the company (or person) desires to deposit
the check in its (or his) own account for collection.

They do not want the check indorsed further and transferred through other forms of business enterprises, they
want to collect the money immediately. Also, they do not
wish to have the check stolen or lost. So they make
the notation, "For collection only" to their bank, making
the bank the indorsee and the indorsement restrictive
so that the check cannot be negotiated further, it must
be collected by the indorsee. It is deposited in their
account for collection only. This is a wonderful safeguard, as an example will show. Say a law firm received
a large check payable to the office for services rendered.
No one in the office had time to take it to the bank for
deposit so a bank messenger was asked to come over to
the firm and pick up the check. But rather than indorse
the check in blank, the firm indorsed the check "For
collection only" to the bank and signed our signature.
In this way, had the bank messenger lost the check,
anyone who found it could not have indorsed the check
further or cashed it. In addition, if the bank's
messenger had been held up or had been dishonest himself, the check would have been valueless to him, because
the firm used a restrictive indorsement, "For collection
only."

Our sixth type of indorsement is the *accommodation
indorsement*. Many times businesses and people doing
business or on a vacation far from home seek funds by
check or seek indorsement of a promissory note where their
credit is not known and where the local bank is unwilling to expend the funds to call the home bank and to
determine if an account is sufficient. But say the
traveler identifies a friend in the community and the
friend will indorse the check as an accommodation party,
then by the indorsement the local person agrees to
guarantee, in effect, the validity of the check. Thus,
an indorser who signs at the time of execution or shortly
thereafter as an accommodation indorser becomes secondarily
liable upon the instrument.

Our seventh type of indorsement is the *waiver indorsement*,
by which the indorser on the instrument agrees that if its
maker or drawer does not pay, the indorser waives specific
notice of the maker or drawer's dishonor before he will
pay the note or check himself. Ordinarily an indorser
is only secondarily liable to the maker or drawer, and
a person who demands payment of the maker or drawer must
generally notify an indorser that the maker or drawer has
dishonored his obligation on the face of the note before

he can make claim of the indorser for payment.   This
rule is to protect the indorser.

     For example, if John Jones holds a note that Sam
Smith has written and there is an indorser named White,
it is incumbent upon the holder to make claim upon the
maker and to demand payment. If the maker does not
make payment, then the holder must advise the indorser,
Mr. White, of the dishonor so as to allow him the opportunity to bring whatever pressure he can bring upon the maker
of the note. After a reasonable time has expired following
notice of dishonor made upon the indorser, then the holder
of the note may make claim directly against the indorser
to pay the liability in full that the maker of the instrument or drawer of the check, Mr. Smith, has incurred by
the instrument itself. But a waiver indorsement waives
notice of dishonor, so that if the note or check was
dishonored on presentation when due, the holder could
immediately make demand upon the indorser without the
requirement of notice of dishonor. That, then, is a
waiver indorsement.

     Our final type of indorsement for discussion is
the *partial payment indorsement*, by which the indorser
indorses the note for only a part of the payment due on
the note. In other words, if Joe Jones wrote a negotiable
promissory note to Sam Smith for $150, and Joe Jones then
paid $75 upon the note, if Sam Smith wanted to negotiate
it by indorsement to Joe Black he would indorse the note
for the remaining balance due on the note. That is, the
indorsement might read, "Received, $75. Indorsed for
balance, $75, Sam Smith." Or he could say, "Pay to the
order of Joe Black, balance on note, $75," which would be
both a special indorsement and a partial payment indorsement.

LIABILITIES OF INDORSER

The blank indorsement is by far the commonest type of
indorsement of negotiable instruments. What does the
indorser undertake when he indorses a negotiable instrument—
either by blank or by special indorsement? The indorser is
bound by law, unless he otherwise specifies, either in
restrictive or qualified language, that upon dishonor
and any necessary notice of dishonor and protest, he,
the indorser, will pay the instrument according to its
tenure at the time of his indorsement. That is to say that

an indorser agrees to pay the note or the check to any
person who takes subsequent to him, provided that the
indorser is liable only after every subsequent indorser
to him has dishonored his particular indorsement.
For example, on an instrument say we have four indorsers.
The fourth indorser presents the check or note to its
original maker or drawee for payment and the maker or
drawer dishonors it. The fourth indorser then presents
notice of dishonor to the third indorser, who in turn
dishonors his indorsement. The fourth indorser decides,
"Well, rather than sue the third indorser, I'll present
the note or check to the second indorser." But this
indorser also dishonors the check or note. So the fourth
indorser gives notice of dishonor and presentation for
payment to the first indorser, who says, "Yes, I'm liable
on the thing, and I'll have to look to the maker or drawer
of the check for payment." This indeed is what the law
states; an indorser, either special or blank, warrants that
he will pay to subsequent indorsers according to the
obligation of the face of the note or check, provided that
subsequent indorsers have been presented with the demand
for payment and have dishonored the face of the note or
the check in turn. Before the first indorser is liable,
the third and the second indorsers must default. Once
such default has occurred the first indorser must look
for his recovery to the original maker or drawer of the
negotiable instrument.

Lest you get too alarmed, an indorser is not liable
for all time. He is liable to a subsequent holder of the
note only if that subsequent holder has used due diligence
in attempting to obtain payment from the maker or drawer
of the instrument and has promptly notified each of the
indorsers in turn of the dishonor following presentation
to the maker or payor. In addition, the holder must make
prompt presentation for payment and notice of dishonor
to each of the subsequent indorsers, or the first indorser
is relieved of his liability. Also, an indorser is
relieved of secondary liability if a holder has extended
a promissory note without the consent of its indorsers for
an unreasonable length of time. For it would be unfair
that an indorser have secondary liability for a long
period of time while a holder was negotiating or allowing
an extension of time to the original maker. At some point
the indorser's liability must be terminated, and when this
is depends upon what is reasonable under the facts and
circumstances of each individual case.

GLOSSARY TERMS

Accommodation indorsement   An indorsement to guarantee the validity of a negotiable instrument.

Blank indorsement   Indorsement by a bearer and subsequent transfer to an unnamed bearer.

Indorsement by delivery   Transfer of a negotiable instrument that is made out to an unspecified bearer.

Partial payment indorsement   An indorsement for a specified amount that is less than the face amount of the instrument.

Qualified indorsement   An indorsement that specifies the bearer but removes the indorser from obligation to cover the negotiable instrument.

Restrictive indorsement   An indorsement by which the negotiation of the note is limited beyond the indorsee.

Special indorsement   An indorsement that makes the instrument payable to a specified person.

Waiver indorsement   An indorsement by which the indorser waives the right to protection from immediate demand for payment to the holder of the instrument if the maker or drawer dishonors the instrument.

SELF TEST

CHAPTER 36

NAME_____

DATE_____

36.1 Contracts are _____. Negotiable instruments
are _____. All documents may be transferred.

36.2 A contract, when assigned, gives the assignee the
same rights and the same _____ as the
_____ party to the contract.

36.3 In negotiable instruments, certain parties who
take possession of the negotiable instrument may
have rights _____ to the original _____.

36.4 A holder in _____ from a payee
may not be subject to the same _____ that
one may have against the _____ payee.

36.5 A negotiable instrument is negotiated by _____.

36.6 The method of indorsement creates or limits the
_____ of the indorser of the instrument.

36.7 The indorsement or transfer of a bearer instrument
may be made merely by _____, because there
is no named _____ on this type of instrument.

36.8 As a matter of practice, most bearer instruments
are indorsed by the people who hold them, because
the person who takes the bearer instrument would
like to have additional _____ on the instrument as additional _____.

36.9 One form of negotiation of negotiable instruments
then, is _____ of bearer instruments.

36.10 Another form of negotiation of negotiable instruments is by _____ indorsement, which is
merely the insertion upon the instrument, generally
on the back, of your _____ only.

36.11 Indorsements are very important, because they make
the indorser liable for _____ of the document
that he has indorsed.

36.12 A/An _____ indorsement is an indorsement which
makes a promissory note or check payable to a
specific person. This type of indorsement can also
make bearer paper become _____ paper, because
it limits the payee to a specific person.

36.13 A/An _____ indorsement qualifies the indorser's _____ to stand behind the negotiable instrument that he is indorsing. An indorsement of this type would usually contain the words "without _____" above the indorser's name.

36.14 A/An _____ indorsement does not make a negotiable instrument nonnegotiable; it merely removes the indorser from _____ upon the face amount of the negotiable instrument.

36.15 A/An _____ indorsement limits the negotiation of a note or check beyond the _____; that is, the person who receives the note (choose either "prior to" or "after") _____ the indorser.

36.16 The most common form of restrictive indorsement is found on checks, and it reads, "For _____ only."

36.17 A local person who agrees to _____, in effect, the validity of another person's check, and who signs at the time of execution is known as a/an _____ indorser. His indorsement makes him _____ liable on the instrument he indorses as a/an _____ indorser.

36.18 A check that is left blank where the name of the party or to his order is supposed to be put in is a/an _____ instrument.

36.19 A/an _____ indorsement is one in which the indorser of the check or promissory note agrees that if the maker or drawer of the note or check respectively, does not pay, then the indorser _____ specific _____ of the maker or drawer's _____ before he will pay the note or check himself.

36.20 An indorser is _____ liable to the maker or drawer, and a person who demands payment of the maker or drawer, must _____ an indorser, generally, that the maker or drawer has _____ his obligation. This rule is to protect the _____.

36.21 A/An _____ indorser only indorses the note for a part of the payment due on the note.

36.22 In quick review the most common types of indorsements of negotiable instruments are:
a) negotiation by delivery of _____ instruments;
b) _____ indorsement, which is by name only;

CHAPTER 36

NAME_____

     c)   _____ indorsements, which mean that they are for a specific purpose for deposit or collection only;

     d)   _____ indorsement, which is an indorsement made near the time of execution of the instrument, and in which the indorser lends his _____ to the original payee of the instrument;

     e)   _____ indorsements naming a particular person to whom the check or note should be paid;

     f)   _____ payment indorsement for an unpaid balance of an instrument which has been partially honored;

     g)   _____ indorsement, which waives, by the indorser, the right to receive notice of _____ and dishonor by the holder to the maker of the instrument; and,

     h)   _____ indorsements, which mean that they may be used for a personal contract between the indorser and _____.

36.23 By far, the most frequent type of indorsement is _____.

36.24 An indorser is bound by law, unless he otherwise specifies, either in _____ or _____ language, that upon _____ and any necessary notice of dishonor and _____, that he, the indorser, will pay the instrument according to its _____ at the time of his indorsement.

36.25 The law states that an indorser, either special or in blank, _____ that he will pay to _____ indorsers according to the obligation of the face of the note or check provided that _____ indorsers have been presented with the demand for payment, and they have in turn _____ the face amount of the note or check.

36.26 An indorser is liable to a subsequent holder of a negotiable instrument only if the subsequent holder has used due _____ in attempting to obtain payment from the maker or drawer of the instrument, and has promptly notified each of the indorsers

in turn of the dishonor following _____ to
the maker or payer. In addition, the holder must
make prompt _____ for payment and notice of
_____ to each of the subsequent indorsers,
or the _____ indorser is relieved of liability.

36.27 An indorser is relieved of secondary liability if a
holder has _____ a promissory note without
the _____ of the indorsers to the promissory
note for an unreasonable length of time.

37 Negotiable Instruments

Collection. Discharge.

LEARNING OBJECTIVES

To learn the rights of a holder-in-due-course of a negotiable instrument.

CHAPTER CONTENTS

In this chapter we will discuss the collection of promissory notes—the obtaining of payment from the maker or drawer of such instruments. The rights of a holder of a promissory note or check depend upon whether he is a holder in due course or is a holder not in due course. A *holder in due course* takes free of defenses that the maker or drawer of the instrument might have against the original payee. For example, Mr. B. sells a horse to Mr. A. and takes a promissory note for payment of the horse from Mr. A. Mr. B is the payee and Mr. A is the maker of the note. Mr. B. negotiates the promissory note to Mr. C by blank endorsement—Mr. C pays value for the note, that is, the face amount of the note or any other value that is agreed upon between Mr. B and Mr. C. At the time for payment of the note, Mr. C goes to Mr. A and demands honor or payment of the promissory note. At this time Mr. A. tells Mr. C that he's not going to pay the note because there has been a lack of consideration, because the horse that Mr. B sold to Mr. A was crippled and died, and Mr. B has defrauded Mr. A. Mr. C advises Mr. A that he (Mr. C) is a holder in due course.; he therefore does not take subject to the defenses that Mr. A might have to Mr. B's making claim upon the note but instead takes free of those defenses.

Why should Mr. C. stand in better position than Mr. A in holding this promissory note? Simply because a promissory note is a substitute for money and is used as a medium of exchange and Mr. C gave value for the promissory note. You'll remember that credit instruments play a much larger part in our commercial society than hard money does. Consequently, the acceptability of such credit instruments must be established by the law, and if every check or promissory note had to be thoroughly checked out with the original maker before it was accepted then our commercial transactions based upon credit instruments would come to an end.

Consequently, the law says that a person who purchases a credit instrument for value with no knowledge of prior defenses or discharge of the maker or drawer of the instrument takes free of defenses that the maker or drawer may have against the original payee of the check or promissory note. (Keep in mind that a contract assignee or a person who receives a contract by assignment takes the contract subject to all of the defenses that the original contracting promisor has against the original contracting party. But this is not the case in promissory notes.) A holder in due course takes free of defenses that the maker or drawer has against

the original payee.   This is an important distinction and
on which our entire credit economy depends.

HOLDERS IN DUE COURSE

Although a holder in due course therefore takes free of
defenses of the maker or drawer of the check, there are some
exceptions to that rule.   But before we examine them let's
find out what it takes to be a holder in due course.   A
holder in due course is a person who takes possession of a
negotiable instrument and pays value, consideration, for
it.   Consideration, as you know, can consist of a promise
to do something in the future, or payment for a past act,
or the delivery of a credit instrument for a credit instrument, or money.   For example, in our example above, Mr. B
could have accepted a promise from Mr. A to do something
in the future and indorsed the promissory note to Mr. C;
or he could have received cash or any other thing of value
from Mr. C and Mr. C would be a holder in due course—if
two other elements are satisfied: Mr. C took the
promissory note in good faith, and without knowledge that
it is overdue.   Good faith means that Mr. C, or any indorser
like Mr. C, is not party to any fraud or was in concert
with Mr. B in defrauding Mr. A in the sale of the horse.
It also means that Mr. C is not knowledgeable about any of
the defenses of Mr. A at the time he took the promissory
note.   In addition, to be a holder in due course of the
promissory note, Mr. C, as we said, must take the instrument without notice that it is overdue or has been dishonored or that any defense or claim has been put on it by
any other person.   Therefore, Mr. C could not be a holder
in due course if he knew that Mr. A had dishonored the
note with Mr. B and made claim for return of his money due
to Mr. A's belief that he was cheated in the sale of the
horse.   Nor could he take as a holder in due course if he
could see from the face of the note that it was overdue.
Nor could he take the note as a holder in due course if
he was aware of any claim or deficiency in the consideration
which was the basis for the issuance of the promissory note
by Mr. A.

Let's review, then, very quickly, who is a holder in
due course: a person who takes the instrument for value,
in good faith, without notice that it is overdue or has been
dishonored, and without knowledge of any defense or claim
to the payment of the note or any claim by any third party.

Using again our example of the sale of the horse by
Mr. B to Mr. A, assume that Mr. A drew a negotiable
promissory note agreeing to pay $500 for the horse, and
that, on the second day, Mr. A came to Mr. B and said,
"That horse isn't worth $500," and Mr. B agreed, and Mr. A
gave Mr. B $250 and said, "Now we're finished with the deal
and I don't owe you any more," and Mr. B agreed. But Mr. A
unfortunately neglected to get back his promissory note.
Thereafter, after he'd been paid in full pursuant to the
subsequent agreement, Mr. B negotiated the promissory note
to Mr. C. Mr. C paid $500 to Mr. B for the promissory note
and then went to Mr. A and demanded payment when the note
became due for the $500. Mr. C gave value for the note in
good faith without notice that it had been paid. Consequently, Mr. A is liable on the promissory note to Mr. C.
Obviously Mr. A has a cause of action for fraud against
Mr. B, who is a crook, but Mr. C is not stuck with the loss
of the $500. Mr. A is, because he is the maker of the
promissory note and Mr. C is its holder in due course.
This may not seem fair to Mr. A, but it certainly wouldn't
be fair to allow Mr. C to be stuck with the loss, for the
rule is that Mr. A allowed Mr. B to keep the note when he
should have taken it back. Mr. A put Mr. B in a position
to defraud someone else, so Mr. A should suffer the loss
rather than Mr. C, who acted in good faith and paid value
for the note. Consequently, you can see that a holder in
due course has rights which are superior to the payee.

But a payee may also be a holder in due course. A
payee who gives value for a note or check or other
negotiable instrument and does so in good faith unaware of
any defense that the maker or drawer of the instrument has
may be able to recover upon the negotiable instrument free
of defenses that the maker or drawer would otherwise have
if it were merely a contract. Consequently, in your dealings
with promissory notes, you should make sure that you're
getting a negotiable promissory note if you're a payee, and
you may very well want to be careful that the note you sign
is not negotiable if you have some doubt about the goods
that you're buying, or if you're buying them on trial, or
if there is a warranty that gives you a free trial inspection
of the goods. You certainly wouldn't want to sign a
negotiable promissory note which would make you liable on
your promise of payment irrespective of the defenses you
would have if the goods were not as warranted. You have seen
a practical example of how the law in its technical distinctions make real differences in our everyday life.

HOLDERS NOT IN DUE COURSE

A person who purchases a negotiable instrument at a judicial
sale, or as a result of a lost lawsuit or a judicial proceeding, cannot be a holder in due course; nor can a person
who acquires a negotiable instrument in taking over an
estate either as an heir or as the administrator be a
holder in due course. Likewise, a purchaser of a business
who also receives certain checks or drafts or promissory
notes in the purchase of the business cannot be a holder in
due course, because a holder in due course has to be a
person who takes possession of a promissory note in the
regular course of his business or of his own transactions.

Similarly, a person who takes possession of a negotiable
instrument cannot be a holder in due course (free of the
defenses of the maker or drawer of the instrument) if the
instrument is so incomplete or bears visible evidence of
forgery or alteration or is sufficiently irregular on its
face that it calls into question the validity or the terms
of ownership or creates any ambiguity on its face. In
other words, if an otherwise negotiable instrument is incomplete, or presents inconsistencies, or is not completely
signed by a maker, or is unclear in its terms or presents
evidence of forgery, then the person who takes possession
of that note, check, or draft cannot be a holder in due
course. The law states that he is under the duty of making
inquiry into any deficiencies because the note or check
itself gives him notice of irregularity.

In addition a purchaser of a negotiable instrument
cannot be a holder in due course if the purchaser has notice
that the obligation of any of the parties thereto is voidable
in whole or in part or that all the parties have been
discharged by a prior party who held the note. (Remember
from our discussion of contracts that a <u>voidable</u> contract
may not be enforced against the promisor although the
promisor may enforce the contract against the promisee; and
remember that a contract is voidable only under certain
circumstances.) But a purchaser who takes the promissory
note with knowledge that it is voidable—for example, it
was issued by a minor—or that the promise has been discharged, cannot take the note as a holder in due course.
Also, a person who purchases a negotiable instrument when
he has knowledge that it is overdue cannot be a holder in
due course; nor can he be if he knows that there has been
a default not remedied by the person who has the right to
demand payment by the maker or drawer. Additionally, he

cannot be a holder in due course if he knows that a demand
has been made upon the maker or payor and it has not been
honored. (At this point you should be informed that a
check that is more than 30 days old is irregular on its
face—it's stale; and any person who takes it as an indorsee
or transferee cannot take that check as a holder in due
course.)

Let's, then, try to redefine a holder in due course.
A holder in due course is one who takes possession of a
negotiable instrument by giving value for it, in good
faith, without notice that it is overdue or has been dishonored, or without notice of any defense or claim to it
on the part of the maker or drawer or any claim by any other
person to the negotiable instrument. For an example of what
this last phrase means, say Mr. Brown has a promissory note
made payable to his order for $500. Mr. Brown negligently
leaves this note out and a thief steals it, indorses it to
himself, and then negotiates it to a bank. The bank pays
value to Mr. Smith, the thief, for the promissory note
since they see no irregularity on the face of the instrument
or in the indorsements even though one was forged. The
bank then makes claim upon the maker of the promissory note,
who pays the promissory note even though he knows that it
was stolen from Mr. Brown, because he is obligated as between
Mr. Brown and the bank to pay the holder of the promissory
note in accordance with its terms.

The bank, in this case, was a holder in due course
entitled to payment even though Mr. Brown had a claim to
the promissory note because it was stolen from him. You
can see that this is different from other forms of personal
property. If an automobile were stolen, the person with
whom the automobile ended up would have to return it to
the person from whom it was stolen. But this is not the
case with respect to negotiable instruments in the hands
of a holder in due course.

DEFENSES AGAINST HOLDERS IN DUE COURSE

Although the holder in due course takes free of personal
defenses of the maker or any preceding indorser on the note,
we mentioned earlier that the rule had certain exceptions,
and that a holder in due course did take subject to some
defenses.

We will examine the first exception by first restating
the rule on holders in due course: A holder in due course

of a negotiable instrument takes free of all claims to it
on the part of any person and free from all defenses of
any party to the instrument with whom the holder has not
dealt. You see in that definition that the holder in due
course does take subject to all defenses that his indorser
or even the maker may have against him if he dealt with
that person in the transfer of the instrument to him. But
the holder in due course does not take subject to any claims
of third parties or to any defenses of third parties even
though it might be the defense of the maker or drawer of
the instrument or any prior indorser of the instrument—
provided that indorser did not deal with him in the indorsement of the instrument to him.

There are four other defenses that the holder in due
course does take subject to with respect to the maker or
drawer or any prior indorser. The holder in due course
does take subject to the defense of voidability based upon
infancy or minority. You will remember that a contract
could be voidable by a minor if the minor was willing to
return the value of the goods or services that he had used
or received and provided that the minor was not purchasing
necessities and was not an emancipated minor, one who lives
away from home and supports himself. A holder in due course
does take subject to the voidability that is available to
a minor.

The holder in due course also takes subject to the
voidability of a contract based upon incapacity of the maker
or drawer of the instrument due to sickness or mental illness or to illegality of the instrument. In other words,
if a promissory note was given in payment of an illegal
contract, it can be voided by the maker. Or if it was for
an illegal purpose, it can be voided. Or if the promissory
note is usurious—that is, an illegal rate of interest is
being charged—it is unenforceable against the maker.

In addition, if the promissory note or negotiable
check is the result of duress—force and violence or threats
and intimidation—it is void and cannot be enforced by a
holder in due course even though when the holder in due
course gave value for the instrument he took in good faith
and without knowledge of the duress or illegality or
incapacity of the maker.

The rule of law is that such contracts cannot be enforced against people who are incapable of contracting or
are forced by duress or engaged in illegal contracts. The
law does not allow or permit the enforcement of such contracts
even though an innocent holder in due course may be trying

to obtain from the maker or drawer compensation for the value
he gave for the negotiable instrument.

In addition, the holder in due course does take subject to a real defense of a maker or drawer or any prior
indorser that is based upon misrepresentations that induced
the maker or drawer or indorser to sign the instrument when
he or they did not know what the instrument meant. This
is a very rare defense because most of us know what a
promissory note is or what a check is, but there have been
cases where a person has signed a document—sometimes as
the result of skillful sales pressure—and didn't know that
he was signing a promissory note or a negotiable draft or
bill of exchange or check for that matter. In such cases
that misrepresentation voids the signature of the maker or
drawer—or the indorser, for that matter—and the promise
implicit in the signature is unenforceable even by a holder
in due course.

Another defense that the holder in due course of a
negotiable instrument takes subject to is the discharge
of the maker or drawer of the instrument·in a proceeding
in insolvency, or bankruptcy. The note is discharged by
operation of law in the adjudication of bankruptcy.

RIGHTS OF HOLDERS NOT IN DUE COURSE

Thus, the holder in due course does take subject to some
defenses because of the policy of the law. But for com-
parison, let's look at the rights of enforcement of a
person who is not a holder in due course of a negotiable
instrument, for he takes subject to the same defenses as
any contracting party, and such a holder not in due course
takes subject to all valid claims to it on the part of any
person, and subject to all defenses of any party which
would be available in the actions on a simple contract.

He takes subject to the defense of want or failure of
consideration, nonperformance of any condition, nondelivery.
He takes subject to the defense of any person through whom
he holds that the instrument was stolen, and also subject
to all of the restrictive or qualified indorsements on the
face or the back of the negotiable instrument. Thus, if
you hold an instrument not as a holder in due course but
only as a person who takes as a transferee or assignee of
the note or check, then you are subject to all of the defenses
that you would be subject to if you had contracted with the
original maker or drawer of the negotiable instrument. But

if you took as a holder in due course—that is, you paid value without knowledge of any of the defenses and you took it in good faith—you would not be subject to the contractual defenses of the maker or drawer except the defenses of voidability due to infancy and voidability due to lack of capacity or illegal purpose, nor subject to the defense of duress.

How does a person go about proving that he is a holder in due course? If he makes claim upon a negotiable instrument, the party upon whom the claim is made must allege in a court of law that the signatures are faulty or there has been a forgery. If the holder in due course can prove that he took the instrument for value in good faith and without notice of any claim or any irregularity, then he may recover. But the burden of establishing these three elements of being a holder in due course rest with the holder.

DISCHARGE OF OBLIGATION

As you know from earlier chapters, every relationship in the law is created, enforced, and discharged by rules of law. How do you discharge or terminate a negotiable instrument? The commonest way to discharge the obligation is by payment of the instrument in accordance with its terms. A maker or drawer or a prior indorser is also discharged if the negotiable instrument is materially altered so that the terms of payment or the time of payment is changed. This discharges the original maker because he did not undertake to pay in accordance with the altered terms of the document, and also it discharges any prior indorser on the instrument.

In addition, a negotiable instrument may be discharged and terminated by cancellation, which means that the person who holds the instrument may mark it paid or destroy it, and not collect on it.

In addition, any time a new note or new obligation is substituted for the old or original note or obligation, the original note or obligation is discharged by novation. If you make a partial payment on a promissory note it is always extremely important to receive the original note back and give a new note for the remaining balance so that there can be no question of the fact that your obligation is reduced by the amount of your payment. If you are an indorser on a note or negotiable instrument of any type and presentation for payment to the original maker or any

prior indorser is unreasonably delayed, and thus no demand
is made at the proper time upon the maker or drawer and
primary indorser of the instrument, then the indorser, who
might be you, is discharged because the law requires a
holder to present the note, or draft, or check to the maker
or drawer for payment at the time that it is due, and
any unreasonable delay results in the discharge of indorsers. The reasons for this rule is that negotiable instruments are the obligations of the makers and drawers primarily,
and if someone who holds an instrument is not diligent in
presentment of the negotiable instrument for payment, then
indorsers who have merely handled the document for value
should not be held liable.

GLOSSARY TERMS

Holder in due course A holder of an instrument who takes free of any defenses that the maker or drawer has against the original payee; a holder who has taken by giving value and in good faith and without knowledge of its being overdue or otherwise having other claims on it.

Holder not in due course A holder of an instrument who has taken it lacking any of the conditions required to hold it in due course.

SELF TEST
CHAPTER 37

NAME_____

DATE_____

37.1 The rights of a holder of a negotiable instrument depend upon whether the holder is a holder in _____ or not a holder in _____.

37.2 A holder in _____ takes free of _____ that the maker or drawer of the instrument might have against the original _____.

37.3 A promissory note or other credit instrument is a substitute for _____, and is used as a medium of _____.

37.4 The law says that a person who purchases a credit instrument for _____ with no knowledge of _____ defenses or _____ of the maker or drawer of the instrument, takes free of _____ that the maker or drawer may have against the _____ payee of the instrument.

37.5 A holder in due course is a person who takes _____ of a negotiable instrument, and pays _____ or _____ for it.

37.6 _____, as you will know, can consist of a promise to do something in the _____, or payment for a/an _____ act, or money.

37.7 The second element required to be a holder in due course is that the holder take the instrument in good _____. Also, the holder must take the instrument without notice that it is _____, or has been dishonored.

37.8 In review, a holder in due course is a person who takes the instrument for _____ and in good _____, without notice that it is _____ or has been _____, or of any defense or _____ to the payment of the note, or any claim by any _____ party.

37.9 You can see that a holder in due course has rights which are superior to the _____, but a/an _____ may also be a holder in due course.

37.10 A person who purchases a negotiable instrument at a judicial sale, or as a result of loss of a lawsuit or a judicial _____, cannot be a holder in due course.

37.11   A person who acquires a negotiable instrument in
        taking over an estate by either _____
        or as an administrator of an estate, cannot be a
        holder in due course.

37.12   A purchaser of a business who also receives negoti-
        able instruments in the purchase of the business can-
        not be a holder in due course, because a holder in
        due course has to be a person who takes possession
        of the instrument in the regular course of his
        _____, or in the regular course of his own
        _____.

37.13   If an otherwise negotiable instrument is _____,
        or there are inconsistencies in the negotiable
        instrument, or it is not completely signed by a/an
        _____, or there appears to be, on the face of
        the instrument a/an _____, then the person who
        takes possession of the instrument cannot be a holder
        in due course. The law states that he is under the
        duty of making _____ into any deficiencies,
        because the instrument itself gives him notice of
        _____.

37.14   A purchaser who takes a credit instrument with
        knowledge that it is _____ cannot take the
        instrument as a holder in due course. An example
        of this type of instrument is one issued by a minor.

37.15   At this point, it should be noted that a check which
        is more than_____ days old is one that is
        _____ on its face; that is, it is stale;
        and any person who takes it as an indorsee or trans-
        feree cannot take the check as holder in due course.

37.16   (Answer "True" or "False") _____ If a holder
        in due course is in possession of a stolen negoti-
        able instrument, he must return it to the person
        from whom it was stolen for no consideration, just
        as he would with any other stolen personal property.

37.17   The holder in due course does take subject to all de-
        fenses that his indorser, or even maker, may have
        against him if he _____ with that person in
        the transfer of the instrument to him.

37.18   The holder in due course does take subject to the
        defense of _____ based upon infancy or minority.

37.19   The holder in due course also takes subject to the
        _____ of a contract based upon _____
        of the maker or drawer of the instrument due to
        sickness, mental illness, or _____ of the
        instrument.

CHAPTER 37

NAME_____

37.20 If the promissory note, or negotiable check, is the
       result of _____, meaning force and violence or
       threats, it is _____, and cannot be enforced
       by a holder in due course.
37.21 In addition, the holder in due course does take sub-
       ject to a/an _____ defense of a maker, drawer,
       or any prior indorser which is based upon _____
       that have induced the maker or drawer to sign the
       instrument, when the maker, drawer, or indorser did
       not know what the instrument meant.
37.22 Another defense that the holder in due course of an
       instrument takes subject to is the discharge of the
       instrument by operation of _____ in the adjudi-
       cation of _____.
37.23 A holder in due course does take subject to some de-
       fenses because of the policy of the _____.
37.24 A non-holder in due course takes subject to the same
       defenses as any _____ party, and is subject
        to all _____ claims against the instrument on
       the part of _____ person; that is, he takes
       subject to all defenses of any party which would be
       available in the actions on a/an _____ contract.
37.25 A non-holder in due course is subject to all of the
       defenses that he would be subject to if he had con-
       tracted with the _____ maker or drawer of the
       negotiable instrument.
37.26 The burden of proof of establishing the status of a
       holder in due course rests with the _____.
37.27 The most common way to discharge the obligation of a
       negotiable instrument is by _____ of the
       instrument in accordance with its terms.
37.28 Another method by which a maker, drawer, or prior
       indorser is discharged is if the negotiable instru-
       ment is _____ altered so that the _____
       of payment, or the _____ of payment is changed.
37.29 In addition a negotiable instrument may be dis-
       charged and terminated by _____, which means
       that the person who holds the instrument may mark it
       _____ or destroy it.
37.30 Any time a new note or new obligation is issued to
       replace the old or original note or obligation, the
       original note or obligation is discharged by _____.
37.31 Negotiable instruments are the primary obligations
       of the _____.

38 Insurance

Introduction. Important Terms—I.

LEARNING OBJECTIVES

To become acquainted with some basic principles of insurance.

To learn some of the terms necessary for understanding insurance.

CHAPTER CONTENTS

The Nature of Insurance   Common Insurance Terminology
Glossary   Self Test

In this chapter we begin our discussion of insurance: how
it applies to property, to persons, to businesses, and how
it affects each of us in our everyday lives. In many ways
insurance seems simple, yet once you are involved with it
in practice it gets more complicated, more exacting, and
trickier.

THE NATURE OF INSURANCE

Basically and most simply, insurance is a system for distributing the losses of a few persons among a large group
of persons. Thus, if you own a home and you want to have
insurance for it, it is better to go to a company that has
millions of home-owners who have insured with that company
and paid a premium in for protection on the home. From
these small premiums that are paid in over many years the
insurance company has literally hundreds of millions of
dollars. Consequently, after you have paid your premium,
you're covered and if your house burns down, that insurance
company can pay out the full amount of the value of the
house or the amount of the value that was destroyed and
not suffer any great loss, whereas it would be a terrific
loss to you if your house burned down and you were not
insured. By insuring you in effect spread the risk of loss
over a great number of people so that in the event of loss,
the entire group pays a very small percentage for each
person in the group. This is how insurance actually
operates as an economic safeguard.

        As you will see in subsequent chapters there is insur-
ance for almost everything today. In fact, some people
feel that there should be an insurance against insurance,
for they have so many policies and the expense of so much
insurance in their businesses.

        Many think that insurance is new, a 20th-century
phenomenon reflecting the very complex world we live in
today, and that this complexity has caused insurance to
become so broadly based and so expensive. The needs for
insurance have expanded in the last 100 years, but the fact
is that insurance is one of the oldest types of risk sharing
known to man. The first forms of insurance were marine
insurance, and these policies, first used in Italy and
Portugal prior to the 10th century, in effect were mutual
marine policies in which all of the sea captains and owners
of vessels contributed 2% of the profits of each voyage to
a common fund, and, if one of the vessel owners lost his

vessel at sea from piracy or any other cause, he was
entitled to withdraw the value of his vessel and cargo
from the fund. This was a mutual protection form of
insurance, which still exists today in mutual companies,
and which we'll discuss in a subsequent chapter.

As marine commerce expanded throughout the Western
world, the Italian and Portuguese navigators brought this
form of insurance to England. In the 14th century insurance
began to be paid by premium rather than through a mutual
company. The risks of navigation were so great that vessel
owners and cargo owners were willing to guarantee against
those risks by paying to a company or a group of underwriters a small premium. These marine policies were settled
and agreed upon at a coffee house in London called Lloyd's
Coffee House. Subsequently, Lloyd's of London became the
center for marine insurance throughout the world, and vessel
and cargo owners pay a premium to underwriters and the
underwriters guarantee the payment of the hull value or the
cargo interest lost by perils of the sea in the event of
loss.

So many people contribute a small premium that the
underwriters make a profit and at the same time guarantee
against loss. So from the 10th century to the present day
this form of insurance—marine insurance—has grown and has
expanded into other types of insurance.

Insurance today is defined as a contract whereby one
undertakes to indemnify another against loss, damage, or
liability arising from an unknown or contingent event. It
has likewise been defined as a contract whereby one party
agrees to wholly or partially indemnify another for loss
or damage which he may suffer from a specified peril. A
policy of fire insurance, for example, has been defined
as an agreement to indemnify the insured against loss by
fire to the property insured, and more exactly, as a
contract of indemnity—to reimburse the insured for his
actual loss not exceeding an agreed sum. And insurance in
relation to property has also been defined as a contract
whereby the insurer becomes bound for a definite consideration to indemnify the insured against loss or damage to
certain property named in the policy by reason of certain
agreed upon perils to which it may be exposed. Even life
and accident insurance has been defined as a contract whereby one party, for a stipulated consideration, agrees to
indemnify another against injury by accident or death for
any cause not excluded from the contract.

We often talk about life insurance or property insurance or liability insurance. Those terms are not accurately

used when we think of them as insuring property or life or
liability. Insurance does not insure against loss of life
or loss of property or liability. All insurance does is
agree to indemnify, or pay back to, the person insured or
a designated party the amount of actual loss suffered by
the insured—either loss of life or the loss or damage of
property or by being held liable for his conduct and acts
if the property or life or acts are specifically covered
in the contract of insurance. Thus, a working definition
of *insurance* for our use would be: a contract whereby one
person agrees to indemnify another person if the second
person suffers a specified monetary loss.

COMMON INSURANCE TERMINOLOGY

We must explore the meaning of several terms so that in
subsequent chapters we will more fully understand insurance
and its effect upon our lives. We have already defined
the first term we must know, insurance, to mean a contract
whereby one person agrees to indemnify another person if
the latter suffers a monetary loss or liability. The
person who agrees to indemnify the other—that is, agrees
to pay or reimburse a person for loss under a stated
policy—is the *insurer*, the company that does the insuring
of the policyholder. The *insured* is the policyholder, the
person whom the company agrees to indemnify in the event
of loss.
     The *subject* of an insurance policy is the thing which
is insured against loss, which can be an automobile, a
life, real property, the title to real property, personal
property, or liability insurance itself, which insures
against loss due to the acts of the insured. The subject
of the <u>life</u> insurance policy is the life of the insured;
the subject of the liability policy on an automobile is the
owner's liability for his acts in the event of his negligence
which results in injury or damage to other persons or
property. The subject of property insurance is real or
personal property specified in the policy.
     Insurance companies assume *risks*. For example, in a
life insurance policy, the company takes the life of the
insured as both the <u>subject</u> and the <u>risk</u> of the policy by
agreeing to pay to the beneficiary a stated sum upon the
death of the insured. So the risk is death.
     In property insurance—for example, fire insurance—the
company specifically insures the owners of property (the

property is the subject of the insurance), against loss
occasioned by the risk of fire and only the risk of fire—
not the risks of tornado, flood damage, hail, lightning,
or whatever, but only the risk of fire. John Jones purchased
from Ace Insurance Company a fire insurance policy upon his
home. John Jones is the insured; the Ace Insurance Company
is the insurer; the subject of the insurance is John Jones'
home; and the risk that the company agrees to bear is the
risk that fire might totally or partially damage John
Jones' home.

The *beneficiary* in an insurance contract is the person
to whom the insurance company will make payment in the
event of a proven loss covered by the policy. In most
insurance policies the beneficiary is the insured himself
or herself. But in a life insurance policy, when the
insured and the risk are the same—that is, payment is to be
made upon the death of the insured—another beneficiary
must be set forth in the policy. That beneficiary, who
can be anyone specified by the insured, is entitled to
the proceeds from the insurance policy in the event the
risk comes to happen—that is, the death of the insured.
(We will discuss in greater detail in a later chapter some
of the technicalities of beneficiaries under life insurance
policies.)

The *policy* is the written contract; state laws require
that insurance contracts be in writing, and most states
have passed laws setting forth certain regulations and
rules as to what the policies may say and may not say.
In fact, some states have form policies that insurance
companies are required to use in the protection of the
citizens of the state so that there will be no doubt as to
the risk covered by the particular policy.

Insurance is an extremely important part of our lives
and the economy of this country. And insurance companies
sometimes spring into existence and do a tremendous amount
of business in a short time through mail-order premium
houses. They are not regulated by the state and they are
illegally issuing policies across state lines. Many, many
thousands of people have paid premiums for coverage that
did not exist, and when it came time to have a claim paid,
either a life insurance claim or a liability claim, the
insurance company was either out of business or was unwilling
or unable to pay. The poor policyholder then must either
hire an attorney in another state to proceed with action
against the insurance company, or forget the claim that he
was entitled to have paid.

This point must be emphasized because insurance is so important in the protection that it affords that it should be one of the most carefully made purchases of your life. Care must be taken to get the type of policy that fits your needs as well as the type of company that will stand behind your problems and pay the claims that are imposed upon you by unfortunate accident, fire, or other loss. Remember that insurance among reputable companies costs about the same and any great saving you're going to make in an insurance policy will generally result in poorer service or poorer claims management.

The *premium* is the agreed consideration that the insured pays to the insurer to bind the risk or issue the policy and take on the obligation of an insurer.

Now the next term is extremely important—*representation*. An insurance policy is a contract, and, like a contract, is entered into as follows: A person who desires insurance makes an application through an agent of the insurance company or a broker who represents several companies. On the application for insurance—whether it be for life, automobile liability insurance, or property insurance—the applicant makes certain representations as to his age or the condition of the property, the type of automobile he wants insured, or any other facts that the application asks information about. Now these representations are the basis upon which the insurance company decides whether it will accept the offer of the applicant to engage in an insurance contract. You, as an applicant for insurance, offer to be insured by the insurance company. It is up to the insurance company to determine whether your risk is one they wish to insure, and the representations in the application are extremely important because they are the facts upon which the insurance company depends in deciding whether the insurance offer will be accepted. (We will discuss representation in greater detail in a later chapter.)

A *warranty* in insurance is some representation that you made as an offeror to be insured and that has been incorporated or made part of the policy itself. If these warranties that you made to the insurance company are discovered to be wrong or untrue, the policy is voided entirely. You remember that a voidable contract is one which may be repudiated at the option of one of the parties, but a void contract had no legal significance at any time and is a nullity and completely unenforceable. So warranties made by an applicant for insurance and incorporated in the insurance policy are extremely important, for if untrue they

will void the policy even if it has been in existence for
many years and thousands of dollars in premiums have been
paid. (Warranty is another subject to be discussed in
greater detail in a later chapter.)

The *application* is the written offer by a person to
become an insured with an insurance company. On the basis
of the application the insurance company makes its acceptance after determining what representations and warranties
are made in the application.

In most types of insurance policies, the insurance
company agrees to pay the actual loss suffered by the
insured up to the maximum amount agreed upon in the policy.
For example, a fire insurance policy will generally state,
"for the actual loss suffered by the insured at its then
market value up to _____ dollars," which is the total
amount of insurance that has been issued; that is a
nonvalued policy. In marine insurance (insurance that covers
cargoes and hulls of vessels) a *valued policy* is occasionally used. A valued policy agrees to pay a fixed sum for
the loss of the vessel or all of the cargo; the insurance
company agrees to pay that amount even though the hull might
have been worth something less than that.

In the insurance field a *stock company* is a corporation
similar to some we studied earlier. It has stockholders
and a Board of Directors, and its business is the issuance
and handling of insurance policies. Its stockholders are
investors, just like those in General Motors or General
Telephone and Telegraph Company. The company issues policies
of insurance, accepts premiums, pays claims, invests funds
from its policy premiums, and turns its profits in the form
of dividends over to its stockholders. It is an organized
corporation for profit just like the other companies that I
have mentioned.

In the insurance business, a *mutual company* is one in
which the profits of the company are held for the operation
of the company and returned to the policyholders in the form
of dividends upon the policies themselves. For example, if
I own a $100,000 life insurance policy and pay $750 a
year in premiums, at the end of the fiscal year I would
receive a certain amount based upon my premium as a dividend
from the profits of the company. I could accept that
dividend in cash or I can have it reduce my premium obligation to the company, or I could have the dividend remain
with the company and use it to purchase paid-up insurance.

A *fraternal association* or society was very common in
the early days of insurance. Clubs were formed and each

member of the club contributed a certain amount of money to cover a casualty or loss of another member of the club. The experience of these fraternal societies has been spotty and they are not as prevalent as they used to be.

GLOSSARY TERMS

Application   The written offer of a person to become an insured.

Beneficiary   The person to whom payment will be made by the insurer in the event of the specified loss.

Fraternal association   A club in which members paid a certain amount to cover the casualty of loss of another member.

Insurance   A contract whereby one person agrees to indemnify another person if the second person suffers a specified monetary loss.

Insured   The person to be indemnified for a specified loss.

Insurer   The person who agrees to indemnify another person for losses.

Mutual company   An insurance company that returns its profits to policyholders as dividends on their policies.

Nonvalued policy   An agreement to pay the actual loss suffered by the insured up to the maximum agreed upon policy amount.

Policy   The written contract for the insurance agreement.

Premium   The consideration paid by the insured to the insurer.

Representation   Statements of fact made on an application for insurance.

Risk   The event or possibility, such as death, fire, specified property damage, etc., that is insured against.

Stock company   An insurance company that, like other corporations, has stockholders and a Board of Directors and turns its profits over to its stockholders as dividends on investments.

Subject   The thing insured against loss in an insurance policy.

Valued policy   An agreement to pay a certain, fixed sum
on an insured loss even though the subject may be
worth less.

Warranty   Representations of fact made by the insured
and incorporated into the policy, the validity of
which is dependent upon the truth of the warranties.

SELF TEST
CHAPTER 38

NAME_____

DATE_____

38.1 Insurance is a system for _____ the _____ of a/an _____ persons among a/an _____ group of persons.

38.2 Insurance, in effect, spreads the _____ of _____ over a great number of people so that in the event of loss, the entire group pays a very small _____ for each person in the group. This is the way that insurance actually operates as an economic _____.

38.3 The fact is that insurance is one of the oldest _____ and oldest types of risk _____ known to man.

38.4 The first form of insurance was _____ insurance, and these insurance policies were first used in Italy and Portugal prior to the _____ century.

38.5 These first forms of insurance policies were, in effect, _____ policies in which all of the sea captains and owners of vessels contributed ____% of the profits of each voyage to a common fund.

38.6 At approximately the _____ century, insurance began to be paid by _____ rather than through a/an _____ company.

38.7 During this period of time, the company of _____ of _____ became the center for marine insurance throughout the world.

38.8 Insurance today is defined as a/an _____ whereby one undertakes to _____ another against _____, damage, or _____ arising from an unknown or _____ event.

38.9 Insurance has likewise been defined as a/an _____ whereby one party agrees to wholly or _____ _____ another for loss or damage which he may suffer from a specified _____.

38.10 Insurance, in relation to property, has been defined as a/an _____ whereby the _____ becomes bound for a definite _____ to indemnify the _____ against loss or damage to certain

property named in the _____ by reason of
certain agreed _____ to which it may be
exposed.

38.11   All insurance does is agree to indemnify, or
_____ to, the person insured the amount of
_____ loss suffered by the insured.

38.12   Let's use the term insurance as meaning a/an _____
whereby one person agrees to _____ another
person if the latter person suffers a specified
_____ loss.

38.13   A/An _____ is one who agrees to pay or reimburse
another person for loss under a stated policy.

38.14   The _____ is the person to whom the company
agrees to indemnify in the event of loss.

38.15   An insurance company is a/an _____, and the
_____ is the insured.

38.16   The _____ of an insurance policy is the thing
which is insured against loss.

38.17   A life insurance policy has as its _____
the _____ of the insured.

38.18   Risk, when discussed in relation to insurance, means
the risk the _____ agrees to _____.

38.19   The _____ in an insurance contract is the
person to whom the insurance company will make
payment in the event of a proved _____
covered by the policy.

38.20   The _____ is the _____ contract, and
state laws require that insurance contracts be in
_____.

38.21   You all know that the _____ is the consideration that the insured pays to the insurer to
_____ the risk, or issue the policy, and take
on the _____ of an insurer.

38.22   A person that desires insurance makes a/an _____
through a/an _____ of the insurance company, or
a broker who represents several companies. On this,
the applicant makes certain _____ concerning
his age, condition of the property, etc.

38.23   The _____ on the application are the basis
upon which the insurance company decides whether it
will accept the _____ of the applicant to
engage in an insurance contract.

38.24   The term _____ in insurance means that some
representation that you make as a/an _____ to be
insured is incorporated or made part of the policy
itself; and these _____ that you have made to
the insurance company, if wrong or untrue, _____
the policy.

CHAPTER 38

NAME_____

38.25 You will remember that a/an _____ contract is
one which may be repudiated at the option of one of
the parties, but a/an _____ contract has no
legal significance at any time and is a nullity and
completely _____.

38.26 The written offer by the insured to become an
insured with an insurance company is known as a/an

_____.

38.27 A/An _____ policy is one which agrees to pay the
actual loss incurred up to the stated limit of the
policy.

38.28 A/An _____ policy is occasionally used in
_____ insurance and it agrees to pay a fixed
sum for a loss, even though the actual loss may be
less than the amount paid.

38.29 A/An _____ company, in the insurance business, is
a company in which the profits of the company are
held for the operation of the company, and returned
to the policyholders in the form of _____
upon the policies themselves.

38.30 A/An _____ company in the insurance business is
an organized corporation for profit similar to the
corporations studied in a previous chapter.

38.31 The difference between a stock company and a mutual
company is that a mutual company distributes its
_____ to its _____.

39

Insurance
Important Terms–II.

LEARNING OBJECTIVES

To learn further terms essential to the understanding of insurance.

CHAPTER CONTENTS

In this chapter we will continue to learn terms essential to your study of insurance.

The next term on your list should be *term* itself. As it is used in insurance policies, term means the length of time for which the insurance itself is issued. Ordinarily a policy has an anniversary date and a termination date. For example, in some forms of life insurance there is a policy of life insurance called term insurance, and it insures the life of the insured for a period of stated years—5-year term, 10-year term, 15-year term. At the expiration date the insurance policy terminates and expires, and new insurance must be obtained in some other form. In the average fire insurance policy upon dwellings, the term of the fire insurance policy is three years, with an anniversary premium date once each year. So the term is the length of time for which the policy has been issued and for which it must remain in force if all of the conditions of the policy have been met and there were no misrepresentations in the application for insurance, and if premiums are paid.

Generally, insurance companies are located a long distance from your home and they do their business in your home town through an insurance agent. You make an offer, by filling out an application, to have insurance issued by this company, you agree to pay the premium for the policy, and you also set forth certain facts about yourself or the property that is to be covered by the insurance policy. These are the representations or warranties about the property which occur in the application.

THE INTRICACIES OF THE BINDER

Most frequently, when we want insurance we want it to be effective immediately so that we know that we have the coverage for the risk that we are paying the premium for. But the offer has to be transmitted to the home office of the insurance company and as much as ten days or two weeks elapse before the company accepts or rejects the offer to issue a policy of insurance. Thus, a *binder* is issued; the agent of the company has authority to temporarily issue the coverage and insurance upon the risk offered for insurance pending the acceptance or rejection by the company of the offer of insurance. The agent who has authority to issue a binder therefore covers you on the risk that you are offering to have insured until the insurance company

accepts your application and issues the formal policy of
insurance. This is temporary insurance pending action by
the company.

The binder is valid only if the agent for the company
has authority to issue it. It is generally held that such a
slip or receipt issued by the duly authorized agent of the
insurance company constitutes the temporary contract of
insurance under which the company will be liable for any
loss occurring between the time of your application and payment of the first premium and the time when the company
issues its policy of insurance to you after its acceptance
of your offer. If the company accepts your offer to be
covered by its policy of insurance, then there is no additional premium for the period of time between your offer and
the company's acceptance. If the company chooses to
reject your offer of insurance the agents will charge a
very small premium for that particular coverage that he
bound the company to provide until it acted officially upon
your offer.

A binder is only temporary insurance—it does not
bind the company to issue the policy of insurance that
you desire; it only protects you during the period of time
that the company has to act upon your application. Where
an agent of an insurance company is entrusted with
certificates, or binders, and delivers a binder to the
applicant upon payment of the premium, the company will be
bound to pay any loss that occurs to the insured even before
the company acted upon the application.

For example, John Jones went into the agent of Ace
Insurance Company and filled out an application for $100,000
worth of property damage insurance upon his business. He
paid the premium as set forth in the rates and schedules
of the company and the agent forwarded the application to
the company together with the premium. In addition, the
agent issued to Mr. Jones a receipt and binder for the
coverage requested, pending the acceptance or rejection of
the application by the head office of the insurance company.

Prior to the receipt of the application by the insurance
company, Mr. Jones' business was totally destroyed by fire.
Mr. Jones went to the agent and advised him of this
catastrophic loss and filled out a proof of loss form,
indicating the fire and the date and the value of the
property which was destroyed, which was the entire business.
The agent forwarded the proof of loss to the company together with a copy of the binder. The company received the
application for insurance and the binder and the proof of
loss all in the same day.

The company replied to Mr. Jones that it was their
policy not to cover the type of business that Mr. Jones
offered to have insured by the company, and additionally
indicated that they would not pay this loss for they would
not have issued the policy in any event to Mr. Jones.
Mr. Jones was so advised by the agent and immediately
went to see his attorney, who advised him that because the
binder was valid the insurance company was liable for the
loss, even though it had not accepted the application for
insurance and, in fact, would have rejected the insurance
offered by Mr. Jones.

The advice of the attorney was based upon the fact
that the agent had authority to issue such a binder, and
the company was temporarily bound by the binder until it
had communicated its acceptance or rejection of the offer
contained in the application of Mr. Jones. The company
would be liable for the loss provided it had not communicated to the agent its policy of not accepting the kind of
risk Mr. Jones' business constituted. If the agent had
known that the company was not covering businesses such as
Mr. Jones' and, on his own, gave a binder against the
company's instructions, there would be a very close
question as to whether Mr. Jones was covered by the
temporary binder. We will discuss the rights and liabilities
of principals through the acts of their agents in greater
detail in later chapters. Suffice it to say here that
binders are temporary insurance policies which will control
the rights of the insured and the rights of the insurer.

One exception to the rule about binders is that in
accident, health, or life insurance policies, a company
will generally not issue a binder to cover the life or
health or accident liability of an insured until it has
received a medical report from a doctor of the insurance
company's choosing. Quite commonly there is a provision
in the conditional binder given to the applicant to the
effect that the insurance shall be considered in force from
the date of the receipt or the date of the medical examination provided the application is approved and accepted at the
home office of the insurer. Such receipts are known in the
insurance business as conditional receipts. It is the
general rule of law that such an instrument is absolutely
ineffectual in providing protection to the applicant until
the application is approved or accepted. In other words, if
Mr. Jones had gone into his agent's office and offered to
buy $100,000 worth of health insurance upon himself, and
the agent had issued a binder and then had told Mr. Jones

to go to his doctor and have a medical examination and have the report of that examination forwarded to the company, the binder would not have been binding upon the insurance company because the insurance company is not held to have issued a temporary insurance policy in life insurance cases or health cases. They have a right to choose their insured according to the health and medical record of the applicant.

To illustrate this very basic distinction between property insurance and personal life and health insurance— that is, that in property insurance a binder can be issued to give temporary insurance until the application is accepted or rejected by the home office, but in personal life, health, and accident insurance, the company is not bound by temporary binders until it has actually accepted or rejected the application—let us assume that Mr. Jones went in for $10,000 worth of life insurance. The company doctor, who was appointed by the insurance company in the town, examined Mr. Jones and forwarded his medical report to the company. The company received the medical report and the application of Mr. Jones together with the premium on the 14th of March. On the 15th of March the company accepted the policy application and began to prepare the formal policy which it would mail to Mr. Jones. On March 16 Mr. Jones had an accidental injury that resulted in his death. On the 17th of March, the formal policy was received by the agent of the company. He took it to the Jones residence and learned that Mr. Jones had died the previous day. At that point, the insurance company was liable for the payment of the policy benefits to the beneficiary on the policy because it had in fact accepted the application the day before Mr. Jones had died even though it had not issued its policy formally to Mr. Jones. Had Mr. Jones died the day before the company had accepted his policy, then the company would not be liable for the loss because there was nothing to insure at the time of acceptance—Mr. Jones was already dead and there was no subject, or risk, that could be covered. The risk, death, had occurred and the subject, Mr. Jones, was nonexistent, so the policy could not have been issued had the true facts been known.

You can see that the technicalities of binder are extremely important. In the event that you have to insure property—your automobile, your home, your business, or your liability for acts that you engage in while driving an automobile or in your employment—make sure that the binder you receive is issued by the agent of the company to cover

you during the time that elapses between your application
and the issuance of the formal policy or the rejection.
In this way you are covered for the risk that you are
insuring, even before the company acts. In life, health,
and accident insurance, you will not be able to receive
such temporary insurance—so you will want to act with
some speed and dispatch in having the medical examination
performed and your application sent back promptly to the
insurance company for their acceptance or rejection.

LOSS

In defining binder, we have also looked at the next term
to define—*loss*. Loss does not necessarily mean only the
loss of the subject, such as in theft insurance, which
covers for total loss of a personal property by theft or
burglary. But loss is a broader term; it means monetary
loss—an actual loss of dollars or dollar value by destruction of property, loss of life, loss of property through
theft or burglary, and loss of dollar or dollar value
through judgments against one for liability to a third
party. Not all loss is insured loss; there are excluded
losses and there are noncovered losses, losses simply not
covered by insurance. To be covered a loss must be the risk
under which the policy was issued. For example, I have
asked my company to issue a policy of insurance upon my
house for fire loss. The application has been accepted
and the policy of insurance has been delivered. After the
policy has been delivered to me and is in full force and
effect by my payment of premiums on it, my house is
severely damaged by windstorm. I put in a claim to my
insurance company for loss and my insurance company advises
me that it is not a covered loss because the risk of the
loss that I covered was fire loss, not windstorm damage.
I could have had that type of coverage had I elected to
apply an indorsement to the policy for extended coverage
that would have included wind damage. But I did not
choose to put on that indorsement, and therefore the loss
was not a covered loss.

    Loss does not mean that all of the property must be
destroyed; there is total loss, but there is also partial
loss. Let's assume that my house was damaged by fire to
the extent of 90% of its true value as set in the policy; it
would be the actual loss of the house that I suffered at
the time. In other words, the cost of repairing the house
would not be covered because the cost of repairs might far

exceed the total value of the house as I had placed it in the policy. We will discuss this concept in fire insurance in greater detail. My loss would have been a partial loss under the policy and I would be paid only the amount of the policy which covered the actual loss I had incurred less than the full value of the home.

PROOF OF LOSS

But before an insurance company has to pay on any loss, it is entitled by law as well as by the contract of insurance to receive a *proof of loss* from the insured. The proof of loss, generally supplied by the insurance company and its agent, is a form that must be filled out by the insured, usually before a notary public and under seal, stating to the insurance company the cause, nature, and the amount of the loss, when it occurred, and many more details of the loss. Here again, accuracy and honesty are extremely important because an erroneous or knowingly false proof of loss may cause the company to cancel the policy and deny coverage and payment upon the proof of loss. For example, if my house had been damaged by windstorm and I had put in a claim for fire damage to my home on the proof of loss, and sworn that that was the truth, and had the company determined that this was erroneous and made by me falsely, not only would they not pay my claim, but they would cancel the policy.

I would have real difficulty in obtaining other fire insurance coverage from other companies because on their applications most companies ask, "Have you ever been cancelled by any other insurance company, or has coverage been refused or rejected by any other company?" Now, if I answer no to that when in fact the answer should be yes, that is a false warranty or misrepresentation, and may make the policy that is issued by the company void. If I answer, "Yes, I have been cancelled by the Ace Company," the company you are making application to will contact that company to determine why you were cancelled, and upon learning that you had filed a false and fraudulent proof of loss they will refuse to offer insurance to you, considering you are a bad moral risk to be covered.

CO-INSURANCE VS. ADDITIONAL INSURANCE

By *co-insurance* we mean that two companies have issued a policy of insurance covering the same risk. For example,

Mr. Jones goes down to the agent for Ace Insurance Company
and files an application for burglary insurance in the
amount of $50,000. The application is accepted by the
company and a policy of insurance is issued to Mr. Jones
covering him for burglary loss. But Mr. Jones decides that
he needs additional insurance for such burglary loss and
goes to the agent for Black Insurance Company and takes a
policy of insurance for $50,000 for burglary insurance. He
now has two policies for burglary insurance, and he thinks
that he has $100,000 worth of burglary insurance, but in fact
he has only $50,000 worth, because both companies are co-
insurers—they have each issued a $50,000 policy for burglary,
and each is liable for the burglary up to $50,000. To
see how it works, say that on Monday Mr. Jones goes to his
factory and finds that over the weekend burglars had broken
in and stolen $30,000 worth of inventory. Mr. Jones con-
tacts both insurance companies and puts in a proof of loss
for the $30,000. The two companies get together and they
pay the loss $15,000 apiece, or a pro-rata amount for the
coverage that they have allowed for this risk. Let's change
the example somewhat: Had Mr. Jones gone to the Ace
Company and bought $50,000 worth of burglary insurance, and
then gone to the Black Company and bought $50,000 worth of
additional insurance (or as it is called in the insurance
business, excess insurance), then he would have $100,000
worth of insurance—$50,000 worth of primary insurance, and
$50,000 worth of excess insurance—and he also would have
saved a tremendous amount in premiums. He would have paid
the flat or regular rate for burglary insurance to the Ace
Company which was the primary underwriter, and he would have
paid a much smaller rate of insurance to the Black Company
which was the excess underwriter, and you can see why:
There is much less risk that the Black Company will be held
liable for a claim for burglary insurance if it has a
$50,000 pad—that is, if it is liable only after the full
$50,000 coverage of the Ace Company is used up.
      Assume that Mr. Jones had used his head and bought
$50,000 worth of burglary insurance from the Ace Company
as primary insurer, and $50,000 excess coverage for burglary
loss from the Black Company. On Monday morning Mr. Jones
goes to his factory and finds that $67,000 worth of
inventory has been stolen by burglars during the weekend.
Mr. Jones then makes a proof of loss upon Ace Insurance
Company for $50,000 worth of benefits for the loss of
$67,000. He then makes application to the Black Insurance
Company for the difference between $50,000 and $67,000, or

$17,000 worth of coverage under the excess policy. Both com-
panies would pay; Ace would pay $50,000 and Black would pay
$17,000 as excess underwriter. Mr. Jones would have full
coverage from the primary insurer and partial loss from
the excess underwriter.

This is the difference, then, between co-insurance
and additional insurance. Co-insurers split the loss on a
pro-rata basis. But what is a pro-rata basis? Assume that
as co-insurers Ace Insurance Company has a $10,000 liability
policy and Black Insurance Company has a $40,000 liability
policy. Assume that the insured had a judgment rendered
against him for $30,000, and that by the judgment the
insurance companies must pay their liability policies.
The two companies would have to pay on a pro-rata basis.
Ace Insurance Company, with a $10,000 policy on $50,000
worth of total coverage, would pay one-fifth of the
$30,000 judgment, or $6,000, and Black Insurance Company,
with $40,000 of the $50,000 total coverage, would pay
four-fifths of the entire judgment—$24,000. Therefore,
the co-insurers would split the loss on a pro-rata basis
as their two policies bear to the total coverage.

But say the insured had additional insurance instead of
co-insurers: let's assume that the first company had the
primary coverage of $10,000 and the second company had the
secondary or excess coverage for such liability. The
first company would pay $10,000 on the $30,000 loss, and the
second company would pay $20,000 on the $30,000 loss because
it was secondarily liable for all liability over $10,000.

GLOSSARY TERMS

Additional insurance   Secondary insurance to cover losses over the specified amount covered by a primary insurance policy.

Binder   Temporary insurance pending final acceptance or rejection by the insurance company.

Co-insurance   The dividing of a loss between two companies with which the same insurer has policies for the same subjects and the same risks.

Loss   Monetary loss of dollars or value through theft, damage of property judgments of liability to a third party, and so on.

Proof of Loss   A report filed by an insured giving the particulars of a claimed insured loss.

Pro-rata   Proportional payment by two co-insurers to share the loss that must be absorbed.

Term   The length of time for which an insurance policy is issued.

SELF TEST

CHAPTER 39

NAME_____

DATE_____

39.1 Term, as it is used in insurance policies, means the length of _____ in which the insurance itself is issued.

39.2 Ordinarily, a policy has a/an _____ date and a termination date.

39.3 An agent who has the authority, issues a binder which covers the applicant on the risk that the applicant is offering to have _____ until the insurance company accepts the application and issues a/an _____ policy of insurance. This is _____ insurance pending _____ by the company.

39.4 A binder is only valid if the agent for the company has _____ to issue the binder.

39.5 A binder does not bind an insurance company to issue a policy of insurance that you desire; it only _____ the applicant during a period of time that the company has to act upon the application.

39.6 Where an agent of an insurance company is entrusted with certificates or binders, and delivers a binder to the applicant upon payment of the _____, the _____ will be bound to pay any loss that occurs to the insured, even (choose either "before" or "after") _____ the company has acted upon the application.

39.7 In accident and health and life insurance policies, a company (Choose either "will" or "will not") _____ issue a binder to cover the life or health and accident liability of an insured, generally, until it has received a/an _____ report from a/an _____ of the insurance company's choosing.

39.8 A provision in a conditional binder issued by health and accident insurance company to the insured which states that the binder will not be considered in force until the receipt of a medical examination is known as a/an _____ receipt. It is the general rule of law that such an instrument is completely _____ in providing protection to the applicant until the applicant is approved or accepted.

39.9   The word loss does not necessarily mean loss of the _____ matter.   In insurance it has a broader definition and means _____ loss, or a/an _____ loss of dollars or dollar value.

39.10   A loss, to be _____, must be the risk under which the policy was issued.

39.11   Losses simply not covered by insurance are known as _____ losses.

39.12   Before an insurance company has to pay on any loss, it is entitled by _____ as well as by the contract of insurance to receive a/an _____ of _____ statement from the insured.

39.13   Co-insurance means that _____ companies have issued a policy of insurance covering the same _____.

39.14   Additional insurance, in the insurance business, is known as the _____ insurance.

39.15   The difference between co-insurance and additional insurance is that co-insurers split any covered law suits on a/an _____ basis; whereas, with additional insurance, one company will be a/an _____ insurer up to a certain limit, and the other company, which will be the _____ underwriter, is liable for law suits above that limit.

40 Insurance

Important Terms—III.

LEARNING OBJECTIVES

To conclude our study of terms essential to under-standing insurance.

CHAPTER CONTENTS

Termination and Cancellation of Policies   Incontest-ability Clause   Glossary   Self Test

In this chapter we will conclude our definition of the terms used in insurance. In an insurance policy, the terms *rider* and *endorsement* should be examined at the same time. A rider to an insurance policy is a separate piece of paper attached, by agreement of both parties, to the policy prior to the policy's issuance to the insured. A rider varies the terms of the policy by adding risk or excluding risk or by changing the terms and conditions of payment, term, or coverage of the policy. An endorsement to a policy, which is made by the insurance company with the consent of the insured prior to the issuance of the policy, appears in the body of the policy as a change in the terms and conditions of the policy.

You can see that the only distinction between a rider and an endorsement is that a rider is a separate piece of paper attached to and made a part of the policy, whereas an endorsement is embodied right in the terms of the policy itself. Most policies of insurance today are printed on forms that the companies have established; and they have literally thousands of forms, for every conceivable type of insurance, and thousands of endorsement slips that they put into their agents' hands for addition to the policies to vary the terms of the policies to fit the insured's needs. So most endorsements today are in fact riders because they are attached to the policy. It doesn't make any difference whether they're riders or endorsements, so long as they are set forth in the policy and attached to it with the consent of the insured at the time of issuance. We will call such additions endorsements rather than riders because the insurance business more frequently uses that term.

TERMINATION AND CANCELLATION OF POLICIES

The insurance company has a right to void, or *lapse*, a policy of insurance upon the breach of the conditions of the insurance by the insured. Most frequently policies lapse through failure of the insured to pay the premiums when they become due or during the *grace period*. Generally speaking, premiums are due on a given date—the anniversary date of a policy of insurance—although by an endorsement the policy premiums may be paid monthly in some policies. If the insured fails to pay the premiums as called for in the policy, a clause in the policy allows the insured 30 days in which to pay the premium. This is called a 30-day grace period.

If the premiums have not been paid within that 30-day grace period, the policy is lapsed and is no longer effective. If there is a loss after that 30-day grace period, the company is no longer liable to cover the risk of insurance which the policy was issued to insure. While the policy is lapsed, the company may reinstate the policy, at its sole option, if the insured pays the premium and in some cases takes a new physical examination upon the order of the insurance company. That is, at its own option the insurance company may reinstate the policy upon the cure of all the defaults by the insured or it may treat the policy as terminated. And if the insurance company, at its own option, determines that the policy should be terminated, then all of the rights and obligations of the insurance company and the insured are terminated following the lapse of the policy due to the default of the insured. This is *termination*.

Under certain conditions the insurance company has the right of *cancellation*, the right to rescind, cancel, surrender, terminate the policy—in other words, to bring the relationship of insurance between the insured and insurer to an end. Now the right of cancellation of an insurance contract can arise from any of the following sources, and either the insured or the insurer may cancel a policy if any one of these conditions occurs: The insurance policy may provide in its terms that either of the parties may cancel the policy without any reason upon giving so many days notice to the other party in writing. (Most states have statutes that prohibit an insurance policy to be cancelled by the insurer, or the insurance company, without written notice—at least 10 days written notice—to the insurer. Thus, in most states no policy can be cancelled by the insurance company without 10 days written notice to the insured.)

Most policies make cancellation available to either party with the consent of the other. Or the insurance company may cancel a policy based upon fraud or misrepresentation in the application and warranties. The insurer or the insured may cancel a policy based upon mistake, provided the mistake is material to the contract itself. The contract may be cancelled if the insurer is adjudicated insolvent, or if the insurer or its company has made an assignment for benefit of creditors or has been merged with another company. But generally the policies provide themselves for cancellation, and the parties to a contract of insurance may include provisions in the policy relative to its cancellation.

Most policies covering property and liability insurance contain provisions permitting either party to cancel the policy on complying with certain conditions. We can see the necessity for these cancellation provisions because the interests in property quickly change. For example, if you have an automobile and you want to have it insured for property damage and theft, you want to be able to cancel that policy when you sell the automobile. This applies also to title insurance or liability insurance for a business that you own, or for liability insurance on your employees or numerous conditions that change requiring the swift cancellation of policies of insurance upon property interests that you have. Similarly, the insurance company may wish to cancel quickly if it determines that any of the warranties or representations made in the application for insurance **were knowingly made falsely or are mistaken** as to facts which substantially change the amount of risk that the insurance company has agreed to undertake in the policy.

INCONTESTABILITY CLAUSE

The *incontestability clause* in policies of insurance provides, in essence, that after a policy has been in effect a given number of years, or even months, an insurance company may not cancel or terminate a policy of insurance, or defend against a claim for benefits by its insured, because of some misrepresentation in the application for insurance. That is, say I made a mistake in my application for insurance and I pay premiums on that insurance for, say, five years, and then I have my first claim under the insurance policy. Checking back very carefully through the policy and making a very careful review of all of the facts, the insurance company discovers that I made a mistake in the application and they cancel the policy and refuse to pay the claim.

Over the years the courts have looked at this practice disapprovingly, and responsible insurance companies have placed in their own policies an incontestability clause that says, "After a given period of time, we will accept your representations as being true and waive any defenses we would otherwise have to a claim based upon false representation in the application for insurance, save and except if there are fraudulent representations and fraudulent warranties in the application."

If you have knowingly and willfully defrauded the
company into issuing a policy based upon fraudulent
statements, then the company does not waive the defense
it has to the issuance of the policy based upon the fraud.
But innocent mistakes or innocent misrepresentations as to
facts within the application are incontestable after a
given period of time. Keep in mind, though, that other
provisions in the policy give the company the right to
cancel the policy on sufficient advance notice. Again,
this is especially true in property insurance.

Many life insurance policies are guaranteed renewable
and noncancellable after a given period of time, wherein
the insured may cancel the policy but the insurance company
may not. This is an important feature of a life, health,
or accident policy because the older the person grows the
greater the risks on life and health policies, and it would
be unfair for the insurance company to take the risk during
a person's earlier years and then refuse to insure the
person or renew the policy in his middle and later years.
Consequently, most reputable life insurance companies and
health and accident companies agree in certain of their
policies to continue the person as an insured for the length
of his life at the stated limit of the life insurance or
health and accident insurance purchase.

You can see, then, that the incontestability clause
in such a policy could be very important. For example,
a person might have a pre-existing medical condition that
he didn't even know about when he applied for insurance and
was accepted, and later in life—5 or 10 years later—that
medical condition would flare up and the doctor would report
that the person had had this condition for many years.
Without the incontestability clause in the contract, the
insurance company might say, "This is a health problem that
pre-existed the application and issuance of the policy,
and we are therefore not liable to pay the medical bills
or death that resulted from this condition." But, with the
incontestability clause the company may not defend against
such a claim based upon a pre-existent condition <u>unless</u>
the insured knew of the condition and did not tell the
company about that condition in an attempt to defraud the
company into issuing the policy.

GLOSSARY TERMS

Cancellation   Termination of a policy by the insurer or the insured.

Endorsement   A change to an insurance policy that appears in the body of the policy.

Grace period   A period after the due date of an insurance premium during which payment can be made to continue the policy.

Incontestability clause   A clause in an insurance contract waiving the right, after the policy has been in force a specified length of time, of terminating the policy for misrepresentation of warranties by the insured.

Lapse   Termination of an insurance policy due to failure of the insured to pay a premium.

Rider   A piece of paper attached to an insurance policy, by agreement of insurer and insured, that alters the policy in some way.

Termination   Ending of all rights and obligations of insurer and insured in an insurance policy.

SELF TEST

CHAPTER 40

NAME_____

DATE_____

40.1 A/An _____ to a policy of insurance is a separate
      piece of paper attached to the policy _____
      the policy's insurance to the insured, and a part of
      the policy to which both parties _____.

40.2 A/An _____ to a policy appears in the _____
      of the policy as a change in the terms and conditions
      of the policy, and the indorsement is made by the
      _____ with the consent of the _____
      _____ the issuance of the policy.

40.3 The only distinction between a rider and an endorse-
      ment is that a rider is a/an _____ piece of paper
      which is _____ to and made a part of the policy,
      whereas an endorsement is embodied right into the
      _____ of the policy itself.

40.4 By the term lapse, we mean that the insurance company
      has a right to _____ a policy of insurance
      upon the _____ of the conditions of the in-
      surance by the insured.

40.5 The term "cancellation," of a contract of insurance,
      means to suggest the right to _____,
      _____, or terminate the policy.

40.6 The right of cancellation of a contract of insurance
      can arise from any of the following sources, or if
      any of the following conditions occur:
      a) if the policy provides in its _____ that
          either of the parties may cancel the policy with-
          out any reason upon giving so many days'
          _____ in writing to the other party; or
      b) if there is fraud or _____ in the appli-
          cation, or the _____ and representations
          of that application; or
      c) if the insurer is adjudicated _____, or
          if the insurer or its company has made an assign-
          ment for benefit of _____, or has been
          _____ with another company.

40.7   The _____ clause in policies of insurance
       provides, in essence, that an insurance company may
       not _____ or terminate a policy of insurance,
       or defend against a/an _____ for benefits by its
       insured, based upon some _____ in the appli-
       cation for insurance after the policy has been in
       effect for a given period of time.

40.8   If an applicant knowingly and willfully defrauded the
       insurance company into issuing a policy based upon
       fradulent statements, then the company does not waive
       the _____ it has to the issuance of the policy
       based upon the _____. But _____ mis-
       takes as to facts within the application are _____
       after a given period of time.

41 Insurance

Life Insurance—I

LEARNING OBJECTIVES

To learn the fundamentals of life insurance.

CHAPTER CONTENTS

Kinds of Life Insurance   Insurable Interest
Application for Life Insurance   Exclusion of the Insurer
from Liability   Glossary   Self Test

KINDS OF LIFE INSURANCE

In the life insurance field the policy most frequently
used for young people just getting their start in life is
called a *term* insurance policy. This is a policy which the
company issues upon the life of the insured for a fixed
premium and for a fixed number of years. At the end of
the term, the number of years, the policy terminates and a
new policy may be instituted by a new physical examination and
at a higher premium, because the insured is older at that
time. A term policy at the outset is the least expensive
type of insurance you can get because it offers you only insurance protection. As a straight insurance policy against
death it has none of the other attributes of insurance
policies. In addition, term insurance can be issued that
is guaranteed convertible at the end of the term to a
different form of policy.

Another common form of insurance policy is the *whole
life* policy (or the straight life or ordinary life policy).
This insurance policy, issued upon application and medical
examination, calls for the insured to pay a premium each
year during his life and calls upon the insurance company
to pay the maximum benefit of the whole life policy upon the
death of the insured to the named beneficiary.

There is also a whole life policy with a limited payment period—sometimes called *limited pay life*; by this policy
the insured is obligated to pay a fixed premium per year
for a given number of years—10, 15, or 20 years. After
that time, no more premiums are required of the insured,
and upon the insured's death the beneficiary receives the
stated value of the policy. This has the advantage that
while the insured is required to pay premiums during his
working years, the insured has no premium to pay once he
has retired and consequently has a reduced income.

Another form of insurance is the *endowment policy*, a
whole life policy that may also call for limited payment of
premiums. But its distinctive feature is that in addition
to a payment of the stated value of the policy upon the
death of the insured, the policy also agrees that if the
insured lives to a stated age, the policy shall pay to him
a fixed sum each month for the remainder of his life and
upon the death of the insured, the remaining balance of
the stated value as a lump sum benefit. For example, an
insurance policy was issued to Mr. Jones requiring
him to pay a premium of $150 a year for 25 years, covering
Mr. Jones' life for $10,000. At the end of 25 years,
Mr. Jones would have to pay no more premiums and the company

would pay an endowment to Mr. Jones of $100 per month for
the remainder of his life. If Mr. Jones dies prior to
the 25th year of the policy, his beneficiary would be
entitled to $10,000 in benefits under the policy. If
Mr. Jones died two years after the 25th anniversary of the
policy, his beneficiary would be entitled to $10,000 less
the sum that had been paid out in endowments—at $100 a
month for two years, $2400. The lump sum benefit would be
$7600. (In addition, the beneficiary could elect to
continue with the endowment payments of $100 per month for
the remainder of the beneficiary's life if he or she so
chose, or to accept the lump sum payment. That policy
would be known as a limited pay whole life endowment policy.)

INSURABLE INTEREST

Insurable interest is a concept basic to all insurance and
is especially important in life insurance. An insurable
interest in the life of another is basically some substantial
hope of benefit from the continued life of another person.
Now most insurable interests mean a hope of pecuniary, or
monetary, benefit in the continued life of another person.
For example, children have an insurable interest in the
continued lives of their parents. Any creditor has an
insurable interest in the life of his debtor to make sure
that he will be paid back the loan.

While all legal authorities agree that an insurable
interest of some sort must exist in the case of life
insurance, they are not exactly agreed on what constitutes
an insurable interest. Some cases hold that the interest
must be monetary, and that mere relationship by blood or
marriage is not enough. But the weight of authority, most
cases agree, is that there must be a reasonable expectation
of benefit or advantage from the continued life of another
person, and this is sufficient to create an insurable
interest. The benefit may not be solely monetary, but
it is enough if there is a continued welfare resulting
from the continued life of the insured party.

For our purposes, an insurable interest will have some
pecuniary benefit or the expectation of continued benefit
in the life of the insured. Clearly, I could not take out an
insurance policy in which I paid the premiums and named
myself as beneficiary, on the life of a movie star whom I
did not personally know, merely because I like the pictures
that he or she made; nor could I take out a life insurance

policy on my favorite political leader merely because I
was a supporter of his. In neither of these cases is the
benefit substantial enough to warrant a life insurance
policy in which I was the beneficiary. That would be known
as a wagering policy—meaning I had merely gambled with the
insurance company that I would outlive the insured under
the policy and therefore be entitled to substantial
benefits upon his death.

Thus, if the only benefit to be derived by the
beneficiary is upon the <u>death</u> of the insured, then there
is not an insurable interest for the insurable interest
must depend upon the <u>continued life</u> of the insured. A
father and mother have an insurable interest in their
children, and a husband and wife have an insurable interest
in each other. And again, often when you borrow money or
purchase a commodity on a time contract, the seller, or
lender, includes in the cost of the loan or the goods an
amount sufficient to put you on an insurance policy so
that in the event of your death he will have payment under
his insurance policy for the amount of your debt paid out
of the proceeds of the benefit on the policy. There is
an insurable interest in this creditor-debtor relationship.

APPLICATION FOR LIFE INSURANCE

The application for life insurance, generally furnished to
the applicant by the insurance company, has a series of
questions on it. Obviously the insurance company is
interested in the health, the age, and the personal habits
of the applicant, and questions about these are phrased for
the applicant to answer honestly and forthrightly. Age
affects the premiums that the insurance company will charge
if it accepts the applicant's offer to be insured, and
certainly the insurance company must know the applicant's
health to determine whether they will accept the application.

If the applicant is actually 27 years old and puts down
that he is 25, this will affect the premium that the
applicant will be required to pay over the years. If the
applicant has knowingly and willfully misstated his age in
order to save some premium expense, the company would be
entitled to cancel the policy upon learning the true age
of the applicant. Remember that, although the incontestability clause protects the insured once the policy has been
in effect a specified period, the insured has no such
protection if the company can establish that the applicant

willfully and fraudulently misstated the facts of his age.
The company can cancel the policy under the terms of most
policies that are issued today.

But if an applicant has misstated his age by, say,
two years, and has had the policy in force and has paid
premiums for 25 years and on his death his true age becomes
known, can the company at that time cancel the policy—
declare it void on the basis of fraud? No. Most courts
have now held that the policy will remain in force but
the benefits payable under the policy shall be reduced
by the difference between the premiums paid and what should
have been paid on the true age of the applicant.

In their application forms insurance companies ask
such questions as "Have you been treated in the last year
by a doctor?" If you answer "Yes" there are generally
some questions that ask what type of treatment and for what
condition. There is usually a series of questions about
whether you have ever had cancer, tuberculosis, trachoma,
and so on through the diseases and conditions that affect
and debilitate a person's health. For an example of the
role such questions play in the relationship between insurer
and insured, an applicant answered "No" to "Have you ever
had treatment for any serious stomach condition or do you
have any stomach or bowel condition at the present time?"
But for two or three years prior to making application the
applicant did have certain upset stomach conditions but
had never seen a doctor about it; he had merely taken some
drug store remedies, thinking he had no more than an upset
stomach or indigestion. Two years after the policy had
been issued, the applicant had to go to the hospital and
have a series of three very serious stomach operations. He
made claim on the health policy for his medical expense
and his lost income, both covered under the policy. The
company denied coverage and cancelled the policy claiming
that by the doctor's diagnosis his condition had been pre-
existent, a chronic ulcer of the stomach and large colon.
When the case was tried the court found that the applicant
did not know of his actual condition at the time he made
application for the policy or when he renewed it, and it was
not until he later went to the hospital that the doctor was
able to diagnose the condition which had then become acute.
Consequently, recovery was allowed upon the contract of
insurance.

Thus, an untrue statement about a material matter
affecting the health or physical condition of an applicant
for life or health insurance is grounds for voiding the

contract by the company if the applicant knew that the
statement was untrue at the time that he gave the answer,
especially if it becomes a warranty under the contract.
But if the applicant did not know his true health at the
time he made application, and couldn't have known in the
exercise of reasonable prudence, then recovery is granted.
In other words, a statement by an applicant for life
insurance or health insurance that he is in good health is
only a representation of his opinion and belief that he is
in good health, and its being proven false by the insurance
company does not allow the company to cancel and avoid
payment. The insurance company must prove one thing more—
that the applicant knew of the existence of the adverse
condition of his health at the time of his application.

Some authorities adopt the strict view that the warranties to the answers in an application for a life or
health insurance policy, are grounds for voiding the policy
if they are untrue. But these views are changing and the
construction of the application becomes more liberal each
year, based upon the notation that the company itself had
its doctor examine the applicant, and if he could not
discover the illness, it is difficult indeed to see how
the applicant could know of the impairment or disease.
But this all assumes the good faith of the applicant. It
is very shortsighted to knowingly falsify an application for
life insurance because the premiums will not gain you
coverage when a claim is made upon the insurance company.

Incontestability provisions in life and health insurance contracts are generally of two kinds: one providing
that the policy shall be incontestable from the date of
its issuance, and the other providing that the policy shall
be incontestable after a specified period of time has
elapsed from the issuance of the policy—generally two
years from the issuance date. The decisions that have
interpreted these clauses hold them valid because they give
the insurance company a reasonable time to determine whether
a misstatement of fact has been made and whether the
applicant has been fraudulent in statements made in his
application. Sometimes fraud may also be incontestable
because of the wording of the clause, but most incontestable
clauses now provide that the assertions made in the application shall be incontestable for a period of two years
except those made fraudulently to induce the company to
issue the policy.

Technically, a policy does not have life until it is
delivered to the actual possession of the policyholder.

It is a contract which is accepted by delivery of the proof
of the contract to the policyholder. Through court interpretation, however, insurance companies have been held
liable on the terms and conditions of their policy even
though actual delivery of the policy to the policyholder
has not occurred. The fact that the policy has been
accepted by the insurance company creates the contract
and makes the insurance company liable in accordance with
the terms and conditions of its policy even though the
policy had not been delivered to the insured prior to the
time of the insured's death or ill health under a health
policy.

As mentioned in a previous chapter, each life insurance
policy has an anniversary date one year after the inception
or original issuance date of the policy. Each year, the
company must renew the policy in accordance with the terms
of its original issuance. If the company chooses to cancel
the policy in accordance with its terms, it must give notice
of the cancellation. As we have discussed before, some
life insurance and health policies are guaranteed to be
noncancellable by the company that issues them. Consequently, if the insured meets all of the obligations and conditions
of the policy—that is, the payment of premiums—and if the
application is factually correct, the policy will be
renewed each year upon its anniversary date.

EXCLUSION OF THE INSURER FROM LIABILITY

Nothing is more certain than death and taxes. However, the
benefit from a death under a life insurance policy may not
be quite as certain as taxes. Let's look at some of the
most common conditions which exclude the liability of the
life insurance company to pay benefits on a death. Almost
without exception, a life insurance policy excludes
liability upon the company for payment of death benefits
to a beneficiary if the insured died while violating a
law or as the result of a judicial sentence of death.
That is, if the insured was robbing a bank and was shot in
the process, no benefits would be paid to his beneficiary;
or if a murderer was caught, tried, and convicted, and
sentenced and the sentence was carried out, to death, no
life insurance benefits would be paid to the beneficiary.

Another exclusion that you should know about has
been interpreted by a court to **exclude liability** of the
company for death which occurred while the insured was

intoxicated—even though there was no proof that the
intoxication directly caused the death. This is something
to really think about if you're going to be driving your
automobile while you're intoxicated. You can kill someone
or someone can kill you and the person who is intoxicated
when he dies may have an exclusion in his life insurance
policy against liability for payment to the beneficiary.

Another common exclusion from liability by the company is if the death of the insured occurs while he is
engaged in the military service of the country. In
addition, a uniform exclusion in all insurance policies
applies to an insured who died as a result of warfare,
even though the insured may have been a civilian.

Another exclusion is that which exempts the company
from payment of benefits to the beneficiary if the death
of the insured resulted from his suicide. However, some
policies exempt the company from liability for suicidal
death if it occurs within two years of the policy's
inception; therefore, the company remains liable for the
death to the beneficiary. But other companies exempt
any liability they might have for any suicidal death, no
matter when it occurs.

So you see that a contract of insurance is a negotiated
contract of rights and obligations—duties and promises.
Merely because an insurance policy is printed on fancy paper
with lots of difficult language and very small print,
don't be confused. It's merely a contract which you enter
into with a company and you have a right to all of the
benefits you can obtain in dealing with any other insurance
company. So you want to obtain the best benefits possible
in your insurance policy.

If you are unfortunate enough to have to make a proof
of loss as a beneficiary under a life insurance policy for
the death of an insured, the law generally states that,
unless the policy requires otherwise, a proof of loss must
be made upon the insurance company within a reasonable time.
In the event of an untimely death, contact your insurance
office and the agent and advise him of the calamity. The
agent will know what the requirements are and generally
furnish you with a proper proof of loss form. But the proof
of loss must be set forth in detail as the terms of the
policy require, or the company again may not be liable.
If the proof of loss is false or fraudulent, the company
may refuse payment on the claim. Keep in mind that some
courts and some policies have taken the view that notification by telephone call or any other reasonable means of

notification puts the insurance company upon the duty of furnishing a proof of loss form to the beneficiary, but the beneficiary or the next of kin must fill out the proof of loss and furnish it to the company. Keep in mind that only <u>after</u> receipt of the proof of loss is an insurance company liable for the payment of the claim pursuant to the terms of the policy.

In the next chapter we will discuss in greater detail who a beneficiary is and what rights the beneficiary has under a life health insurance policy.

GLOSSARY TERMS

Endowment policy   A whole life, and sometimes also limited pay, policy that in addition to death benefits will pay monthly sums to the insured if he lives beyond a stated age, and at his death the remaining balance will go to the beneficiary in a lump sum.

Insurable interest   A substantial hope of benefit from the continued life of another person.

Limited pay life   A life insurance policy with the benefits of the whole life policy but with a fixed number of years in which premiums are due.

Ordinary life insurance   Whole life insurance.

Straight life insurance   Whole life insurance.

Term insurance   A life insurance policy for a fixed premium and a fixed number of years.

Whole life insurance   A life insurance policy requiring the insured to pay a premium every year of his life and requiring the insurer to pay the maximum stated benefit to the beneficiary.

SELF TEST

CHAPTER 41

NAME_____

DATE_____

41.1 The policy that is most frequently used for young people just getting their start in life is called a/an _____ insurance policy.

41.2 A term policy is a policy which the company issues upon the _____ of the insured for a fixed _____ for a fixed term of _____.

41.3 A term policy, at the outset, is the most (choose either "expensive" or "inexpensive") _____ type of insurance you can get because it only offers you _____ protection.

41.4 Term insurance can be issued which is guaranteed _____ at the end of the _____ to a different form of policy.

41.5 A whole life policy is also called a/an _____ life policy or _____ life policy.

41.6 A whole life policy is a policy of insurance issued upon application and _____ examination which calls for the insured to pay a premium each year during _____, and calls upon the insurer to pay the _____ benefit of the whole life policy upon the death of the insured to the named _____.

41.7 A/An _____ pay life policy is a policy in which the insured is obligated to pay a/an _____ premium per year for a/an _____ number of years and upon his death, the insurer pays the benefits under the policy to the named beneficiary.

41.8 An endowment policy is a whole _____ policy which may also have a feature of calling for _____ payment of premiums. In addition to the payment of the _____ value of the policy upon the death of the insured, the policy also agrees that if the insured lives to a stated _____, the policy shall pay to the insured a fixed sum each month for the remainder of his life, and upon death of the insured, the remaining _____ of the stated value as a lump sum _____ to the named beneficiary.

41.9   An insurable interest in the life of another means,
        basically, some substantial hope of _____
        from the _____ life of another person.

41.10   Most insurable interests mean a hope of _____
        or monetary benefit in the _____ life of another
        person.

41.11   Any person who is a/an _____ of a debtor has an
        insurable interest in the life of the debtor to make
        sure that he will be paid back the loan.

41.12   If the only benefit to be derived from an insurance
        policy by a beneficiary is upon the death of the
        insured, then there is not a/an _____ interest.

41.13   An insurable interest must depend upon the _____
        life of the insured.

41.14   If an applicant for life insurance has knowingly and
        _____ "falsified" his age in order to save
        some premium expense, the insurance company would
        be entitled to _____ the policy upon learning
        of the _____ facts and age of the applicant.

41.15   An untrue statement in regard to a/an _____
        matter affecting the health or physical condition of
        an applicant for life or health insurance is grounds
        for _____ the contract by the company if the
        applicant knew that the statement was untrue at the
        time the statement was given, especially if the
        statement is a/an _____ of the contract.

41.16   If an applicant did not know the true condition of
        his health at the time he made application for life
        and health insurance, and could not have known in
        the exercise of reasonable _____, then
        _____ of a claim would be granted.

41.17   In order for an insurance company to cancel a policy
        or avoid a claim because of misrepresentations on
        the application, it must prove that the applicant
        _____ at the time of the application of the
        _____ of the condition which affected his
        health so adversely. This assumes _____ on
        the part of the applicant.

41.18   Incontestability provisions in life and health
        insurance contracts are generally of two kinds:
        one providing that the policy shall be incontestable
        from the _____ of its issuance, and the other
        providing that the policy shall be incontestable
        after a specified _____ of _____ has
        elapsed from the _____ of the policy.

CHAPTER 41

NAME_____

41.19 Incontestability clauses have generally been considered valid, because they give the insurance
company a reasonable time to determine whether a/an
_____ of fact has been made, or whether the
applicant has been _____ in statements made
in his application.

41.20 Technically, a policy does not have life until it
is _____ to the actual _____ of the
policy holder; however, through court interpretation,
it is enough that the policy has been _____ by
the _____.

41.21 Most life insurance policies have a/an _____
date of _____ year after the inception or
original issuance date of the policy.

41.22 Each year, a life insurance company must _____
the policy in accordance with the _____ of
the original issuance of the policy. If the company
chooses to cancel the policy in accordance with its
terms, it must give notice of _____.

41.23 Very frequently, almost without exception, a life
insurance policy excludes _____ upon the
company for payment of death benefits to a beneficiary if the _____ died during the _____
of a law, or if his death resulted from the _____
of a/an _____ sentence.

41.24 An exclusion in one policy that has been interpreted
by a court excluded _____ of the company for
death which occurred while the insured was _____,
even though there was no proof that the _____
directly caused the death.

41.25 Another common exclusion which excludes liability
by the company is if the death occurs while the
insured is engaged in the _____ _____
of the country. In addition, a/an _____
exclusion in all insurance policies excludes liability
where the insured died as a result of _____,
even though the insured may have been a/an _____.

41.26 Another exclusion which exempts the company from
payments of benefits to the beneficiary is if the
death of the insured resulted from _____;
however, some policies will maintain liability for

this cause of death if it occurs two years after
the issuance of the policy.

41.27 When we talk about a contract of insurance, we are
really talking about a/an _____ contract of
rights and _____.

41.28 Keep in mind that it is only after _____ of a/an
_____ of _____ statement that an
insurance company is liable for the payment of a
claim pursuant to the terms of the policy.

42 Insurance

Life Insurance—II. Health and Accident Insurance

LEARNING OBJECTIVES

To conclude the study of life insurance and learn the rights of a beneficiary to a life insurance policy.

To discuss some important points of accident and health insurance policies.

CHAPTER CONTENTS

Rights of Beneficiaries to Life Insurance Policies
Health and Accident Insurance Policies   Glossary   Self Test

In the law of insurance a beneficiary is, broadly, the one
to whom the insurance is payable, or who is entitled to the
proceeds of the policy or the benefits of the insurance
fund. Ordinarily, in insurance, the term beneficiary is
used in referring to the person who is designated in a
contract of life, health, or accident insurance as the one
who is to receive the benefits which become payable
according to the terms of the contract upon the death of
the insured.

Remember that some people cannot be beneficiaries of
a life insurance policy. A person who does not have an
insurable interest in the life of the insured cannot be
a beneficiary, since we cannot have wagering contracts. A
beneficiary must be one who had an insurable interest in
the life of the insured. In addition, a person who has
intentionally caused the death of the insured may not be
a beneficiary, for a murderer may not prosper by the
murder through insurance benefits.

RIGHTS OF BENEFICIARIES TO LIFE INSURANCE POLICIES

But if the person named in the life insurance policy on
Mr. Jones has an insurable interest in Mr. Jones and did
not intentionally cause the death of Mr. Jones, what right
does the beneficiary have prior to Mr. Jones' death? The
law states that a beneficiary named in the life insurance
policy has a property right or expectancy in the proceeds of
the life insurance policy; the beneficiary has an interest
in the policy and life of the insured. Thus, unless the
policy sets forth on its face that the insured reserves
the right to change the name of the beneficiary, the
beneficiary may not be changed on the policy without the
consent of the beneficiary.

You can well imagine the problems that have arisen
when the insured has not reserved the right to change the
name of the beneficiary upon notice to the company. In
this country there have been literally hundreds of court
cases to decide this question, and uniformly they have
held that if the insured does not reserve the right to
change the beneficiary,the beneficiary named in the policy
has a right to the proceeds unless he has consented to a
name change of beneficiary. Men and women have been
divorced; there have been all kinds of disagreements between insured people and the parties named as beneficiaries. It has been adjudicated that a man can leave all

of his estate, including his insurance policies, to a son,
and yet the named policy beneficiary receives all of the
insurance policy proceeds because the insured did not
reserve the right to change the name of the beneficiary.

Fortunately, most insurance policies today reserve
for the insured the right to change the name of the beneficiary. Consequently, if before his life ends, the
insured sends formal, written notice to the company that
the beneficiaries on his policies are to be changed and
gives the accurate new names for the beneficiaries, and if
the insurance company changes the names of the beneficiaries prior to the death of the insured, the new
beneficiaries will receive the proceeds from the death or
accidental death provisions of the policy.

Let's assume that the policy of insurance has reserved
unto the insured the right to change the name of the beneficiary, and let's assume that the insured has stated
"in the event of my death the beneficiary is to my wife."
Let's further assume that when the insurance was taken
out, the insured was married to Jane but that when he died
he had been married to Barbara. Who should recover the
benefits of the policy at the time of death—Jane, the
wife when the policy was taken out, or Barbara, the wife
when death occurred? The beneficiary who is entitled to
the recovery in this case would be Barbara, the wife at
the time of death. The rule of law is that the beneficiary entitled to recovery is the beneficiary occupying
the status described in the policy at the time of death.
Let's assume that Mr. Jones has a life insurance policy
and he states, "The beneficiaries are to be my children."
Two of his three children die before he does. Consequently
his sole remaining child would be entitled to all of the
proceeds of the policy as the sole remaining beneficiary.
Mr. Jones would have been wiser to have stated, "To each
of my children and to their heirs. My children presently
living are Jane, John, and Joe." In that case, even though
Jane and John had died prior to Mr. Jones, his grandchildren
would have received a proportionate interest in the proceeds
or benefits under the life insurance policy.

Another example of how the naming of the beneficiary
is very important is if Mr. Jones states in his life
insurance policy that the beneficiaries are to be his
wife, Jane, and their children, John, Jane, and Joe. If
Mr. Jones dies and his wife and three children survive
him, all four of them are entitled to equal share of the
benefits payable under the life insurance policy. Mr. Jones

may have intended to provide fully for his wife, rather
than for his children. But each child would take one
quarter of the insurance benefits. A life insurance
policy is a contract and therefore its terms are binding,
so you must pay particular attention to the terms and the
provisions of the contract to make sure that they meet
with the desire of the insured, and the desires of the
beneficiaries.

One last point with respect to beneficiaries: Since
a beneficiary must have an insurable interest in the life
of the insured at the inception of the policy, and since
the contract names the beneficiary specifically and,
unless the beneficiary has been properly changed (by the
insured's reservation of right to change the name of the
beneficiary), the beneficiary is entitled to the proceeds
of the policy even though the insured had a different
intent prior to his death, you will not be shocked and
dismayed to learn that the mere fact that a husband and
wife have become divorced does not affect the rights of
the spouse to be a beneficiary in the ex-spouse's insurance
policy. Although some states have passed statutes to the
effect that divorce does terminate the rights of the
beneficiary to the policy, in most states the law remains
that unless the beneficiary is changed on the policy, the
ex-spouse is entitled to the proceeds payable upon the
death of the insured ex-spouse, even though the insured
has remarried and intends that his or her present spouse
be entitled to the proceeds of insurance that they have
maintained on their life. There are numerous cases to
this effect.

HEALTH AND ACCIDENT INSURANCE POLICIES

More and more people are finding it advisable to be
insured under major medical or health or accident policies
which sometimes include disability income provisions.
Texts on business law and even on insurance unfortunately
do not spend a great deal of time examining some of the
problems that occur in such policies. Most health and
accident policies have incontestability clauses, most of
them provide a time limit in which the insurance company
may cancel or contest any claim based upon mistaken or
untrue statements in the application itself. The same
problems that apply to insurance in general and to life

insurance in particular are just as important in health
insurance—in fact a little more so because health
insurance is so new and is growing so rapidly.

Let's look at some of the rules of law as to which
diseases are covered and which are **excluded**. Assume that a
policy explicitly covers blood poisoning. Blood poisoning
would be covered whatever its cause (except a pre-existent
condition that you willfully and fraudulently failed to
mention). Although the policy might say that it does not
cover accidental injury, if the blood poisoning resulted
from an accidental injury, the policy would still cover for
the blood poisoning, even though it would not cover for
the medical and doctor and hospital expenses for the treatment of the injury itself—only the blood poisoning which
resulted therefrom.

In addition, if the policy excludes all coverage for
any condition which is chronic in nature—whether it be
deformity, infirmity, condition, or disease—then any
condition which flares up, say, after ten years of paying
premiums on the policy but turns out to be a chronic
condition—one you were born with or one that had long
existed undiscovered in your body—you will not be covered
under the policy. Many policies exclude such chronic
conditions or diseases only until a period of time has
elapsed after the policy was begun. These, of course, are
more valuable policies to have because you or your doctor
may not know that you have a chronic condition that may
cause you severe difficulty over the next 20 years. For
example, you're 26 years old and have never had any back
trouble or joint problems in your legs or arms. But at
age 29 you suddenly have stiffness in the back, shoulders,
and arms and you see your doctor, who says that you have
serious rheumatoid arthritis, a chronic condition which
for you has only now flared up. This is not an unusual
situation; many, many people suffer from arthritic problems
at a very young age, and the condition had been quiescent
most of their lives and then flared up for no obvious
medical reason. It is a chronic condition but not a
disabling condition. Consequently, the very best health
insurance policies provide for exclusion of chronic
conditions for only a limited period of time after which
they are covered. Obviously, the insurance company is
endeavoring to keep people from its coverage who know they
have a chronic condition and are seeking to have someone
else pay for their medical expenses; this is a proper self-
protection for the companies, for otherwise insurance rates

would be too high for any of us to afford them. But the
responsible insurance companies and the best policies
provide for coverage of said chronic condition after a
two, three, or four year period, depending on the particular
policy.

What is meant by *accident*? What type of injury is covered
Accident insurance is a part of health insurance.
(We are not talking about liability insurance, but about
health and accident insurance wherein the insured is
covered for accidental injury or death to himself.) Most
health policies in their terms or an endorsement include
coverage for accidental injury or death as part of the
health program of the policy.

What is meant by *accident*? What type of injury is covered
under an accidental injury policy? The words accident and
accidental have never acquired any true technical precision
in law, and are used in insurance contracts as they are
used in the ordinary speech of people generally. The
courts are pretty much agreed that the words accident and
accidental mean that which happens by chance or fortuitously,
without intention or design, and which is unexpected,
unusual, and unforeseen. The courts usually define an
accident as an event that takes place without one's foresight or expectation—an event that proceeds from an unknown
cause or is an unusual effect of a known cause and therefore
not expected. Some accident and health policies cover for
injury resulting from external, violent, and accidental
means. The courts have held that an accident policy that
describes its coverage for bodily injury resulting from
external, violent, and accidental means covers an accident
of a violent nature occurring from an external cause. The
death or injury need not directly be caused by the external
force or a violent agency. For example, if I am driving
my car down the road and around a curve comes a logging
truck driving in the middle of the road and forcing me to
drive off the road and seriously injure myself, I would
have a right to compensation under the accidental injury
portion of my health policy. No one could argue that what
I did was intentional because I was forced into that
external, violent, and accidental activity; I reacted
quickly to save my family, myself, and my automobile. The
cause of my accidental injury was my pulling off the road,
and yet it was external because the cause of my pulling
off the road was the negligent driving of the logging truck
operator.

Another problem that you'll want to look to when you are
reviewing an accident and health policy is the requirement
in an accident policy that there be bodily injury resulting

from the accident. This portion of the policy is not a
health policy but an accident policy. Consequently,
injury must result from the accident. If you buy an accident
policy, you expect to be covered for the injuries that
result from accident and not to be covered for disease, for
if you expect the contrary you will discover your mistake
when your claim is presented to the company and denied.
Bodily injury is distinguished from a disease or chronic
condition.

For recovery under bodily injury by accidental means
some policies require some visible mark or injury; there
must be some abnormality of the body—either externally
or internally—that can be distinguished by a trained
medical practitioner using X ray or some other technique
to establish that an accidental means has caused injury as
distinguished from disease or chronic condition. If the
external or internal mark was visible to a medical practitioner or to any independent person and notice and proof of
loss was given to the insurance company, then you have every
right of recovery. It is not necessary that you be examined
by an insurance company medical examiner for you to be
entitled to recovery. The intent of this language is to avoid
the sham claims sometimes made by unscrupulous people.

While an accident policy covers only for accidents,
you are not excluded from coverage if you accidentally injure
yourself through negligence. We will discuss accidents and
negligence in greater detail under liability policies, but
here we can say that within our own accidental and health
policies the courts have uniformly held that even though we
were negligent in exposing ourselves to danger or in how
we conducted ourselves, we are not precluded from recovery
under our own accidental injury policies. We must not have
deliberately inflicted the wounds upon ourselves, and after
we have been hurt by accidental means we are under a duty
to use discretion and every care necessary for the preservation of our health; that is, we cannot have sliced a
finger and then fail to medicate it, allowing it to become
infected and then require amputation of the finger, and
expect the insurance company to pay for all of that medical
expense, unless we can show that we used reasonable care
in the preservation of our own health, after the accidental
injury.

An accident policy does not make the insurance company
liable to our beneficiaries if you and I are intentionally
murdered by some individual, unless the individual is insane
and therefore does not have any legal ability to form a
murdering intent. Remember that this is an accidental

injury policy and not a life insurance policy. Additionally,
the coverage does not apply if the insured voluntarily and
deliberately engages in a fight unless he is defending his
own property or person and is in fear of danger to his
property or person. You can defend yourself and be covered
under such an accidental policy but you cannot go out and
pick a fight and expect the insurance company to pay for
the medical expenses if you lose it. The same thing applies
to injury in the service of your country, and to suicide,
as we discussed in relation to the life insurance policy.
One final caution is that some accident insurance policies have
exclusions for certain occupations. You will want to check
on the policy provisions to make certain that your occupation
is not excluded.

GLOSSARY TERMS

Accident   An event that occurs without one's foresight or expectation, that proceeds from an unknown cause or is an unusual effect of a known cause and therefore not expected.

Bodily injury   Some physical, either external or internal, abnormality that is discernible and is not caused by disease or chronic condition but by accident.

SELF TEST

CHAPTER 42

NAME_____

DATE_____

42.1 The term beneficiary, as used in the law of insurance, may be defined broadly as the one to whom the insurance is _____ or who is entitled to the _____ of the policy, or the _____ of the insurance fund.

42.2 A beneficiary must be one who has a/an _____ interest in the _____ of the insured. We cannot have _____ contracts.

42.3 In addition, a beneficiary may not be the one who has caused, _____, the _____ of the insured.

42.4 The law states that a beneficiary named in the policy of life insurance has a/an _____ right or _____ in the proceeds of the life insurance policy. The beneficiary has an interest in the _____ and _____ of the insured.

42.5 Unless the policy sets forth on its face that the insured _____ the right to change the name of the beneficiary, the beneficiary (choose either "may" or "may not") _____ be changed on the policy without the _____ of the beneficiary.

42.6 The rule of law is that the beneficiary entitled to recovery is the beneficiary occupying the _____ described in the policy at the time of death.

42.7 We have noted that the contract of insurance names the beneficiary _____, and unless the contract is changed by the insured pursuant to a/an _____ of the rights to change the name of the beneficiary, the beneficiary is entitled to the _____ of the policy, even though the insured had a different _____ prior to his death.

42.8 Most health and accident policies have the _____ clause that we have discussed earlier.

42.9 In reference to the incontestability clause, the rule is that your knowledge and intent of any illnesses you may have is to be judged at the time of _____;

not at some future time when your health may deter-
iorate to a point where you know you are sick.

42.10 Many policies exclude _____ conditions or
diseases for a period of time after the policy has
been in existence.

42.11 The accident and health insurance discussed in this
chapter is insurance wherein the insured is covered
for accidental _____ or _____ to him-
self.

42.12 The definition of an accident that has usually been
adopted by the courts is that an accident is an
event that takes place without one's _____
or _____—an event that proceeds from a/an
_____ cause or is a/an _____ effect of a
known cause and, therefore, not _____.

42.13 An accident policy requires that there be _____
injury resulting from an accident, and would not,
therefore, include diseases or chronic conditions
covered by a health policy.

42.14 With respect to accident and health policies, the
courts have uniformly held that even though we were
_____ in the manner in which we conducted
ourselves, this will not preclude _____ under
our accidental injury policies; however, we must
not _____ the wounds upon ourselves, and we
are under a duty after injury by accident to use
_____ and every care necessary for the _____
of our health.

42.15 Under an accident policy, the insurance company is
not liable to the beneficiary if the insured is
intentionally _____ by some individual unless
the individual is _____.

42.16 One final caution on the subject of accident policies
is that some policies exclude certain _____.

43 Insurance

Fire Insurance. Homeowner's Insurance.

LEARNING OBJECTIVES

To learn the basic concepts of fire insurance.

CHAPTER CONTENTS

In this chapter we will discuss the standard fire insurance
policy that applies to business premises as well as to
residences. Fire insurance contracts date back to the 16th
century and the great fires of London, after which merchants
and capitalists got together and agreed upon a form of fire
insurance policy in which all of the merchants and businessmen of the community contributed a premium to underwriters
and the underwriters insured their premises against fire.

In those days fire was a major calamity because there
was no fire fighting equipment of any size, and once a fire
got started it was extremely likely to burn to the ground
all of the buildings in a very wide area. That fire insurance was adopted in England was natural, for the English had
had successful experience with total losses in the marine
insurance field. (Remember that around the 14th century
marine insurance was introduced to the English by Italian
merchants and seamen.)

THE STANDARD FIRE INSURANCE POLICY

Today fire insurance policies are far more standardized
than life insurance, liability insurance, or automobile
insurance contracts. Fire insurance policies are much
like marine policies—they have become standardized over
the years. In fact, most states have adopted by law the
New York standard fire insurance form, which from time to
time to time has been amended and modified. The New
York standard fire insurance form is a relatively
simple insurance form.

We will use as an example for study a modified form
of the New York standard fire insurance form. We'll begin
with the insuring clause, which is the undertaking by the
insurance company and sets forth the term, the subject,
the insured, the risk, and the premium. It begins, "In
consideration of the provisions and stipulations herein or
added hereto, and of the premium charged this company,
for the term from" (say January 1, 1974 to December 30, 1976,
the term of the insurance, a three year term, and the term
expires) "at noon, standard time, at location of property
involved, to an amount not exceeding that shown in the
declarations at $12,000." Often in our present form of
policy are declarations of a policy on a separate piece
of paper showing the premium, the dwelling, and the amount
of insurance on each dwelling. Assume that we have a
$12,000 amount of insurance on the particular property.

Let's see what the insurance company will do. "...does insure the insured _____ and legal representative." What amount will they insure for? "... to the extent of the actual cash value of the property at the time of loss but not exceeding the amount which it would cost to repair or replace the property with material of like kind and quality within a reasonable time after such loss, but without allowance for any increased cost of repair or reconstruction by reason of any ordinance or law regulating construction or repair, and without compensation for loss resulting from interruption of business or manufacture. Nor, in any event, for more than the interest of the insured."

Let's try to understand that language. The amount of the insurance is $12,000, but the company is liable only to the extent of the actual cash value of the property at the time of loss and not to exceed the amount of cost to repair or reconstruct the property or replace it with like kind and quality within a reasonable time after the loss. So, assume that the house insured has a value and the amount of insurance is $12,000. The insurance company does not have to pay $12,000 if the house is burned down and the cost of replacing the house is $10,000. If the house is burned down and the cost of replacing the house is $20,000, the insurance company has limited its coverage and the extent of its liability to $12,000. If only part of the $12,000 house is burned and the part destroyed may be replaced, the insurance company, at its own option, may hire a contractor to come in and make replacement of the damaged portion of the house, and it is liable only for the actual cost of said replacement of like quality and kind. It is not liable to the insured for any increased cost based upon zone change or building code requirements that increase the cost of replacement—it is only liable for the actual replacement cost itself at the time of the fire.

You will also note that the company is not liable for loss resulting from interruption of business or manufacture. A separate insurance policy, called business interruption insurance, is available to businessmen. Obviously, if a factory burns down, the businessman would suffer very large consequential damages as a result of being out of business during the time it took to have the factory replaced. Thus, a specialized policy of insurance will pay the manufacturer for this loss of manufacture or inter-ruption of business. But such coverage is not in a fire insurance policy.

Finally, you will remember that the company is not liable for more than the interest of the insured. What

does this mean? An example will make it clear: As
husband and wife, Mr. and Mrs. Jones own a house valued at
$12,000. They have an $8000 mortgage on the premises.
The mortgage company always insists on fire insurance upon
the premises at least in the amount of their mortgage loan.
The mortgage company in this case has a mortgage for
$8000. They have insisted that Mr. and Mrs. Jones obtain
fire insurance upon the home for $8000. Mr. and Mrs.
Jones do so; they obtain fire insurance on the house in the
amount of $8000 and pay the premium. Unfortunately the
house is burned down and a total loss results. Mr. and Mrs.
Jones make claim upon the fire insurance company. After
receiving the proof of loss the fire insurance company
comes out and appraises the property and determines that it
is a total loss. They therefore pay to Mr. and Mrs. Jones
the amount of $8000, but the Joneses say the value of the
house was $12,000 and they want payment for the full value
of the home. Their interest is $12,000. The mortgage
company says, "No, the limit of this policy was $8000."
Mr. and Mrs. Jones could have insured the property to their
full interest of $12,000 but they chose only to take
insurance for the mortgage amount. The mortgage company,
on the other hand, could not insure the building for more
than $8000 for that was the limit of its interest in the
building itself. From this you will see that it is
extremely important when you're buying a home to insure
it for your full interest and not just the interest of the
mortgage company. The mortgage company may only insure
up to the value of its loan, whereas the owner or mortgagor
of the property, may insure it for its full value. In
this case, unfortunately, Mr. and Mrs. Jones foolishly only
insured for the protection of the mortgage, or the lending
institution, and they have lost the additional $4000 that
they paid for the property, and in the meantime have no
place to live.
      Let's find out now what the policy insures against—
what is the risk that the policy underwrites. The company
insures "against all direct loss by fire and lightning."
Now direct loss by fire and lightning means just what it
says; all damage to the property directly caused by the
fire is covered by the insurance policy. In addition, it
is generally held in most policies that damages resulting
from efforts made in good faith to save the property from
a fire—that is, damage by breakage or removal of the
property from the premises, or water or chemical damage
caused by the efforts of fire fighters to put out the fire—
are also covered by the fire insurance policy. In fact,

in the standard form of coverage, there is an insuring
clause that covers for theft or damage of property which
has been removed from the dwelling to a place of safety.
    The standard fire insurance policy does exclude
liability by the company for damage to the building caused
by explosion unless the explosion causes a fire; but if
a fire results from the explosion, then all of the damage
is covered by the insurance policy. Also, unless the fire
insurance policy specifically covers loss by lightning,
lightning damage is not covered. (The standard form that
we examined did cover for lightning loss.) In addition,
the fire insurance policy does not cover deterioration or
rust, mold, or dry rot, cracking or shrinking, bulging or
expansion of pavements or foundations—unless these losses
resulted from fire or lightning damages. It does not
cover for earthquake, landslide, earth sinking or settling,
mud flow—unless, again, the loss by fire or explosion
results from any of these conditions. The policy does not
cover for flood damage, tidal waves, overflow of streams
or other bodies of water, for water backing up through
drains or sewers, for ground water that rises—unless,
in each case, loss by fire or explosion results from the
flood or the backing up of water. The policy does not
cover for loss of property by theft or for malicious mischief—that is, vandalism. The policy does not cover for
damage from wind, snow, hail, or ice, or sleet, nor does
it cover for trees or shrubs damaged by wind, rain, sleet
or hail. However, it does cover for damage to shrubs,
trees, and fences that results from fire or efforts to
protect the building or personal property resulting from
fire.

HOMEOWNER'S INSURANCE POLICY

Many insurance companies have now gone to a homeowner's
policy, which includes many types of insurance in one
policy. This is a good form of insurance, provided all
of the coverage that the homeowner really needs is included.
The basic part of the homeowner's policy is the standard
form of fire insurance policy, but as you'll remember,
many of the damages that a home can suffer are not covered
by fire insurance. Consequently, a homeowner's policy can
have in it such things as an *extension of coverage
endorsement*, which covers for such things as wind, rain,
sleet, and hail damage, and riots or civil commotion.

Several years ago some of our major cities experienced
riots. Those homeowners and business premise owners who
had extended coverage were covered for damage done by
rioters, whereas homeowners and business premise owners who
did not have extended coverage were unable to recover their
losses from the insurance company who issued their basic
fire policy.

There is also a broad form endorsement, sometimes also
called dwellings and contents, which is, in effect, a
separate insurance policy that the homeowner can buy.
Such *broad form and contents coverage* insures the dwellings
for minor fires—for example, a stove fire or the blazing
up of curtains through a child's playing with matches.
This coverage generally has a deductible clause in it.
You can get the deduction for $50, $100, or any other amount,
but not less than $50. A deduction works as follows: If
damage is done to my sofa by my child's playing with
matches, I pay the first $50 of damage and after receiving
proof of loss the insurance company pays all of the damage
in excess of the $50.

This broad form coverage on contents covers windstorm, hail, explosion, vandalism, burglars, falling air-
craft, or even vehicles that drive into a home or business
premise. In many cases broad form coverage for dwellings
and contents also covers collapse, and extensive water
damage from explosion of steam boilers or water heaters
or pipes, or from their rupture or explosion due to freezing.

In some homeowner's policies you will find included
a different form of insurance called *comprehensive personal
liability insurance*, the insuring clause of which says
that the company will pay on behalf of the insured all
sums that the insured shall become legally obligated to
pay as damages for bodily injury or property damage
(covered by this insurance) caused by an occurrence; and
the company shall have the right and duty to defend any
suit against the insured seeking damages on account of
such bodily injury or property damage, even if any
allegations of the suit against the insured are groundless,
false, or fraudulent; and the company may make such investigation and settlement of any claim or suit as it deems
expedient. But the company shall not be obligated to pay
any claim or judgment or to defend any suit after the
applicable limit of the company's liability has been ex-
hausted by payment of judgments or settlements.

This particular coverage is liability insurance. It
is not indemnity insurance for the insured himself; it
is insurance protection for the insured in the event his

conduct or his premises cause injury to another person or to
another person's property. The insurance company undertakes
to defend the insured against any lawsuits or claims by
third parties; and in the event the insured is held liable
to the third person, then the insurance company agrees to
pay the third person the amount of the judgment or settlement
sufficient to settle the case or the claim. Here, then,
you see a very important distinction: Some insurance is
indemnity insurance, which means that it will pay to the
insured the amount of his loss, while some insurance is
liability insurance, which means that the insurance company
will take over the defense of the insured and protect him
against liability to a third person.

The insurance company thus has two duties: one, to
defend the insured against the claim of a third person; and
two, to pay the third person the amount of the judgment or
settlement necessary to settle the claim or demand (but
only to the extent of the limits of the policy). For
example, Mr. and Mrs. Jones, who own their home, have
invited a guest in to have dinner with them. That evening,
the downspout on their front porch breaks and water falls
on the front steps. The guest is not advised of this and the
light isn't working on the front porch, and as the guest
comes up to ring the doorbell, he slips on the very wet
steps, falls, and breaks his back. The guest brings suit
against Mr. and Mrs. Jones for negligence in not advising him
of the water, in not keeping the downspout in good repair,
and finally in not having the steps lit so he could see the
dangerous condition they were in. Mr. and Mrs. Jones
fortunately have comprehensive personal liability insurance.
The insurance company makes an investigation and talks with
the guest's attorney in an effort to settle the case. They
are not able to reach an agreement as to the fair amount to
be paid, so the insurance company hires its own attorney
and that trial attorney and the guest's attorney litigate
the case in court. The insurance company advises Mr. and
Mrs. Jones that the guest has brought suit for $25,000,
whereas the insurance policy has limits of $10,000.
Consequently the insurance company advises Mr. and Mrs. Jones
that while they will defend the suit, if the judgment goes
over $10,000, then Mr. and Mrs. Jones will have to pay the
excess over $10,000 and the insurance company will not be
liable. This is what is meant by the limits of the insurer's
responsibility. You can see from this that it is important
to have sufficient limits in your policy to guard against
just the kind of claim that could bring you to financial ruin.

Another part of many homeowner's policies is the deductible broad form personal theft policy. The broad form indicates that personal property shall be covered even though it is unscheduled; in other words, you place a value on your personal property: furniture, $4000; appliances, $2000; jewelry, $1000; clothing $3000; etc. The deductible provision of the policy says that you will pay the first $50, $100, or $200 worth of theft, and the insurance company will pay the remainder. The personal property covered is all of the property that you own in the premises—and you may also get a policy that covers personal property stolen from you away from the premises.

A personal property theft policy covers only items that have a replaceable value; you would not insure a very valuable heirloom or an extremely valuable painting under such a policy because it is stated that the limit of the company's liability for loss shall not exceed the applicable limit of the insurance in this policy, nor what it cost at the time of loss to repair or replace the property with other of like kind and quality. If you had a very valuable painting or heirloom that was, in effect, irreplaceable, you would want to put a separate endorsement in the policy for it so that its value would be stated on the policy itself and in the event of its loss the company would pay you the stated value of the item. This would therefore be a valued policy.

Many other elements can be included in a homeowner's policy—personal property floaters, credit card theft, riders for plate glass damage to the property, riders for malicious prosecution or false arrest, and on and on and on. Clearly, you can get just about any kind of insurance you need.

Three very important points must be made about property insurance: One, again, if you willfully conceal a fact about the property or about yourself in the application for insurance, the insurance will be void and the company will have no liability. Second, if the risk that the company has agreed to take on in the insurance policy is materially increased during the policy period, the policy is in suspension. Most commonly, if you leave your home for six months on a vacation and do not advise the company that you will be gone, the company is not liable for damage to the property because the risk of damage was so greatly increased by your absence. You should advise the company of your absence and pay the additional premium required for untended premises.

Finally, if you have insured personal property and real property and you sell either or both, do not attempt to transfer the insurance on the property to the purchaser. The insurance company has insured <u>you</u> for the property loss—it is not insuring the property itself; the company has the right to reject or accept a new application for insurance from your purchaser. But keep in mind that insurance is not transferable unless it has the consent of the company. Consequently, if you sell real property or personal property that is insured specifically by a policy, advise the company and cancel the policy as to the property you have sold and get a reduction or rebate in your premium.

GLOSSARY TERMS

Broad form and contents coverage   Additional coverage on
a homeowner's policy for protection in case of minor
fire damage or minor damage from other sources.

Comprehensive personal liability insurance   An insurance
supplementing a homeowner's policy that protects the
insured against loss due to property damage or personal injury to others on or because of the property
of the insured.

Extension of coverage endorsement   An endorsement in a
homeowner's policy that covers property damage resulting from sources other than fire.

SELF TEST

CHAPTER 43

NAME_____

DATE_____

43.1   Fire insurance contracts date back to the _____
        century, and the great fires of _____.
43.2   Fire insurance policies are much like _____
        policies, in that they have become _____ over
        the years.
43.3   Most states have adopted the _____ standard
        fire insurance form.
43.4   The _____ clause in a standard fire insurance
        policy is the undertaking by the insurance company,
        and it sets forth the term, the _____, the
        insured, the _____, and the premium.
43.5   The amount of insurance in a policy will be a
        stated amount, but the insurance company is liable
        only to the extent of the actual _____ of
        the property at the time of _____, and not to
        exceed the amount of cost to _____ or re-
        construct the property.
43.6   When a fire loss occurs the insurance company is
        not liable to the insured for any increased cost
        based upon _____ change or _____ code
        requirements that increase the cost of replacement;
        it is only liable for the _____ replacement
        cost itself at the time of the fire.
43.7   Under a fire insurance policy, if a fire occurs,
        the insurance company is not liable for loss result-
        ing from _____ of business insurance that is
        available to a businessman, called business
        _____ insurance.
43.8   A mortgage company may only insure property up to
        the value of its _____, whereas the owner,
        or mortgagor, of the property may insure it for its
        _____ value.
43.9   (Answer "true" or "false") _____ The standard
        form of fire insurance will cover damages caused by
        water or chemicals used by firefighters to put out
        the fire.

43.10   (Answer "true" or "false") _____   The standard
        form of fire insurance will cover loss from explo-
        sions, earthquake, flooding, mudslides, or vandalism.

43.11   A/An _____ policy can have in it such things
        as an extension of _____ endorsement to
        cover such things as wind, rain, or riot damage.

43.12   Broad form coverage on dwellings and contents
        usually has a/an _____ clause.

43.13   Many homeowner's insurance policies include _____
        personal _____ insurance to protect the
        insured against third party claims for damages that
        occurred on the insured property.

43.14   Some insurance is _____, which means that the
        insurance company will pay to the insured, the
        amount of his loss.

43.15   Some insurance is _____ insurance, which
        means that the insurance company will take over the
        defense of the insured, protect the insured against
        liability to a third person.

43.16   The broad form of personal theft insurance indicates
        that personal property shall be covered even though
        it is _____.

43.17   A personal theft policy only covers items that have
        a/an _____ value.

43.18   Heirlooms and other valuable items should be listed
        separately in a personal theft policy, and be insured
        for a stated value, thereby making the policy a/an
        _____ policy.

43.19   If an applicant conceals a fact about property
        which is going to be insured, the insurance company
        can _____ the policy and have no liability.

43.20   If the _____ that an insurance company has
        agreed to take in the insurance policy is _____
        increased during the policy period, the policy is
        _____.

43.21   Keep in mind that insurance is not _____
        unless the company consents to it.

44 Insurance

Automobile Insurance

LEARNING OBJECTIVES

To learn the law of automobile insurance.
To learn how the law works, how a policy is issued, and what are the types of coverage.

CHAPTER CONTENTS

In this chapter we will review the law of automobile
insurance—how it works, how a policy is issued, and the
coverage in a common automobile policy. Most grown
Americans operate an automobile, and with 80 million private
automobiles in this country it is not surprising that
thousands and thousands of accidents occur each year.
Obviously, then, the primary function of automobile insurance
is as liability insurance to protect the owners of automobiles for the possible human injury and property damage
that results from the operation of their automobiles.

THE USES OF AUTOMOBILE INSURANCE

But automobile insurance has several other functions. It
covers against theft; if your automobile is stolen and
not recovered you will be reimbursed for the cost of the
automobile at the time of its theft. Automobile insurance
also covers against fire, and also for collision damage
to the automobile itself. There is also extended or comprehensive coverage. These are the various parts of the
policies that we will be looking at in this chapter.
    In most states you don't have the option of buying or
not buying automobile insurance, for legislation called
financial responsibility laws has been passed that requires
the owner of each automobile to insure its operation against
property damage and personal injury to other people. When
we lose between 30,000 and 40,000 people a year on our
highways, the problem has grown beyond all proportion.
So most state legislatures have required each automobile
owner to insure its operation to very basic minimums.
The minimum coverage in most states is $5000 for each
accident and personal injury, and $10,000 for the total
injury, or each occurrence. (We will discuss such coverage
a little later in the chapter.)
    Automobile insurance varies somewhat in the policies
available. We will talk about pooled risk, and about
uninsured motorist coverage, because thousands of people
disobey the law and do not have the minimum automobile
insurance. This brings up an important distinction:
Automobile insurance, is not primarily insurance on the
<u>automobile</u> (although fire and theft are included cover-
ages), it is really <u>liability insurance</u>—protection for the
<u>operators</u> and <u>occupants</u> of the automobile itself, much like
liability insurance in a business.

The procedure for issuing an automobile policy is the
same as for any other insurance contract. An application
is made with an insurance company, or underwriter, for the
issuance of an insurance policy on an automobile owned by
the applicant. But already we see a difference. Whereas
in most policies we wanted to be covered ourselves for our
life or liability, in this situation it is the automobile
and its operators that we cover. We don't insure ourselves
personally, we insure the operation of the automobile and
our operation of other automobiles. But the basis of
automobile insurance is, of course, the ownership of the
automobile itself.

In the application for automobile insurance, facts are
required so that the insurance company may determine whether
they will issue the insurance to the applicant. Such
things as driving record, age, type of automobile, year,
the accident record of the applicant and the members of
his family, where the operation of the automobile is going
to occur, that is whether it would be in the countryside
or downtown or in a large city. In addition, the insured has
to inform the company who will be driving the automobile
as members of the family. For example, if a husband and
wife want to have joint coverage for their use of the
automobile, the insurance company will want to know whether
any member of the family who will be using the automobile
is under the age of 25 years.

If one of the users and operators of the automobile
will be under the age of 25, then the company will substantially increase the premium because the risk of
damage to the automobile or injury to a third party or his
property is substantially increased. The cold, hard fact
is that young people between the ages of 16 and 25 are
the largest group of killers in this country by their
improper use of automobiles. That's why insurance premiums
on automobiles driven by people under 25 years of age are
so terribly high.

Again, a misstatement in the application for the
insurance as to the age of the automobile, how it is
equipped, the use that will be made of the automobile, the
ages of its owners and operators, or any other material
representation in the policy itself will allow the company
to void the policy and deny any benefits or claims that
are made under the policy which was issued upon false application information. In addition, unreported change in
condition which materially increases the risk under an

automobile policy will void the policy as to any damage or
injury resulting from the use of the automobile under
that increased risk.

RISK POOLS

There are growing numbers of people in this country who have
demonstrated that they are unsafe drivers under any cir-
cumstance. Their own record proves this. They have had
a number of accidents, perhaps even accidents that have
caused physical injury or even death or extensive property
damage. These people are such poor insurance risks and
such poor drivers that insurance companies will not voluntarily insure them. They make application after application
to insurance companies to obtain the necessary insurance
as required by the state law in which they live.

But the insurance companies deal on a contractual basis
with their insured, and they reject or do not accept the
offer to issue insurance to these very poor risks. At
the same time the state requires that all owners of automobiles have insurance. Consequently, the insurance
companies have formed a pool wherein all of the insurance
companies doing business in a state that has mandatory
insurance requirements agree to take an equal percentage of
the very bad risk drivers. For example, if the Ace Company
and the Black Company are the only insurance companies doing
business in a particular state, and that state has mandatory
insurance requirements, then Ace and Black will share the
bad risk drivers on a basis equal to the amount of
business they do in that state. If Ace has 40% of the business
of automobile insurance in the state, and Black has 60%,
then Ace will take 40% of the bad risk drivers and Black will
take 60%, and the insurance commissioner of the state or
the State Highway Department in some cases administers the
program of assigning the bad risk driver to the insurance
pool. You can well imagine that the insurance premium
charged in the insurance pool is extremely expensive. It
is almost like self insurance. Say a young man was a
dangerous driver—his attitude was extremely poor and he
shouldn't really have had a license—but he did have a
license and he had to obtain insurance through the insurance
pool. The insurance premium on his driving record was
$850 a year. You should also keep in mind that merely
because your record is such a terrible record as a driver
and you have been assigned to an insurance pool and you do

have insurance, your record is still with you and if you
have further difficulties as a driver and demonstrate again
that you are a poor driver, you can be cancelled by your
company and be reassigned to the insurance pool with a
further upward adjustment of your premium. Consequently,
it is absolutely essential that as a driver you maintain
good faith with other motorists on the highway, but it also
makes good sense as a matter of personal economics.

STANDARD FORM OF AUTOMOBILE INSURANCE

A standard form of policy in its first part of the policy
states that, based upon the premiums paid and the conditions
kept by the insured, the company shall pay for an insured
all damages which the insured shall be legally obligated
to pay because of, one, bodily injury sustained by any
person, and, two, injury to or destruction of property.
Thus, the risk is bodily injury and property damage but
it's limited to damages arising out of the ownership, maintenance or use, including loading and unloading of the owned
automobile or a nonowned automobile. From this part of the
insuring agreement you can see that as an insured your
liability or duty to pay damages to a third party—that's
what liability means, legal duty to pay damages to a third
party—is covered in the event of bodily injury, death,
or property damage arising out of the ownership, maintenance,
or use, including loading or unloading of an automobile
you own or in your maintenance or use of a nonowned automobile. The company says that it will defend any lawsuit
even if groundless, false, or fraudulent against any
insured for such damages that are payable under the terms
of this policy, and makes such settlement of any claim or
suit that the company deems proper.
    Let's look in greater detail at the exact coverage that
this liability policy provides. First, who is insured
under this policy? With respect to automobiles owned by
the insured, the company undertakes as follows: It says
that, with respect to an owned automobile, those insured
are the named insured and any resident of his household.
So, if I have a policy, my wife is covered if she is stated
on the policy, and the members of my household who use the
automobile. So is any other person using such automobile
with my permission, provided the person using the automobile with my permission operates it within the scope of
such permission.

This is a very important part of the policy. For
example, Mr. Jones asks me if he may borrow my car to go
across town to the cleaners. I tell him that he may use
the car to go across town to the cleaners. Mr. Jones takes
my car, and after going to the cleaners he proceeds east
out on the freeway to pick up a friend of his whom he had
forgotten to tell me about. While he is driving out in
the countryside to pick up a friend of his, a collision
results and serious bodily injury ensues as a result of
the negligence of Mr. Jones. Now, Mr. Jones had permission to take my car to the cleaners but he did not have
permission to proceed east out of town to pick up a friend
of his. As a result of his exceeding the scope of the
permission granted, Mr. Jones is not covered for his
liability under my policy of insurance, because at the
time of the accident he was exceeding the scope of the
permission granted.

Who is insured under nonowned automobiles? With
respect to a nonowned automobile, a policy provides the
following are insured: One, the named insured; two, any
relative but only with respect to a private passenger
automobile or utility trailer, provided that the relative
using the automobile or trailer uses it with the permission
of the owner or other person in lawful possession, and
such use is within the scope of such permission. Again
we have an extremely important situation. I have borrowed
a car from Mr. Black. I loan the car to my wife to go to
the grocery store. The car in my possession is covered
by my liability policy. The lending of the car to my
wife to go to the grocery store to do some shopping is
also covered by my liability policy provided my wife uses
the car within the scope of the permission granted.

This is an example of a double loan of an automobile.
Remember, the policy says that with a nonowned automobile
I'm covered as a named insured, and any relative of mine
is covered so long as the relative using the automobile
has my permission and uses the automobile within the scope
of that permission. I borrow a car from Mr. Black, who
has advised me that he wants the car back at 4 p.m. because
he has to make use of it. He wants to know where I'm
going to take the car and I tell him I'm going to take the
car across town to the cleaners and that I will have it
back by 4 o'clock. I go across town to the cleaners and
I have the car back at my home at 3 o'clock. Upon my return
home my teenage son advises me that he needs the car to
go down to a friend's house and pick up his baseball glove

to use that afternoon in the baseball game. I tell him to
drive carefully because the car does not belong to us and
that I have to have it back to the house at 3:30 to return
it to Mr. Black. My son negligently drives the car and
collides with another automobile. Is my liability and my
son's liability covered by the policy? The answer to that
is yes. You'll remember that the policy says that with
a nonowned automobile, any relative of mine is covered with
respect to the automobile when the relative has actual
permission from the owner or person in lawful possession.
I had lawful possession of the car because Mr. Black lent
it to me, and the coverage provides that the bailee, or
person in possession of the automobile, is covered if his
operation is within the scope of permission. The automobile was being used with my permission within the scope
of the permission and therefore my son's liability would be
covered under my policy. The liability would not be
covered under the policy of Mr. Black's because he did not
give permission to my son to use the automobile—he
gave permission solely to me to make use of that automobile
for the purpose of going across town to the cleaners.
You can see here that coverage is extremely important in
various situations.

    Another aspect of the use of an automobile is covered
under the standard policy: With respect to a nonowned
automobile, I am insured, as any relative of mine is who has
my permission to use the automobile and uses it within the
scope of permission. But in addition, any other person,
or organization, that does not own the automobile, may
have liability insurance if they use the automobile with
my permission and within the scope of the permission
granted. Consequently, if I returned at 3:30 with Mr. Black's
car and a neighbor of mine called up and asked to borrow the
car to take her son to the doctor's, and I lent her the
car and she drove the car negligently and collided with
another car, her liability would also be covered under my
policy—not under Mr. Black's, but under my policy. It
would also be covered under her policy in the event she had
a standard form of automobile insurance on her own automobile,
because, you will remember, the named insured on an automobile policy is covered even though that named insured
does not own an automobile. Now here's a good point to
remember. When you're married, you and your spouse should
both be named as insureds under the policy because then if
you, as a spouse, drive another person's automobile, you
are named insured under your automobile policy and any use

you make of any other person's car with the person's permission will be covered under your policy.

One of the exclusions on this liability policy leads into another coverage that is commonly included and should be included in your automobile policy: The exclusion says that this insurance does not cover bodily injury to any person if such person is related by blood, marriage, or adoption to, and is a resident of the same household as the insured. Consequently this liability insurance does not cover my responsibility to pay for the medical expenses of any member of my family who is injured in an automobile that I or my wife is driving. We have no protection at all, only third parties.

Medical coverage, which is always a good part to put on your own automobile coverage, covers the cost of medical expenses to occupants of your car who are related to you; it says, "The company will pay all reasonable expenses incurred within one year from the date of accident for necessary medical, dental, surgical, X ray, ambulance, hospital, professional nursing and funeral services, pharmaceuticals, eyeglasses, and prosthetic devices to or for an insured who sustains bodily injury caused by accident." The named insured and each relative who sustains bodily injury caused by an accident are covered.
This is not liability insurance; it is indemnity insurance: It agrees to pay in the event of loss. It does not require you to be legally liable to pay; it will pay in the event of loss—a basic distinction between liability insurance and indemnity insurance: Liability insurance protects you from the claims of third parties, while indemnity insurance reimburses you your actual loss—it pays you.

Coverage for collision insurance is not mandatory. But it is coverage that you should look at very carefully if you have a late model car. Collision covers loss to the automobile by collision with another object, which includes an automobile. The company will pay for loss to the owned or nonowned automobile caused by collision, less the deductible amount stated in the declaration. Now the deductible, as you well know, says that you will pay the first $50 or the first $100 or any amount you want to state; of course the more the deductible is the less your premium will be.

Another form of coverage is called comprehensive. (Under fire policy it was called extended coverage.) Under comprehensive insurance the company will pay for loss caused other than by collision to the owned or nonowned

automobile. For the purpose of this coverage, breakage
of glass and loss caused by missiles, falling objects, fire,
theft or larceny, explosion, earthquake, windstorm, hail,
water, flood, malicious mischief or vandalism, riot or
civil commotion, or colliding with a bird or animal shall
not be deemed to be a loss caused by collision; in other
words, just about every type of accident or malicious
vandalism that can occur to your car is covered by the
comprehensive portion of the policy. This is indemnity
rather than liability protection. Keep in mind that an
automobile policy is a mixture of indemnity policies and
liability policies.

There are duties upon the insured in the event of an
accident under an automobile policy. You are not to admit
your liability to another driver of an automobile in the
collision. To do so is viewed by the insurance company as
failure to cooperate with the company—and may be grounds
for voiding the policy, because the law determines who is
liable in any given situation. You are to report the loss
immediately to the insurance company and upon their request
fill out a proof of loss and accident report on the insurance
company's form. It is very important that you cooperate
with the insurance company in the event of a loss or they
may be able to cancel the policy. After all, they are
seeking to protect you from liability and your cooperation
is essential. In addition, most states require that you
fill out an accident report with the local police station
when there has been an accident. You should check your
own state law on this because failure to file an accident
report in most states may result in the suspension or
revocation of your driver's license.

SELF TEST

CHAPTER 44

NAME_____

DATE_____

44.1   The primary function of automobile insurance is as
_____ insurance to protect the owners of automobiles for the possible human injury or property
damage that results from the _____ of their
automobiles.

44.2   In the field of auto insurance, there is also extended
or _____ coverage available for automobiles.

44.3   (answer "true" or "false") _____ In most states,
automobile owners have the option of buying or not
buying automobile liability insurance.

44.4   In most states, legislation has been passed called
_____ laws which require that each
owner of an automobile insure that automobile's operation against property _____ and personal
_____.

44.5   With automobile insurance, it is the _____ and
the _____ of the automobile that is insured,
not the life of the driver.

44.6   The basis of automobile insurance is the _____
of the automobile itself.

44.7   People between the ages of _____ and _____
are responsible for more deaths due to improper use
of their automobiles than any other age group.

44.8   Any change in conditions which _____ increase
the _____ under an automobile policy will
_____ the policy as to any damage or injury
resulting from the use of the automobile underneath
that increased _____.

44.9   An insurance _____ is a condition where in all
of the insurance companies doing business in a state
that has _____ insurance requirements agree to
take an equal _____ of all bad _____
drivers.

44.10   The risk assumed by the insurance company under an
automobile liability insurance policy is the risk of
bodily injury or property damage, but it is limited

to those injuries or damages arising out of the
_____, _____ or use of the _____
or _____ automobile.

44.11 With respect to owned automobiles, the insureds are
the _____ insured, and any resident of his
_____. Any other person would be covered that
uses the automobile if he has the insured's
_____, and operates the automobile within the
_____ of such _____.

44.12 With respect to nonowned automobiles, the insureds
are the _____ insured, and any _____,
but only with respect to a private passenger automobile, provided that the relative using the automobile
uses it with the permission of the _____ or
other person in _____ possession.

44.13 A named insured on a policy is covered for all use
the named insured makes of any other automobile, provided the named insured has _____ to make use
of the automobile. Obviously, a thief has no insurance _____ in the operation of an automobile.

44.14 _____ coverage is a good part to have in your
automobile insurance policy, because it does cover the
cost of medical expenses to occupants of your car who
are _____ to you.

44.15 _____ insurance covers loss to the automobile
resulting from collision with another object.

44.16 Under _____ coverage, the insurance company
will pay for loss or damage caused other than by collision to the owned or nonowned automobile. An
example would be a loss caused by fire.

44.17 An automobile policy is a mixture of _____
policies and liability policies.

44.18 One of the duties owed by the insured to the insurer
is that if the insured is involved in an accident, he
is not to admit his _____ to another driver of
an automobile in the collision. Also, after the accident, the insured should report the loss _____
to the insurance company, and upon their request, fill
out a/an _____ of _____ and accident
report.

45 Agency

Introduction

LEARNING OBJECTIVES

To become acquainted with the laws of agency.
To examine the effects of the laws upon a principal and agent.

CHAPTER CONTENTS

Necessity of the Agency Relationship   Parts of the Agency   Agency and Liability   Glossary   Self Test

NECESSITY OF THE AGENCY RELATIONSHIP

In this and the next two chapters we will discuss principals
and agents and the law of agency. The statement "There
just isn't time enough in the day" is the basis for all of
agency law. Business and our everyday affairs could not
really be run by each of us individually. Companies could
not do what they need to do in their ordinary business
affairs without the hiring of employees to do work, and
employees could not fulfill all of their tasks unless some
of the employees became agents to act on behalf of the
company with third parties. By the same token, some of the
work that you have to have done in your daily lives cannot
be performed individually by each of you. Consequently, you
appoint others to act for you with third persons. The
law of agency is extremely complicated and is very important
in our daily affairs. Any time you or I have someone else
represent us to a third person there are risks involved
and there is a tremendous amount of liability imposed upon
us by the acts of our agents.

Some examples will best illustrate what an agent is
and is not and what a principal is and is not. Mr. Jones,
the owner of Jones' Bakery, hires Sam Smith to drive his
delivery truck and deliver bakery products to the stores
that sell Mr. Jones' products on their shelves. Now, Sam
Smith, as a truck driver delivering products to the various
stores, is an employee. The law describes an employee as
a person employed to perform a service for another in his
affairs and who, with respect to the physical performance
of the service, is subject to the other's control or right
to control. Mr. Jones, the owner of Jones' Bakery, hires
Sam Smith to drive a truck and deliver products to the
bakery's stores. Mr. Jones has the right to control Sam
Smith and direct which way he will travel and the route he
will travel and the time he has to travel and how many
products to deliver to each store.

The crucial element of determining when one is an
employee of another is whether the person who is the employee
is subject to the control of the employer. Control may be
looked at in terms of the maximum possible for that particular type of employment. For example, if an employee of mine
is a salesman who works 300 miles away from me, the extent
of control I will exercise upon that employee may be limited
to reports as to what he has done over a period of a month,
his expense account, whom he has called upon, and his list
of sales. But if I employ Sam Smith as a truck driver, my
control over his physical activities is much more direct and

more complete. So you may be an employee working for an
employer even though you're in a foreign country thousands of miles away—if you are subject to the control of
the employer.

Isn't an agent an employee of an employer? Sometimes
he is and sometimes he is not. For example, Mr. Jones
hires Sam Smith to drive his delivery truck to his stores
and deliver bakery products. Now, with just that Sam Smith
is an employee. But let's assume after several months that
Sam Smith has proven himself to be a reliable employee,
so Mr. Jones calls Sam into the office and advises him that
henceforth he will not only deliver goods to the stores,
but he will make the charge list against the stores. He
will attempt to sell more products to each of the grocery
stores, and keep the accounts of the stores that he services.
In other words, he will not only be a deliveryman, but he
will also be a sales promotion man for the company.
Sam Smith, therefore, becomes both an employee of Jones' Bakery
Company as well as an *agent*. The difference is that an
agent is a person who acts for and in behalf of another
in dealing with third persons; he is subject to the control
of the person for whom he is working but he has the authority
to deal with third persons on behalf of his employer, or
principal. In an employee-employer relationship, the person
who has the right to exercise control over the employee
is known as the employer. But in an agency relationship—
that is where one person may engage in business contracts
on behalf of another person—then the principal has the right
to control the activities of the agent. The agent speaks
and acts on behalf of the principal, and the principal is
bound by the acts of the agent within the scope of the
agent's authority. The agent is subject to the control of
the principal.

PARTS OF THE AGENCY

In an employment relationship, two parties are necessary—
the employer and the employee. In an agency relationship,
three parties are necessary: one, the principal, the person
with the right to control the agent and who authorizes
the agent to act for him; two, the agent himself, a person
who speaks on behalf or works on behalf of another; and
three, the third person with whom the agent will negotiate
and engage in business dealings on behalf of the principal.
A third type of relationship (that is, in addition to
employment and agency relationships) is the relationship of

independent contractors. For example, the Jones Bakery
Company has hired Sam Smith as the deliveryman for its
products and subsequently it has authorized Sam Smith to
become a sales promotion person for the company as an
agent. Now let's assume that Sam Smith decides that he
can do better for himself and his family if he works for
himself. So he goes to Mr. Jones and says, "You know that
there are a lot of communities around town that don't have
any representation by your company. What I propose to do is
buy my own truck. You can then sell me your bakery products
wholesale and I will resell them to the grocery stores
using your name and your company's products. I will make
a profit because I will add a penny or two to the wholesale
price in the price I charge the grocery stores." The Jones
Bakery Company agrees that this is a good idea. Sam Smith
buys his own truck, comes to the Jones Bakery Company,
buys products from it, and resells them on his own. He
is now an independent contractor. He is not subject to
the control of the Jones Bakery Company, nor when he sells
the products to the grocery stores does he speak for the
Jones Bakery Company. He does not negotiate on behalf of
a principal because he negotiates in his own right or in
his own behalf. He is therefore an independent contractor.

AGENCY AND LIABILITY

The significance of the difference is that in an agency the
principal is liable to third persons for the acts of the
agent when the agent is acting within the authority given
to him. This in part is the same thing as an employer-
employee relationship. An employer is liable for the acts
of the employee in tort, but a principal is liable for
the acts of the agent both in tort and contract. Let's get
that distinction in mind before we move on. You will
remember from our business organization chapters that an
employer cannot be bound by the contracts of his employee
because the employee had no right to make contracts for
the employer. For example, if Sam Smith, when he was just
a delivery driver, drove up to a service station and ordered
new tires for the truck and the station attendant put the
tires on without the authority of the Jones Bakery Company,
the service station could not recover the cost of the tires
from Jones Bakery Company. They would have to take the
tires off and replace the old used tires back on the truck
because the employee, Sam Smith, did not have authority to
bind the company in the purchase of these new tires. On the

other hand, if Sam Smith, the delivery driver, while driving down Ash Street, collided with the back of another car, the employer would be liable for Sam Smith's acts as an employee if he was negligent in causing the accident.

So you see that the tort liability of the employer exists for all of the physical acts of the employee, but the employer is not liable for the contractual acts of the employee. On the other hand, as soon as Sam Smith became a sales agent for the Jones Bakery Company, the company could be held liable for the acts of Sam Smith, its agent, because he was authorized to engage in the sale and billing for bakery products.

The distinction is, of course, that an agent binds the principal to contractual as well as tort acts, whereas an employee only binds his employer for his negligent conduct, that is, for tort acts. In the first chapter we talked about the difference between contractual and tortious acts: A tortious act is one that imposes liability upon the person who did not use reasonable care in his conduct. Most frequently, tortious acts are ones that cause bodily injury or property damage to a third party. However, tortious conduct can also include words, not only physical acts that cause bodily injury. Slander, or libel, is a tortious act. For example, if Sam Smith the delivery driver went into a store and swore at the store owner for not selling enough products or not paying a bill on time and called him names and went around town saying that the man was a deadbeat and a liar and a cheat, he might impose liability upon his employer, the Jones Bakery Company, for the slander and libelous conduct of the employee, Sam Smith.

On the other hand, if Sam Smith becomes the agent his conduct in dealing with the store owners in the billing and collection of the money due the Jones Bakery Company imposes liability upon the company. Sam Smith agrees that he will deliver 40 dozen loaves of bread on Thursday to one of the grocers. Instead of making that delivery, Sam forgets all about it. The grocery company can hold the Jones Bakery Company liable for failing to deliver as promised.

An agent can be anyone who is physically capable of carrying out the authority granted to the agent. That means simply that Mrs. Jones can send her 10-year-old daughter to the store to buy the groceries that week and if the daughter is able to get herself to the store and buy the groceries, she is an agent of Mrs. Jones. Not quite anyone

can be a principal. A principal may be any person who
has the legal capacity to contract. You will remember
that a minor or person under 21 years of age does have
the capacity to contract but his contracts may be voidable
at the option of the minor with the exception of a minor
who is emancipated or who is buying necessities. Consequently, a minor may be a principal, but a person who is
suffering from insanity may not be a principal because
their contracts are void at the beginning, they do not have
the legal capacity to form a contract. Consequently, a
person who is mentally unable to contract is also unable
to be a principal.

GLOSSARY TERMS

Agent   A person who acts for and in behalf of someone in dealing with third persons.

Independent contractor   A person who negotiates with third parties on his own behalf in matters in some way involving second parties but not making second parties liable to the third parties.

Principal   The person on whose behalf and under whose control an agent acts with third parties.

SELF TEST

CHAPTER 45

NAME_____

DATE_____

45.1 "There just isn't _____ enough in the day."
      That statement is the basis for all _____
      law.
45.2 The law says that a/an _____ is a person employ-
      ed to perform a service for another in his affairs,
      and who, with respect to the physical _____ of
      the service, is subject to the other person's
      _____ or right of _____.
45.3 The crucial element of determining when one is an
      employee of another is whether the person who is the
      employee is subject to the _____ of the employer.
45.4 A/An _____ is a person who acts for and in behalf
      of another in dealing with _____ persons.
45.5 An agent is subject to the control of the _____.
45.6 In an agency relationship, there are three parties
      necessary: the _____, the _____, and
      _____ persons.
45.7 A/An _____ is not subject to the
      control of, nor does he act on behalf of, a principal.
      He _____ in his own right, or in his own behalf.
45.8 The underlying notion of an agency is that the _____
      is liable to third persons for the acts of the _____,
      when the agent is acting within the _____ given
      him.
45.9 An employer is liable for the acts of the employee
      in _____, but a principal is liable for the
      acts of the agent both in _____ and _____.
45.10 A/An _____ act is an act which imposes liability
      upon the person who did not use reasonable care in
      his conduct.
45.11 An agent may be anyone who is _____ capable
      of carrying out the _____ granted to the agent.
45.12 A principal may be any person who has the _____
      _____ to contract.
45.13 A minor (choose either "may" or "may not") _____
      be a principal, and a person suffering from _____
      may not be a principal, because their contracts are

void at the beginning; that is, they do not have
the legal _____ to form a contract.

45.14   In review, a/an _____ is one who acts for and
in behalf of another, called a _____, in
dealing with third persons, and is subject to the
_____ of the person for whom he is acting.

45.15   An agent may create _____ for his principal
by the agent's acts and contracts within the
scope of the agent's _____.

46 Agency

Creation of Agency Relationship. The Legal Relationship—I.

LEARNING OBJECTIVES

To learn the ways in which an agency relationship is created.

CHAPTER CONTENTS

Agency by Appointment   Agency by Appearance   Agency by Ratification   Agency by Necessity   Duties of Agents and Principals   Glossary   Self Test

In this chapter we will discuss how the agency relationship
is created, and what are some of the effects of the
relationship on the principal and on the agent. An agency
relationship in the law is created by one of four basic
methods: appointment, appearance, ratification, and
necessity. The first and commonest method is by express
authorization or, as the lawyers say, by appointment.

AGENCY BY APPOINTMENT

An agency relationship being created by appointment is
comparable to an express contract. An *agency by appointment*
is created by the giving of an express authority by the
principal to an agent to act for the principal. Mr. Jones
asked Mr. Smith to please go downtown and purchase 100
bales of hay and gave him the necessary funds. This is an
example of an express agency; Mr. Jones has expressly
authorized Mr. Smith to act for him with a third person. He
has given Mr. Smith the money and has instructed him to
purchase 100 bales of hay. Consequently, Mr. Jones has the
right to control Mr. Smith's expenditures of the money,
and he has expressly controlled the expenditure of the money
by instructing his agent, Mr. Smith, to purchase 100 bales
of hay.
        Although an agency need not be created in writing,
there are certain limitations upon that rule. Some agency
relationships must be set forth in writing: The first,
the appointment of an agent to buy property for the principal; second, the appointment of an agent for more than one
year.
        As to this first requirement of an agency in writing,
the transfer of real property must be made in writing so
that all the world will know who holds title to property,
and the proof of ownership of property, that is real property,
is beyond doubt. Proof of ownership is by deed. Consequently, if I am the principal and I appoint or authorize an
agent to purchase real property in my behalf, then the
authority of the agent to purchase property in my name must
be expressed in writing, because the agent cannot buy
property for me in my name without having proof of the
authority to put my name on the real property. (However,
in some circumstances real property may be purchased by an
agent in his own name and later transferred to me. In
that case the proof of the agency need not be in writing,
but this is a very technical point and we will not discuss it

in great detail.) For most purposes, if an agent is going
to purchase property on behalf of a principal, his authority
to make such purchase on behalf of the principal must be
in writing.

As to the requirement that if the appointment of the
agent is for more than one year, the authorization or
appointment must be in writing; the Statute of Frauds requires
any contract that has a duration of more than one year for
performance must be in writing. Consequently, an agency
relationship that is going to extend beyond one year must
also be in writing.

This power for agency document is called simply a Power
of Attorney—one person asks another to act for him in his
absence. Many people believe that a Power of Attorney
authorizes a lawyer, or attorney, to act on his client's
behalf. Many times this is true, but most frequently people
who are absent from a city or on a long vacation or who are
otherwise not able to attend to their business affairs
appoint a bank or a close friend or a relative as their
attorney in fact, which is merely a legal term for an
agency and the person armed with such a Power of Attorney
may act on behalf of the principal in so far as the Power
of Attorney authorizes. There are two types of written
authorization for agent: a Special Power of Attorney, and
a General Power of Attorney. A Special Power of Attorney
merely authorizes the local agent to act in a specific
matter, that is, "I hereby authorize John Blow to sign a
deed in my absence if the sale of my house is consummated
after I leave town," or "I hereby authorize John Blow to
sign all papers and do all deeds necessary for the transfer
of my real property in the sale thereof after I have left
town on the 12th day of March." That is a Special Power of
Attorney because it limits the agency to a specific function
or a specific subject.

A General Power of Attorney grants to the agent or
attorney in fact the power to do all things necessary for
the protection of the business interests of the principal.
Most frequently such a legal document is carefully drawn
so that the agent knows exactly his authority, and people
dealing with the agent and aware of the General or Special
Power of Attorney are completely aware of the agent's
authority.

Those are the two types of situations in which a written
agency relationship is created. They are not very frequent—
probably less than one tenth of one percent of all the agency
relationships created from day to day. Certainly every
housewife has sent her children to the store to purchase a

commodity. This is an agency relation and it certainly
doesn't require a written Power of Attorney, and most
frequently business agencies or business principal and
agent relationships are not subject to the rule of a
written Power of Attorney.

AGENCY BY APPEARANCE

The second most common method of creating an agency relationship is an agent by appearance or, as used by lawyers,
an *apparent agency*. Say Mr. Jones runs a used car lot and
has several employees working for him. He has expressly
told the employees that they are not to sign any sales
contracts with any people without his prior approval. Well,
Mr. Jones is out of town frequently, making car purchases for
sale to customers. One of his employees, Mr. Schwartz, has
numerous car buyers that he wants to have the sales on, so
Mr. Schwartz signs the sales contracts. When Mr. Jones
returns to town he rescinds all of the car contracts
because he did not give his prior approval to them before
they were signed.

Meanwhile the purchasers, who had paid their money and
taken their cars, go to a lawyer and say, "We don't have to
return our cars and get a refund of our money. This man
said he had authority to act for the principal and we
weren't given any notification that he didn't have that
authority." When Mr. Jones clothed Mr. Schwartz with the
apparent authority to engage in business dealings with third
persons, he will be held to have appointed Mr. Schwartz as
an agent. Mr. Jones gave Mr. Schwartz all of the appearance
of an agent for the sale of cars by employing him on the
car lot with no notification to anyone that Mr. Schwartz
did not have the authority to sell cars for Mr. Jones to
the customers.

However, that apparent authority would not have
existed had Mr. Jones used the foresight to place on the
sales contract itself, "This contract is void (or
nonenforceable) unless signed by Mr. Jones, the owner of
Jones' used car lot." That would have been notice to the
third persons, purchasers, that they must deal with Mr. Jones
directly in the purchase of automobiles. But no such warning
was given to third persons that Mr. Schwartz did not have
apparent authority. Consequently, they have the right to
deal with Mr. Schwartz and Mr. Jones is liable for the acts
of his agent and is bound to the contract that his agent
entered into with the apparent authority to do so. We

will talk a little later about the rights between Mr. Schwartz, the agent, and Mr. Jones, the principal. But as between Mr. Jones, the principal, and the third party who relied upon the apparent authority of Mr. Schwartz, the agent, the third person has a right to enforce the contract of sale.

AGENCY BY RATIFICATION

Another form of agency is created in the law, agency by *ratification*. Say Mr. Jones, the owner of the used car lot, goes out of town again, and again before he leaves he gives instructions to his employees that they may enter into negotiations for the sale of used cars, but they may not sell any car without his prior approval. Upon his return to town Mr. Jones finds that two of his employees have in fact sold cars and taken the money for them. Again he states that he is not bound to the contract made by his employees without authority.

However, Mr. Jones takes the money that his employees received for the contracts and uses it in the business to pay expenses. By accepting the benefits of the contract, knowing that sales have been made and knowing that they benefited him to the extent of the purchase price, the principal, Mr. Jones, has ratified the contract made by his employee even though at the time the employee didn't have authority to enter into the contract.

The law views Mr. Jones as having ratified the contract of sale when he, knowing the full facts, accepted the benefits of the bargain. The law says you can't take the benefits of the bargain and repudiate the contract that was made by your employee and insist that you're not bound to the contract.

However, ratification does not occur if the principal does not <u>fully</u> ratify the acts. That is, say Mr. Jones returns to the city and finds out that one of his employees has sold a car; the car was a used car but the employee had stated to the purchaser that the car was new. If Mr. Jones did not know of this unfair and untrue warranty his retention of the money would not ratify the acts of the agent, for as soon as he finds out the true facts of what the employee had said Mr. Jones has a reasonable time to repudiate the contract his agent entered into, by returning the money to the purchaser. So an agency by ratification is created by the principal accepting the benefits of the contract made by his apparent agent and having full knowledge of all of the facts of the contract and accepting all parts of the contract as made by his acceptance of all the benefits of the contract.

AGENCY BY NECESSITY

Another form of agency quasi-contract or contract implied in law is agency created by necessity. *Agency by necessity* is almost self-defining. As an example, Mr. Jones once again leaves town. While he was gone a fire occurred in his building. The employees had the fire department put out the fire, they made notice to the fire insurance company of the fire, and they were smart enough to know that they had an absolute duty to protect the building and its contents from further damage. They had to use reasonable effort to minimize the loss, so they called in a roofer to replace the roof as soon as possible for fear that snow and rain would damage the rest of the merchandise and records of the building, and Mr. Jones' business.

Mr. Jones returned, found out about the fire, and furnished the proof of loss to his insurance company. He then received the bill from the roofer. He called the roofer and told him that he had not authorized the roofing of the building and was not going to pay the bill; the roofer could look to Mr. Jones' employees for payment of this expense. But the law says that in the event of an emergency, a person who does not have authority may act reasonably for the protection of a third person, and the third person, the principal, is deemed to have ratified the acts because the law says that had the third person or principal been there, he would have done the same in the same circumstances. In this case, the roofer should be able to recover from Mr. Jones under the theory that he was the principal of an agent by necessity.

Another, less common form of agency by necessity is one in which a parent has not taken care of his or her child as required by law. The child does have the right to obtain by credit of his or her parent the necessities of life and the child may charge certain necessities at stores where the parents' credit is good because the law makes it mandatory that parents support their children. This is another, but very infrequent, form of agency by necessity.

DUTIES OF AGENTS AND PRINCIPALS

The agent has the general duty under the law of good faith
to the principal. This means many things, but specifically
it means that an agent clothed with authority must act
for the principal's benefit; an agent may not serve two
masters. For example, an employee given agency authority
may not use that authority to hurt his principal for the
benefit of a third party; he must represent the principal's
interest. By the same token an agent may not profit by
his agency. He may be paid as agreed by the principal but
he may not use his authority or his privileged information
to turn a private profit for his own benefit at the expense
of the principal.

In addition, the agent is under a duty to obey
instructions. For example, if Frank gave Jim $25 and
asked him to drive his car to Pittsburgh and Jim drove the
car to Cedar Rapids, Iowa, instead of to Pittsburgh, he
would have breached his agency relationship with Frank.
The duty of obeying instructions is implicit in an agency
relationship, as is the duty of advising the principal of
any difficulty that arises which makes it impossible for
the agent to perform. If a car breakdown or a flat tire
made it impossible for him to continue on to Pittsburgh he
was under a duty to advise Frank, his principal, of the
difficulty and request additional instructions.

Also, anyone employed or appointed as an agent has
the duty by law to exercise reasonable care, not only for
his own welfare and safety, and liability, but also to
protect the liability and welfare of his principal. In
effect, this is a double duty. The standard of due care
is always with every citizen, but the standard of due
care for the principal is imposed upon the agent by the
agency relationship. If you are given money to go to the
grocery store, or to make a purchase for any other person
at any other place, you're under a duty to make that purchase
and in the process not to lose the money or not to get
cheated in the purchase of the product. You are held to a
high standard of care on behalf of your principal and you
are liable to the principal if you have not exercised due
care and exercised your instructions and authority with
all of the care possible.

In addition, if the principal asks you to hold money
for him for a specific purpose, the law prohibits you from
mingling the principal's funds with your own, even though
you have sufficient funds to cover both if the principal calls

you. You are to keep the principal's money separate and distinct from your own.

Finally, you are under an affirmative duty to the principal in all situations to inform the principal of material facts. That is, say a principal once retained an agent to negotiate the purchase of a large piece of equipment from a third party. The agent went to the seller and began negotiation for price. He soon learned that the seller would sell for a little bit more than the principal was willing to pay but not very much more and it was a very attractive price. The agent went back and told the principal that he could not accomplish the purchase of the equipment.

Once released from his obligation to negotiate the purchase, the agent then went to the seller and with his own funds bought the equipment and sold it on the open market at a substantial profit. The principal sued the agent for the profit, alleging that the agent was under an affirmative duty to tell him of the fact that the seller would have sold for slightly more than the principal had offered. The court awarded the principal full damages for the profit the agent had realized for two reasons: First, the agent had not dealt with the principal in good faith; and second, the agent had not told the principal of the material fact which he was duty bound to do.

Thus, as an agent you have several negative and affirmative duties: the duty of good faith with your principal; the duty to obey instructions; the duty to use reasonable care; the duty not to mix your funds with those of your principal; and the duty of informing your principal of all material facts.

The duties of the principal to the agent are basically three in number: First, the principal has the duty of good faith to the agent. When Frank gave Jim the car and gave him $25 to drive it to Pittsburgh, he would be liable to Jim if he knowingly gave the car to Jim in a terrible condition so that Jim would be stranded in the countryside.

Second, the principal has the duty of paying agreed or reasonable compensation to the agent. If there is an agreed compensation to be paid for the duties of the agent, that must be paid as agreed in the contract or understanding. If there is no fixed compensation, then the agent is entitled to reasonable compensation.

Third, the principal must pay the agent the necessary and reasonable costs that the agent has incurred in undertaking to represent the principal on the specific authority given by the principal to the agent.

GLOSSARY TERMS

Agency by appointment Agency created by express authorization of the principal to the agent to act for the principal.

Agency by necessity Agency created by the acts of a person otherwise without authority, to act reasonably to protect the interests of a third person, the principal, in an emergency.

Apparent agency A method of creating agency whereby the principal has not taken due precaution to prevent the appearance that some person has the power to act of his agent.

Attorney in fact A legal term applied to a person authorized to act in behalf of another, the principal, who appointed him.

Power of attorney The authority, created by an agency by appointment, of one person to act for another.

Ratification A method of creating agency whereby the principal, having full knowledge of the fact, accepts the benefits of the contract entered into by his apparent agent.

SELF TEST
CHAPTER 46

NAME_____

DATE_____

46.1 The first and most common method of creating an agency relationship is by express _____, or as the lawyers say, by _____. As most commonly used, we refer to an agency relationship created by _____.

46.2 An example of an agency relationship that must be set forth in writing is the appointment of the agent to buy _____ for the principal.

46.3 Another example of where an agency relationship must be set forth in writing is when the appointment of the agent is to be for more than _____ in time.

46.4 The writing, or power of agency document, is called a/an _____ of _____.

46.5 The two types of written authorization for agents are: a) a/an _____ power of _____, which authorizes the agent to act in a specific matter; b) a/an _____ power of _____ which grants to the agent the power to do all things necessary for the protection of the business interests of the principal.

46.6 (Answer "true" or "false") _____ Most frequently, business agency relationships require a written power of attorney.

46.7 The second most common method of creating an agency relationship is an agent by appearance, or a/an _____ agent.

46.8 Another form of agent is created in the _____, and this is called an agent by _____.

46.9 _____ does not occur if the principal does not _____ ratify the acts.

46.10 An agency by ratification is created by the principal accepting the _____ of the contract made by his _____ agent, and having full _____ of all the facts of the contract, and accepting all parts of the contract as made by his _____ of all the _____ of the contract.

46.11   An agency is created by _____ when, in the
        event of a/an _____, a person who does not have
        authority may act reasonably for the protection of
        a third person, in this case the (choose either
        "principal" or "agent") _____, who is deemed to
        have ratified the emergency action.

46.12   Another less common, but apart, form of agency by
        _____ is one in which a parent has not taken
        care of his or her child as required by law.

46.13   The agent has the general duty, under the law, of
        good _____ to the principal.

46.14   An agent is under a duty to obey _____,
        which is _____ in an agency relationship.

46.15   Not only does an agent have a duty of obeying exact
        _____, but he also has a duty of advising
        the principal of any difficulty that arises which
        makes it _____ for the agent to perform.

46.16   If a principal asks his agent to hold money for
        him for a specific purpose, the law prohibits the
        agent from _____ the principal's funds with
        his own.

46.17   An agent has a/an _____ duty in all situations
        to inform the principal of _____ facts.

46.18   The principal has the duty of good _____ to
        the agent.

46.19   The principal has a duty to pay the agreed, or
        reasonable, _____ to the agent.

46.20   The principal is responsible and must pay the
        agent the _____ and reasonable _____
        that the agent has incurred in undertaking the
        _____ of the principal within the specific
        authority given by the principal to the agent.

46.21   If an agent _____ authority, and acts with
        authority, then the principal is liable.

Agency

The Legal Relationship—II. Termination of Agency.

LEARNING OBJECTIVES

To examine the power and authority of an agent.

CHAPTER CONTENTS

In this chapter we will explore the authority of an agent;
how a principal becomes bound to a third party on a
contract; the rights of the principal; the rights of a third
party against both the agent and the principal; the rights
of the principal against the agent; and the rights of the
agent against the principal.

DISCLOSED AND UNDISCLOSED PRINCIPALS

For our purposes we will assume that an agent has express
authority to act on behalf of his principal (that is, he
has oral authority or has written authority through a Power
of Attorney or agency contract to represent the principal
in a business relationship). It is important to realize
that an agent may represent either a disclosed or an
undisclosed principal. This distinction is very important
in our understanding of the rights of the principal and
of the third party. A disclosed principal is one who is
represented by the agent to the third person as being in
existence; an undisclosed principal is one whose existence
is unknown to the third person. When you go into a large
chain store you deal primarily with a sales agent—either
a clerk, a sales manager, or the store manager. But in
each case, unless you deal with the owner of the store,
you are dealing with an agent for a disclosed principal.
For example, J. C. Penney Company is a large, national
retail establishment. Each store has a store manager,
department managers, and sales clerks. You know that you
are not dealing directly with J. C. Penney or the family
that owns the company, but are dealing with an agent of
the company. In most situations you are dealing with an
agent who is acting for a disclosed principal, in this case,
of course, the J. C. Penney Company.

UNDISCLOSED PRINCIPALS

You may someday be dealing with an agent who you think is
bargaining and negotiating for himself but in fact is
dealing for an undisclosed principal, a principal whose
existence you don't know anything about. For example, if
an ad in a newspaper offers a used car for sale by a private
owner, a man may come to the door of the seller and say,
"I'm interested in this car," and begin to negotiate back
and forth with the seller on the purchase price and so on,
and not in fact be buying the car for himself. He is an

employee of a used car lot and is buying the car on behalf
of the lot. But he does not make that fact known. He
pretends (for purposes of our illustration) to be buying
the car for his own benefit. Consequently, the sale of
that automobile is made to an agent of an undisclosed
principal—the used car lot that employs this purchasing
agent. Principals who are undisclosed have different
rights and liabilities from principals who are disclosed.
An undisclosed principal may sue upon the contract made
by the agent, but if the third party repudiates the contract,
the principal may not enforce the contract. Let's take a
look at that. Mr. Jones had a sawmill for sale on the
market. He had been offered a very handsome price for the
sawmill by his major competitor, but Mr. Jones and this
competitor had very harsh feelings toward each other and
Mr. Jones refused to sell him the sawmill. So the competitor offered a third person $10,000 if he could negotiate
the sale on his own behalf and in his own name. After the
sale was negotiated and signed, then the agent was to assign
the contract to the principal so that he could end up with
the sawmill. Everything went fine—the agent was able to
successfully negotiate the sale of the sawmill by Mr. Jones
to the agent. The agent then transferred, assigned, the
contract to the principal, receiving his $10,000. The
principal then advised Mr. Jones by letter that he is the
purchaser in fact and would be making the payment on the
sawmill, and he asked Mr. Jones to vacate the premises.
Mr. Jones then rescinded the contract completely, saying
that he would sell to the agent as agreed but not to the
undisclosed principal. The case went to court and the court
held that Mr. Jones had a right to rescind the contract, for
he did not have to deal with the undisclosed principal and
could deal with just the agent if he saw fit. Mr. Jones
was therefore sustained in rescinding the contract, and
the principal was out $10,000. He could not recover the
$10,000 from the agent because the agent had fully per-
formed his part of the bargain—it was not his fault that
Mr. Jones had rescinded the contract with the principal.
The agent had performed all of the duties he had undertaken.

But an undisclosed principal may enforce a contract
when the contract promisor does not repudiate the contract
on good grounds.

When an agent contracts and negotiates in his own name,
the party dealing with the agent may hold him personally
liable on the contract, and if the contract is assigned
to an undisclosed principal, the third person may also hold

the principal liable on the contract. In other words,
the party dealing with the agent, and later with the
undisclosed principal, has the option of enforcing the
contract against either of the parties—the party that
signed the contract, the agent, or the undisclosed principal
who took subsequently the benefits of the contract.

The third party cannot recover twice but he has a choice
of remedies against either the principal who is undisclosed
at the time the contract is made or the agent. Thus, if
someone asks you to purchase property, personal or real,
or engage in a contract in your own name but in their behalf,
make sure that you disclose and have the authority to
disclose the name of the principal for whom you are acting
and that you are acting solely as agent for the principal.
For if you do not do that, you may be held personally
liable on the contract even though you were engaging in
the contract of sale, purchase, or services on behalf of
an undisclosed third party. A contractor once asked a
friend of his to purchase a great amount of steel for a
particular job that he was bidding on. The steel was at a
very low price and was a very attractive offer; although
the contractor could not afford to buy the steel at that
time he didn't want to lose the price. So he talked his
friend into ordering the steel at the attractive price but
he didn't want the other contractors to see his name on
the contract. So this friend went down to the steel company
and ordered the steel in his own name and using his own
credit. At delivery time the friend contacted the contract-
or and said, "I have the steel ready. Where do you want it
delivered?" The contractor had meanwhile gone broke.
There the agent was—liable on the contract for the purchase
of steel with really no place to use the steel. He took
a tremendous financial beating on this particular deal.
The steel company held him to the contract as they had
every right to do, and the price was not as attractive
as he had been led to believe. He had very grave difficulties
in selling the steel for enough money to get him out short
of bankruptcy. So again, remember that you will be held
personally liable on any contract you make in your own
right and in your own name even though you are working on
behalf of an undisclosed principal.

DISCLOSED PRINCIPALS

The rights and duties of a disclosed principal can be very
simply stated; a disclosed principal has the same rights

and duties under a contract entered into for him by an agent
as if he had entered into the contract himself. All of
the warranties, promises, and obligations undertaken by
the agent are binding upon the principal if the agent has
made those assertions, obligations, warranties, and promises
within the scope of his authority. By the same token, the
contract promisor, or promisee, who deals with an agent
for an undisclosed principal is subject to all of the
duties and obligations as if he had dealt directly with the
principal.

In the disclosed principal relationship you have the
true go-between or middleman, but he is only acting on
behalf of his principal. You can see that we've now come
full circle. We have surrounded the topic of an agent's
authority and what effect it has on the principal and the
third party who deals with the agent. This is a very
touchy and extremely difficult field of law. On the one
hand, the third party who deals with an agent does so
at his own risk and peril. If the third party knows that
a person represents a principal, then he is under a duty
to inquire and determine what the scope of the agent's
authority is.

If he does not, he may be in trouble later on, because
the principal is not bound for acts of the agent that exceed
the agent's authority when the third party knew or should
have known that the agent had limited authority. This
is very very common in the purchase of real estate, or
homes, and appliances and automobiles. The courts are
filled with suits in which purchasers have sued principals for
breach of warranty wherein a sales agent had stated the
land, or the house, or the car to be something other than
what it turned out to be. But in almost every case, the
purchaser is rudely shocked to find out that right on the
sales contract, and as part of the inducement and purchase
money on the contract, the agent's authority was severely
limited to just the terms of the contract as printed. So
it is terribly important if you deal with a sales agent or
an agent for any other purpose, that you determine pre-
cisely what that agent's authority is and have that authority
spelled out in writing if possible so that you know exactly
which parts of his warranties, promises, and negotiations
you can rely upon as if the principal were there, and which
parts you cannot rely upon.

You should also know that when you see a written agency
agreement or document, or when you see a Power of Attorney,
you should read that document very narrowly. The courts and

the law interpret a Power of Attorney or agency agreement
very strictly. It limits, as far as the language can be
read, the power of the agent to do <u>exactly</u> what the agency
agreement sets forth and no more, because the law is
based on the belief that we do not authorize people to
speak or act for ourselves except as is absolutely
necessary. Consequently, if you have to deal with an agent
upon an express written agency, read carefully the terms of
his agency agreement.

For example, a real estate agent is the agent of the
owner and you will note that on the listing agreement the
agent has no authority to make warranties with respect to
the house itself. If you have doubts about the foundation,
roof, chimney, or any other part of the structure, you
should ask that agent to obtain from the principal, the
seller in this case, a written statement as to the construction that you're in doubt about, because the agent himself
has no authority to bind the principal as to warranties
with respect to construction of the house itself other than
those things that you can see.

Thus, for your own protection you have to know that
the agent has the authority to deal on behalf of the
principal, and the extent of his power to bind the principal,
and you have to narrowly or strictly construe his power.
But all is not as black as it might seem. There is a
doctrine in the law that holds an agent personally liable
for holding himself out with more authority than he
actually has. Stated simply, the rule is that if an agent
makes a contract on behalf of his principal but in excess
of the agent's authority, the agent is personally liable
on the contract if the principal repudiates it even
though the agent made no false express representations as
to his power and authority, since by signing the contract
on behalf of the principal the agent impliedly warranted
that he was empowered by the principal to make the contract.
(Don't breathe a sigh of relief here because in most real
estate or home purchases, the agent doesn't sign the contract
on behalf of the owner, the agent merely takes the contract
to the owner for signature. Thus, the real estate broker
or really, real estate agent, is not personally liable to
you unless you can prove that the agent who sold you the
house expressly misrepresented, materially, facts about the
house. That is a lot easier said than done.)

The point should be clear: You deal with an agent at
your own risk. The agent's power and authority are limited,
and if the agent exceeds his authority the principal may

repudiate or rescind the contract, in which event you may not enforce the contract against the principal. By the same token, a principal is not bound by special warranties or promises made by the agent in excess of the agent's authority. Consequently, if special warranties are made in a contract of purchase for any kind of property, you must make sure that on the contract of purchase the agent and the owner sign the promise as to the special warranty that you rely upon. For example, say the agent advises you that a new roof was put on the home a year and a half ago, and you have that put in the earnest money agreement; then you have both the agent and the owner sign that part of the earnest money agreement. By so doing, you are thereby assured that the owner has made the representation and has ratified the agent's authority to make such representation, and your offer of purchase is conditioned upon the truth of that assertion. In the event the assertion is untrue, you have all of the remedies that we have previously discussed in the contract cases—the remedy of recision and return of your money, the remedy of suit for damages for the replacement of the roof if it's totally defective, or even the remedy for punitive danger in the event of fraudulent dealings with you.

There is another doctrine in the law that gives you recision of a contract, and even damages, if a principal can be found to know or to have reason to know of the false dealings with other people conducted by a person who has been an agent for that principal for a long time. If you have been defrauded by such an agent, you may enforce the contract against the principal, you may rescind the contract and get your money back from the principal, or you may sue the principal and agent for damages. In such a situation, the principal is held to ratify the acts of the agent by taking not only the benefit of the contract but by having an agent with the authority to make such representations when the principal knew or should have known that his agent made dishonest representations.

TERMINATION OF AGENCY

A principal or an agent may terminate an agency in accordance with the terms of the original agency. For example, if an agency is limited in time, then the agency automatically terminates at the expiration of the time. If an agency is orally made for a specific act, the principal may cancel the agency or the agent may renounce the agency prior to

the consummation of the act undertaken. In addition, if
the acts undertaken by the agency have been accomplished,
then the agency is terminated. For example, when Frank
gave Jim $25 to go to Pittsburgh, upon delivery of the car
in Pittsburgh the agency would be terminated.

A revocation by the principal or a renunciation by
the agent may be made at any time by either party. The
principal has the duty of paying the agreed upon or reasonable compensation, if none has been agreed upon, and the
cost of the agency. And the agent has the duty of returning all of the goods and assets that the principal has put in
the agent's hands.

In addition, an agency is **terminated by operation of law**
if the agent assigns his agency without the consent of the
principal. An agent may not assign the duties put upon
him by the principal without the principal's knowledge and
consent. An agency is also terminated by operation of
law upon the death of either the principal or the agent.
If you appoint an agent to sell your home for you and, prior
to the time of the sale, you pass away, the agent has no
principal; consequently, there can be no agency. Or if the
agent dies prior to the confirmation of the sale, then,
of course, the agency is also terminated.

Many times you appoint an office or a group of
people to be your agents, especially in the sale of a
house. Since you appoint the office of the real estate
agent to be your total agent, the death of one of the
realtors in the office will not terminate the agency.
(But the death of the principal will terminate the agency.)

Some agencies are irrevocable, such as an employment
contract for a term of years. We have studied contracts
of employment and employment in business organizations,
and you know well enough that if you are hired, or you
hire another, for a period of five years to be your agent,
you may not revoke the agency, or the agent may not renounce
the agency, without good cause or in accordance with the
terms of the written contract of agency.

Our final note on termination of the agency: Upon
termination of the agency, it is absolutely essential that
all of the agent's appearance of authority be removed, or
a third party may deal with the agent as an apparent agent.
For example, if you go out of business in the sales field,
but you leave one of your sales agents with your name on
the door, an innocent third party may deal with that agent
as an apparent agent of yours, and hold you liable for the
contracts that the agent wrongfully entered into.

GLOSSARY TERMS

Disclosed principal   A principal known to the third person to be dealing through an agent.

Undisclosed principal   A person not known by the third person to be the principal for the agent with whom the third person is dealing.

SELF TEST

CHAPTER 47

NAME_____

DATE_____

47.1   A/An _____ principal is one who is represented by the agent to the third person as being in existence.

47.2   A principal who is _____ is not known to exist in an agency relationship by "third" in an agency relationship.

47.3   A principal who is _____ may sue upon the contract made by the agent, but if the third party _____ the contract, the principal may not enforce a contract when he is undisclosed and has the _____ of the contract against a willing seller or contract promisor if the contract promisor does not _____ the contract on good grounds.

47.4   A third party dealing with an agent and an undisclosed principal has the _____ of enforcing the contract against _____ of the parties.

47.5   An agent acting for an undisclosed principal may be held _____ liable on any contracts he enters into on behalf of the undisclosed principal.

47.6   A disclosed principal has the same _____ and _____ under a contract entered into for him by an agent as if he had entered into the contract _____.

47.7   If a third party knows that the person with whom he is dealing represents another principal, then he is under a duty to _____ and determine what the scope of the agent's _____ is.

47.8   A principal (choose "is" or "is not") _____ bound by the acts of the agent which exceed the agent's authority when the third party knew or should have known that the agent had _____ authority.

47.9   The courts or the law interpret a Power of Attorney or agency contract very _____; it limits, as far as the language can be read, the _____ of the agent to do exactly what the agency agreement sets forth and no more.

47.10   The law states that an agent who makes a contract
         on behalf of his principal, but the contract is in
         _____ of the agent's authority, is _____
         liable on the contract upon the principal's _____
         of the contract, even though the agent made no false
         _____ as to his power or authority. By
         signing the contract on behalf of the principal,
         the agent impliedly _____ that he or she was
         enpowered by the principal to make the contract.

47.11   A principal or agent may terminate an agency in
         _____ with the terms of the original agency.

47.12   A/an _____ by the principal, or a/an _____
         by the agent, may be made by either party at any
         time, unless it is otherwise agreed.

47.13   An agency is terminated by operation of _____
         if the agent _____ his agency without the
         consent of the principal.

47.14   An agency is terminated by operation of law upon the
         _____ of either the principal or the agent.

47.15   Some agencies are irrevocable, such as a/an _____
         contract for a term of years.

48 Wills

Introduction. Testacy—I.

LEARNING OBJECTIVES

To explore the transfer of property at death.
To become familiar with wills.

CHAPTER CONTENTS

Importance of Wills   Elements of a Will   Purpose of
Witnesses   Changing a Will   Transfer of Assets by Will
Glossary   Self Test

In this and the next chapters, we will discuss the transfer
of real property and personal property at the time of death.
In our earlier chapters on real and personal property we
discussed the transfer of property during life—transfer by
gift, by sale, by law. The transfer of property at death
can be by *testaments* or *wills*, or by operation of law when
there is no will involved. A person who dies with a will
that is valid is said to have died *testate*. In the law the
transfer of property by will is called a *testamentary
transfer*. A person who dies without a will has died *intestate*.

IMPORTANCE OF WILLS

To an unmarried person or one without an estate of any
size, a will perhaps is not important. But upon a person's
marriage or accumulation of real and personal property a
will becomes important because without a will the law
transfers property in your behalf and the transfer may
not be in accordance with your wishes for the transfer of
the property. In addition, a will is extremely important
if there are children, for a will serves an additional
purpose other than the mere transfer of property. In the
event that husband and wife are killed in an accident, then
who takes the guardianship of their minor children? Remember that a person under 21 years of age (or in some states
18 years of age) does not have legal capacity to contract
and engage in certain business relationships.

A minor must have a guardian, someone who is responsible for the upbringing, support, and training of the minor
child. Say Sally and Joe Black, at age 28, were killed
outright in an automobile collision. They left a minor
daughter, Deborah, age 3. Both Sally's parents, 60 years
of age, and Joe's parents, 68 years of age, are willing to
take the responsibility of raising Deborah. But Sally
and Joe had very good friends who they desired to have
raise the child if something happened to them—in fact they
had an agreement with these friends to that effect. But
without a will Sally and Joe's wishes are not before a
probate court. Consequently, Deborah may go to Joe's or
to Sally's parents, both elderly couples who might not be
alive when Deborah most needs their counsel and help in
going on to college or in getting married or making
decisions in life.

Had Sally and Joe made a will in which they appointed
their good friends to be the guardians of Deborah, the
court, while not being bound by their wishes, would take

those wishes into consideration and have the friends come
into court and be interviewed by the judge so that the
court could determine if Deborah's best interests would be
served by having Sally and Joe's friends appointed guardians.
This provision in a will also avoids very bitter feelings
between grandparents on occasion. Sally and Joe could have
shown both sets of parents the will and explained to them,
"You will also have a part in Deborah's life and will be
included in her life, but the responsibility for raising
Deborah will go to our friends because we believe that
they are younger and will be able to better include
Deborah in their family with their own children and support
and help her through her life."

ELEMENTS OF A WILL

What is a will? A will is a document executed or signed
by a person during his or her lifetime that provides for
the disposition of his or her property at his or her death.
It also, as I have indicated, sets forth the testator's wishes
with respect to guardianship for any minor children who
may survive the testator. While a gift in life transfers
title to property during life, a will transfers property
at death, and the gift occurs only at the time of death.
If you make a gift during life, that is an executed gift
or a gift that has taken place. But a will that transfers,
say, a diamond ring to a niece is an unexecuted gift until
the time of death and the passage of the ring through the
processes of the probate of the estate.

Who may make a will? Anyone may make a will who is
above a minimum age set by the statutes of the state in
which the person resides and who owns property and has
legal capacity to contract. There are three separate parts
of this definition of who may make a will: First, the
person must be over the minimum age set by statute;
second, he or she must have property subject to transfer
by will; and third, the person must have the contractual
capacity to make a will. The minimum age for a person to
make a will varies from state to state. In all states any
person over 21 years is old enough to make a will, but
in some states any person over 18 may make a will, and in
the state of Georgia any person over 14, in Louisiana, any
person over 16.

The second requirement is that the person must own
property. The person need not own property at the time he
makes the will, but to be valid on his death the will

must transfer some property. For example, say Sally and
Joe made a will, the primary purpose of which was to make
their wishes known that their friends would be the guardians
of Deborah, and in that will Sally and Joe had both stated
that they transferred by devise and bequest all of their
property, both real and personal, unto the guardians for
the benefit of Deborah. If at the time of their death
they owned an automobile or they had had a claim against
the negligent driver who caused their death, that would be
property which would pass to the estate of Deborah for
her benefit. So you can see that even though Sally and Joe,
at the time they made their will, didn't have property,
they could very well have property at the time of their
deaths which would pass under the will to the guardian of
the estate of Deborah for Deborah's benefit.

The final requirement for a will is that the person
must have legal capacity to contract. That is, the person
cannot be insane or be subject to undue influence or fraud
or intimidation. The legal capacity to make a will is
the same capacity as is required to make a valid contract—
freely, voluntarily with knowledge of and intent to perform
a particular act.

Can a will be oral? If Sam Jones says to Pete Smith,
"Sam, when I die, I want you to have my horse," is that a
will? Such a gift, to take effect at the time of death,
would be the testamentary transfer without a written will.
It would merely be an oral gift to be effective upon the
time of death. Such a gift would not be valid and enforceable by Sam Smith upon the death of the testator because
there is no written document that proves that the gift
was made. An oral will may be enforceable in some states
but only very, very rarely, such as when there has been an
emergency situation. In some states an oral or *nuncupative will* is enforceable if a person is severely injured by
an accident and his life is threatened; he may make a
testamentary transfer to a witness that is enforceable.
The same thing applies in some states to oral wills made
by soldiers and sailors during time of war if they are
shot or injured in combat. These wills are sometimes given
effect; but generally an oral or nuncupative will is not
enforceable.

Thus, the requirements that a will must satisfy to
be valid are: first, the will must be in writing;
second, the written will must be signed by the *testator*
(or, if female, *testatrix*)—the person who signs the will
and provides for the transfer of his or her property by the

will itself; third, the will must be witnessed by at least
two witnesses (in some states three witnesses).

PURPOSE OF WITNESSES

Why must a will be witnessed? For three reasons: First,
the witnesses attest to the fact that the person signing
the will did so freely and with understanding of what he
or she was signing; second, the witnesses attest to the
fact that the testator or testatrix was of sound mind at
the time that he or she executed the document; third, the
witnesses, their addresses, and whereabouts are noted so that
when the will is offered to the probate court the witnesses
may sign an affidavit, or appear in person if there is a
contest, and prove by their own testimony that the testator
or testatrix did sign the will freely and voluntarily with
the disposing intent that is set forth in the will, and at the
time of the execution the testator or testatrix was of sound
and disposing mind—was not intoxicated, insane, or senile,
and knew what she or he was doing.

A look at an *attestation clause* in a will should show
us exactly the purpose that witnesses have in witnessing
the execution of a will by a testator. "This instrument,
consisting of four typewritten pages, including this page,
each bearing the signature of the testator, John Jones,
was by him on the date which it bears, signed, published,
and declared by him to be his last will and testament
in our presence, who at his request, and in his presence,
and in the presence of each other we, believing him to be
of sound and disposing mind and memory, have hereunto
subscribed our names as witnesses." Beneath this is a
place for the signature of two witnesses and a place for
their residence addresses.

You can see that the witnesses have identified the
document and the number of pages in it; they have identified the testator; and they have declared that in their
presence the testator published the will by stating it was
his intent to sign it and dispose of the property as set
forth in the will, and that each of the witnesses in
each other's presence saw the testator sign the will and
that each was of the opinion that the testator was of
sound and disposing mind. The validity of this will is
thus very clear and the witnesses will be available,
hopefully, at the time of the testator's death to prove the
validity of the will and the intent of the testator to
pass his property by the provisions of the will.

A will can be very simple or very, very complex.
A will is a very important document to save taxes for a
testator upon his or her death, for the taxes—income,
estate, and inheritance—have a great impact upon an estate
at the time of a wealthy person's death. In addition, if
all of the requirements of the state's statute are not
met a will is not valid. Consequently, the average person
who tries to prepare his own will creates more problems and
difficulties for his heirs than if a skilled attorney
had been employed to prepare such a document.

CHANGING A WILL

What do you do if as very young people you had a will
executed on your behalf by a lawyer and then later you
changed your wishes substantially? You'll remember in
the insurance chapters we talked about a husband who
divorced and changed his will to leave everything to his
new wife, and the insurance company was not bound by such
a provision. Well, how do you go about changing your
will? A will may be changed by two methods: first, by
amendment; second, by revocation. In an amendment the
basic document may stay in existence but be amended by
preparing a *codicil*. A codicil is nothing more than an
amendment to a will, but to be valid the amendment must
be prepared and executed with all of the formalities and
technical requirements of a will—that is, it must be
signed by the testator or testatrix before the number of
witnesses required to make a will valid. It must also be
physically affixed to the will to become a valid amendment
to the will.

A will may also be changed by revocation of a prior
will and the execution of a new will. Now, revocation has
caused a tremendous amount of dispute and despair in the
law. When a prior will is revoked it must be physically
destroyed so that there is never any question as to which
will was to be offered to the court for the disposition of
the estate at death. This is why most people have their
lawyers retain their original will; when they come back to
their lawyer to have the will revoked and changed, the
lawyer himself may then destroy the first will after the
second will has been properly executed. Many times a person
forgets to destroy his first will, and upon his death two
different people offer two different wills as the last will
and testament of the deceased person. This creates long

and sometimes very costly and bitter disputes in the probate
court as to which will is the valid will. This can simply
and easily be avoided by the destruction of the prior will
and all copies may be in the person's, the insurance
company's, or the bank's possession.

TRANSFER OF ASSETS BY WILL

We begin with a definition: A *decedent* is a person who has
died, and we will use this term from here on. A decedent
who has left a valid will is known as a testator or testatrix,
while a dead person who does not have a will is known as
an intestate decedent. A will that has been properly
drawn and executed by the testator before the necessary
number of witnesses always provides for an executor—or if the
executor is a woman, an executrix—a person appointed by
the decedent upon his death to take under his or her
management all of the estate. Such management includes
paying the bills of the decedent that are outstanding at
the time of his death, including funeral and burial
expenses; after the payment of all the necessary bills
and claims against the estate, then the executor or
executrix is charged with the distribution of the remaining estate to the deposees and legatees in the will.

The executor does not take possession or title to all
this property; a will is first offered to the probate
court as the last will and testament of the decedent.
The executor or executrix is then appointed by the court
and often is required to furnish a bond through an insurance
company, insuring that the executrix will faithfully and
fully perform all of the duties imposed upon him or her
for the undertaking of the execution of the will.

Once appointed, the executor or executrix, after
publication to claimants in a newspaper, takes all of
the claims against the estate, and puts all assets in a
bank account, or if necessary sells some of the real
property to satisfy claims against the estate. The executor
or executrix then files an accounting or inventory with
the court showing all of the assets—real and person
property, accounts and monies due the estate—and all monies
owing by the estate. After this is performed, the
executrix or executor files with the court a motion to
allow him or her to pay the claims against the estate, first
out of the personal property of the estate, and if that is
not sufficient, then, with authorization, by selling some
of the real property to satisfy bonafide claims against the
estate.

Once permitted, the executor or executrix pays all of the claims against the estate and a final accounting for the estate is rendered to the court showing all the bills that have been paid, all of the assets that have been received. The remainder of the estate, over and above the bills that have been paid, is then subject to distribution to the *legatees* and *deposees* in the will. (A *legatee* is a person who takes personal property under a will, and a legacy is the transfer of personal property by a testator to a legatee. A *disposee* is a person who takes real property under a will by the wishes of a testator, and such transfer is called a *devise*.)

After all of the claims of the estate have been paid by the executor, and the final accounting has been rendered, then the executor or executrix must compute the amount of the estate tax that the federal government and the state of the decedent's residence at death may impose upon the estate. Only after the taxes have been paid are the legacies transferred to the legatees and the devises to the deposees.

GLOSSARY TERMS

Attestation clause   The statement by witnesses to the signing of a will that the circumstances of its drawing and signing render it valid.

Codicil   An amendment to a will that meets all the requirements for validity placed on the will itself.

Decedent   Any dead person.

Deposee   Recipient of real property under a will.

Devise   Transfer of real property by a will.

Executor   A male appointed by a will to dispose of the estate.

Executrix   A female appointed by a will to dispose of the estate.

Intestate   Having died without a will.

Legacy   Transfer of personal property by a will.

Legatee   Recipient of personal property under a will.

Nuncupative will   An oral will.

Testament   A will

Testamentary transfer   Transfer of property by will.

Testate   Having died and left a valid will.

Testator   A male signer of a will.

Testatrix   A female signer of a will.

Will   A document executed and signed during life providing for the disposition of property and the care of minor children after the person's death.

SELF TEST

CHAPTER 48

NAME_____

DATE_____

48.1 When a person dies with a will that is valid, that person is said to have died _____.

48.2 In the law, the transfer of property by will is called a/an _____ transfer.

48.3 If a person dies without a will, he is said to have died _____.

48.4 A will is a document _____ or signed by a person during his lifetime that provides for the _____ of his _____ at the time of his death. It also sets forth the _____ wishes with respect to _____ for any minor children who may survive the testator.

48.5 A/An _____ during a person's life transfers title to property during life, but a will transfers property at _____.

48.6 Anyone above a minimum _____ set by the _____ of the state in which the person resides, and who _____ property, and has legal _____ to contract may make a will.

48.7 If a person is over _____ years of age, he is old enough in any state to make a will.

48.8 For a will to be valid, it must, at the time of _____, transfer some _____.

48.9 The legal capacity to make a will is the same capacity as is required to make a valid contract; that is, freely, _____ with knowledge of an _____ to perform a particular act.

48.10 A/An _____ will is enforceable in some states, but is usually when the will was made in an emergency situation.

48.11 Generally speaking, an oral or _____ will is not enforceable.

48.12 The first requirement to have a valid will is that the will must be in _____.

48.13 The second requirement to have a valid will is that the will must be _____ by the _____.

48.14 When a man signs a will to provide for the disposi-
       tion of his property, he is known as a/an _____;
       however, when a woman signs a will, she is known as
       a/an _____.

48.15 The third requirement for a valid will is that the
       will must be _____ by at least _____
       witnesses.

48.16 The two methods of changing a will are by:
       a) amendment; that is, the basic document may
           stay in _____, but it may be amended by
           preparing a/an _____; or
       b) _____ of a prior will, and the _____
           of a new will.

48.17 A/An _____ is nothing more than an amendment
       to a will.

48.18 A person who is deceased is known in the law as a/an
       _____.

48.19 The _____, or if a woman, the _____,
       is a person appointed by the decedent to manage,
       upon his death, all of the estate and pay all of
       the bills of the decedent which are outstanding at
       the time of his death; and, after all expenses have
       been paid, to make the distribution of the remainder
       of the estate to the _____ and _____
       set forth in the will.

48.20 A/An _____ is a person who takes personal
       property under a will.

48.21 A/An _____ is a person who takes real property
       under a will.

49 Wills

Testacy—II. Intestacy. Trusts.

LEARNING OBJECTIVES

To learn how the transfer of property differs according to whether or not there is a will.

CHAPTER CONTENTS

In this chapter we continue our discussion of wills and the transfer of property by testate succession and intestate succession. (You will remember that a testator is one who executes a written will with the necessary attestation of the required number of witnesses. A person who dies without a will dies intestate. In this chapter we will discuss in detail the differences of transfer of property when a will exists and when one does not exist—that is, when a person dies testate and when a person dies intestate.

CONDITIONS ON TESTATE LEGACY AND DEVISE

A person who dies with a will may make any disposition of property that he or she desires, with certain minor exceptions. The first exception is that a person may not dispose of his or her property by will when the disposition of the property is against public policy. For example, I obviously could not leave my son $30,000 on the condition that he goes into the manufacture of dangerous narcotics. Such a legacy would obviously be against public policy and the condition would be void, and my son would probably take the $30,000; if he did the legacy would definitely be free of the condition.

Another restriction, this one upon the transfer or devise of land, is known as the rule against perpetuity. This is a very complex and technical rule difficult to administer by anyone but a lawyer. Simply stated, a devise of land may not be under the control of the testator for longer than a life in being. At the time of the will's probate—that is, when the will is probated—the will may transfer the property to a then living deposee and thereafter the will may provide that upon the death of the deposee the property shall be transferred to a third person—say a great-grandson—and so long as the great-grandson is living at the time of the probate of the will, the property may be transferred to him. But after that the will may not provide for a further transfer of the property unless the great-grandson was living at the time of the will's probate and after that for no longer than 21 years.

Restrictions on the transfer of land are not favored in the law, and real property cannot be controlled from the grave for all time. So the conditions in a will, or life estate in wills, terminate after a given period of time, that is, a life in being and 21 years. This does not mean that Mr. B, the son of Mr. A, cannot, in addition,

impose restrictions upon his son in his tranfer of the
property if he had more than a life estate in real property.
Nevertheless, there can be no complete control of property
for centuries by devises in wills.

Another condition upon the unrestricted transfer of
property by will is called the rule against *pretermitted
heirs.* Say Mr. Antupit has three sons, and decides, for
reasons of his own, that he will disinherit his son Dick.   In
his will, Mr. Antupit gives his son Chas one-half the
property, and his third son Davey the other half.   He
does not mention Dick in his will at all.   Dick may contest
the validity of the will under the rule that a pretermitted
heir—an heir who is omitted from any mention in the will—
has been inadvertently forgotten by the testator.   The son
might be able to establish this and take one-third of his
father's estate.

Thus, the rule is that if you are going to disinherit someone, you must specifically mention him in your
will and either specifically disinherit the person or leave
him a paltry sum, such as $10.

One further condition upon a testator's rights to
unconditional transfer of property is the law that no heir
(by either intestate or testate succession) who lives in
a foreign country or is an alien in this country can
take the intestate succession or the devise or bequest
unless the country in which that alien lives reciprocates
and allows a United States citizen to take by bequest or
devise or intestate succession.

This sprang up chiefly because of the cold war, when
many states passed statutes in which a citizen of Russia
may not take a devise or bequest from an American citizen
unless Russian law allows an American citizen to take a
property by devise or bequest or intestate succession from
a Russian testator.   This reciprocity statute is important
because many U.S. citizens have come from countries that
are, or, until recently, were, enemies of the United States
and have not allowed their citizens to devise or bequest
property to American citizens.

Aside from the qualifications we've listed, a testator
may leave real and personal property by devise and bequest
virtually unconditionally, may make any program or proceeds
available not only to relatives but to people who are not
related to the testator.   A testator may leave property
to corporations or to trusts, to government agencies or to
charities by gift upon his death, and to almost any conceivable association or group of people.   Thousands and

thousands of dollars have been left to veterinarian hospitals to take care of the cats and dogs of very old people. In some cases, the amounts that have been left to a cat or a dog have been so large that the probate court has viewed the will with suspicion and has concluded that the testator signed the will when they were not of sound mind. But if the bequest or devise is to an animal hospital or a university for research into animal sicknesses, these bequests and devises have generally been upheld. If a million dollars is left outright to a cat or to a person to take care of the cat, the will is not likely to be followed and the testamentary bequest or devise will be ruled improper. But with these qualifications, a testator may make such provisions as he or she desires.

INTESTATE SUCCESSION

The succession of property by intestacy varies from state to state, so only some general rules can be given. Basically, the property of a person who dies intestate goes to that person's heirs. Most people believe that heirs are the sons and daughters of a decedent, but this is not always true. For example, Mr. Antupit is a widower—his wife has predeceased him; he has three children and he dies intestate. The laws, generally, in each state provide that the three children will succeed to Mr. Antupit's estate equally—that is, each of the children will take one-third of the estate after all the debts, taxes, and claims against the estate have been paid. But what happens if one of Mr. Antupit's children died before his father and the deceased child had two children of his own? (That is, Mr. Antupit had two children still living and two grandchildren by his third child who was no longer living.) The heirs of the deceased child would take their share of the estate by right of representation.

If Mr. Antupit died leaving his wife and three children the intestate succession would generally be that the wife would take one-third of the estate and the three children would split up equally the remaining two-thirds of the estate. If Mr. Antupit dies intestate leaving only his wife as a survivor, the wife would take one-third of the estate and Mr. Antupit's parents would take two-thirds of the estate equally. If they were no longer living, then the two-thirds of his estate would go to his brother and sister, and if he had none living, then to their children—his nieces and nephews.

Clearly, intestate succession does not probably cor-
respond with Mr. Antupit's real intentions; if he died
leaving only his wife it may be presumed that he would
intend that she inherit all of his estate during her lifetime so that she would have the benefit of their common
labors through life in acquiring the property that they
held when Mr. Antupit died. Thus, it was important that
Mr. Antupit have a will, and unfortunate that he did not.
Assume that Mr. Antupit has a large estate, his wife
has predeceased him, he has no children, no brothers and
sisters, and his parents have predeceased him, and
throughout his life he has been too busy to prepare a will
conveying by devise and bequest his estate to charitable
organizations or to his friends. Mr. Antupit dies
intestate, without heirs at law, and his property goes to
the state in which he dies, his money and proceeds of his
estate going into the general fund of the state to run
the government. Without a will the court would have no
authority but to allow the property go to the state
government by *escheat*.

TRUST ADMINISTRATION

A will may provide for monthly payments for the education
or support of a family of children or it may provide for
the administration of a trust for the benefit of a wife
who is unable to manage the affairs of an estate. By
establishing a trust for the benefit of a wife or for the
benefit of minor children, a skilled trust officer of a
bank or other institution may manage the affairs of the
estate and pay to the children for their education and the
wife a monthly income from the principal and interest
of the estate. Again, there are many ways in which the
affairs of an estate may be governed by the proper execution
of a will.

GLOSSARY TERMS

Escheat   Succession by a state government to the property
    of an intestate.

Heir   A person who succeeds to intestate property.

Pretermitted heir   An heir who is omitted from any mention
    in the will.

SELF TEST
CHAPTER 49

NAME_____

DATE_____

49.1 We discussed that a testator is one who executes
a/an _____ will with the necessary _____
of the required number of witnesses in attempting
to transfer the testator's _____, and make
his wishes known with regard to the _____ of
his minor children at the time of death. A person
who dies _____, dies without a will.

49.2 The first exception in regard to the disposition of
property by will, is that a person may not dispose
of property by will when the disposition is against
_____ policy.

49.3 Another restriction upon the transfer or devise of
land is known as the rule against _____.

49.4 This rule states that a devise of land may not be
under the control of the testator for longer than a/an
_____ in being and _____ years.

49.5 Another condition upon the unrestricted transfer
of property by will is one which is called the rule
against _____ heirs, or heirs who have been
_____ from a will.

49.6 If you are going to disinherit someone, you must
_____ mention that person in the will, and
either specifically _____ the person, or
leave him a paltry sum.

49.7 Another restriction upon the unrestricted transfer
of property by will is the law that states that an
heir by intestate succession, or a devisee or legatee
by testate succession, who lives in a foreign
country, is not allowed to take the property unless
the country in which that alien lives _____,
and allows a United States citizen to take property
in that foreign country by bequest, devise, or
intestate succession. This law is known as the
_____ statute.

49.8   Basically, the property of a person who dies without
        a will, or who dies _____, goes to that
        person's _____.

49.9   (Answer either "true" or "false") _____ A
        decedent's heirs are always the sons and daughters
        of a decedent.

49.10   If a person dies intestate, without heirs at law,
        the property of the decedent usually goes to the
        _____ in which he dies. This process is
        called _____.

49.11   A will may provide for monthly _____ for
        the education or support of a family, or it may
        provide for the administration of a/an _____
        for heirs who do not want to be bothered with the
        administration of the estate.

49.12   An heir is a person who _____ to the intestate's
        _____.

49.13   (Answer either "true" or "false") _____ A testator
        may leave property to persons not related to the
        testator, or even to corporations.

50 Bailment

Introduction. Standard of Care.

LEARNING OBJECTIVES

To learn the general law of bailment.
To learn the various types of bailment.

CHAPTER CONTENTS

Bailments   Duties of the Bailee   Glossary   Self Test

BAILMENTS

Bailment is a legal term for the transfer of <u>possession</u> of personal property without the transfer of <u>title</u>. Any time you borrow personal property from a friend or acquaintance, or any time you lend personal property to another person, a bailment exists. A bailment exists any time personal property is in the possession of someone who is not the rightful owner.

You will remember that in the sale of personal property title passes with the sale. Sometimes title remains in the seller and is secured by a promise to pay for the price of the goods, and this is a conditional sale of personal property. However, in a bailment only possession of the personal property is transferred—never title. Any time a housewife goes next door to borrow a cup of sugar, she has created a bailment: There is a promise that the cup she has borrowed from her neighbor will be returned, as will an equal amount of sugar. An implied promise is created that the goods or similar goods will be returned to the bailor. Now the *bailor* is the person who has legal title to the personal property and is the one that loans the personal property to the *bailee*, the person who takes possession of the personal property. When I go to the cleaners and leave my clothes to be cleaned I am primarily interested in having my clothes cleaned in a reasonably professional manner, but I am also interested in the return of my clothes in good condition. I have engaged in two legal relationships: First, I have contracted for the cleaner to clean my clothes and have promised expressly or by implication to pay for that service. Second, a relationship of bailment exists. The cleaner holds possession of my clothes during the term that he is to hold them for cleaning and he has made an implied promise to return the clothes in a cleaned condition. A bailment arises whenever we loan personal property to another to have it worked on or fixed, whether you take your car to a garage to have it fixed or leave your coat and hat at a checkstand in a restaurant or park your car in a private parking lot, and so on.

Bailments are not always contracts; bailments may be created when you walk down the street and find a valuable piece of personal property such as a wristwatch, a diamond ring, or a wallet. When you pick up that personal property you don't have automatic title or the right to own it. When the true owner comes for the personal property, either because we advertised that we had found it or the owner discovered we possessed it, a bailment is created and we are under an implied duty to return the personal property to the true owner upon demand.

Most bailments are coupled with a contractual interest. That is, something is to be done; there is a promise by the bailee to do something with the personal property—to hold it safely, or to repair or clean it, or to act with the personal property in some way. Thousands of bailments occur in any year of our everyday lives in the lending and borrowing of personal property, but most bailments occur through business transactions. A safety deposit box is a form of bailment. In many cases, property left in the hands of a third party to be managed is a bailment (sometimes they are trusts as well).

Bailments apply only to personal property. It is not possible to have a bailment of real property.

Bailments should not be confused with debtor-creditor relationships or with conditional sales relationships. For example, Antupit loans $500 to Brickyard, who signs a promissory note agreeing to repay the $500 in 90 days at 6% interest. Is a bailment created of the $500? You remember that he promised to repay the $500 plus interest. May Antupit, at the expiration of 90 days, demand $500 back in the form of a bailment and be entitled to the return of the $500 plus interest? In other words, is a bailment situation created or is some other legal situation created? A bailment is not created because when Antupit loaned the $500 to Brickyard, he gave him legal <u>title</u> to the $500. He did not expect the return of the $500 he lent—he merely expected a return of 500 U.S. dollars plus 6%. The legal relationship is one of debtor and creditor, not bailor and bailee.

As another example, Antupit purchased an automobile from Brickyard and signed a conditional sales contract by which Brickyard, the seller, holds the legal title to the automobile and the legal title is still registered in his name. Does Antupit hold the automobile as a bailee or is there some other legal relationship created? A bailment was not created because the seller holds legal title under a conditional sales contract only as security for the payment of the debt—that is, the purchase price of the automobile. It is merely a security on the loan created by the sale. Consequently, a conditional sales relationship does not create a bailment. They sometimes look alike but they are very different.

DUTIES OF THE BAILEE

When you hold property that belongs to someone else you
have certain duties and obligations for the protection
of that property; the standard of care or the extent of
your liability as a bailee is governed by the nature of
the bailment situation that prevails. There are three
categories or classifications of bailments. The first
is the bailment .that benefits the bailee. I ask my
neighbor, "May I borrow your lawn mower this Sunday to mow
my lawn?" I'm not going to pay for the use of the lawn
mower, and it's for my sole benefit, as bailee, that I've
asked for the possession of the lawn mower. Any time a
borrower asks for the use of personal property for his
own benefit, this is a bailment for the benefit of the bailee.

In such situations, the law requires that the bailee
exercise great care in the protection of the personal
property so that it can be returned to the owner, the
bailor, in the same condition in which it was originally
bailed to the bailee.

There's a rule that the bailor, even though he receives
no benefit from the bailment, may be held liable if he
gives personal property to the bailee (at the bailee's
request) which the bailor knows has a defect that may
create a hazard to the bailee's personal safety. Say
my neighbor comes over and asks to borrow my stepladder.
I grant him permission to borrow the stepladder and get it
out of the tool shed for him. I momentarily forget to
tell my neighbor that two of the rungs on the stepladder
have been weakened and are cracked and that he should be
very careful to not step on those rungs. While my neighbor
is up on the ladder he steps on one of the weakened rungs
and falls, sustaining severe and permanent injuries. I
may well be liable for those injuries even though I was
being a good neighbor in loaning my stepladder. I knew
that the ladder had a defect in it that could cause injury
and I failed to advise the bailee of that fact.

The second type of bailment is one for the sole benefit of the bailor, the legal owner of the property. For
example, we're all at the football game together and I
ask my neighbor to please watch our coats while my wife and
I go up to get a cup of coffee. When we return to our
seats we find that our coats have been stolen. In this
situation, the bailment was one which totally benefited the
bailor, that is me, but not the bailee. In that situation
the bailee has a very low standard of care that is imposed

upon him by law because he gets no benefit out of the bailment—it is solely for the bailor's benefit. The same thing
applies when your family goes on vacation and asks the
neighbor to take care of the dog or the cat or leaves the
car keys with the neighbor so that he can turn over the
engine every so often to keep the battery charged. This
is a bailment for the sole benefit of the bailor, and the
bailee has a relatively low standard of care to insure the
return of the bailed article to the bailor.

For the bailee to be liable for the loss or damage
to the personal property, the bailor would have to prove
that the bailor was grossly negligent in failing in any
way to protect the property. However, even in a bailment
for the sole benefit of the bailor, the bailee does have
a duty not to misuse the property left in his or her care.
For example, Mr. and Mrs. Jones are planning on leaving
town for an extended vacation. They ask their neighbor,
Mr. Smith, to please take the keys to their car and turn
the engine over once a week while they're gone so that the
battery will not go dead. But the bailee not only runs
the engine in the driveway, he uses the automobile to go
to and from work and also takes it to the beach on a weekend
trip.

Of course, during this trip the car is damaged. Even
though the accident itself was not his fault, the bailee is
liable to the bailor for the damage that resulted from the
bailment. For the bailee must return the car in as good
a condition as when he took possession under the bailment.
Of course, if the car had been sitting in the driveway
and been damaged by a milk truck that went out of control,
the bailee would not be liable to the bailor, for there
was no negligence of any sort on the bailee's part. It
should be obvious why. When the bailor is being benefited
by someone's looking after his goods and the bailee
receives no benefit for taking on that responsibility, he
should not be personally liable unless he has misused the
goods or been grossly negligent in taking care of them.

The third category of bailment and the commonest
form of bailment, is mutual benefit bailment, in which both
the bailor and the bailee are benefited by the bailment
itself. This is generally a business bailment, such as when
you take your clothes in for cleaning or your car or your
watch in for repairs, or park your automobile and an
attendant gives you a claim slip. Both the bailee and the
bailor benefit.

Another common type of bailment is called a bailment
for hire, such as when we rent a car in another town to get
about when we're on a business trip or a vacation. When
we rent the car, the bailor, the owner of the car, rents
us the automobile and we are in possession for a period of
time.

When the bailment is for mutual benefit, the bailee
is under the duty to exercise reasonable care in the protection of the goods and to return the goods in the same
condition in which they were bailed. In a bailment in
which repairs or services are to be performed on the article
in the possession of the bailee, the bailee has the duty of
making reasonably professional repairs or cleaning on the
article and returning it to the bailor upon the bailor's
payment of the service or repair charge. You're not
entitled to your car from the parking lot until you've
paid the parking fee, or to your watch or clothes until
you've paid the watch repairman or the tailor. By the same
token, the bailee—the parking lot attendant, the cleaner, or
the watch repairman—is responsible for the protection of
your goods, and if he has not exercised reasonable care
in the protection of the goods, then he is liable for the
value of the goods to you.

The law presumes that a bailee has not exercised due
care in a mutual benefit bailment if the bailee cannot
produce the article bailed upon demand by the bailor. There
is a presumption that if he exercises ordinary care, a
bailee will not lose or destroy the article bailed. But
if the bailee can show that he has exercised reasonable
care in the protection of the article, then he may not be
liable even if some damage occurs.

In mutual benefit bailments there are certain implied
promises. When we take our articles in to have them worked
upon or stored in a warehouse, we warrant to the bailee
that the articles are not inherently dangerous. For
example, we cannot store a can of gasoline in a warehouse
without advising the warehouseman of its presence in
the package that we bail with him.

As bailors for mutual benefit bailments, we also
promise by implication to pay the reasonable charges for
the bailment itself. That is, we agree to pay the warehouse charges before we have a right to the return of our
goods; in a service or repair contract we make an implied
promise to pay the reasonable charges for the service
performed on the article bailed before we are entitled to
a receipt or return of the articles bailed. This is why it's

very important when you take your automobile into a garage
to make sure of the charges that will be made upon it for
the services performed, because in most states a service
bailee has a right to retain possession of the article
until his reasonable charges are paid—you can't get your
car, your watch, or your clothes back until you've made
the payment. This can create some real difficulties if
the charge seems unreasonable or excessive. So it's a good
idea to have a written estimate before the car is put in
the hands of the bailee.

The bailee on the other hand, warrants that his repair
work is reasonably sound, that the car or any other
personal property left in his possession will receive
reasonable care in its protection, and that he will return
it to you in as good a condition as that in which you left
it with him. Because the bailee has no legal title to the
property, creditors of the bailee may not seize the goods
in his possession, because they do not belong to him.
In addition, if fire or some catastrophe occurs in a mutual
benefit bailment, there is a presumption that the bailee
is liable to the bailor for the return of the goods unless
he can affirmatively show his exercise of great care in
the protection of the goods for the return to the bailor.

GLOSSARY TERMS

Bailee   The person who receives possession of property
    under a bailment.

Bailment   The transfer of possession of personal property
    without transfer of title.

Bailor   The person who gives possession of property under
    a bailment.

SELF TEST

CHAPTER 50

NAME_____

DATE_____

50.1   A bailment is a/an _____ term for the transfer of _____ of _____ property without the transfer of _____ .

50.2   A bailment may exist any time _____ property is in the _____ of someone who is not the rightful _____ .

50.3   The _____ is the person who has _____ title to the personal property of the _____ .

50.4   The _____ is the person who takes possession of the property.

50.5   The bailor is the person who gives momentary or _____ possession of the personal property to the bailee, but who expects the property, or similar property, to be _____ .

50.6   It is not possible to have a bailment of _____ property, only _____ property.

50.7   If party A lent party B $500, on a 6%, 60-day note, the legal relationship would be that of a/an _____ and _____ , not bailor and bailee.

50.8   When title to personal property is held as security on a loan created by a sale, a bailment does not exist, because a/an _____ relationship does not create a bailment.

50.9   A bailor has the right to make _____ upon the bailee for the return of the possession of the personal property that was loaned.

50.10   Any time a borrower asks for the use of personal property for his own _____ , this is a bailment for the benefit of the _____ .

50.11   Any time a borrower _____ the bailment for his own benefit, the bailment is for the benefit of the _____ .

50.12   In a bailment for the benefit of the bailee, the law requires that the bailee exercise _____ care in the protection of the personal property.

50.13   In a bailment for the benefit of the bailor, the
        bailee has a relatively _____ standard of
        care to insure the _____ of the bailed article
        to the bailor. For the bailee to be liable for the
        _____ or damage to the personal property,
        the bailor would have to prove that the bailee was
        _____ in his care of the
        property.

50.14   In a bailment which is for the sole benefit of the
        bailor, the bailee does have a/an _____ not to
        _____ the property left in his or her care.

50.15   The bailee, in a bailment for the sole benefit of
        the bailor, is not liable for damage to the bailed
        property unless he is _____ negligent, except
        when the bailee makes a/an _____ or _____
        use of the bailed property.

50.16   In a bailment for the benefit of the bailee, the
        bailor may be held _____ if he gives
        personal property to the bailee at the bailee's
        request which the bailor knows has a/an _____
        that may create a/an _____ to the bailee's
        personal _____.

50.17   In review, in a bailment for the sole benefit of
        the bailor, the bailee has only a duty of exercising
        _____ and _____ care, but he may
        not make an unwarranted use of the property for his
        own benefit, or he will be liable if he has been
        guilty of _____ negligence, or has not used
        _____ care.

50.18   A person who borrows something for his own use must
        exercise _____ care in the protection of the
        personal property bailed, but the bailor in that
        situation must use _____ care in advising the
        bailee of any known defects in the property bailed.

50.19   The third category of bailment is the _____
        _____ bailment, where both the bailor and the
        bailee are benefited by the _____ itself.
        This is the most _____ form of bailment, and
        is generally a/an _____ bailment.

50.20   If a person rents an automobile for a trip or
        vacation, this bailment would be a/an _____ for
        _____.

50.21   In bailment situations that are for the mutual bene-
        fit of the bailee and the bailor, the bailee is
        under the duty to exercise _____ care in the
        protection of the bailed goods.

NAME_____

DATE_____

50.22   There is a presumption that a bailee, if he exer-
        cises _____ care, will not lose, or have
        destroyed, the article bailed.

50.23   Of the implied promises made by the bailer, one is
        that he warrants to the bailee that the bailed
        articles are not inherently _____.   There is
        also a promise, by implication, to pay, if any, the
        _____ charges for the bailment itself.

51 Credit and Interest

Introduction. Installment Sales.

LEARNING OBJECTIVES

To examine interest and the cost of borrowing money.

CHAPTER CONTENTS

Simple Interest   Compound Interest   Repossession
The Hazards of Installment Contracts   Glossary   Self Test

The cost of borrowing money is the *interest* charge or finance
charges levied by the lender for the use of the money by
the borrower. It is extremely important that all of us
have a clear understanding of the charges that we pay for
the use of someone else's money. Far too many of us spend
a great deal of time shopping for needed goods and services
to get the best price possible but spend far too little time
shopping for the credit that we need, and we pay exorbitant
amounts of interest for the use of the borrowed capital.
Too many families say, "What are the monthly payments that
I have to make on this purchase?" instead of looking at the
monthly payment of principal and actual interest they are
paying.

Before we look at interest charges some current U.S.
statistics on over-financing and over-interest charges should
be revealed. Credit buying costs more than cash purchases.
Young families are the biggest users. Two out of five
families in America under 45 years of age pay out between
10% and 40% of their net income (after tax income) on
installment payments. About 65% of all new cars and 75% of
all used cars are bought and paid for through some form of
installment sales contract, as is about 85% of all the
furniture and appliances bought.

The **greatest danger** in personal **credit practices** is
that a number of families always consider only that a
desired article costs just so much per payment, and therefore tend to overload their family budgets. A surprising
number of families never seem to understand that there is
no excuse for nonpayment. Even if the family is ill or
has emergency expenditures, or even if the income earner
loses his job, they still must make the payments or be
in default on the installment sales contract. Another
group does not understand that even repossession of the
article they purchased on credit does not necessarily cancel
the debt.

SIMPLE INTEREST

We will look into the various forms of credit purchasing
and installment sales, and the interest charges on this,
the commonest and most expensive form of credit available.
We will look first at simple interest. If you borrow
$100 or purchase a $100 item and the credit charge, or
interest, is stated at 6% per year, you may think that the
cost of borrowing the hundred dollars or having the $100

item for a year would be $6. This is not generally true,
however, the actual interest rate on the $100 purchase is
12% per year. For example, I go into a store and purchase
on credit a $100 radio. I agree to pay back the store in
12 equal installments at 6% interest. Now, I have not had
the use of the $100 for a period of one year; I've had the
average use of only $50, because by the end of six months I
will have repaid $50 of the original loan; but the interest
rate is figured on $100—that is, the original purchase
over the entire 12-month period. The loan cost is $6 on
$100 but actually I had only an average of $50. So the
true interest rate is 12%—not 6%.

Any time you borrow money or purchase a commodity and
the interest rate is figured on the original loan, double
the amount of interest you are paying and you'll find the
actual interest rate. Let's assume that we borrowed $500
and agreed to pay it back in 12 equal installments. The
rate of interest was 7%. Now actually, at the end of six
months we would have repaid $250 of the original loan but
the interest would still be running on the $500 original
loan balance. Consequently, we had only $250 for six months,
but we would be paying a 7% rate on $500. Consequently,
our interest rate would be 14% on the money we had borrowed
or the goods we had purchased on credit.

In home loans for mortgage financing, the actual
interest rate and the stated interest rate are the same,
because the interest is figured on the declining balance
owed—not on the original purchase price or mortgage amount.
That is one of the few areas where interest as stated is
the actual interest charged. Home financing loans are one
of the least expensive of interest charges in our economy,
while installment interest on purchases or on short term
financing is generally double the amount of the stated
interest.

COMPOUND INTEREST

As you know, most stores have two forms of credit accounts.
One is a 30-day charge; that is, your family charges
certain purchases and next month receives the bill. If
you pay that bill there is no financial or interest charge
on the credit that has been extended, except a little higher
price for the goods (which everyone, including cash customers,
absorbs). But if the purchase price is not paid on the
revolving credit account within 30 days, then there is an

interest charge, generally, 1½% per month on the balance
each month up to $500, or 1% of the amount over $500.
    Notice that the interest charge is assessable monthly.
Now, if the interest charge is 1½% per month, the actual
interest charge on the balance is 18% per year, or if 1%
per month, then 12% per year, because we multiply the
monthly interest rate times the number of months that the
interest is charged to the principal. Consequently, if I
have a credit charge with our local department store of
$100, the interest charge against that $100 at 1% for a
period of one month would be $1, but at the end of the year
my interest paid on the $100 balance would be $12 or 12%.
In addition, if the interest is not paid on the first
month's balance, the $101, then the second month's interest
compounds—it becomes part of the principal, and thus
interest is charged on the interest. This is known as
compound interest. This is how it works. If I have a $100
balance with a department store, at the end of a year I
will have a principal balance of $112. But actually the
balance outstanding at the end of the year will be in
excess of $112 because each month's unpaid interest goes
to the principal, and the succeeding month's interest is
charged against the new principal balance. Say I owe a $100
balance at the local store which charges 1% per month on the
balance outstanding at the end of the month. At the end
of the first month, $1 interest would be charged on the $100
principal, and that interest amount would be added to the
principal for a total of $101. The second month's interest
would be charged not against $100 but against $101, for
the interest would be compounded into the principal.
This would leave a balance at the end of the second month of
$102.01; at the end of the third month, a principal balance
of $103.03; the fourth month, $104.04; the fifth month,
$105.08; the sixth month, $106.13; the seventh month,
$107.19; the eighth month, $108.26; the ninth month, $109.34;
the tenth month, $110.43; the eleventh month, $111.53; the
twelfth month, $112.64.
    The rate of interest would be in excess of 12%
because the interest was compounded each month. If simple
interest had been charged on the monthly balance, the total
cost for the use of the $100 would be $12, but because the
interest was compounded, the yearly charge for the use of
the $100 was $12.64. Again, remember that on installment
purchases we should double the rate of interest if the
interest is charged on the original loan amount. Because
you are repaying each month, over the life of the loan you

really owe <u>an average of about one-half the original loan</u>; if you repay in 12 monthly installments a $1000 debt at a stated rate of $12 per $100, and thus a finance charge of $120, your true interest cost would be 24% because your average debt during that year is $500—not the original $1000.

You can see that credit financing of purchases is an expensive use of money. Personal and auto loans are available from banks across the country at a rate of between $4.50 to $6 per each $100 purchased, plus a charge of 25¢ to 50¢ for insurance that automatically repays the debt if the debtor dies. These annual loan charges run from between 9% to 13% of true interest charged. Credit unions charge from three-quarters of one percent to 1% a month on the unpaid balance, putting the true interest rate at about 9% to 12% per year, slightly less than the bank rates. Depending on where you live, true annual interest charges can range from between 18% to 40% at small loan companies and between 12% and 34% on car loans arranged through auto dealers or finance companies, and between 18% and 20% on installment purchases of appliances through retail stores.

If your family has an ordinary life insurance policy, it has a loan value after it has been in effect several years. Life insurance loans are very attractive because the stated rate is the actual rate; that is, the rate of interest, generally between 5% and 6%, is charged on the declining balance of the principal. This is also true of home loans through mortgage banks; the stated charge is the actual charge. But in most home loans there is a prepayment penalty. That is, if you prepay your loan before the normal termina- tion, the lending institution may charge you a penalty roughly equal to half of the interest the lending institution would have earned had the loan gone to its normal duration date. In addition, such lending institutions as mortgage companies and savings and loan companies, which do a great deal of home financing, have service charges for setting up the loan and handling the papers. These may run between ½% and 1% on the total balance of the loan. This is another charge which should be considered as one of the costs of borrowing the money.

REPOSSESSION

As you know, almost every type of good or service can be purchased today on installments—everything from clothing,

dishwashers, automobiles to an ocean cruise, an airline
ticket, and on and on. When the service or goods are
purchased from the seller on an installment basis, the
contract is usually called an installment sales contract,
or conditional sales contract. In these contracts the
seller has very good protection. If it is personal property
he holds the title to it as security until all of the
installments plus interest are paid in accordance with the
terms of the contract.

Under the Uniform Conditional Sales Act, the seller
has the right to repossess the goods if the contract
balance is not paid as required in each installment.
Repossession does not end the relationship between the
buyer and the seller. After the goods have been repossessed,
the seller must auction the goods and sell them to the
highest bidder. If the seller receives more for the goods
than the remainder of his contract balance and interest,
he will then turn over to the buyer that excess amount.
This very rarely happens. If the seller does not receive
the amount that is left on his contract, which is what
almost always happens, then the seller may bring suit
against the buyer for the deficiency. At this point you
can see that the buyer has to pay for the deficiency for
goods that he no longer has, and a judgment including court
costs and attorney's fees, in some cases, may be taken
against the unwary buyer. And his wages may be garnished
or other property of his may be attached.

THE HAZARDS OF INSTALLMENT CONTRACTS

If you are going to make an installment purchase and sign
a conditional sales contract, it's extremely important to
know exactly what you're signing. There are certain
pitfalls that you must avoid to stay out of trouble yourself and get the value of the goods that you have purchased.
First, make sure that all of the blank spaces on the form
contract are filled in and executed by the seller before
you sign the contract itself. Don't leave it to chance as
to what may be put in the blank spaces after you have
signed the contract.

Second, in such contracts look for a clause known as
a wage assignment clause. This clause may give the seller
or his assignee power to collect all or part of your wages
if an installment payment is missed. This legal process,
known as *garnishment*, obliges your employer to withhold all
or part of your wages until the debt is paid. Most states

prohibit by law garnishment beyond a certain percentage of a person's wages.

Unfortunately, some buyers sign such contracts and miss one payment; thereafter their employer is garnished and has to go through the difficulties and disruption of filling out a garnishment form and sending the money to the creditor, so often the employee may lose his job. Garnishment generally is only available after judgment is obtained, but an imprudent buyer may sign such a wage assignment clause in a conditional sales contract, not knowing that it is strictly unenforceable in most states. The employer may also not know that it is unenforceable, but the buyer may be stuck and have his wages garnished.

Third is a clause that is sometimes used in unscrupulous sales, the *add-on clause*. This clause is often included in a contract to cover a series of installment purchases such as for furniture, and it makes earlier purchases security for the present installment purchase. For example, I buy some livingroom furniture on an installment sales contract. I pay off that contract in accordance with its terms. I then go back to the store and negotiate a purchase of a washing machine. The seller says, "Why don't we use your earlier furniture as security for this sale in addition to the washing machine?" He does this by the insertion of an add-on clause for the purchase. In other words, the title to the washing machine remains in the seller, but in addition, all of my front room furniture is used as additional security. If I am injured and am unable to work or for some other reason unable to make payments on the washing machine, the seller may come and repossess not only the washing machine but all of the front room furniture. Such an additional assurity or add-on clause is clearly unfair to the buyer.

Another clause quite common in conditional sales contracts is the *acceleration clause*, which you may not be able to avoid but which is unfair nevertheless. This clause provides that if you default on one payment, then all installment payments that are subsequently due become immediately due and payable. If you are unable to pay the total unpaid balance, then the goods that you purchased may be repossessed. If you defaulted on the second payment of a $100 conditional sales contract, you then might have to make not only that payment but the entire $90, or else lose the entire purchase price as well as the clothes or goods that you had purchased. In addiition, you may be held liable for the remainder of the installment sale balance which

is not recovered by the seller on the auction of the goods.
The final clause we will look at in a conditional sales
contract is known to lawyers and financial people as the
balloon clause, which has been used frequently by unscrupulous car salesman.   The contract provides for payments
of, say, $70 per month on principal and interest on the
automobile.   But the payments balloon, or increase, for the
last three payments, which go up to $140 per month.   Now,
let's assume that the contract is for two years and you
have paid $70 per month for almost two years.   You're within
three months of paying off the contract and the interest at
between 18% and 24% when you see in your payment book that
you must come up with $140 this month and the next two
months.   You can't make those payments, and you weren't aware
that you were going to have to.   The seller may repossess
the car even though $1688 has been paid on it and only
$420 remains to be paid.   These balloon payments are
notorious in the automobile industry and although reputable
dealers do not use them they are something to be extremely
careful about.

   Finally, a word of caution about credit cards, which
most of you have used or will use at some time.   View a
credit card as a check that has been signed by you but is
blank in amount.   Credit cards are cash—you merely pay a
little later for the credit cards.   You will pay interest
on your credit card purchase and the person who accepts
your credit card will pay some interest to the credit card
company.

   If you lose your credit card, you must promptly notify
the credit card company in writing because any charges that
are made by the thief or finder of your credit card are
assessable to your account between the time your card
was lost or stolen and the time the credit card company was
advised by you in writing that the card is lost so the
company can cancel it.   Be extremely careful in your handling
of your credit card and if you lose it or it's stolen from
you, advise your company immediately so that you will not be
responsible for literally thousands of dollars that may be
charged against the card without your authorization or
knowledge.

   There are four rules that you should follow when
purchasing money—that is, borrowing funds.   First, borrow
the least amount you need, not the most you can get.
Second, make monthly payments as large as you can, not the
smallest amount the creditor will permit.   Third, don't
borrow unnecessarily in advance of actual need.   Fourth,

borrow from the lowest-cost source—which is not necessarily
the handiest or quickest.   If you're going to pay 18% more
for a product at one store than at another, obviously
you're going to purchase at the lower cost store, but you
should use the same discretion on shopping for credit because
you are paying 18% more than the list price of the article
in interest.   Finally, keep in mind that installment credit
at stores runs approximately 18% to 24% a year.

GLOSSARY TERMS

Acceleration clause   A clause whereby failure to make one
    installment payment makes the purchaser liable to
    immediately pay the entire unpaid balance.

Add-on clause   A clause added to an installment sales
    contract that makes earlier purchases security for
    present installment purchases.

Balloon clause   A clause whereby the regular monthly
    payments are made with larger monthly payments
    due at the end of the contract period.

Compound interest   Interest that periodically is entered
    as part of the unpaid principal.

Garnishment   Extraction from a person's salary or wages
    of the amount not paid on an installment contract.

Interest   The cost of, or charges for, borrowing money.

SELF TEST

CHAPTER 51

NAME_____

DATE_____

51.1   The cost of borrowing money is known as _____
       or finance charges.

51.2   _____ buying costs more than cash purchases.
       _____ families are the biggest users of
       credit.

51.3   Two out of _____ families in America under
       _____ years of age, pay out between ____ and ____ %
       of their net income on installment payments.

51.4   If you borrow $1,000 for one year at 5% per year,
       and pay back the $1,050 in 12 equal installments,,
       your true, or effective, rate of interest is ____ %.

51.5   In home loans for _____ financing, the actual
       interest rate is the _____ interest rate,
       because the interest is figured on the _____
       balance owed, not on the _____ purchase price.

51.6   The type of loan with the·least expensive financing
       charge is the _____ financing loan.

51.7   Installment payment interest is generally _____
       the amount of the stated interest.

51.8   If the interest on a charge account is 1½% per
       month, the annual rate of interest is ____ %.

51.9   When interest is charged on the principal, plus
       interest that has accrued, the interest is known as
       _____ interest.

51.10 In reference to interest on installment purchases,
       if the rate of interest is stated as a yearly
       percentage of the _____ debt, the true yearly
       rate of interest is approximately _____ what
       is stated as interest.

51.11 Usually, interest that a/an _____ union charges
       is usually less than bank rates of interest.

51.12 Life insurance loans are very attractive because
       the stated interest rate is the _____ interest
       rate.

51.13 With home loans, you must be aware that there is
       usually a/an _____ penalty in the loan.

51.14   With a conditional sales contract, under the Uniform
        Conditional Sales Act, the seller has a right to
        _____ the goods if the contract balance is
        not paid as required in each installment.

51.15   After repossession, unless it is otherwise agreed
        upon, the seller must _____ the goods, and
        sell them to the highest bidder. If the seller
        receives more for the goods than the remainder of
        his contract _____ and _____, he
        will then turn over to the _____ that excess
        amount. If the seller does not receive the amount
        that is left on his contract, then the seller may
        bring suit against the buyer for the _____.

51.16   When signing a contract, make sure that all the
        _____ spaces on the form contract are filled
        in and _____ by the seller before you sign
        the contract yourself.

51.17   A/An _____ clause in a contract
        gives a seller or his assignee the power to collect
        all or part of your wages if an installment payment
        is missed. This legal process is known as _____.

51.18   A/An _____ clause in a contract makes earlier
        purchases security for a present installment purchase.
        This is common with installment purchases for furniture.

51.19   A/An _____ clause provides that if you default
        on one payment, then all installment payments that are
        subsequently due become due and payable _____.

51.20   (Answer either "true" or "false") _____ If you
        lose your credit card, or it is stolen, you are liable
        for any subsequent charges made with the card until
        you notify the credit card company in writing.

51.21   Some rules to think about when borrowing money are:
        a)   borrow the _____ amount you need;
        b)   make monthly payments as _____ as you can;
        c)   borrow from the lowest _____ source; and
        d)   remember that installment credit interest rates
             at stores run approximately 18 to ____ % a year.